Auditing Information Systems

Second Edition

Jack J. Champlain

John Wiley & Sons, Inc.

Copyright © 2003 by John Wiley & Sons. All rights reserved.

Published by John Wiley & Sons, Inc., Hoboken, New Jersey
Published simultaneously in Canada

For general information on our other products and services, or technical support, please contact our Customer Care Department within the United States at 800-762-2974, outside the United States at 317-572-3993 or fax 317-572-4002.

Wiley also publishes its books in a variety of electronic formats. Some content that appears in print may not be available in electronic books.

Library of Congress Cataloging-in-Publication Data:

Champlain, Jack J.
    Auditing information systems / Jack J. Champlain.—2nd ed.
      p. cm.
    Includes bibliographical references and index.
    ISBN 0-471-28117-4 (cloth : alk. paper)
      1. Electronic data processing—Auditing. I. Title
  QA76.9.A93 C48   2003
  658'.0558—dc21   2002034202

Printed in the United States of America

10 9 8 7 6 5 4 3 2 1

While creativity and innovation are what drive new technology,
they are also what must secure it.

Jack J. Champlain

List of Registered and Trademarked Names

Access

ACF2

ACL

AFS 2000

Alpha

AltaVista

Amazon.com

AS/400

Baan

Black Hole

BlackICE

BorderWare

Checkpoint Firewall-1

Consumer Reports

Cookie Cutter

Cookie Monster

Cop-Only

CRYPTOCard

Cyber Patrol

CyberCash Wallet

CyberCop Scanner

Cyberguard Firewall

DB2

Defender

Digimark

Diner's Club

EOPACS

Excel

Experian

Explorer

Fedline II

Fedwire

FOCUS

GFX Internet Firewall Systems

Gummi Bears

IDEA

Interceptor

Internet Scanner

J.D. Edwards

Java

Jurassic Park

Lawson

Lotus 123

Macintosh

MareSpider

MasterCard

Micro-ID

Monarch

MVS

Net Nanny

Netbuilder Router

Netscape

NetWare

Norton Utilities

ON Guard

Option Finder

Oracle

OS/2

Paradox

PC Tools

Pentium

Pentium II

Pentium Pro

Pentium MMX

PeopleSoft

PGPcookie.cutter

PICK

Pipeline Router

PIX Firewall

Playboy

Portus

PowerBook

PrivateNet

RACF

Retina

SafeBack

Sagent

SAINT

Secure Network Gateway

SecurID

Sidewinder

Star Trek

Star Wars

Tiny

Turnstyle Firewall System

Unix

VAX

VeriSign

Visa

VMS

WebSense

Windows

Windows NT

Windows 95

Windows 2000

Word

WordPerfect

ZoneAlarm

Contents

Preface

Auditors have always been responsible for consulting with management to help ensure that sufficient and adequate internal controls exist within organizations to mitigate major risks to a reasonable level. Auditors identify and quantify risk using professional judgment based on knowledge, education, experience, and even history. As major events occur, the auditing profession retools its approach to risk assessment to adapt to the new environment.

When the first edition of this book was published (October 1998), it seemed as if the biggest risks organizations faced were insider abuse, hacking, viruses, and the Year 2000 problem. The newspapers were flooded daily with stories of new hacks and viruses, and the creators sometimes were idolized. Huge amounts of human and financial resources were devoted toward Y2K projects. Looking back, the United States and many other western countries were indeed spoiled by the dot-com success and thus became ignorant, complacent, and self-centered. Many businesses worried only about profits, and many individuals worried only about themselves and their antigovernment messages. It was a "me" world. An aura of invincibility existed.

Over the last four years, several new events have forever reshaped the social and business environment of the world. These events have had a direct impact on the internal control environments in which we auditors exist, in both the public and the private sector. Although previously I did not think it was possible, some of these recent events were so significant that they actually have redefined the way most of us view risk. I will discuss three events in particular.

SEPTEMBER 11, 2001

Terrorism suddenly became the number-one risk among all risks. It is more disturbing than even war. While war is somewhat predictable in where it is fought and whom the enemy is, terrorists are often faceless and can strike anywhere, at any time, even in the heartland of America. No longer can any organization overlook the possibility of being impacted by a terrorist act.

In the first edition of my book, the 1995 bombing of the Federal Building in Oklahoma City and the 1993 bombing of the World Trade Center in New York City were the most serious terrorist acts against the United States. America was outraged that the Oklahoma City bombing was carried out by two of our very own citizens. But these evil acts paled in comparison to the thousands who lost their lives on September 11, 2001. Nobody can forget the horror and feeling of helplessness as we watched the once-mighty twin towers of the World Trade Center buckle from the intense heat caused by the fuel of jets-turned-missiles by Osama bin Laden. A successfully coordinated simultaneous jet missile attack on the seemingly impenetrable Pentagon was beyond anyone's wildest imagination.

Not only did this terrorist act cause great physical and emotional damage, it concurrently struck at the heart of the world economic system. The airline industry was suddenly in jeopardy of being permanently grounded. Commercial airline manufacturers were immediately forced to cut production and reduce workforces. Many businesses within the World Trade Center itself were destroyed, and government resources suddenly had to be diverted to homeland defense and away from social services. Already reeling from the dot-com bust, the stock market tumbled further, and thoughts of any return to economic health were snuffed. Investors lost billions of dollars. All of us were impacted, either directly or indirectly.

Even our seemingly well-prepared disaster recovery and business resumption plans no longer looked so thorough. Many of them were based on the assumptions that people and data storage devices can be flown to hot sites, that automobile traffic would be available and free flowing, and that cell phones would work. The 9/11 attack has shown us that none of these conveniences can be assumed. Post 9/11 disaster recovery and business resumption plans should have backup procedures for each assumption.

DOT-COM BUST

The dot-com stock market house of cards that ignored Alan Greenspan's famous "irrational exuberance" description began tumbling down in late 1999. By the end of 2001, even the most bullish dot-com princesses became bears struggling to survive. Even many blue-chip stocks lost more than half their value. As it turns out, Mr. Greenspan was correct. Most dot-com business models had no basis in making profits, only in generating revenues and intangible market capitalization. Many dot-commers had no business or management skills, only technical skills. Yet they were being rewarded with billions of dollars from venture capital firms as well as Wall Street investors who themselves had no technical skills to realize that the business models were destined for long-term failure. Although many people initially made millions of dollars on dot-com stock, only those few who were fortunate enough to cash in their stock and options before 1999 were able to retain wealth. Many others lost their life savings. Institutional investors running retirement plans, mutual funds, and 401(k) funds lost billions on behalf of their investors. Many individuals will never recover their losses.

ENRON COLLAPSE

As if things could not get worse, the Enron collapse that materialized in late 2001 pointed out that auditors need to look in the mirror and reevaluate themselves and their ethical practices. Enron is the most recent and noteworthy example of how unethical practices by top management can quickly destroy a seemingly magnificent firm in a very short time. There are accusations that Enron and other energy trading firms manipulated energy prices, leading to the doubling and tripling of energy bills to individual consumers. The ramifications affected nearly everyone in the United States, either directly through increased energy bills or indirectly through reduced values of stock holdings or investments in 401(k) plans, mutual funds, and retirement plans. State and local governments that invested in mutual funds holding Enron stock suffered, thereby reducing investment revenues and increasing the need for such governments to reduce services and increase taxes to make up the difference.

ROLE OF INTERNAL CONTROLS

As a result of these events alone, all the world's organizations had to reassess risk and rethink their internal controls. Because of the Enron collapse, ethical practices by senior management, board members, external auditors, and even internal auditors are more important now than ever before. The tone at the top should be foremost on every auditor's list of internal controls. Had proper internal controls been exercised at Enron, the firm would not have incentivized growth at any cost and there would not have been a meltdown from so much artificial overvaluation.

The dot-com bust has caused venture capitalists and other investors to closely scrutinize the management skills and business models of new and existing companies. The companies themselves have had to carefully review their internal controls, including corporate governance controls, to help ensure they remain viable businesses. Auditors must play a key role in this assessment.

While better internal controls within the U.S. government might have deterred some or all of the 9/11 attack, likely there would have been too many skeptics to prevent something equally as sadistic from happening later. But better internal controls, such as more timely and accurate communication and coordination among governmental agencies, could have slowed the movement of terrorists and stymied their operational and financial networks. Fully developed and tested disaster recovery and business resumption plans could have saved some organizations and helped lessen the impact on others that managed to survive the attack.

ROLE OF AUDITORS

Each of the three events just described—the September 11 attack, the dot-com bust, and the Enron collapse—points out the need for everyone to heed the devastating effects of these new twenty-first century risks. It is the role of auditors to make sure that management and indeed world leaders never overlook potential risks by eliminating important and necessary controls. Never again should any of us view risk in the same way. We must learn from history, since eventually it will repeat itself. The types of potential risks are limited only by our imaginations and the imaginations of heinous people and organizations around the globe. Throughout our careers, each time we hear a manager or executive downplay the significance of risks and controls, we should maintain our resolve and continue to remind ourselves never to become complacent or succumb to ignorance or arrogance. Otherwise we risk putting the future of our organizations as well as the future of our families and our way of life in jeopardy.

All organizations must perform complete risk assessments and implement adequate internal controls to help manage all significant risks. The need to do so has always existed, but the urgency has increased dramatically. The western world is under imminent attack, not only by terrorists, but more commonly by thieves and other criminals who will stop at nothing to make money and create havoc at the expense of law-abiding citizens.

Since computing systems play a critical role in all organizations, protection of these systems and the information stored in them is a strategic requirement. Physical security controls over all facilities, including those that house computing systems and information, must be diligently applied. The same is true of logical security controls over computing systems and the information stored in them.

There is good news in all this mayhem. The audit approach to assessing the adequacy of the physical and logical security controls of computing and information systems is basically the same as it has always been. The approach presented in this book can be applied to virtually any information systems environment. It works now; it worked 20 years ago; and it will work well into the future.

With the proliferation of thousands of different types of computing systems since the 1980s, mostly in end-user environments, critical computing system applications are multiplying at an exponential rate in many organizations. The phenomenal growth in the processing speed of computers has helped propel the productivity of businesses to never before thought of heights. It is this same enormous processing power that can exponentially magnify the significance of a control weakness to truly worldwide proportions if a computer system is not adequately protected. As a result, more and more nontechnical auditors are being relied on to identify the risks and evaluate the adequacy of controls over critical computing systems in their companies. Furthermore, in today's litigious society, audit managers, audit committee members, senior management, executives, and board members must also be able to understand how adequate assessment of controls over critical computing systems in their organizations can be accomplished. Otherwise, they risk being held personally accountable in the event their organizations suffer significant losses or fail as a result of inadequate controls over critical computing systems.

A major challenge exists because many auditors are not familiar with techniques and resources that they can use to efficiently and effectively perform audits of computing systems. The situation has been further accentuated in many companies by the flattening of reporting structures, which results in the downsizing of audit departments, and budget reductions arising from cost-control efforts. Many organizations do not have the luxury of retaining specialized information systems auditors on staff or the financial resources to contract outside specialists or consultants to evaluate the adequacy of controls over critical computing systems and related processes. Without these resources or the skills necessary to evaluate the controls and security over critical computing systems, however, organizations are facing significant risks by leaving ominous gaps in their control environments.

The intent of this book is to help fill these gaps by presenting readers with an easy, practical approach to understanding how to assess the adequacy of controls over virtually any type of computing system, whether it be a large mainframe computer supporting hundreds of applications, a midrange computer running vendor-supported applications, a wide/local area network supported by in-house technicians, a stand-alone desktop computer that transmits/receives critical information, or a vendor's computing system that processes data for other organizations (such vendors are sometimes referred to as service organizations, service bureaus, or third-party processors). This book is not intended to be an all-encompassing technical encyclopedia of information systems auditing, as there have already been many such books published. Instead, I attempt to provide an easy-to-implement approach to auditing information systems. This approach is then coupled with real-world situations and examples that demonstrate how the techniques were applied. Finally, the book is supplemented with discussions about control self-assessment, encryption and cryptography, computer forensics, humanistic aspects of IS auditing, IS project management, and a variety of other IS auditing challenges as we begin our journey into the new millennium.

The techniques in this book are intended to be of interest to nontechnical auditors, audit managers, audit committee members, senior managers in charge of critical computing systems, executives, and board members. It is my hope that after reading this book, these people will feel more comfortable auditing or evaluating audits of computing systems they are likely to encounter in their organizations. It is also intended that this book be a source of reference to auditing students, new auditors, and those aspiring to become information systems (IS) auditing specialists. Even for experienced IS auditors, this book should provide a unique perspective, and at least some of the scenarios should prove to be interesting, informative, and somewhat entertaining.

This book assumes that readers have at least a basic understanding of the various components of the auditing process. These components include planning, risk assessment, entrance memos (also known as engagement memos), system descriptions or narratives, flow charts and schematic diagrams, audit programs (i.e., a list of audit steps to be performed), testing, management review of work papers and other test materials, exit meetings with client or auditee management, preparation of audit reports, acquisition of management responses to recommendations in the report, postaudit surveys, and recommendation tracking to ensure proper resolution.

The book is organized into three parts. Part One contains chapters discussing the basics of computing systems and how to identify the universe of computer systems in an organization. Part Two is based largely on a generic IS audit program I have developed that addresses the primary risks associated with any computing system. If the steps in the program are properly performed, the reader should be reasonably comfortable that key controls over critical computing systems have been deployed. Readers should also be able to obtain sufficient information to determine whether these controls adequately protect the computer hardware, software, and data in an organization against unauthorized access and accidental or intentional destruction or alteration. Mitigation of these risks will help an organization achieve its strategic business objectives.

The steps in the audit program are grouped into four general categories: (1) tests of environmental controls, (2) tests of physical security controls, (3) tests of logical security controls, and (4) tests of IS operating controls. The concepts in each category are discussed in detail in Chapters 4 through 9. The chapters applicable to each category are indicated on the audit program.

This organization enables readers to quickly locate a chapter that discusses an audit area of specific interest without having to search through the entire book. Some of the steps on the audit program may or may not be applicable to one particular computing system, but the steps collectively address the risks and controls of virtually all computing systems. Chapter 3 presents the generic IS audit program. Chapters 4 through 9 cover the concepts pertaining to IS security policies, standards, and guidelines; service organization applications; service organization and vendor assessments; physical security; logical security; and information systems operations.

The first section of Chapters 4 through 9 begins with a discussion of the theory as to why the particular step should be performed. In the second section of each of these chapters, one or more scenarios are presented that illustrate the primary concept of the chapter. These scenarios are based on actual findings, situations, and occurrences that I have encountered during my auditing experiences. Also included are descriptions of and references to various other incidents where IS control weaknesses resulted in losses to companies or exposed organizations to significant risks.

Part Three includes six chapters that discuss contemporary auditing techniques and issues that are highly relevant as we progress through the new millennium. Chapter 10 is a detailed discussion about control self-assessment, a leading-edge auditing technique that has taken the worldwide auditing community by storm. Chapter 11 discusses encryption and cryptography, which are the keys to secure electronic exchanges of information throughout the world. Chapter 12 discusses computer forensics. Chapter 13 discusses a variety of IS auditing challenges, including computer-assisted audit techniques, computer viruses, software piracy, electronic commerce, Internet security, and information privacy. Chapter 14 discusses some of the humanistic aspects of IS auditing, which is an area that is often overlooked in auditing literature. After all, even auditors are human beings who experience many of the same wants, needs, and anxieties as everyone else does when performing their jobs.

Because of my belief in the importance of the need for all auditors to become active in audit-related professional associations, a section in Chapter 14 is devoted to this topic. Information in this section should stimulate readers to become active in one or more associations to increase their knowledge and expertise, expand their network of professional contacts, and enhance their careers.

Chapter 15 discusses the risks and controls pertaining to the management of IS projects.

Appendixes have been included to provide additional reference information. Appendix A provides a list of selected professional associations and other organizations related to IS auditing and computer security. Included for each organization are the name, mailing address, phone number, web address, and mission statement. Appendix B provides an overview of the Common Criteria for Information Technology Security Evaluation. Appendix C briefly discusses the ISO seven-layer Open Systems Interconnection (OSI) model. A list of selected reference publications pertaining to IS auditing and computer security has also been included.

Additional appendices containing background information of interest to readers of this book are available online at *www.wiley.com/go/information systems*. Appendix D begins with a post mortem of the Year 2000 problem. The last part of the appendix preserves the original chapter 12, "The Year 2000 Problem," from the first edition of this book. This is included because the Year 2000 project was essentially an enormous enterprise-wide IS project that was wildly successful for the world as a whole.

Appendix E, also available online, contains the U.S. Department of Defense "Orange Book" Trusted Computer System Evaluation Criteria.

While the term *information technology* (*IT*) has been in vogue for a few years, I still believe the phrase *information systems* (*IS*) is more accurate because we do not audit just the technology. Technology must not be viewed in a vacuum. Rather, it must be examined within the context of the entire system in which it exists, including all human interfaces. Therefore, I will continue to use the phrase "information systems" (IS) throughout this book.

To facilitate an interactive style that is not technically overwhelming, this book has been written in the first and second person.

Acknowledgments

I would like to acknowledge the following individuals who were instrumental in the completion of this book project:

> *My lifelong companion, Shannon*, for her patience, love, and understanding during the many 3 A.M. writing sessions we endured
> *My two sons, Jonas and Joshua*, for their love and for motivating me to be a better father
> *Sheck Cho*, for his dedicated direction
> *Steve Kirschbaum*, for his guidance and instruction on network and Internet security

I would also like to thank the following partial list of computer pioneers, some posthumously, for creating a technology that has revolutionized the way humans live and has created a huge industry in which we as IS auditing professionals can make a wonderful, interesting, challenging living.

> *Robert "Bob" Bemer* The father of ASCII, who made it a worldwide technology standard. In the 1950s he also developed a key component of the COBOL programming language.
> *Tim Bernets-Lee* A British physicist who in 1989 invented the World Wide Web at CERN, a major particle physics lab in Geneva, Switzerland.
> *Dr. Fred Cohen* As a University of Southern California student in 1983, he wrote the first computer virus to demonstrate the concept. Unlike most virus writers, his mission is to help mankind, not hurt it. Dr. Cohen also designed protocols for secure digital networks carrying voice, video, and data, and created the first Internet-based information warfare simulations.
> *Seymore Cray* Cofounded Control Data Corporation in 1957 and then built the first computer that used radio transistors instead of vacuum tubes, thus making the machines more reliable and allowing for miniaturization of components, which enhanced the performance of desktop computers.
> *Frances "Betty" Snyder Holberton* Programmed the groundbreaking ENIAC digital computer for the army in the 1940s and later helped create the COBOL and FORTRAN languages.
> *Claude Shannon* Referred to by some as the "father of the Digital Revolution," he outlined a series of mathematical formulas in 1948 to reduce communication processes to binary code, known as "bits," and calculated ways to send the maximum number of bits through phone lines or other modes of communication.
> *Ray Tomlinson* Invented e-mail in 1971 when he merged two programs he had written earlier (Sndmsg/Readmail and CYPNET) into a single program that enabled messages to be sent between two computers via a net-

work. He chose the @ symbol to separate the user's name from the host computer name.

Unisys Corporation Introduced the first UNIVAC commercial computer on June 14, 1951.

The many other computer pioneers whom I have yet to discover and recognize.

PART ONE

Core Concepts

CHAPTER 1

Basics of Computing Systems

Before performing an audit of a computing system or assessing the adequacy of an audit that was performed on a computing system, there are a few basics that one must understand about how a computing system functions. A computing system is essentially comprised of three basic components: the central processing unit, the operating system, and application programs. Many systems also have a fourth system where the data resides and is managed. This is called a database management system. Each of these components is described in the following sections of this chapter.

CENTRAL PROCESSING UNIT

A central processing unit (CPU) is essentially a box of interconnected electronic circuits. There are literally thousands of CPUs in the world today. They include stand-alone microcomputers such as the IBM family of personal computers and their clones, the Apple Macintosh family of microcomputers, mini and mid-range computers such as the IBM AS/400 and the Compaq Alpha family, mainframe computers such as the IBM System 390 series, and even experimental supercomputers. The brains of these CPUs are computer chips. Among other things, chips determine the speed and efficiency with which computers operate. For computer chips, operating speed is usually measured in terms of megahertz (MHz) and more recently in gigahertz (GHz) and teraflops. One MHz is equivalent to one million operations per second. One GHz is equivalent to one billion operations per second. One teraflop is equivalent to one trillion operations per second. There are hundreds of computer chip manufacturers, both large and small. Some of the more well-known chip manufacturers include IBM, Sun, Intel, Motorola, Hewlett Packard, Advanced Micro Devices, NEC, Hitachi, Compaq, Mitsubishi, and Apple. One of the most widely recognized computer chip manufacturers is Intel, maker of the Pentium® family of chips, which are installed in many personal computers and file servers. Pentium 4 chips enable personal computers to run at speeds over 2.5 GHz.

Recent History of Processing Speeds

In January 1997, Intel launched the Pentium MMX™ computer chip, which was touted to run existing programs 10 to 20 percent faster than previous same-speed processors. Programs written to take advantage of the new multimedia-enhancing technology reportedly could run 60 percent faster.[1] In July 1997, the Apple PowerBook® 3400 laptop was reportedly capable of running at speeds up to 235 MHz.[2]

Computer chips installed in more sophisticated commercial computers were attaining speeds in the 300 to 500 MHz range in 1997. For example, in May 1997, Intel introduced the Pentium II®, a sixth-generation processor that can run at 300 MHz and also incorporates the MMX technology. This chip was based on the Pentium Pro®, a powerful commercial-use chip.[3] In 1996, Digital introduced its new midrange Alpha® computer. The Alpha chip, which crunches 64 bits of data at a time,[4] is capable of processing at 440 MHz. In October 1996, a small computer chip maker announced that it had developed a chip purported to be able to operate Apple Macintosh software at up to 533 MHz.[5]

In December 1996, news was released of a supercomputer developed jointly by Intel and the U.S. Energy Department that could perform at a speed exceeding one teraflop, or one trillion operations per second.[6] This was almost three times faster than the previous supercomputing record held by Hitachi of Japan. The $55 million computer was primarily to be used by government scientists at Sandia Laboratories in Albuquerque, New Mexico, to simulate nuclear weapons tests that are now banned by international treaty.[7] This application reduced the need to detonate live nuclear explosives to assess their destructive powers. It also eliminated the risk of damage to humans and the environment, and thus avoids the many political ramifications associated with live nuclear testing. The technology can be applied to any commercial applications requiring high-speed calculations. Examples of such applications include weather forecasting and genetic mapping. The tremendous speed of the supercomputer was achieved by clustering 7,264 high-end Pentium Pro computer chips into modules, using a technique called "massively parallel computing." The system eventually included 9,200 of the computer chips and was able to operate at 1.4 teraflops. Using this technology, Intel expects to be able to configure networks to utilize the processing power of far more chips than before, thereby vastly increasing their computing power. By the year 2000, Intel expected the supercomputer to be able to break the three teraflop barrier.

Since 1997, computer chip manufacturers have continued to keep pace with Moore's Law, which asserts that computer processing speeds will double every 18 months. Intel cofounder Gordon Moore predicted in 1965 that each new memory chip could perform about twice as many processes as its predecessor, and each new chip would be released within 18 to 24 months of the previous chip. The following article snippets bear this theorem out:

- In June 2002, the National Centers for Environmental Prediction, a division of the National Weather Service, orderd a $224 million IBM computer that will be able to run at 100 teraflops.[8]

- In April 2002, the Japanese NEC Earth Simulator computer had 5,104 processors that could reach a speed of 35.6 teraflops. This beat the existing computer speed record of 7.2 teraflops achieved by the ASCI White-Pacific computer at the Lawrence Livermore National Laboratory in California using 7,424 processors.[9]
- In 2002 IBM built the world's fastest single microchip, which runs at more than 100 GHz.[10]
- In 2001 Intel devised a new structure for transistors (chips) that eliminated the speed-limiting problems of power consumption and heat. The chips reportedly can operate at one terahertz, or one trillion operations per second.[11]
- Britain purchased a supercomputer made by Sun Microsystems that has a memory equivalent to 11,000 CD-ROMs and runs at 10 GHz.[12]
- Intel introduced its two fastest chips, which run at 1.8 and 1.6 GHz, and offered a 2 GHz chip in the third quarter of 2001.[13]
- Intel has developed what it says is the fastest and smallest transistor ever. The new transistors are ony 20 nanometers, or .02 microns, in size compared to the .18 micron chips in use today. The breakthrough means that silicon will be able to be used to make chips until at least 2007 and will make possible microprocessors containing close to 1 billion transistors running at 20 GHz by that year. It also means that Moore's Law will remain on the books until at least 2007.[14]
- Advanced Micro Devices, Inc., introduced two new Athlon chips that run at 1.2 and 1.0 GHz.[15]
- Intel introduced the long-awaited Pentium 4 processor, which runs at 1.7 GHz.[16]
- Intel rolled out its Pentium 3 chip for laptops, which runs at 1 GHz.[17]
- Intel is introducing two Celeron chips that run at 766 MHz and 733 MHz.[18]
- IBM scientists plan to spend five years building the fastest computer in the world. The "Blue Gene" computer will be 500 times faster than anything in existence today.[19]
- Apple unveiled new iMac computers that run at 400 MHz and 350 MHz.[20]
- IBM unveiled a new high-speed mainframe computer that runs at 1.6 GHz. It will be used for mapping human genes.[21]
- IBM has developed the world's fastest computer capable of running at 3.9 teraflops to simulate nuclear explosions.[22]

Future of Processing

The potential processing speed of supercomputers, and eventually commercial and consumer computers, is limited only by the amount of space available to house the computers and the size of the materials used to create chips. Conventional technology uses silicon-based chips. However, these chips are projected to reach their maximum size-reduced potential by 2010 to 2015. A newer, promising technology is based on quantum technology. This technology uses individual atoms as semiconductors.

It is fascinating to try to comprehend the potential capabilities of robots and other computer-based machines, which, in the near future, could have multiple high-speed computer chips clustered in a manner that enables processing speeds in excess of one quadrillion operations per second or more. It is only a matter of time before many of the science fiction events depicted in productions like *Star Trek* and *Star Wars* are no longer fiction. Teleporting is already being experimented on. As higher- and higher-speed computers materialize in the workplace, auditors will need to understand their potential capabilities and be prepared to evaluate the controls and security over them. Auditors will also need to be able to help organizations maximize the benefits from the processing capabilities of these computers. Governments will need to minimize the risks of such technologies. Imagine the chaos that could ensue in a battle where enemies could teleport bombs and even troops behind each other's lines and even into each other's headquarters. The race for technology truly is on.

Computer Memory

Other CPU components determine the amount of memory available in a particular computer. Memory is usually measured in terms of the number of bytes of data that can be stored in memory at any one time. Two primary types of memory are usually referred to with regard to computers: processing memory and storage memory.

Processing memory is often referred to as random access memory (RAM) or temporary memory. The amount of RAM available in computers is commonly stated in terms of megabytes (MB). As of this writing, new retail home computers were boasting available RAM sizes of up to 512 MB. The more RAM a computer utilizes, the more applications it can process concurrently, thus allowing users to switch from one application to another without having to exit previous applications. Once a computer is turned off or the power is interrupted, most of the information residing in RAM is not retained, hence the term *temporary memory*. Many have found this out the hard way when their systems went down and they had not saved their work recently. After a few instances of suffering the loss of hours of work because I had not saved, I developed the habit of saving every 5 to 10 minutes to both the hard drive and a diskette or read-writable CD (CD-RW) in an external drive. Numerous applications can permanently reside in RAM. For example, a security software package exists that resides in RAM and requires the user to enter a password before the computer can proceed with the initialization process. This software can prevent an unauthorized user from initializing a computer by placing an initialization diskette into an external drive, such as the A drive. An unauthorized user could use this technique to initialize a computer, circumvent a less sophisticated sign-on security application that is not resident in RAM, and then access the hard drive from the external drive. Unfortunately, many computer viruses can also reside in RAM. They usually gain residence when an unsuspecting user accesses an infected file. Once viruses are resident in the RAM of a computer, they are able to infect other computers and file servers by infecting a diskette that is accessed by another computer and by traveling through intranets and the Internet. For example, attaching an infected file to an e-mail message can cause the recipient's computer to become infected. To combat viruses, many virus-checking applications have been developed and marketed. Some are available from computer manufacturers upon the purchase of computer equipment and operating systems while others are available over the counter. The best virus checkers can be set to examine any incoming data files for viruses in their inventory, regardless of source, remove the infected files, and notify the user or system security administrator of any detected viruses. Obviously, the virus inventory needs to be updated periodically as new viruses are identified. Some virus application developers offer a service that provides subscribers with updated virus inventories on a periodic basis (e.g., daily). Viruses are discussed in greater detail in Chapter 13.

Storage memory refers to the number of bytes of data that can be stored on the hard drive of a computer. The phrase *hard drive* is synonymous with the phrases *hard disk*, *fixed disk*, and *fixed drive*. Storage memory has increased to the point where it is usually stated in terms of gigabytes (GB). As of the writing of this book, retailers were advertising new home computers with hard drive capacities of up to 100 GB. Unlike RAM, storage memory is retained even after the power is turned off or interrupted. Thus, storage memory is sometimes referred to as permanent memory. However, it is permanent only until the information has been completely deleted. Note that the act of deleting a file does not actually delete the data. It simply removes the file location reference. The data remains on the storage medium until it is overwritten. Since most computers store data sequentially, it can take several weeks, months, or years to overwrite a previously deleted file, depending on the amount of data that has been saved and deleted and the size of the storage medium. Many organizations have a backup data storage program to help ensure data recovery in the event of a disaster. Depending on the frequency of rotation and the storage period of the backup media, data can be proliferated indefinitely. For this reason, especially when working with highly sensitive, classified, or confidential information, it is extremely important to adequately secure access to the computer storage media.

Computer forensics companies have recently come into existence to search through the mines of data in existence at virtually all businesses, governments, and other organizations. These forensics firms provide a variety of services. They can be hired by plaintiffs in lawsuits against organizations. After performing the necessary legal proceedings, they can secure a search warrant, which grants judicial authority to obtain control over all the computer resources of an organization, regardless of size, for the purpose of searching for incriminating evidence. Computer forensics firms can also be hired by organizations to assist in developing data storage and retrieval policies and procedures that help minimize or maximize the incidence of data proliferation, depending on the objectives of the organization. Law enforcement agencies have also utilized the services of computer forensics companies to help recover data from confiscated computer equipment and storage media obtained during raids. See Chapter 12 for additional information on computer forensics.

The main concept to keep in mind when assessing controls over a computer is that no matter how physically large it is or how fast it operates, all computers function in basically the same manner. Thus, the audit approach and many of the controls that can be applied are generally the same.

OPERATING SYSTEM

Central processing units are usually connected to various peripheral devices that assist in storing, accessing, and transmitting data and also in the production of information output. Examples of peripheral devices include external disk drives, single CD-ROM and CD-RW drives, multiple CD-ROM drives (sometimes called "jukeboxes"), magnetic tape drives, disk packs, printers, routers, bridges, gateways, controllers, visual monitors, keyboards, terminals, and others. These devices are collectively referred to as *computer hardware*.

Operating systems are programs that are required to make hardware devices function. They are usually loaded into computers during the manufacturing process. Operating systems typically include an assortment of utility programs that assist in the functioning, maintenance, and security of the various hardware devices. The operating system and utilities are collectively referred to as *system software*. Examples of common operating systems include DOS, Windows, OS/2, NetWare, OSX, Unix, VMS, and OS/390.[23] Certain features within the system software can be customized by the purchaser. For example, most sophisticated operating systems possess system access control features that enable the purchaser to adequately protect the system against unauthorized access. Manufacturers usually set the system access control parameters to allow virtually unlimited access during initial installation. This is necessary so that the user performing the initial installation can set up other users, configure the system, and customize available system parameter settings. However, because of how wide open newly installed systems are, it is important that the system access control features be properly deployed as soon as possible after installation. Although computer manufacturers usually assist in the initial installation of complex systems, they tend to concentrate more on making the system operational rather than ensuring that it is adequately secured. In fact, many vendor technicians usually create user identifications (IDs) for themselves, which have the same privileges as a system security administrator. Often they do not delete the user IDs after they have completed the installation. As a result, the organization is subjected to the risk of unauthorized access by the installing technicians. This is one of the reasons it is important for auditors to participate in new system implementation projects. These and other issues will be discussed in greater detail later in the book.

APPLICATION PROGRAMS

Application programs are required to make a CPU and system software perform business functions. Many off-the-shelf application programs have been written to perform general tasks such as word processing (e.g., Word, WordPerfect), spreadsheets (e.g., Excel, Lotus 1-2-3), and data analysis (e.g., Access, Paradox). Many other applications have been written to perform specific business functions in a variety of industries (e.g., loan and deposit applications in financial institutions, credit card applications in card issuing companies, computer design applications in automobile and airplane manufacturing firms, and claims processing applications in insurance companies). Several enterprise resource planning (ERP) applications exist that help perform common business functions such as financial accounting, accounts payable, human resources, payroll, fixed assets management, and so on. Examples of these ERP applications include PeopleSoft, SAP, Oracle, Baan, J. D. Edwards, and Lawson. Literally millions of other applications have been developed internally by companies and externally by vendors to perform a myriad of business functions, some of them in multiple languages. Each of these applications may or may not have control features designed to help prevent unauthorized access to them. To assess the adequacy of controls over these applications, detailed knowledge of the control features available within the particular applications currently deployed in an organization must be obtained.

DATABASE MANAGEMENT SYSTEMS

A database management system (DBMS) typically consists of a suite of programs that are used to define, query, secure, and generally manage large volumes of data. Having data located in a separate DBMS offers several benefits, including the flexibility to change applications without affecting the data, the ability to eliminate data redundancy formerly required by nonopen applications, and the ability to better secure and monitor the data.

Some applications perform tasks that do not require a DBMS. For example, an application that specifically controls the raising and lowering of cooling rods in a nuclear power plant does not need a database. However, data about the raising and lowering needs to be recorded, monitored, and analyzed, most likely by another application. Depending on the amount and complexity of data being recorded, a DBMS may be necessary.

In fact, a majority of complex computing applications have some sort of DBMS associated with them. In some cases, applications are written to function with a specific DBMS and to rely solely on the DBMS to implement security. In other cases, applications are written to function with a variety of different DBMSs and have security features within the application software as well as the DBMSs. Examples of common DBMSs include Microsoft SQL Server, Oracle, and IBM DB2.

PHYSICAL SECURITY CONTROLS

Computer hardware includes the CPU and all peripheral devices. In networked systems, these devices include all bridges, routers, gateways, switches, modems, hubs, telecommunication media, and any other devices involved in the physical transmission of data. These pieces of equipment must be adequately protected against physical damage resulting from natural disasters, such as earthquakes, hurricanes, tornadoes, and floods, as well as other dangers, such as bombings, fires, power surges, theft, vandalism, and unauthorized tampering. Controls that protect against these threats are called *physical security controls*. Examples of physical security controls include various types of locks (e.g., conventional keys, electronic access badges, biometric locks, cipher locks); insurance coverage over hardware and the costs to re-create data; procedures to perform daily backups of system software, application programs, and data; as well as off-site storage and rotation of the backup media (e.g., magnetic tapes, disks, compact disks [CDs]) to a secure location; and current and tested disaster recovery programs.

LOGICAL SECURITY CONTROLS

Computing systems must also be adequately protected against unauthorized access and accidental or intentional destruction or alteration of the system software programs, application programs, and data. Protecting against these threats is accomplished through the deployment of logical security controls. Logical security controls are those that restrict the access capabilities of users of the system and prevent unauthorized users from accessing the system. Logical security controls may exist within the operating system, the database management system, the application program, or all three.

The number and types of logical security controls available vary with each operating system, database management system, application, and in many types of telecommunication devices. Some are designed with an extensive array of logical security control options and parameters that are available to the system security administrator. These include user IDs, passwords with minimum length requirements and a required number of digits and characters, suspension of user IDs after successive failed sign-on attempts, directory and file access restrictions, time-of-day and day-of-week restrictions, and specific terminal usage restrictions. Other operating systems and applications are designed with very few control options. For these systems, logical security controls often seem to be added as an afterthought, resulting in control settings that are weaker than what is reasonably desirable, even when the maximum available access restrictions have been implemented.

Many systems are programmed with controls that are commensurate with the degree of risk associated with functions performed by the systems. For example, a high-risk wire transfer transaction processing system at a financial institution should have significantly more extensive controls than a lower-risk nontransactional record-keeping system at the same institution. However, be alert to high-risk systems with poor controls. Many high-risk systems have been programmed with inadequate control features or have adequate control features available but the features are inadequately implemented. Problems can occur when programmers and/or process owners are not aware of one or more significant risks facing the organization during the use of the system.

LOCATION OF PHYSICAL AND LOGICAL SECURITY CONTROLS

Exhibit 1.1 visually depicts the concept of a basic computing system and the location of physical and logical security controls. Physical security controls pertain to the central processing unit and associated hardware and peripheral devices. Logical security controls exist at the operating system level and within database management systems and application programs. This basic model can be applied to virtually any type of computing system. For example, Exhibit 1.2 presents a

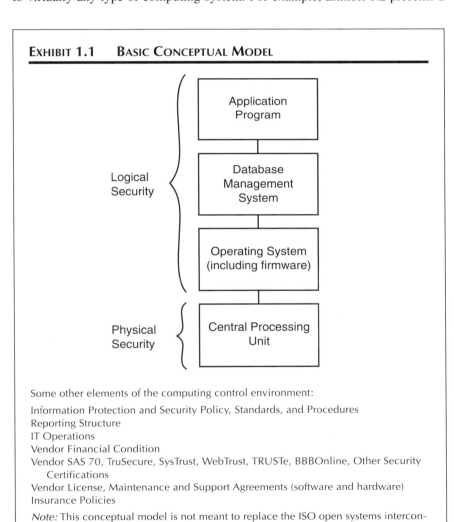

EXHIBIT 1.1   BASIC CONCEPTUAL MODEL

Some other elements of the computing control environment:

Information Protection and Security Policy, Standards, and Procedures
Reporting Structure
IT Operations
Vendor Financial Condition
Vendor SAS 70, TruSecure, SysTrust, WebTrust, TRUSTe, BBBOnline, Other Security
    Certifications
Vendor License, Maintenance and Support Agreements (software and hardware)
Insurance Policies

Note: This conceptual model is not meant to replace the ISO open systems interconnection (OSI) model. It is a simplified approach meant to help nontechnical auditors to quickly ascertain the adequacy of controls over the most common risks associated with computer systems. See Appendix C for a brief overview of the ISO-OSI model.

EXHIBIT 1.2   CONCEPTUAL MODEL OF OPEN-NETWORKED SYSTEM

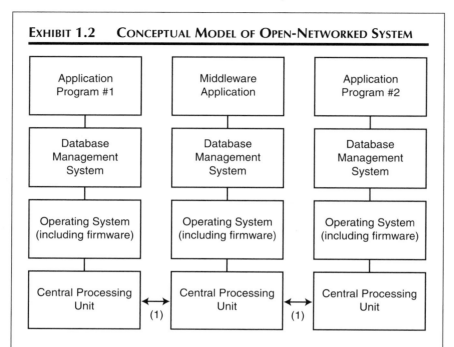

(1) Includes all telecommunications devices and media that are involved in the transmission of data, such as bridges, routers, gateways, switches, hubs, modems, telecommunications media, etc. Each potentially has some logical security controls associated with it.

Some other elements of the computing control environment:

Information Protection and Security Policy, Standards, and Procedures
Reporting Structure
IT Operations
Vendor Financial Condition
Vendor SAS 70, TruSecure, SysTrust, WebTrust, TRUSTe, BBBOnline, Other Security
    Certifications
Vendor License, Maintenance and Support Agreements (software and hardware)
Insurance Policies

Note: This conceptual model is not meant to replace the ISO open systems interconnection (OSI) model. It is a simplified approach meant to help nontechnical auditors to quickly ascertain the adequacy of controls over the most common risks associated with computer systems. See Appendix C for a brief overview of the ISO-OSI model.

---

conceptual model of one way to view the physical and logical security controls over a system that has three applications, each with its own CPU. In this configuration, data redundancy can be eliminated if managed properly because applications 1 and 2 are able to exchange data via the middleware application.

Firmware includes memory chips that contain frequently used operating programs and data so they can be processed more rapidly than if the programs had to be loaded and executed in RAM. Unlike RAM, the programs and data are not erased when the power to the CPU is turned off. The firmware typically performs computer processing and thus has logical security controls associated with it.

Audit steps to test physical and logical security controls over computing systems are presented in the audit program in Chapter 3. Each audit step is discussed in greater detail in subsequent chapters.

This chapter should give the reader a grasp of the basics of how computing systems operate and the types of physical and logical security controls that may be available. The next step is to identify the computing systems within an organization.

NOTES

1. Walter S. Mossberg, "MMX Has Much to Offer, but Less Than Hype Suggests," *Wall Street Journal* (February 13, 1997): B1.
2. Paul Salzman, "P.S. The Mac: I'm Back!" *Computer Source Magazine* (July 1997): 25.
3. "Intel to Introduce Sixth-Generation Pentium Chip," *KIRO Radio News Fax* (May 5, 1997): National Business page.
4. Don Clark and Jon G. Averbach, "Microsoft, H-P to Unveil Broad Alliance over Windows NT, Business Computing," *Wall Street Journal* (March 18, 1997): B4.
5. "Fastest Chip to Be Shown," *KIRO Radio News Fax* (October 22, 1996): National Business page.
6. Bill Richards, "Intel, U.S. Build Most-Powerful Computer Yet," *Wall Street Journal* (December 17, 1996): B6.
7. Rajiv Chandrasekaran, "New Supercomputer Breaks Record, Using Chips from Desktop," *Seattle Times* (December 17, 1996): A9.
8. "Business Briefs," *Seattle News Fax* (June 3, 2002): 5.
9. "Japanese Own Fastest Computer," *Seattle News Fax* (April 22, 2002): 5.
10. "IBM Unveils Fastest Microchip," *Seattle News Fax* (February 26, 2002): 5.
11. "Intel Touts New Transistors," *Seattle News Fax* (November 26, 2001): 5.
12. "Supercomputer May Unlock Origins of Universe," *Seattle News Fax* (August 1, 2001): 5.
13. "Intel Introduces Fast Chips," *Seattle News Fax* (July 3, 2001): 5.
14. "Intel Develops Fastest, Smallest Transistor Ever," *Seattle News Fax* (June 11, 2001): 5.
15. "Business Briefs," *Seattle News Fax* (June 6, 2001): 5.
16. "Intel Unveils 1.7 GHz Processor," *Seattle News Fax* (April 2, 2001): 5.
17. "Intel Rolls Out 1 Gig Laptop Chip," *Seattle News Fax* (March 19, 2001): 5.
18. "Business Briefs," *Seattle News Fax* (November 13, 2000): 5.
19. "'Blue Gene' Will Dwarf All Other Computers," *Seattle Times* (June 5, 2000): A1.
20. "Apple Computer Unveils New iMac hardware," *KIRO Radio News Fax* (October 7, 1999): 6.
21. "Business Briefs," *KIRO Radio News Fax* (May 4, 1999): 5.
22. "Fastest Computer Developed," *KIRO Radio News Fax* (October 28, 1998): 2.

23. The list of computer and operating system manufacturers is included for illustration purposes and is by no means intended to be exhaustive. Those listed are simply intended to provide readers with a general idea of the vast number and types of computers and operating systems in existence today.

CHAPTER 2

Identifying Computer Systems

Before performing any assessment of computing system controls, all of the computing systems utilized by an organization must be identified. Creating an inventory of computing systems is essential so that the size and complexity of the computing system environment, or "universe," within an organization can be assessed. The inventory should include systems that have been developed internally as well as those purchased from vendors. It should also include systems in which an organization's data is processed by an external vendor's computer system (these vendors are often referred to as service bureaus, third-party processors, or service organizations). An organization's computing system inventory may prove to be quite challenging. Do not be surprised if the number of computing systems reaches into the thousands.

GETTING STARTED

For purposes of this book, a computing system is generally defined as any computer software application that performs a business function; the supporting database management system, if any; the hardware on which it resides and that provides access to it; and the operating system that controls the hardware. Computing systems include hardware devices that reside within an organization or at a vendor site as well as software programs that are written and maintained by internal programmers, purchased from and maintained by vendors, or reside at third-party processor sites. This book focuses on those computing systems that have or should have some form of auditable security associated with them. Although even basic calculators could be considered computing systems, they are insignificant in terms of the risks associated with their use. Thus, they are excluded from the scope of this book.

Once the "universe" of computing systems in an organization has been identified, the systems must be categorized by criticality; essentially a risk analysis must be performed on them. The risk analysis could prove to be very time consuming. The best method for evaluating the risk of the computing systems must be determined. For some it may be in terms of total dollar value of items processed by the system, while for others it may be the total number of items processed, total cost or investment in the system, potential losses if the system were corrupted, a combination of these criteria, or some other factors that may be deemed appropriate. The method that makes the most sense for the industry, the size of the organization, and the number and complexity of the computing systems in the organization must be determined. Software packages can assist in performing risk analyses. Although risk analysis software can be useful for obtaining general risk rankings, human judgment must always be exercised to make the final determination as to what systems are the highest risk and should be audited next.

One way to create an inventory is to begin by surveying managers within each work group. If the organization is large, a written survey form may need to be created and sent to the managers. In a small organization, telephoning managers and verbally asking them for the required information may be a more efficient way to complete the survey.

As the term *auditor* implies, one can often identify computing systems, especially those being proposed or those that are in the early stages of development, by what one hears during conversations with others in the organization or even through the grapevine. Case study 2.1 describes a situation in which an unknown aspect of an e-mail system was identified through the company grapevine.

Another way of identifying computing systems is to deploy some sort of network search program that identifies all executable files. Such a tool is also helpful in identifying pirated or other unauthorized software. However, this method will not identify all third-party processor systems or Internet-based applications. Optimally, a combination of methods should be used to identify all systems.

CASE STUDY 2.1

Identification of Unknown E-mail System

During an audit of a company's electronic mail process, it appeared that there were only two available methods through which employees could send and receive electronic messages. The primary electronic mail system was part of a mainframe application to which all employees were assigned access. Some users were also assigned access to the company's wide-area network. However, an electronic mail application was not installed on the network since a large number of employees were not network users.

All network users could send and receive electronic messages up to 240 characters long via a network operating system feature. This practice was discouraged by the network management group because it could disrupt certain file update procedures. Many employees found this feature amusing because the message would appear on the recipient's workstation screen and require him or her to click "OK" before continuing work, thus ensuring immediate reading unless the recipient was not at his or her workstation, in which case there was the risk that a passerby could read the message. These operating system messages were also less incriminating than regular e-mail messages because they could not be retrieved once the recipient had clicked "OK." (As a matter of note, it was possible to create a permanent record of these messages by pressing the "Print Screen" key before clicking "OK." This action would copy the screen and the message to the Windows clipboard. One could then open a word processing application and click "Paste" to copy the screen printed file. At that point, the file could be saved and printed. Thus, senders of these types of messages ran the risk of having the content of their messages re-created.)

As far as anyone in the Internal Audit Department was aware at the time, Internet electronic mail access was only in the planning stages, with general availability to all staff over one year away. Near the end of the audit, the manager heard from some colleagues that several areas, including all of the executives, had the capability to send and receive messages on the Internet. It was subsequently discovered that in addition to the executives, users in four departments, including marketing and network management, were assigned Internet electronic mail access. To our relief, the Internet electronic mail access was limited in that the company owned a file server that was installed at an off-site vendor location and was connected to the Internet through the vendor's mainframe. Thus, the vendor assumed the responsibility for deploying a firewall between its system and the Internet. To send or receive messages via the Internet, users had to dial in to an off-site network file server and sign on. The risk was primarily limited to that of viruses being attached to any messages that were sent to a user and subsequently downloaded to the user's workstation. Fortunately, this risk was already adequately controlled by a virus detection software application, which was installed on the wide-area network. The virus detection software was programmed to examine all incoming files for viruses in its virus database. Furthermore, the virus software vendor provided a quarterly update to help ensure that its virus inventory could adequately protect against new viruses.

It was not believed that there was any intent to deceive the Internal Audit Department. However, this example illustrates how people in many organizations sometimes may not think to notify internal or external auditors of a new system. In this case, the network management group and the users apparently did not consider that an internal audit group would be concerned about the risks associated with Internet electronic mail access (e.g., hacking, viruses, probing, data damage) and the controls to mitigate such risks (e.g., firewalls, system monitoring, logging, virus protection software, backup procedures). In their minds, the system was a new service that was made available on a limited basis to select employees until the infrastructure for company-wide Internet electronic mail access was in place. They believed that the system had a relatively low risk and that the risks were mitigated. They did not consider the fact that it is the job of information systems (IS) auditors to independently assess the risks and adequacy of related controls over computing systems, preferably prior to the installation of the systems.

BENEFITS OF A COMPUTING SYSTEMS INVENTORY

Once completed, the computing systems inventory can provide several useful benefits. First, as mentioned previously, it will help in assessing the size and complexity of the computing systems environment within the organization. Some computing systems of which one was unaware may be identified. Some of these systems may subject the organization to significant risks due to the relative ease and rapidity with which new systems can be purchased or developed internally at end-user sites. Often managers in end-user areas are too busy or may intentionally neglect to inform an auditing department or other interested parties of the development of new computing systems.

A second benefit of the computing systems inventory is that it can help to identify work areas where the same or similar data is being stored and utilized. In these cases, there may be opportunities for consolidation of data storage resources and data processing resources, potentially resulting in reduced expenses and increased efficiency.

A third benefit is that the inventory can help both internal and external audit management in planning what computing systems to examine and in budgeting human resources and the necessary dollars to perform the examinations. Case study 2.2 describes a situation in which a computing systems inventory was developed and utilized.

CASE STUDY 2.2

Preparing and Utilizing a Computing Systems Inventory

Several years ago, as the only IS auditor in a financial institution, the external audit manager requested a list of all the computing systems in the organization that had some form of logical security associated with them. The external auditors planned to use this inventory to ensure that internal audits designed to assess the adequacy of controls and security over the highest-risk systems were being performed on a regular basis. The external auditors also performed additional independent tests to enable them to attest as to the adequacy and effectiveness of the general controls over these high-risk systems, thus helping them gain assurance that the risk of material errors in the financial statements was minimal. Each year the external auditors requested an updated inventory.

The computing systems inventory is a very useful tool in preparing the annual internal audit plan for information systems. More recently, the list has become an item of interest to management in the IS division of the organization because it helps identify stand-alone computing system applications that may be candidates for being networked, thereby reducing data redundancies and software costs. The cost of a multiuser license for network software allowing, for example, 20 concurrent users, is usually more economical than purchasing 20 single-user copies of the same software.

The list also included any computing systems that were scheduled to be replaced or new systems that were being developed. Again, the IS division management was interested in these systems because some end-user organizations may have been considering the purchase and/or installation of systems to meet needs that existing systems may have been able to address.

Exhibit 2.1 provides an example of what part of the computing systems inventory looked like in a financial institution. It is sorted by type of operating system or platform on which the computing system exists, the name of the department process owner, and the business application. Normally, another column indicating the name by which the system is commonly known would be listed. The name is usually the name of the actual product, service, vendor, or developer. However, since the name is usually trademarked or otherwise protected, that column has been omitted from the exhibit. This list is by no means comprehensive, but it is intended to give readers an idea of the wide variety of operating systems, database management systems, and applications they are likely to encounter.

RISK ASSESSMENT

Now that the computing systems in an organization have been identified, one has the necessary information to begin performing a risk assessment of the IS environment. Additional data regarding the dollar amounts, transaction volume, and other information should be obtained to enable ranking of the computing systems from most risky to least risky. It is a good idea to record all the computing system demographic information in a spreadsheet, database, or other audit planning application. The computing systems can then be sorted by various criteria, such as process owner, dollar volume, operating system, and application type. Often this can aid in audit efficiency and effectiveness by assisting in determining which audits need to be performed and the order in which they should be performed. As previously mentioned, special over-the-counter software applications are available to assist in the risk assessment process. However, such software is by no means a requirement. An internally developed spreadsheet or database application may be quite sufficient.

Examine the application description column in Exhibit 2.1. You will notice some very high-risk computing systems. For example, wire transfer systems present the single highest risk that financial institutions face.[1] Automated clearing house (ACH) transactions are also a high-risk process. In many U.S. financial institutions, wire transfer and ACH transactions are processed through a single personal computer (PC)–based application that is developed and distributed by the U.S. Federal Reserve. Other high-risk systems on the inventory list include telecommunications systems, incoming and outgoing check processing systems, and automated teller machine (ATM) systems.

Sometimes even seemingly obscure systems can present significant risks. For example, the credit report request workstations listed in Exhibit 2.1 may, at the surface, appear to require minimal security. However, if these terminals are not adequately secured, either physically or logically, an unauthorized user could request credit reports through the terminals. Since most credit report database companies record inquiries by creditor organizations, the person whose credit information was obtained by the unauthorized user could find out that an unauthorized credit report on his or her name had been requested by a particular creditor organization. The person may then be able to successfully sue the creditor organization for privacy violation if he or she can prove that the unauthorized inquiry

EXHIBIT 2.1   SAMPLE INVENTORY OF COMPUTING SYSTEMS WITH LOGICAL SECURITY

Primary Operating System(s)	Department/Process Owner	Application Description
3rd Party/Compaq VMS (formerly DEC)	Support Services	Insurance claims/payments via client web browser that communicates with vendor host computer
3rd Party/IBM OS/390	Customer Service	Travelers' check inventory; client workstation direct-dials into vendor host computer
3rd Party/IBM OS/390	Lending/Collections	Credit report requests via stand-alone direct dial workstations located in Loan and Collections Departments
3rd Party/IBM OS/390	Lending/Consumer	Paperless vehicle title processing via client web browser that communicates with vendor host computer
3rd Party/IBM OS/390	Lending/Credit Card	Credit card accounting and operations via frame relay communications with vendor host computer
3rd Party/IBM OS/390	Support Services	Wire transfers, ACH, cash orders through the Federal Reserve
3rd Party/IBM OS/390	Support Services	Send/receive consumer credit history dispute information via web browser that communicates with vendor host computer
3rd Party/IBM OS/390	Support Services	Outgoing check processing; DB2 DBMS
3rd Party/Tandem	Operations/ATM	ATM hotcards, adjustments, PIN orders/reorders via client web browser that communicates with vendor host computer
Cisco	IS/Telecommunications	Bridges and routers connecting various servers and telecom devices
DOS	Facilities	Heating, ventilation, and cooling

EXHIBIT 2.1 *(continued)*

Primary Operating System(s)	Department/Process Owner	Application Description
IBM OS/400, OS/2	Support Services	Incoming check processing; DB2 DBMS
NetWare 5/Mac OS X	Information Systems	Subnetwork used in Marketing Department with MacIntosh OS X workstations
Unix	Information Systems	Firewall
Unix	Information Systems	Physical security to data center (electronic access badges)
Unix	IS/Telecommunications	Voice response for rate line, fax line, other miscellaneous applications
Unix	IS/Telecommunications	Voice mail
Unix	IS/Telecommunications	Reports incoming and outgoing ECS calls; controls some ECS call routing
Unix	IS/Telecommunications	Primary telephone system (ECS or enterprise communications server; formerly called PBX or private branch exchange)
Unix	Operations/Customer Service	Primary deposit and lending system; uses Oracle 9i DBMS
Windows 2000	Accounting	PeopleSoft ERP (financial accounting, accounts payable, fixed assets inventory & reporting); uses SQL Server DBMS
Windows 2000	Finance	Asset and liability management
Windows 2000	Human Resources	Lawson ERP (payroll; human resources demographic/statistical reporting); uses SQL Server DBMS
Windows 2000	Information Systems	Primary internal network; Windows 2000 workstations
Windows 2000	Information Systems	Internet

(continued)

EXHIBIT 2.1   *(continued)*

Primary Operating System(s)	Department/Process Owner	Application Description
Windows 2000	Information Systems	E-mail
Windows 2000	Information Systems	CRYPTOCard token card authentication
Windows 2000	Information Systems	Audio response (telephone) banking
Windows 2000	Information Systems	Wide-area network (WAN) for local and remote facilities
Windows 2000	Information Systems	Internet home banking
Windows 2000	IS/Records Management	Electronic records storage/ retrieval; includes electronic imaging
Windows 2000	IS/Telecommunications	Tracks incoming and outgoing calls to monitor for abuse
Windows 2000	Investments	Electronic investments safekeeping
Windows 2000	Lending/Real Estate	Mortgage loan origination
Windows 2000	Marketing	Demographic information on customers

was the result of poor internal controls. Case study 2.3 describes a situation in which an unauthorized credit report was obtained at a financial institution.

CASE STUDY 2.3

Unauthorized Credit Report

An employee at a financial institution was found to have requested an unauthorized credit report via a terminal that had no physical or logical security controls to prevent such access. The terminal was located in an unrestricted area of the building and a user ID and password were not required to initiate a credit report request. Seizing this opportunity, the employee requested a credit report on her ex-spouse's new love interest. The unauthorized credit

(continued)

EXHIBIT 2.2   SAMPLE RISK ASSESSMENT MATRIX FOR A GENERAL NETWORK AUDIT

Risk Description[a]	Probability of Occurrence[b]	Impact of Occurrence[b]	Overall Risk Ranking	Control Descriptions[c]
1. Accidental or intentional loss, damage, alteration, insertion, disclosure, fraudulent use, or other compromise of information by an authorized or unauthorized LAN user or internal or external hacker	3	4	12	
2. Lost, damaged, and/or inaccessible data due to system failures or disasters (e.g., computer viruses, worms, fire, flood, earthquake, volcano, terrorism, etc.)	3	4	12	
3. Cost overruns and excessive maintenance and upgrade costs	2	3	6	
4. Theft of computer hardware, peripherals, laptops, etc.	2	2	4	
5. Software piracy or copyright violations (e.g., Digital Millennium Copyright Act)	2	2	4	
6. Failure to comply with other laws and regulations (privacy, disclosures, etc.)	1	2	2	

[a]Risks should be described at the 10,000- to 20,000-foot level to avoid getting caught up in too much detail and minutia. Unless the process is extremely complicated or the scope is very large, there should only be about 5 to 10 major risks. Risks should not be stated as control failure statements (this is a common mistake).

[b]Probability of Occurrence and Impact of Occurrence should each be quantified on a scale of 1 to 5. A probability of 5 would mean the risk is certain to happen or already happened. An impact of 5 means that it would likely cause the organization to cease operations (e.g., Enron). The overall risk ranking is the product of the probability and impact. It has a maximum risk ranking score of 25. The above quantifications are provided only as examples. Each organization's quantifications will be different. List risks in risk order.

[c]List all significant controls within the scope of the network audit. The controls should be cross-referenced to each step in the network audit program as well as to the internal control model being applied (e.g., COSO, CoCo, Cobit, etc.).

report was identified by the violated person when she applied for credit and was informed that there had been a recent inquiry from the financial institution in question. The ensuing investigation by the financial institution revealed that the employee had the opportunity and the motive to request the unauthorized credit report. The employee was summarily terminated, although the damage had already been done. Fortunately for the financial institution, the violated person did not sue.

Based on the results of the risk assessment, the highest-risk computing systems can be selected and audits of their controls can be performed. The audit program presented in Chapter 3 is designed to help one obtain reasonable comfort that key controls over the computing systems have been deployed and that these controls are functioning adequately enough to protect the computer hardware, software, and data in an organization against unauthorized access and accidental or intentional destruction or alteration.

Exhibit 2.2 presents a template risk assessment matrix for a general network audit.

NOTE

1. Jack Champlain, "Is Your Wire Transfer System Secure?" *Internal Auditor Journal* (June 1995): 56–59.

PART TWO

Standard Information Systems Audit Approach

CHAPTER 3

Information Systems
Audit Program

Audit programs are necessary to perform an effective and efficient audit. Audit programs are essentially checklists of the various tests that auditors must perform within the scope of their audits to determine whether key controls intended to mitigate significant risks are functioning as designed. Based on the results of the tests performed, the auditor should be able to determine the adequacy of the controls over a particular process.

OTHER BENEFITS OF AUDIT PROGRAMS

Audit programs can also assist audit management in resource planning. For example, management can estimate the total number of hours required to perform an audit based on the expected amount of time required to perform each of the steps in the audit program. Another benefit of audit programs is that they can help promote consistency in tests performed on audits of the same process from one cycle to the next. During planning and preparation for an audit, audit programs used during the previous audit usually can be employed as the basis for the steps to be performed during the current audit. This obviously does not apply in cases in which the process has never been audited before or where the process has changed significantly. In these cases, new audit programs must to be created.

Audit programs can also promote consistency in tests performed on controls that are common to all processes. For example, in many organizations, system security administrators perform additions, changes, and deletions of users and their access capabilities. Department managers are responsible for authorizing the access capabilities granted to their employees by these system security administrators. In these cases, it may be more practical to examine the system access capabilities of users as each particular process or department is audited rather than trying to examine the access capabilities of all users at one time. If an audit department elects to examine user access capabilities on a process or department basis, it would be useful to develop a standard audit program to help ensure that auditors are evaluating such capabilities on a consistent basis.

INFORMATION SYSTEMS AUDIT PROGRAM

Exhibit 3.1 shows the information systems (IS) audit program that is the foundation of Part Two of this book. The audit program is designed to address the primary risks of virtually all computing systems. Therefore, the objective statement and steps in the program are general by design. Obviously, computing systems can have many different applications running on them, each with its own unique set of controls. However, the controls surrounding all computing systems are very similar. The IS controls in the audit program have been grouped into four general categories:

EXHIBIT 3.1   INFORMATION SYSTEMS AUDIT PROGRAM

Objective: To assess the adequacy of environmental, physical security, logical security, and operational controls designed to protect IS hardware, software, and data against unauthorized access and accidental or intentional destruction or alteration, and to ensure that information systems are functioning in an efficient and effective manner to help the organization achieve its strategic objectives.

TESTS OF ENVIRONMENTAL CONTROLS (CHAPTERS 4 THROUGH 6)

Step 1.   Assess the adequacy and effectiveness of the organization's IS security policy. In addition, assess whether the control requirements specified in the organization's IS security standards adequately protect the information assets of the organization. At a minimum, the standards should specify the following controls and require them to be applicable to all information systems:

   a.   The maiden password should be changed after the system is installed.
   b.   There is a minimum password length of eight or more characters.
   c.   Passwords require a combination of alpha and numeric characters.
   d.   The password is masked on the screen as it is entered.
   e.   The password file is encrypted so *nobody* can read it.
   f.   There is a password expiration period of 60 days or less.
   g.   Three or fewer unsuccessful sign-on attempts are allowed, then the user ID is suspended.
   h.   User sessions are terminated after a specified period of inactivity (e.g., five minutes or less).
   i.   Concurrent sign-on sessions are not allowed.
   j.   Procedures are in place to remove user IDs of terminated users in a timely manner.
   k.   Users are trained not to share or divulge their passwords with other users, post them in their workstations, store them in elec-

---

EXHIBIT 3.1   *(continued)*

---

           tronic files, or perform any other act that could divulge their passwords.

    l.   Unsuccessful sign-on attempts and other logical security-related events (e.g., adding and deleting users, resetting passwords, restarting the system) are logged by the system, and the log is reviewed regularly by system security staff.

    m. Fully developed and tested backup and recovery procedures exist to help ensure uninterrupted business resumption in the event of a full or partial disaster.

    n.   New information systems are required to be designed to enable the aforementioned controls to be implemented by system security administrators. New systems include those developed in house, those purchased from vendors, and third-party processor systems. In the case of software vendors and third-party processors, the above control requirements should be specified as requirements in the contract.

Step 2.   For service organization applications, examine the most recent report on the policies and procedures placed in operation at the vendor's data processing site as prepared by its external auditors. In the United States, the format and testing requirements are dictated by Statement on Auditing Standards 70 (SAS 70), issued by the American Institute of Certified Public Accountants. SAS 70 reports may also describe tests of the operating effectiveness of the policies and procedures if the vendor has contracted the external auditor to do so.[a]

    a.   Assess the adequacy of controls described in the report and determine whether applicable control recommendations have been implemented at your organization.

    b. If applicable, determine whether another type of security or privacy certification exists (e.g., TruSecure, SysTrust, WebTrust, BBBOnline, TRUSTe).

Step 3.   If the system was purchased from and supported by a vendor, assess the financial stability of the system vendor using the most recent *audited* financial statements prepared by the vendor's external auditors. (Optimally, this step should be performed prior to when the decision is made to purchase the system. Otherwise, significant resources could be wasted on a system for which the vendor will no longer exist.)

---

[a]See Chapter 5 for a discussion on SAS 70 and the equivalents in Canada, the United Kingdom, and Australia. Chapter 5 also contains a discussion of other security and privacy certifications.

(continued)

EXHIBIT 3.1   *(continued)*

> a.   Select a sample of recent invoices from the system vendor and determine whether costs have been properly recorded and classified on the financial statements of your organization. Costs should normally be amortized over the expected useful life of the system.
>
> b.   For IS development projects, determine whether applicable internal development costs (e.g., programmer hours) have been capitalized and amortized over the estimated useful life of the internal use system in accordance with AICPA Statement of Position (SOP) 98-1 (does not apply to software sold to external parties). See Chapter 15 for details on IS development projects.

Step 4.   Examine the vendor software license agreement and any agreements for ongoing maintenance and support to ensure that they are current, address service needs, and do not contain or omit any wording that could be detrimental to your organization. Where applicable, the agreements should also require that a copy of the programming source code of the current version of the software be stored in escrow by an independent third party so that it is available to your company in the event the vendor goes out of business or another stipulated event occurs (e.g., breach of contract; software no longer supported by vendor).

TESTS OF PHYSICAL SECURITY CONTROLS (CHAPTER 7)

Step 5.   Assess the adequacy of physical security over the computer system hardware and storage media.

Step 6.   Determine whether an adequately trained backup system security administrator has been designated.

Step 7.   Assess the adequacy and effectiveness of the written business resumption plan, including the results of mock disaster tests that have been performed.

> a.   Assess the adequacy of backup procedures for system software and data. The procedures should include periodic backups as necessary (daily, weekly, monthly), off-site storage at a secure location, and rotation of backup media.
>
> b.   Verify that at least one alternative set of processes exists for each key assumption (transportation, communications, staffing, processing facilities, etc.).

Step 8.   Assess the adequacy of insurance coverage over the hardware, operating system, application software, and data. Hardware should be covered at replacement cost. The costs of re-creating any lost software and data should be covered. Optimally, coverage should include lost revenues directly resulting from hardware failure and loss

EXHIBIT 3.1   *(continued)*

of the operating system, application software, and data during covered events.

TESTS OF LOGICAL SECURITY CONTROLS (CHAPTER 8)

Step 9.   Determine whether the maiden password for the system has been changed and whether controls exist to change it on a periodic basis in conformity with the computing system security policy, standards, or guidelines identified in Step 1.

Step 10.   Observe the system security administrator sign on and print a list of current system users and their access capabilities. Alternatively, if you can obtain appropriate system access, you can obtain the list of users independently.

    a.   Assess the reasonableness of the access capabilities assigned to each user.

    b.   Confirm that user IDs of terminated employees are suspended in a timely manner.

    c.   Confirm that system access capabilities of transferred employees are adjusted accordingly.

Step 11.   Document and assess the reasonableness of the default system security parameter settings. The settings should conform to the organization's computing system security policy, standards, or guidelines tested in Step 1. (Be alert to the fact that in some systems, individual user parameter settings override the default system security parameter settings.)

Step 12.   Test the functionality of the logical security controls of the system (e.g., password masking, minimum password length, password expiration, user ID suspended after successive invalid sign-on attempts, log-on times allowed, and session time-outs).

Step 13.   Determine whether the file containing user passwords is encrypted and cannot be viewed by anyone, including the system security administrator.

Step 14.   Determine whether sensitive data, including passwords, are adequately encrypted throughout their life cycles, including during storage, transmission through any internal or external network or telecommunications devices, and duplication on any backup media.

Step 15.   Assess the adequacy of procedures to review the log of system security-related events (e.g., successive invalid sign-on attempts, system restarts, changes to user access capabilities and user parameter settings).

(continued)

EXHIBIT 3.1 *(continued)*

Step 16. Assess the adequacy of remote access controls (e.g., virtual private networks [VPNs], token devices [CRYPTOCard, SecurID, etc.], automatic dial-back, secure sockets layer [SSL]).

TESTS OF INFORMATION SYSTEMS OPERATING CONTROLS (CHAPTER 9)

Step 17. Determine whether duties are adequately segregated in the operating areas supporting the information system (e.g., transactions should be authorized only by the originating department, programmers should not have the capability to execute production programs, procedures should be adequately documented, etc.).

Step 18. Determine whether there have been any significant software problems with the system. Assess the adequacy, timeliness, and documentation of resolution efforts.

Step 19. Assess the adequacy of controls that help ensure that IS operations are functioning in an efficient and effective manner to support the strategic objectives and business operations of the organization (e.g., system operators should be monitoring CPU processing and storage capacity utilization throughout each day to ensure that adequate reserve capacities exist at all times).

---

1. Environmental controls
2. Physical security controls
3. Logical security controls
4. IS operating controls

Environmental controls are more general than physical or logical security controls. They often dictate the extent to which physical and logical security controls are deployed. Environmental controls include such items as IS security policies, standards, and guidelines; the reporting structure within the IS processing environment (including computer operations and programming); the financial condition of service organizations and vendors; vendor software license, maintenance, and support agreements and warranties; and the status of computing system policies and procedures placed in operation at service organizations, if applicable. (See Exhibit 1.1 for conceptual model including environmental controls. Environmental controls are discussed in Chapters 4 through 6.)

Physical security controls pertain to the protection over computer hardware, components, and the facilities within which they reside. Although somewhat of an environmental control, insurance coverage over computing system hardware and the costs to re-create or replace lost or damaged software programs and data will be discussed in association with physical security controls since they are closely related. Chapter 7 delves into the various aspects of physical security.

Logical security controls are those that have been deployed within the operating system and applications to help prevent unauthorized access and accidental or intentional destruction of programs and data. They include system access capabilities of users, system access profiles and parameters, and logging mechanisms. Logical security controls are discussed in more detail in Chapter 8.

Chapter 9 is dedicated to information system operating controls, which are those designed to help ensure that the information system is operating efficiently and effectively. These controls include the timely and accurate completion of production jobs, distribution of output media, performance of backup and recovery procedures, performance of maintenance procedures, documentation and resolution of system problems, and monitoring of central processing unit and data storage capacity utilization.

Throughout Chapters 4 through 9, the theory supporting why each step in the audit program should be performed is presented in the first part of each chapter. The second part of each chapter includes one or more descriptions of real-world situations that illustrate how the concepts were applied in practice. These chapters are presented in the order they appear in the audit program. To provide flexibility to readers when using the audit program as a reference, each chapter has been designed as an independent module.

CHAPTER 4

Information Systems Security Policies, Standards, and/or Guidelines

One of the key elements of the internal control environment within any organization is its information systems (IS) security policy (see Exhibit 1.1). An IS security policy provides the high-level framework from which all other IS security-related controls are derived. Many of us assume that nearly all organizations have an IS security policy or something that would qualify as such. Shockingly, this is not the case. According to a 1996 Datapro Information Services Group survey of over 1,300 organizations from the United States, Canada, Central and South America, Europe, and Asia, only 54 percent had an IS security policy. This was down from a high of 82 percent in 1992 and was the lowest figure since Datapro began the survey in 1991.[1] The survey also indicated that only 62 percent of respondent organizations had assigned a specific person to be responsible for computer security, and the majority of respondents reported that less than 5 percent of their organization's information technology (IT) budget is allocated for security.

A separate worldwide survey by Xephon of England confirmed Datapro's findings. Xephon found that fewer than 60 percent of responding organizations had IS security policies. Of those that did, Xephon found that the policies were essentially made in a vacuum, with only one in five based on external standards.[2]

More recently, a July 2000 industry survey conducted by *Information Security* magazine found that 22 percent of organizations did not have a security policy and 2 percent of respondents did not know if their organization had a policy.[3] Similarly, a 2000 *Internet Week* survey of IT and security managers found that 25 percent had no formal IT security policy.[4]

The results of these surveys are alarming. They indicate that many organizations are complacent with regard to information security in an age when computers and information systems are proliferating at an exponential rate and the risks are critical. If an organization does not have an IS security policy, a significant internal control weakness has been identified. A security policy should be developed and implemented as soon as possible.

Furthermore, procedures should be implemented to ensure that the policy and supporting standards are updated to include new laws and regulations as well as changes in technology and business practices. The policy and any updates should be communicated to all employees on a regular basis (at least annually). Applicable portions of the policy and standards should also be communicated to all contingent staff (vendors, consultants, temps, etc.).

The terms *policies*, *standards*, and *guidelines* are frequently used interchangeably in many companies. This is also the case when members of an organization are discussing IS security documents. However, differences among these terms are important to understand before evaluating the adequacy of IS security within an organization. The following sections define and discuss each of these terms to clarify the differences

INFORMATION SYSTEMS SECURITY POLICIES

Information systems security policies are high-level overall statements describing the general goals of an organization with regard to the control and security over its information systems. Policies should specify who is responsible for their implementation. Policies are usually established by management and approved by the board of directors. Because most boards meet only monthly, changes to policies can often take several months to become official. If the change is significant, the board may request additional information or research before it will vote on the change. If the change is relatively minor, there may not be sufficient time in their agenda to address minor policy changes. For these reasons, it is important that the IS security policy not be too specific. For example, the policy should require that the organization provide adequate physical and logical security controls over computer hardware, software, and data to protect them against unauthorized access and accidental or unintentional damage, destruction, or alteration. However, the policy should not specify detailed controls, such as the minimum number of characters required for passwords or the maximum number of unsuccessful sign-on attempts allowed before suspending a user ID. If this were the case, senior management would be constantly submitting policy change requests to the board. As we all know, often controls that were thought to be strong have been rendered inadequate by advances in technology. At one time, five-character passwords were thought to be sufficient for business applications. With hacking software available at little or no cost on the Internet, passwords of eight or more characters are now required in many organizations. Therefore, it is more practical to include detailed IS control requirements in the IS security standards of an organization. Standards are discussed in the next section.

Exhibit 4.1 provides an example of an IS security policy. The policy is divided into five sections:

1. Purpose and Responsibility
2. System Procurement and Development
3. Access Terminals

4. Equipment and Information Security
5. Service Bureau Programs

In general, this policy is reasonably adequate. However, there are a number of opportunities where the policy could be changed to increase its overall effectiveness. Each section of the policy that contains an area that could be improved will be critiqued to demonstrate how an auditor could assess the adequacy of a policy and formulate recommendations to improve its overall effectiveness.

EXHIBIT 4.1   INFORMATION SYSTEMS SECURITY POLICY EXAMPLE

SECTION 1: PURPOSE AND RESPONSIBILITY

The Company operates various forms of computing and telecommunications systems throughout its operations. For purposes of this policy, the term "systems" shall refer to all computer operations (mainframe, minis, micros, personal computers, and telecommunications) and any other functional areas in which data is transmitted via an electronic or telecommunications medium.

The purpose of the Company's Information Systems Security Policy is to provide the essential guidelines for efficient electronic transaction processing and reporting services, management information systems, and appropriate customer information capabilities for management and the Board of Directors to effectively operate the Company. In addition, this policy is designed to ensure continuous support and improvement of the computing and telecommunications systems of the Company.

It shall be the responsibility of the President or his/her designated individual(s) and Senior Management Committee to manage the Company's computing and telecommunications systems. The President shall establish an operating structure that optimizes the systems capabilities of the Company consistent with sound business practices. The various systems will be continually monitored to ensure proper functioning and the ability to meet the current and future needs of the Company. The President and Senior Management Committee shall be responsible for and direct the feasibility studies regarding development, implementation, and system conversions, as well as the continued operation of the Company's computing and telecommunications systems.

SECTION 2: SYSTEM PROCUREMENT AND DEVELOPMENT

The Company's procurement, development, and operation of data processing systems (hardware and software) shall be managed by the President or his/her designated individuals and the Senior Management Committee. The computing systems of the Company shall be constantly monitored, and should a current and/or future need for change be identified, the Company should follow the system life-cycle evaluation steps outlined on the next page.

(continued)

EXHIBIT 4.1   *(continued)*

---

 a. Scope definition—A description of the needs to be addressed
 b. Requirement definition—A description of the requirements of the end user and the objective of the new development
 c. Review of alternative solutions
 d. System design
 e. System development
 f. System testing
 g. System monitoring

SECTION 3: ACCESS TERMINALS

Management is authorized to install other dial-up access online terminals as may be required in operations of the Company.

SECTION 4: EQUIPMENT AND INFORMATION SECURITY

The establishment and maintenance of a complete security program covering computing systems is the responsibility of the President or his/her designated individual(s). The systems and related information will be protected and provided a safe operating environment. The controls and security that shall exist include, but are not limited to, the following:

a. Equipment and Environmental Security

Proper security for the computer and telecommunications systems shall be established and maintained as necessary to protect the equipment and related data. The primary intent of protecting these systems from a breach of security shall be to limit unnecessary interruptions in system processing time and to prevent the corruption of Company data. The Company's mainframe computer room, as well as appropriate other computing and telecommunications system facilities as determined by management, shall be supported by an uninterrupted power supply, which will also function as a temporary source of power in the event of a power failure. The physical environment for these system facilities will be adequately protected from fire, smoke, and water. In addition, the Company will maintain and support the proper heating, ventilation, and air conditioning required by the various systems. Access to the systems will also be properly maintained and monitored by security personnel. All systems hardware and the costs of re-creating any lost data will be adequately insured.

b. Information and Communication Security

The Company is to maintain integrity and security controls for protection of all computing and telecommunications systems, which is intended to also address the risks that arise from potential misuse of computing system resources. The establishment of these controls shall include, but not be limited to, the following steps:

 i. Logical access controls
 ii. An information resource classification method

EXHIBIT 4.1 *(continued)*

---

iii. Network and local access security
iv. Retention and disposal of information
v. An incident reporting system to analyze errors and develop procedures to prevent future occurrences

Measures used to establish and/or enhance such controls should be appropriately justified as to their cost and financial benefit relative to criticality and sensitivity of the information resources being protected.

c. Contingency and Recovery

Backup systems support contracts shall be established to protect the Company in the event of an unforeseen breakdown or catastrophe. The Company is to develop and maintain a plan that addresses the risk that such events can occur. This shall require planning for alternate computing system processing options (facilities, equipment, etc.) and that the necessary procedures be established in order to successfully achieve each of these alternatives. This is to ensure that the Company can provide for business continuity. Minimum contingency requirements should include, but not be limited to, the following steps:

i. Identification of critical applications to determine their priority for recovery.
ii. Documented backup and recovery plan(s) that include all related or potentially affected information assets (and their probable/potential) effects on any/all operational areas).
iii. Test procedures at least once each year to evaluate the plan's effectiveness on information assets, personnel, and all other potentially affected operational areas.
iv. The Company shall maintain backup data at an off-site location to limit risk and allow for the timely recovery of data should on-site information be destroyed, corrupted, or for whatever reason made unusable.

SECTION 5: SERVICE BUREAU PROGRAMS

The Company's service bureau agreements shall be drafted to require that such bureaus retained by the Company indicate a commitment to developing and maintaining computer application software in such a manner that system capabilities, as specified by the Company, are ensured and that appropriate record-keeping checks and balances are in place. The agreements should detail the level of support the service bureaus will provide with existing programs, new programs developed, and program updates. Consequently, the following steps are designed to facilitate a positive interaction with all service bureaus being utilized:

a. Programming requests by the Company shall be monitored as to the timeliness of response by the service bureaus, and where timeliness

(continued)

EXHIBIT 4.1 *(continued)*

---

or quality of performance is questionable, the President or his/her designate shall evaluate alternative for better performance.

b. The Company, through its own as well as the service bureaus' verification systems, will ensure that the new system's software is operating correctly before conversions are made to standard operational use.

c. The service bureaus' system software supplied will be supported by detailed documentation instructing the Company on operating and error recording procedures.

Section 1: Purpose and Responsibility

The second sentence in the first paragraph provides a definition of the term *systems*. However, the definition is somewhat dated in that it does not specify certain types of computers and methods of data transmission commonly in use today. To provide a more universal definition that encompasses recent technological advances, a recommendation could be submitted to management to change the definition of systems to read:

> For purposes of this policy, the term *systems* shall refer to all computer operations within the company, including, but not limited to, mainframes, midranges, minis, local- and wide-area networks, personal desktop and laptop computers, telecommunications, any new technologies currently under development, and any other specialized computers residing in functional areas where data is transmitted or processed via electronic, telecommunications, satellite, microwave, or other media.

The third paragraph appropriately specifies that the president or his or her designated individual(s) and Senior Management Committee are responsible for managing the company's computing and telecommunication systems. Readers should note that in some large organizations with complex computing systems environments, an IS *steering committee* consisting of various members of senior management and other key managers is assigned the responsibility for managing and directing all computing system resources. In fact, the external auditors of this organization recommended that an IS steering committee be created. When an organization decides to create a steering committee, the policy must be adjusted accordingly.

Section 2: System Procurement and Development

Section 2 specifies the steps required when new information systems are being considered in the organization. These steps represent a fairly standard systems development life-cycle approach. However, one major step is missing between system testing and system monitoring. There should be a step called *system imple-mentation*. System implementation is the culmination of all previous planning and development stages. It is where a new system is placed into production and where the project development team finds out how well the system performs under a continuous load of live data. The effects of a new system implementation on an organization can vary significantly, depending on the number of hardware com-ponents, programs, and amount of data processed by a new system. Major imple-mentations are often performed over weekends to provide more of a time cush-ion should unforeseen problems arise. Some implementations can take place over a period of weeks or months, as different parts of a system are brought online. Organizations often elect to keep an old system operating concurrently with a newly implemented system to provide additional assurance that the new system is fully capable of processing data without any significant problems. Due to the importance of the implementation phase in the life cycle of a new information system, a recommendation to add a system implementation step to the IS secu-rity policy would be warranted.

Section 3: Access Terminals

Section 3 does not contain enough information to warrant a separate section. Therefore, the section should be deleted or consolidated into Section 4.

Section 4: Equipment and Information Security

Section 4 divides security into three subsections:

a. Equipment and environmental security
b. Information and communication security
c. Contingency and recovery

Subsection b requires the establishment of at least five specific controls (items i through v). Among these controls, item i (logical access controls) and item iii (network and local access security) are critical for inclusion in any IS security policy. However, a deficiency exists in that these two statements are essentially referring to the same type of controls. Readers of the policy in Exhibit 4.1 could become confused when they see logical security and network and local access security listed as separate controls.

As discussed in Chapter 1, logical security controls are those that restrict the access capabilities of users of the system and prevent unauthorized users from accessing the system. Logical security controls may exist within the operating system, the database management system, the application program, or all three. Since operating systems and application programs exist in any computer perform-ing specific functions, the existence of logical security is not dependent on the size or type of computer. Logical security should exist in mainframes, midranges, minis, wide- and local-area networks, networks, stand-alone computers, and any other type of equipment that allows electronic access to data within an organization.

Networks were included in the definition of systems in the Section 1 of the policy, along with all other types of computing systems. Since network security can be considered a subset of the overall logical security environment of the organization, it should not be specifically mentioned as a separate set of controls under Section 4, subsection b.

In the reference to local access security in item iii, it is not clear what the term *local* refers to. Access to any system can take place from a variety of locations, including where the central processing unit (CPU) resides, at an end user workstation, or from a remote location via a dial-in communication connection. Depending on one's point of view, any of these locations could be considered local. Therefore, it would be better to combine the two control statements in items i and iii into a single, all-encompassing phrase, such as "logical access controls over the operating systems, database management systems, and applications of all company computing and telecommunication systems."

Section 5: Service Bureau Programs

Section 5 addresses most policy-related issues pertaining to service bureaus. However, one important risk that is not addressed pertains to the disposition of the original application source code in the event the service bureau ceases operations or otherwise fails to fulfill a significant aspect of its contract with the client organization. Many companies require the source code of the application version currently in use to be held in escrow by an independent third party. The third party would be authorized to release the source code to the client organization if specific aspects of the contract are not fulfilled. If applicable, the source code escrow requirement should also apply to contracts with software vendors who supply and maintain programs for the organization but who are not service bureaus. By specifying this requirement in contracts, the client organization can reduce the risk of business interruption if a service bureau or software vendor ceases operations. The organization would be able to continue to maintain and modify the vendor's application source code until a suitable replacement could be developed or purchased from another vendor.

A good idea would be to add a fourth step in policy Section 5 that reads: "Contracts with service bureau organizations and external software vendors shall specify that the original source code is to be held in escrow by an independent third party and that the source code shall be released to the Company in the event the service bureau or software vendor discontinues operations, ceases to support the software, or otherwise violates any *significant* terms of the contract." (*Note*: Further details of items to be specified in contracts with service bureaus and outside software vendors should be included in IS security standards. Such standards are discussed in the next section.) Since many of the risks associated with service bureaus are also applicable to software programs purchased from outside vendors, an additional recommendation would be to change the name of Section 5 to Service Bureau Programs and Outside Software Vendor Programs or to add a separate policy section to address any unique risks to which the organization may be exposed as a result of outside software vendor programs.

The following list summarizes the general concepts that were included in the IS security policy in Exhibit 4.1 as well as corrections of the noted deficiencies. Each of the items in the list should be included in the IS security policies of all organizations. If an organization does not utilize service bureaus or custom vendor software programs, they can be excluded from the policy. However, including them makes the policy more flexible by reducing the need to update or revise it when an organization decides to employ the services of a service bureau or custom software vendor.

Items to include in an information systems security policy:

- Statement of Purpose and Responsibility
- System Procurement and Development Approach
- Equipment and Environmental Security (i.e., physical security)
- Information and Communication Security (i.e., logical security)
- Contingency and Recovery (This is a subset of physical security, but it is acceptable to have a separate section due to its importance.)
- Service Bureau Programs (if applicable)
- Custom Vendor Software Programs (if applicable)

An organization's IS security policy should be examined to ensure that it contains at least the concepts presented in this list. Depending on the nature of the organization and the complexity and size of its computing systems environment, it may be necessary to recommend adding or deleting certain items from the IS security policy. In some cases, it may even be appropriate to have separate policies for each subsidiary, division, or other operating unit.

INFORMATION SYSTEMS SECURITY STANDARDS

Information systems security standards are minimum criteria, rules, and procedures established by senior management that must be implemented to help ensure the achievement of the IS security policy. They are implemented by staff (e.g., system security administrators and users) under the direction of management. Information systems security standards should specify the detailed requirements of each IS control. A few examples of detailed controls that should be specified in the standards would be an eight-character minimum password length, a 30-day password expiration period, and a requirement that passwords be composed of at least two alpha and two numeric characters. Standards should not be specific to any particular computer platform (i.e., make, model, or operating system). Instead, they should be general enough to apply to all existing and proposed information systems that possess some form of logical and/or physical security. Whenever management deems that the standards need to be changed, the changes can be communicated to staff and implemented without the need for the approval of the board of directors. This enables the organization to react more quickly to technological advances that may have weakened preexisting standards.

With regard to auditing, IS security standards provide a management approved benchmark or baseline against which the adequacy of controls applied to individual information systems can be assessed. Exhibit 4.2 provides an example of IS security standards that can be applied to many information systems. Management should ensure that the standards are applied to existing systems, that they are part of the design specifications for systems currently under development internally, and that contracts with external software vendors and service bureaus specify that their programs must comply with the standards. Occasionally situations may arise that warrant deviation from the standards. These deviations should be documented and approved by management responsible for the system and related processes.

EXHIBIT 4.2   SAMPLE INFORMATION SYSTEMS SECURITY STANDARDS

The following minimum IS security standards have been approved by senior management and are to be applied to applicable information systems within the organization:

1. Upon completion of initial installation of software, the maiden password shall be changed by the system security administrator.
2. A backup system security administrator shall be designated and trained to ensure continued operation of the system, even in the absence of the primary system security administrator.
3. System security administrators shall set parameters to require passwords to be a minimum of 8 alpha-numeric, case-sensitive characters in length.
4. Systems shall be designed so that passwords are masked (i.e., invisible) on workstation screens as they are entered by users.
5. Systems shall be designed so that password files are encrypted by a secure algorithm so that nobody, including system security administrators, can view them.
6. System security administrators shall set passwords to automatically expire within 60 days or less.
7. User IDs shall be suspended after three consecutive unsuccessful sign-on attempts. Users shall be required to contact system security administrators to have their user IDs reset. Only system security administrators shall have the capability to reset user IDs.
8. User sessions shall be terminated after five minutes of inactivity.
9. Users shall not be allowed concurrent sign-on sessions.
10. System security administrators shall remove the user IDs of terminated or transferred users immediately upon notification from the user department manager and/or the Human Resources Department. Procedures shall require department managers to notify all applicable system security administrators when users terminate or transfer.

EXHIBIT 4.2   (*continued*)

11. Department managers shall be responsible for training users not to share or divulge their passwords to anyone, write them down, post them in their workstations, store them in an electronic file, or perform any other act that could potentially result in their password being divulged.

12. System security administrators shall request user department management to review user access capabilities and certify in writing that the access capabilities of the users in their department are necessary to perform normal duties. This certification shall be performed at least annually, or more often if deemed necessary by senior management.

13. Logical security related events shall be logged by the system, and the log shall be continuously monitored by system security administrators for potential acts of unauthorized access. Examples of logical security-related events include unsuccessful sign-on attempts, addition/deletion of users and changes to their access capabilities, resetting of passwords, and system restarts. There are probably many other events that could be logged.

(*Note*: There is a trade-off between control and efficiency on this standard. The more events that are logged, the more memory that is required to store the events in the log file. In some systems, this "overhead" can lead to significant reduction in system performance or even a system failure if the log file is not purged. Also, system security administrators must spend more time reviewing the log file. Therefore, the system security administrator should work with management to determine the most critical events that their particular systems can log and that can be reviewed in a reasonable amount of time.)

14. Business resumption procedures shall be fully developed, tested, and documented by management in collaboration with system security administrators and other key staff members. The business resumption plan shall provide for complete system backups on a weekly basis, complete data backups on a daily basis, and rotation of backup media to a secure off-site facility on a three-or-more generation rotation cycle.

15. Adequate insurance coverage shall be maintained over the hardware, operating system, application software, and data. Hardware should be covered at replacement cost. The operating system, application software, and data shall be covered for the costs of re-creation. Lost revenues directly resulting from hardware failure and/or loss of the operating system, application software, and data during covered events shall be fully covered.

16. For custom applications developed by external software vendors, contracts shall specify that the original source code shall be held in escrow by an independent third party and that the source code shall be released to the purchaser in the event the vendor ceases to support the software or otherwise violates any "significant" terms of the contract.

(*continued*)

EXHIBIT 4.2   *(continued)*

Other items to be included in vendor contracts shall include the contract period, annual maintenance costs, types of maintenance provided, service level standards (i.e., response time requirements), and so on.

17. Vendor-developed applications acquired in the future should be contractually required to include programming that enables the standards to be deployed upon installation.
18. Confidential information, including passwords, shall be encrypted by a secure algorithm during electronic transmission.
19. System security administrators shall install software that automatically checks for viruses using a current virus pattern file. The virus software parameters should be set to examine all memory sectors of computers, including boot sectors, all permanent storage devices, and all incoming files. The software shall also be set to notify the system security administrator of any viruses identified.

OPTIONAL STANDARDS IF WARRANTED BY RISK (AND IF SYSTEM IS CAPABLE)

20. User access shall be restricted to normal work hours and days (e.g., 6 A.M. to 6 P.M., Monday through Friday). Overnight and weekend access shall require advance written approval from management responsible for the system.
21. User access shall be restricted to specific workstations. (*Note:* Each workstation is identified by a unique node number.)

The above list of IS security standards is fairly general by design. Depending on the nature of the organization, it will likely be necessary to recommend additional standards that will help strengthen the IS control environment. As with policies, it may be necessary to recommend a different set of standards for each subsidiary, division, or operating unit.

INFORMATION SYSTEMS SECURITY GUIDELINES

Information systems security guidelines are also established by senior management and are intended to help ensure the achievement of the IS security policy. Guidelines are similar in format to standards in that they provide detailed specifications for individual IS controls. Where they differ from standards is in their implementation. In some firms, management may direct staff to implement only those guidelines that they judge to be pertinent or useful. In others, they may be understood to be the equivalent of standards. Since guidelines are not necessarily required by management to be implemented, they can prove to be somewhat of an anomaly to auditors. For example, in a firm that has IS security guidelines but no standards, an auditor may use the guidelines as a benchmark against which the adequacy of controls of a particular information system can be assessed. When recommending improvements in those controls to line management in charge of the system, using the guidelines as the benchmark, the auditor may encounter resistance to change because line management does not consider the guidelines to be requirements. It is for this reason that the use of the term *guidelines* is inappropriate when referring to IS security controls. All firms should develop IS security standards that are clearly defined and enforceable.

It should not be surprising when one is unable to locate adequate IS security policies, standards, or guidelines within an organization. Based on personal experience and discussions with numerous colleagues in various professional auditing associations, it appears that many companies do not have any IS security policies, standards, or guidelines. Even in firms that do, the policies, standards, and guidelines are often inadequate or do not address many risks associated with information systems. In many cases, the so-called policies, standards, or guidelines are actually just a conglomeration of procedures in various locations, each prepared independently of the other (see case studies 4.1, 4.2, and 4.3).

CASE STUDY 4.1

Inadequate Information Systems Security Standards

In one organization being audited, there were IS security standards in an employee handbook, other standards in a microcomputer user manual, and still other standards that were applicable to each of the major computer platforms in the organization. There was also a one-page sheet on password guidelines that was handed out to new employees by the Human Resources Department upon hiring. Each of these documents was prepared independently by separate departments. Nowhere did there exist a comprehensive set of standards. After hiring, employees did not receive any additional training on IS security. Most employees were not even aware of the existence of the standards for the major computer platforms or the location of the other standards. As a result, IS security awareness was inconsistent throughout the organization. In some departments management was very conscious of IS security, while in other areas IS security was viewed as more of an operational inconvenience.

It was recommended that the directors of each of the major IS processing areas jointly develop a comprehensive set of IS security standards that would provide consistency in the application of controls over all of the information systems within the organization. It was also recommended that, once completed, the standards be communicated to all staff members. One suggestion for communicating the new standards was to develop a reference brochure or pamphlet that details the standards and then distribute the document to all existing staff members. It was further recommended that the new standards be included as part of the training that all new employees were required to attend.

CASE STUDY 4.2

Development of an Information Protection Program

For years, a banking organization had inadequate information systems security standards that were based on the types of computing systems in existence within the organization. One part of the standards addressed various general controls over the mainframe environment, another part addressed the network, another part addressed stand-alone personal computers, another part addressed the telecommunications systems, and so on. Each part of the standards was essentially a copy of the same general standards, with slight wording modifications to adapt them to the type of computing system. This resulted in an unnecessarily long set of standards with redundant information. Furthermore, the general controls did not specify any logical security controls (passwords, encryption, system security administration, etc.), which are arguably the most important standards. The general standards only covered things like physical security and system procurement. As one would expect, the lack of logical security standards resulted in inconsistent implementation of logical security controls throughout the organization, thereby subjecting the organization to excessive risk. The other standards were poorly worded at best.

The internal IS auditors made consistent recommendations regarding logical security and other controls during each individual audit. Since no internal standards could be referenced, the IS auditors defended their recommendations as sound business practices common within the industry. Over a number of years, the IS audit manager recommended several times to the head of information systems that a single set of company-wide general standards be developed. Each attempt was unsuccessful. Each year the IS audit manager discussed the issue with the external IS auditors who supported the annual financial statement audit. Finally, the internal IS audit manager convinced the external IS auditors to recommend to the organization's senior management that a comprehensive set of IS security standards be developed. About 10 months later, in 1997, senior management commissioned a team of representatives from various areas of the organization, including IS audit, to craft company-wide standards that addressed not only IS security but also the protection of information in general, regardless of whether the information existed in electronic, paper, microfilm, or other forms. Senior management was concerned that with the increasing prevalence of telecommuting and the existence of large amounts of information in nonelectronic form, IS security standards would not be comprehensive enough. The team also hired a consultant from the external audit firm to facilitate the development of the standards.

In late 1998, the end product was completed. The team had developed a comprehensive information protection (IP) program and a set of procedures that would require all employees, regardless of whether they worked in IS or business units, to perform those IP practices applicable to their work environments. The team had identified about 125 general IP standards. These were divided into three categories: departmental, system administration, and system capability.

Departmental standards are those that employees in all departments could perform. They include about 25 commonsense standards like locking workstations when leaving the immediate vicinity, storing confidential information out of sight and locking it up when necessary, not writing passwords down or using easily guessed passwords, and logging off the network at the end of a shift. Each department was also required to classify the information it receives into three general categories: public, restricted, and confidential. *Public* information could be shared with anyone. Examples included things like marketing and promotional materials. *Restricted* information could be shared among all employees but not with the public. Examples included the employee phone book, intranet information, and all-staff e-mails. *Confidential* information could be shared only with those individuals who had a legitimate business reason for needing the information. A large majority of information fell into the confidential category. Management was required to communicate the information classifications to their employees and to exercise appropriate controls over each type of information.

System administration standards are those that all system administrators could perform. They include about 50 standards, such as: reviewing security event logs; ensuring that restricted or confidential information is encrypted while being electronically transmitted; protecting system hardware from fire, electrical surges, and theft; designating and training backup system administrators; and installing automatic virus-checking software. Depending on the risk and significance of the systems, some standards would not be applicable.

System capability standards are those that are desirable in systems. They include about 50 standards, such as the ability to: restrict access to information and segregate duties; enforce an eight-character minimum password length and 60-day password expiration; store passwords in encrypted format; change maiden passwords on new systems; and create audit trails.

A critical procedure was built into the IP program to make sure that the IP standards do not just collect dust: An annual certification to be completed by March 31. The manager of each department is required to review a certification checklist of the departmental standards with staff. The checklist requires the manager to specify "yes," "no," or "not applicable" to each standard. There is room for a brief comment next to each response. The manager must sign the certification indicating that the standards were communicated and discussed with staff and have the division manager approve the certification. Similarly, the administrators of each unique system in the organization are required to complete system administration and system capability assessment checklists. All completed certification checklists are sent to the security officer who ensures that all departments and system administrators have completed them. About one month prior to the certification, an organization-wide team, including the IS audit manager, convenes to review and update the IP standards and associated procedures.

For some systems, especially less sophisticated applications, not all of the system administration and system capability standards could be met. So long as the risk of noncompliance is acceptable to management, no action is required. The annual certifications act as reminders to management to reassess the risks of the systems.

(continued)

CASE STUDY 4.2 (*continued*)

As a standard audit step early within each audit, the most recent annual certifications are examined to ensure they have been completed and approved, and the responses to each checklist standard are reviewed for reasonableness and accuracy. The checklist responses often provide the IS auditors with an idea of the knowledge level of the system administrators and the sophistication of the system being audited.

Fortunately for the organization, the new IP program was ahead of its time. After deployment of the IP program in late 1998, the Gramm-Leach-Bliley (GLB) Financial Services Modernization Act of 1999 was passed. It requires, among other things, that financial institutions fully disclose their practices regarding the distribution of personal financial information of their customers, distribute such customer information only if customers give them permission, and implement adequate security practices to protect personal customer information. Full compliance with GLB information privacy and protection requirements was required by July 1, 2001. The GLB requirements were mapped to the IP program, and only a handful of new standards or adjustments had to be made. While most banking organizations had to develop comprehensive information protection programs from scratch, this organization had the foresight to develop one as a sound business practice, primarily at the urging of the internal IS audit manager.

CASE STUDY 4.3

Government Organization without an IS Security Policy or Standards

A large U.S. city government did not have an information systems security policy and standards. As a result, security was implemented inconsistently and inadequately among the various existing networks and application systems scattered throughout the many city agencies and business units. Even mainframe operating systems centralized at the data center lacked consistent and adequate security. The lack of a policy and standards also affected new systems being developed. During audits of two major enterprise-wide application systems development projects, it was found that the project request for proposals (RFPs) for software vendors did not include specific logical security design requirements considered necessary to adequately protect confidential information. The project teams also did not identify adequate postimplementation procedures for system security administration until after the internal auditor recommended them. While some types of IS security standards or guidelines existed within a number of different procedures located in different city agencies, they were not well communicated or not communicated at all, and thus were usually overlooked by all except the agency that developed them. Therefore, during each of the two application systems development audits, the internal auditor recommended that senior IS management create a city-wide information security policy with supporting standards.

The centralized IS department of this city recently hired a chief information security officer (CISO). One of the CISO's first challenges will be to develop a city-wide IS security policy and standards. But the CISO faces many obstacles. For example, political gain often diverts resources away from areas where they are needed most. Systems are often implemented without security in mind, often because politicians would rather make services available to the public than defer services until adequate system security controls can be deployed. Also, deploying security increases the cost of the service. A third difficulty is that the CISO reports to the head of IS and ultimately to the mayor, while the owners of many other systems report to different senior managers and in some cases to the city council. Within these two basic reporting structures, city agencies are often operated as separate, independent business units, with separate IS reporting and funding structures. This makes it difficult to agree on city-wide IS security standards or to even fund an attempt at developing centralized standards. A fourth challenge is that the CISO lacks a staff and will need to lobby for funding within the city and from the state and federal governments to be able to develop and communicate the policy and standards adequately.

The CISO will need to emphasize that despite these obstacles, it is in the best interests of the city and its citizens to put politics aside and work together as a team to develop an IS security policy and standards that can be implemented by all city workers, especially system security administrators. The future security and reputation of the city are at risk if IS security standards are not developed and implemented. So far the city has been fortunate that it has not suffered major losses from a security breach.

Information systems security policies, standards, and guidelines should be designed in conjunction with one another to ensure continuity and consistency in their application to all information systems throughout the company. They should also be worded to allow some flexibility in their deployment. For example, a low-risk, nontransaction processing system would obviously not warrant the degree of controls of a high-risk financial transaction system such as wire transfers. For low-risk systems, adherence to specific items within the standards could be waived with written approval of senior management.

Information systems policies, standards, and guidelines should be documented and readily available to all employees of an organization in written or electronic form. They should be as concise as possible so that staff members are not intimidated when they read them. The documents should be updated at least annually. In addition, all staff should be educated as to the content and location of these documents and how to access them. Such communication should occur at least annually.

NOTES

1. "Policy Use Hits New Low." *Infosecurity News* (January/February 1997): 14.
2. "Policies Made In a Vacuum, Survey Finds," *Infosecurity News* (January/February 1997): 14.
3. "Security Policies," *Information Security Magazine* (September 2000): 60.
4. "Do You Have an IT Security Policy?" Institute of Management and Administration *Newsletter* (October 2000): 9.

CHAPTER 5

Auditing Service Organization Applications

Many firms employ the services of external organizations to provide business applications and data processing resources that would otherwise be too expensive or time consuming to develop and maintain internally. These external organizations are often referred to as service organizations, service bureaus, or third-party processors. Numerous service organizations provide a variety of applications to virtually all sectors of industry and government. These include services for payroll processing, mortgage loan servicing, investment safekeeping, software development and maintenance, automated teller machine (ATM) transaction processing, check processing, electronic bill payment, wire transfers, credit card operations, and trust services.

Service organizations enjoy economies of scale by developing and maintaining applications and computer systems that may be used by hundreds or thousands of client companies. By processing high volumes of client transactions, the cost to process each individual transaction through a service organization often is significantly less than if each client were to hire a programming and development staff and purchase or lease the computer hardware necessary to process the transactions. As a result of technological advances, changes in laws and regulations, and other business risks, a company might invest significant financial resources in a major computer system only to find it obsolete in a few years. Similarly, a company may hire a programming staff to develop and maintain one or more custom applications internally. Only after years of project delays and application design flaws does the firm realize that it would have been more cost effective to have contracted with a service organization to provide the application. This is not to say that companies should not maintain internal systems development and maintenance staffs and computer systems. In fact, many large organizations are very successful at creating their own applications. There are benefits and drawbacks to both alternatives.

While service organizations often process transactions at a lower cost than their clients, they must try to maintain applications that meet the needs of all their clients. Some clients may require the service organization to develop customized modules and modifications to the original application to meet unique product and service needs. Service organizations can partially offset these needs by incorporating tables and parameters into their applications. These tables and parameters can then be customized by each client. However, there will always be clients whose needs cannot be anticipated when the tables and parameters are designed or whose needs are so unique that changing the primary application to meet those needs could adversely affect other clients. In these cases, special modules must be designed and integrated with the primary application at the client site while the primary application is left intact. Thus, service organizations must constantly monitor the changing needs of their clients and update their applications to meet those needs.

If there are a large number of clients with specialized requirements, service organizations often become backlogged and thus are not able to meet the needs of all their clients in a timely manner. They must prioritize their client requests. Clients that are the greatest source of revenue to the service organization are often given top priority. This places smaller clients at a disadvantage with their competitors who may be utilizing a different service organization or who develop and maintain their own applications. Sometimes the backlogs can be months or even years. In the worst cases, service organizations may simply have to reject a client request. Fortunately, most client companies form user groups to discuss their successes and difficulties with the service organization application. If several small firms have the same programming change request, they may be able to form an alliance that is strong enough to leverage their request ahead of a large client. The threat of clients leaving and taking their business to a competing service organization is an effective means of getting programming requests implemented. As with any business, a service organization can survive only if it is managed in such a way that it is able to satisfy the requirements of its clients in an efficient and effective manner. The aforementioned problems are not unique to service organizations.

Many companies maintain internal staffs of application development and maintenance personnel. These companies are able to create their own customized applications without relying on outside service organizations. They do not have to compete with other firms to implement specialized programming requests. These benefits often enable companies to tailor their applications to meet the exact needs of their products and services in a timely manner. However, the same pitfalls that face service organizations can occur within companies that program their own applications. For example, many firms have numerous departments, each utilizing different applications to process their information. When new systems or programming changes to existing systems are necessary, each department submits a request to the information systems (IS) development or maintenance area for action. Information systems areas are faced with limited resources and, like service organizations, must prioritize the requests of the individual departments. In theory, the requests promising the most financial benefit to the organization are given top priority. Often, however, the departments with the greatest financial or political leverage get their requests completed ahead of other departments. When a company is significantly downsizing, the backlog can reach into the months or years, as evidenced in case study 5.1.

CASE STUDY 5.1

Backlog of Programming Requests

A large banking corporation that was consolidating data processing centers located in various individual states into regional data processing centers was being audited. Since the corporation was also implementing extensive staff downsizing, IS development and maintenance staff resources were devoted almost exclusively to the data processing consolidation efforts. Only in cases in which a system became nonfunctional or required a change to comply with government laws and regulations would programming requests be honored in a timely manner. All other requests were still accepted and placed in a queue. The standard backlog for completion was two years. Therefore, when audits of information systems were performed and recommendations submitted that required programming changes, management was often unable to implement the recommendations, even if they agreed that the changes needed to be made as soon as possible. Top management had elected to assume the risks of not enhancing the controls over their information systems. Fortunately, no significant losses were known to have occurred as a result of the two-year backlog for completing most programming change requests.

Another risk of programming applications internally is that they may become obsolete. Sometimes changes in technology, in the regulatory environment, or in the products and services offered by competitors are so significant or numerous that it is no longer cost effective to maintain a customized internal application. Because their internal application and related operational procedures are so unique, the firm may find that contracting with a service organization and revising operational procedures could prove very costly in terms of money, impact of changes to products and services on customers, and stress on operational staff. For these reasons, management of each company must perform detailed analyses to determine whether their product and service needs can best be met by contracting with a service organization or hiring a specialized staff to develop and maintain applications internally. The next section of this chapter provides a background on reports prepared by independent external auditors (also known as service auditors) on the adequacy of IS control policies and procedures in place at service organizations.

SERVICE AUDITOR REPORTS

Most major service organizations contract with an independent auditing firm to express an opinion on the adequacy of policies and procedures within the service organization that may affect the internal control environment at the client organization. In some cases, the independent auditor may be contracted to perform additional tests to determine whether such policies and procedures are operating effectively within the service organization. These service auditor reports provide some assurance to clients that adequate controls exist within the service organization to ensure the reliability, integrity, and confidentiality of client customer information. Professional auditing standards pertaining to the issuance of service auditor reports in most developed countries are similar but by no means identical. Some standards provide more assurance than others. Therefore, when examining a service auditor report, the reader must be cognizant of the country in which the service organization is domiciled. The following paragraphs examine the current status of professional auditing standards pertaining to the different types of service auditor reports issued in the United States, Canada, the United Kingdom and Australia.

United States

In the United States, a service organization may hire an independent external auditor to express one of two types of opinions on policies and procedures at the service organization that may be relevant to the internal control structure of organizations that utilize its services. The reporting and testing requirements for external auditors who perform such engagements are dictated by Statement on Auditing Standards 70 (SAS 70), issued by the Auditing Standards Board of the American Institute of Certified Public Accountants (AICPA). SAS 70 is entitled "Service Organizations" and is effective for service auditors' reports dated after March 31, 1993. (*Note*: The SAS 70 name was amended, effective December 1999, from "Reports on the Processing of Transactions by Service Organizations" by SAS 88 entitled "Service Organizations and Reporting on Consistency.") The first type of report expresses, among other things, the auditor's opinion as to whether relevant policies and procedures were placed in operation at the service organization "as of a specific date."[1] This type of report *does not* express an opinion as to the operating effectiveness of such policies and procedures. The second type of report expresses the auditor's opinion as to whether relevant policies and procedures were in place at the service organization *and whether such policies and procedures were in fact operating effectively*. To formulate an opinion under the second type of report, the auditor is required to perform various tests to confirm that the policies and procedures at the service organization are functioning properly. SAS 70 goes on to state that "To be useful to user auditors, the report should ordinarily cover a minimum reporting period of six months."[2] SAS 70 supersedes SAS 44, which was entitled "Special-Purpose Reports on Internal Accounting Control at Service Organizations" and was required for special-purpose reports on internal accounting control dated after December 31, 1982. The primary difference between SAS 70 and SAS 44 is that SAS 70 specifies a minimum reporting period of six months. Under SAS 44, a required time period was not specified. Rather, the necessary testing period was left to the judgment of the auditor. SAS 44 reports usually covered a period of approximately two to four months, except in cases in which significant control weaknesses were identified.

Canada

The Canadian equivalent of SAS 70 is Section 5900 of the *Handbook of Auditing* published by the Canadian Institute of Chartered Accountants (CICA). Section 5900 is entitled "Opinions on Control Procedures at a Service Organization" and is effective for engagements covering periods on or after July 1, 1987. Like SAS 70, Section 5900 details two types of opinions that external auditors may express. One pertains to the "design and existence of control procedures at a service organization," while the second pertains to the "design, effective operation, and continuity of control procedures at a service organization." The first type of opinion requires auditors to attest only to the design and existence of control procedures "as at a point in time."[3] No opinion is expressed regarding the operating effectiveness of the control procedures. The second type of opinion requires auditors to perform tests and obtain management representations regarding the effective operation of control procedures "throughout the specified period."[4] Unlike SAS 70, Section 5900 does not specifically recommend a six-month testing period. The time period necessary to obtain assurance as to whether control procedures were operating effectively is left to the professional judgment of the external auditor. However, a six-month testing period may be inferred from the example service auditor's report in Section 5900, which states that the auditor "performed tests of the effectiveness of those control procedures for the period from January 1, 19X1 to June 30, 19X1."[5]

United Kingdom

In September 1994, the Faculty of Information Technology (FIT) of the Institute of Chartered Accountants in England and Wales (ICAEW) issued Technical Release FIT 1/94, which bears the same name as SAS 70, "Reports on the Processing of Transactions by Service Organizations." FIT 1/94 is intended to apply only to matters relating to service organizations that provide data processing services, although some of its principles may also be relevant to other types of services provided by service organizations. FIT 1/94 is quite similar to SAS 70 and Canada's Section 5900. The auditor may issue an opinion on the policies and procedures of the service organization only or on the policies and procedures as well as tests of compliance to the policies and procedures. Control objectives for the service organization are to be specified in the report, including their source. For opinions with tests of compliance, FIT 1/94 specifies that "In order to be effective for user auditors, the report would normally need to cover a minimum reporting period of six months."[6]

A guidance document similar to FIT 1/94 was released by the Financial Reporting and Auditing Group (FRAG) of the ICAEW in May of 1994. Technical Release FRAG 21/94, entitled "Reports on Internal Controls of Investment Custodians Made Available to Third Parties," is smaller in scope than FIT 1/94. It focuses primarily on custodial activities related to investment businesses. Other activities of such businesses are not addressed. The report under FRAG 21/94 includes the auditor's opinions on whether "control policies and procedures were suitably designed to achieve the specified control objectives" and that "the related control objectives were achieved during the period."[7] Unlike FIT 1/94, FRAG 21/94 does not require a minimum reporting period. Also, the adequacy of the control objectives is not assessed by the auditor. Appendix III of FRAG 21/94 includes an illustrative example of a management report, which includes a section on control policies and procedures established to ensure that the control objectives are achieved. Among these control policies and procedures, FRAG 21/94 includes a section on the "security and integrity of computer systems" objective.[8] This section lists 11 control areas:

1. Unauthorized admission to data processing areas
2. Restricted access to operating systems, utility software, applications, communications software, and data
3. Logging and detection of unauthorized system access attempts
4. Data entry accuracy and integrity of information transmitted over networks
5. Reconciliation of data output
6. Definitions and descriptions of all reports
7. Written procedures to ensure the accuracy, completeness, and authorization of all transactions
8. Accurate audit trails
9. Adequate documentation of all data processing systems
10. Adequate archiving and safe storage of records and programs
11. Implementation of adequate contingency procedures

These control areas are fairly comprehensive and can be applied to almost any type of IS control environment. Therefore, they can serve as a useful reference to external auditors.

Australia

Australia did not have an auditing standard applicable to service auditors as of the writing of this book. The Australian Accounting Research Foundation (AARF) has recognized the lack of such a standard as a deficiency and is in the process of drafting an Audit Guidance Statement (AGS) on Outsourcing Entities.[9] The AARF Project Manager responsible for the new AGS on outsourcing entities reported that it focuses on three concepts:

1. Applicable to outsourcing arrangements, including but not limited to service entity arrangements (i.e., service organizations)
2. Encourages "effectiveness" reporting of controls rather than "design-only" reporting
3. Encourages "period-of-time" reporting rather than "point-in-time" reporting

Item 1 is more comprehensive than SAS 70, Section 5900, or FIT 1/94. Items 2 and 3 are consistent with the second type of SAS 70 report, which expresses the auditor's opinion regarding whether relevant policies and procedures were in place at the service organization and whether such policies and procedures were in fact operating effectively.

The Australian AGS project manager also stated that the new AGS is based largely on an AARF invitation to comment (IC) document entitled "Reporting on Internal Control," which was prepared by the Auditing Standards Board of the AARF in April 1996. Some of the pertinent highlights of the IC document include:

- Reporting on internal controls is considered a specific type of performance auditing and should be read in conjunction with AUS 806, "Performance Auditing," and AUS 808, "Planning and Performance Audits," to obtain a more comprehensive understanding. AUS 806 and AUS 808 provide generic principles, practices, and guidance relevant to auditors reporting on internal controls.
- The report on internal controls is a separate engagement from the financial report audit. Although they may be conducted in conjunction with each other, each requires a separate report.
- The IC adopts a broad definition of internal controls, which includes:

  1. Effectiveness, efficiency, and economy of operations
  2. Reliability of management and financial reporting
  3. Compliance with applicable laws and regulations and internal policies

  This definition of internal controls is consistent with the frameworks of the Committee of Sponsoring Organizations (COSO) in the United States, the Criteria of Control Board (CoCo) in Canada, and the Cadbury Committee in the United Kingdom. These internal control frameworks are discussed in greater detail in Chapter 10.
- The IC document is based on the premise that any evaluation of the effectiveness of internal controls is inseparable from a consideration of the objectives to which the internal controls are directed and the risks that threaten achievement of those objectives. Criteria that take into account these objectives and risks must be clearly identified before a meaningful opinion about effectiveness can be expressed. Without such criteria, an auditor's report would be open to widely divergent and subjective interpretations of individual users.
- The tests of operating effectiveness should be performed over a period of time that is adequate to determine that the internal controls are operating effectively. The period of time over which the auditor would perform tests of operating effectiveness is a matter of judgment.[10]

Based on the foregoing information, it is reasonable to expect that the AARF Audit Guidance Statement on Outsourcing Entities will provide as much or more guidance to external auditors who prepare reports on the internal control environments of Australian service organizations as do SAS 70, Section 5900, and FIT

1/94. As part of the AGS, it would also be reasonably expected that internal controls over information systems within service organizations will be adequately addressed.

In January 1997, the Auditing Standards Board of the AARF issued AGS 1026 entitled "Superannuation Funds—Auditor Reports on Externally Managed Assets." AGS 1026 is very similar to the FRAG 21/94 document in the United Kingdom in that it provides some guidance on IS controls, albeit only for a specific type of entity. AGS 1026 is directed primarily at superannuation (pension) fund auditors and is limited to an explanation and application of existing standards to circumstances in which superannuation fund auditors may need to obtain necessary audit evidence concerning externally managed assets through reports issued by the auditor of an external manager. The guidance is intended to provide a clearer indication of the needs of superannuation fund trustees and auditors and seeks to achieve greater consistency in their requests for reports by the auditors of external managers.[11]

The report under AGS 1026 includes the auditor's opinions on whether the external superannuation fund manager maintained effective internal controls for the assets under management as of the period ending date, based on the criteria set out in a Management Report on Internal Controls, which is attached to the audit report. AGS 1026 does not specify a minimum reporting period, and the adequacy of management's control criteria are not required to be assessed by the auditor. Like FRAG 21/94, Appendix 3 of the AGS 1026 includes an illustrative example of a Management Report on Internal Controls, which includes a section on control policies and procedures established to ensure that the control objectives are achieved. Among these control policies and procedures, AGS 1026 includes a section on the objective entitled "Security and Integrity of Computer Systems."[12] This section lists 10 control areas, most of which are specified in FRAG 21/94:

1. Unauthorized admission to data processing areas
2. Restricted access to operating systems, utility software, applications, communications software, and data
3. Logging and detection of unauthorized system access attempts
4. Data entry accuracy and integrity of information transmitted over networks
5. Written procedures to ensure the accuracy, completeness, and authorization of all transactions
6. Accurate audit trails
7. Adequate documentation of all data processing systems
8. Adequate archiving and safe storage of records and programs
9. Formal process for testing new programs before they are released
10. Implementation of adequate contingency procedures

Item 9 is a control area not included in the FRAG 21/94. Formal process for testing new programs before they are released is a control area worthy of specific mention. This control area is applicable not only in the context of superannuation funds but for all IS control environments. Another difference between AGS 1026 and FRAG 21/94 is that the AGS excludes the two control areas pertaining to reconciliation of data output and definitions and descriptions of all reports (control areas 5 and 6 under FRAG 21/94). It appears that these items were excluded because they are more operational in nature rather than specifically pertaining to the security and integrity of computer information systems. Therefore, their exclusion should not be considered a significant detriment to the guidance of AGS 1026.

Like FRAG 21/94, the control areas of AGS 1026 are quite comprehensive and can serve as a useful reference and be applied by auditors and interested parties to almost any type of IS control environment.

Internal auditors and other interested parties who utilize SAS 70, Section 5900, FIT 1/94, and similar reports should be alert to the fact that even if an external auditor expresses an unqualified or unreserved opinion as to the operating effectiveness of relevant policies and procedures at a service organization, there may exist relevant policies and procedures upon which the external auditor was not hired to express an opinion. In fact, SAS 70 states, "The management of the service organization specifies whether all or selected applications and control objectives will be covered by the tests of operating effectiveness."[13] This is why it is important to carefully examine the report to understand the areas tested and to determine whether an organization should request additional assurance from the service organization regarding the existence and operating effectiveness of policies and procedures that were not tested in the original service auditor's report. Case study 5.2 discusses a situation in which a significant risk affecting the control environment of its clients existed with a service organization's application, but the risk was not mentioned as a control consideration for client organizations. Readers should be aware that the issue presented in that case study is rare. Most service auditor reports are of high quality and are very useful in evaluating internal controls at client organizations and in understanding the control environments at service organizations. Other than the issue described in case study 5.2, the rest of the service auditor's report in question was very good.

CASE STUDY 5.2

Significant Risk with Service Organization Application

An internal audit was performed of the logical security controls of an application that was licensed from a service organization and installed on computer hardware at a client organization. The service organization provided ongoing maintenance and support for the software and also processed data for smaller client organizations. Once every two years, the service organization hired an independent auditor to prepare a SAS 70 report on the relevant policies and procedures placed in operation *and the operating effectiveness of such policies and procedures.* One of the steps of the audit was examination of the SAS 70 report on the service organization. In the opinion of the service auditor, the policies and procedures were operating with sufficient effectiveness to provide reasonable, but not absolute, assurance that the con-

(continued)

CASE STUDY 5.2 (*continued*)

trol objectives specified in the report were achieved during the six-month period tested. In other words, no significant control issues affecting client organizations were identified in the service auditor's report.

Detailed tests of the logical security controls of the application that were in place at the client organization were then performed. During the course of testing, it was noted that a major control deficiency existed in the design of the application that affected every client who used the service organization's application. (At the time there were about 600 client organizations.) The weakness was that the password file at each client location was not encrypted. As a result, users with system administration access capabilities at each client location could view the passwords of all the users in their organization. The viewing could be performed routinely within the application software. System security administrators did not even have to search for a password file at the operating system level. Furthermore, since the support technicians at the service organization required system administration capabilities when they dialed in via modem to a client organization, they too could view the passwords of all the users if they wished. Because the clients of this service organization were all financial institutions, the control weakness was considered to be a major issue.

An example of one of the risks associated with this weakness is that tellers at the client organizations rely on a password to ensure that only their transactions are posted under their unique teller identification number. One purpose of password controls is to provide an audit trail if any transactions require research, including situations in which a fraudulent transaction may have been posted. However, anyone with system administration access capabilities or any service organization technicians who dialed in to a client organization could look up a teller's password and then perform an unauthorized transaction using the teller's identification number, thereby negating the sole ownership of transactions posted on the system. Also, if a teller became aware that others could look up his or her password, the teller could perform an unauthorized transaction and later claim that a system security administrator or service organization technician had looked up his or her password and performed the transaction. In a court of law, the teller could prove that there were several persons who had the ability to view the password and thus create a "reasonable doubt" as to whether the teller had performed the transaction.

It was recommended to the appropriate management in the client organization that a request be submitted to the service organization to modify the application so that the password file was encrypted. After three years, client management still had taken no action. The weakness was discussed with a few other auditors at client organizations; only one was even aware of the control weakness. Unfortunately, the other client organizations also did not appear to be concerned enough with the control weakness to strongly suggest to the service organization that the password files be encrypted.

The internal audit manager of the service organization was asked whether she was aware of the weakness and why it was not mentioned in the service auditor's report. She stated that she was not aware of the issue and had to confirm it with a technician. After discussions with a technician, the internal audit manager stated that a new authorization system module had been available for over a year and that this new module had an encrypted password file. She stated that the module at the client organization being examined was an old version. The service organization did not promote the fact that password file encryption was one of the enhancements of the new authorization system module. Although it was recommended to the client organization's management that the new module be adopted, they did not see enough compelling reasons to adopt the new module. Since the service organization did not require its clients to migrate to the new authorization system, many client organizations were still exposed to the risk that users with system administration capabilities could view the passwords of other users and perform unauthorized functions.

As to why the password file weakness was not mentioned in the most recent service auditor's report, the service organization's internal audit manager stated that the external auditors had tested only the new authorization system module. She was not able to explain why service auditor reports prior to the creation of the new authorization system module did not identify the fact that the user password file was not encrypted. She then said that the external audit manager in charge of preparing the service auditor's report had more details on the preparation of the service auditor's reports. As a matter of note, the internal audit manager at the service organization had previously been an auditor with the external auditing firm that prepared the service auditor's report.

The manager at the external audit firm was asked whether he was aware that system security administrators could view user passwords under the old authorization system module. He stated that the service organization did not identify the weakness to the service auditor, and the service auditor's tests did not identify the weakness. He agreed that it was a significant internal control issue and appreciated the fact that this control weakness had been identified so they could test it during the next examination of the service organization's application. The test would be applied to the new authorization system module and any old modules still in use at client organizations. Depending on the outcome of their tests, they may identify the control weakness in the next service auditor's report. The service auditor manager stated that he wished he had known of the weakness prior to completion of testing for the most recent service auditor's report, because the next one will not be prepared for another two years.

Both the internal audit manager at the service organization and the manager at the service auditor firm stated that we were the first client organization to mention the control weakness to them. It is very unsettling to think that with over 600 client organizations, all of which are financial institutions, only one was aware of the control weakness and found it significant enough to discuss with the service organization and service auditor. The issue apparently had not even been discussed at any annual user group conferences at which client organizations and the service organization discussed desired enhancements to the application.

(continued)

CASE STUDY 5.2 (*continued*)

Another design flaw of the service organization's application was that access capabilities were determined by hierarchical security levels. A user with a security level of 8, for example, could perform all access functions mapped to security level 8 as well as all those mapped to any of the lower levels (0 through 7). With hundreds of functions, many of which were required for use in multiple departments, it was virtually impossible to assign security levels to users in certain areas without granting them additional access capabilities that were not necessary for their normal duties. An alternative would have been to assign the lowest security level to all users and then, on an individual basis, specifically assign each additional access function necessary for them to perform their normal duties. With hundreds of users, this alternative was operationally impractical to the area performing the system administration duties at the client organization I was examining.

To complicate matters, data processing management at the client organization elected not to segregate the duties of security administration, computer operations, and system software analysis. (The client organization did not have any in-house programmers.) The client organization mapped all functions necessary to perform these different duties to the highest hierarchical security level. Each user in the data processing department was assigned this security level. Therefore, all the users in the data processing department had the capability to run jobs, install and test software, add and delete users, change user access capabilities and system security parameters, and perform a myriad of other functions. In addition, the entire data processing department had the capability to look up the passwords of any users they wished and then perform unauthorized transactions. We presented this issue to data processing management and recommended that these duties be segregated. Management elected not to implement the recommendation under the guise that all the users in the data processing department could be trusted.

Again, the service auditor's report did not identify the hierarchical security level table as a client control consideration or a control weakness. At least with the new authorization system module, the hierarchical security level table was abolished. Instead, independent groups of users could be established, each with its own set of access functions mapped to it. Since the groups are nonhierarchical, access to one group does not grant access to any access functions of any other user group. Unfortunately, client organizations that do not adopt the new authorization system module will be at significantly greater risk of unauthorized access than those that do adopt the new module. The service organization did not require clients to migrate to the new module, most likely because of the potential inconvenience to client organizations. This inconvenience, coupled with other service problems, could lead client organizations to seek a new service organization.

Because of situations like the one discussed in case study 5.2, service auditors always include the statement that their tests do not provide absolute assurance that all significant internal control issues affecting client organizations will be identified. Such a disclaimer statement may relieve service auditors of some or all of the liability in lawsuits against them for losses occurring as a result of control weaknesses not identified in their reports.

USE OF SERVICE AUDITOR REPORTS FOR INTERNAL AUDITS

Once an organization has determined that it will contract with a service organization, one of the first steps that the project development team at the client organization should perform is to examine a copy of the most recent service auditor's report from each of the bidding service organizations. This examination should take place before any contract is entered into with the service organization. Significant control weaknesses in a service auditor's report could signal that the service organization cannot provide client organizations with an adequate level of service and information protection. If a service organization does not have a service auditor's report prepared, the client organization should seriously consider dropping that service organization from consideration. The lack of a service auditor's report may also signal that internal controls at the service organization could significantly jeopardize client operations. The internal control environment can change over time at a service organization, as with any organization. Therefore, even after a service organization has been contracted and its services have been deployed, process owners and internal auditors at the client organization should examine each service auditor's report that is prepared. Although professional auditing standards do not require the preparation of a service auditor's report for all service organizations, most reputable service organizations have one prepared annually or at least biannually. To help defray a portion of the costs of hiring service auditors to prepare the reports, some service organizations charge client organizations a fee for each copy of the service auditor's report. The internal audit department should obtain a copy of the service auditor's report for each service organization utilized by the client organization on an annual basis or whenever the reports are prepared.

Service auditor reports can be quite lengthy (up to 100 pages or more) and consist of several sections. Although professional standards do not specify how service auditor reports are to be organized, they generally include four pieces of information:

1. Report of independent auditors
2. Description of relevant policies and procedures (provided by client organization management)
   (a) General description of operations, including an organization chart
   (b) Description of control environment elements
   (c) Description of transaction flow, including flow charts
   (d) Application overviews
   (e) Program change procedures
   (f) Regulatory compliance information (if applicable)
3. Control objectives as specified by client organization management and

results of service auditor's tests of the operating effectiveness of the control objectives
4. Client control considerations

REPORT OF INDEPENDENT AUDITORS

The independent auditor's report includes an opinion statement on the adequacy of policies and procedures and, if contracted by the service organization, an opinion on whether the policies and procedures were operating with sufficient effectiveness during the specified period. Internal auditors at client organizations should examine the opinion closely. If the opinion is "qualified" due to one or more significant control weaknesses at the service organization, the internal auditor should determine whether the weaknesses significantly affect the internal control environment at the client organization. If so, the internal auditor should recommend that management communicate their concern to the service organization and determine whether the service organization has implemented necessary changes to resolve the control weaknesses.

If the necessary changes have not been implemented, the internal auditor should recommend that management consider changing to another service vendor that does not have any significant control weaknesses that adversely affect the internal control environment at its client organizations. If the original service organization states that the control weaknesses have been corrected, the internal auditor should perform alternative tests to confirm the changes. The internal auditor should also confirm that the same control weaknesses are not mentioned in the next service auditor's report. The existence of perpetual control weaknesses within a service organization could be an indication that its overall control environment is weak, thereby increasing the risk that transactions could be improperly processed; service could be interrupted; data could be lost, damaged, or divulged to unauthorized parties; and the service organization could suffer a significant enough loss to drive it out of business. Case studies 5.3 and 5.4 present qualified opinions of two different service organizations by their respective service auditors.

CASE STUDY 5.3

Qualified Opinion of an ATM Network Service Organization

During an internal audit of an ATM network switching service to which numerous financial institutions belonged, the service auditor's report was examined, and the following qualified opinion was noted:

> The accompanying description of policies and procedures includes general computer controls related to data processing and selected services but does not include application system control objectives for the application systems processed by the client organization. We believe

that these control objectives, and the related policies and procedures that might achieve these control objectives, are relevant to those user organizations and user auditors intending to rely on control policies and procedures for these application systems.

In our opinion, except for the matter described in the preceding paragraph, the accompanying description of the aforementioned controls presents fairly, in all material respects, the relevant aspects of the client organization's policies and procedures that have been placed in operation as of [date].

In this particular case, the chief executive officer (CEO) of the switching service was commonly known to dislike auditors and was not far from retirement. He likely believed that the control objectives specified in the report and the tests of their operating effectiveness were sufficient for purposes of the service auditor's report. Therefore, he chose to accept a qualified opinion rather than submit to the recommendation of the service auditor and include at least a description of the application system control objectives for the application systems processed by the service organization.

The service auditor's report did describe control objectives and procedures in the areas of organization and administration; card production; network settlement; computer operations; physical access and security; logical access and security; systems acquisition, development, and maintenance; and systems management. Since the service auditor's opinion regarding these control areas was unqualified, and since extensive testing of internal ATM processing procedures was performed, the internal auditors did not recommend that the process owner at the client organization request that the service organization explain why application controls were not included in the scope of the service auditor's report.

CASE STUDY 5.4

Qualified Opinion of a Credit Card Service Organization

A financial institution has used the same credit card service organization for over a decade. The financial institution utilized the credit card application supplied by the service organization as well as the data processing resources at the service organization's data center. For the period 1984 to 1995, service auditor reports were prepared in the following years: 1984, 1986, 1988, 1991, 1992, 1993, 1994, and 1995. Examination of these reports revealed that the service auditor had issued qualified opinions on the consecutive reports from 1986 to 1991. It is interesting to note how deficiency number 3 in the 1986 report was resolved but led to numerous new deficiencies in 1988, as the service organization was still in the process of learning how to adequately secure its mainframe and deploy its new access control software. Although qualified opinions were issued in three consecutive service auditor reports, a large

(continued)

CASE STUDY 5.4 (*continued*)

majority of the control objectives were achieved by the service organization and the identified weaknesses were corrected over time. Also, the weaknesses were not considered to be an indication that the overall control environment at the service organization was suspect. As you read through these weaknesses, consider whether they may exist within your organization. Many of the control weaknesses are fairly generic and could exist in almost any organization.

Deficiencies Noted in 1986 Service Auditor's Report

1. The quality assurance department does not review output from each plastic card production run for either embossing or encoding accuracy. Without quality assurance or other review, incorrectly embossed or encoded credit cards could be distributed to user institution customers. A possible ramification of an encoding error is that the daily withdrawal limit located on track 3 of the card's magnetic strip could be greater than the amount intended.
2. Programmer manuals describing file layouts, record layouts, subroutine calls, and other pertinent information are not consistently prepared. After initial development, program modifications or enhancements are more difficult and prone to error without detailed program documentation.
3. Although the service organization has a policy that authorizes only appropriate individuals to make program or other modifications, only rudimentary password protection exists to ensure that the policy is followed. System security application software, such as RACF® or ACF2®, is not installed to help prevent unauthorized modifications to application software, data files, or system software.

Deficiencies Noted in 1988 Report

1. The internal audit schedule is not adhered to and the areas actually audited are subjectively determined. Audit reports are not always issued on a timely basis, management responses are not documented, and follow-up audits to determine the implementation status of recommendations are not performed. The internal audit department does not consistently review system design, development, and maintenance controls for program changes. Information systems audit personnel do not routinely attend meetings in which system enhancements and major rewrites of the systems affecting all user institutions are determined.
2. The service organization does not have a consistently applied systems development methodology in place. Client organization sign-off on systems prior to implementation is not solicited by the service organization. Program documentation is not consistently prepared. Program modifications are often placed into production without supervisory review or user approval.
3. Programmer manuals describing file layouts, record layouts, subroutine calls, and other pertinent information are not consistently prepared. After initial development, program modifications or enhancements are more difficult and prone to error without detailed program documentation.
4. Programmers are able to write and authorize their own program changes

to be placed into production without consistent review or approval. Once a program is assigned to a programmer for modification, the completion of testing is generally at the programmer's discretion. System validation tests are not routinely performed to ensure that no source code was accidentally deleted or otherwise improperly modified.

5. The service organization does not have a designated person who has responsibility for administering security. No formalized, documented security procedures exist for the assignment of key cards allowing access to critical operational areas, access to application systems by service organization employees through the in-house security system, or control of programmer access through the ACF2 access control software. Security violation reports are not routinely reviewed, passwords are not routinely changed, terminated and transferred employee passwords and key cards are not always removed or modified on the appropriate systems on a timely basis, and an excessive number of individuals are capable of performing password maintenance. Groups of programmers share the same user IDs and passwords for time-sharing functions, thus decreasing the personal accountability for the use of the system. The service organization has recently implemented an access control facility program to control access to programs and data in the batch and time-sharing environments. However, the access control facility was not installed on the test computer, which was connected to the production computer and all disk files.

6. System and production tapes, which would be required in the event of a recovery of data processing service, are not always maintained in the off-site storage facilities. The service organization disaster recovery plan is incomplete and lacking in detail in a number of areas.

7. Systems programmers are given unrestricted access to the System Management Facility (SMF), which is the primary audit trail in the MVS® operating system used at the service organization. This facility is used to journal a wide variety of system events, including ACF2 access control software information.

8. No method exists to authorize or document changes made by systems programmers to sensitive areas such as the System Parameter Library (SPL), which contains key information for the audit, control, and security of the MVS operating system.

9. The Authorized Program Facility (APF) is provided by IBM to control access to libraries of programs that can circumvent all security mechanisms of the operating system, including the access control software. Most APF-authorized libraries can be accessed only by systems programmers whose job it is to maintain the programs in those libraries. However, one test library was APF authorized and also allowed application programmers unrestricted access to it. As a result, the possibility existed that an application programmer could run an unauthorized program.

10. The production library for application programs is APF authorized and contained 25 APF authorized programs, some of which were old and un-

(*continued*)

CASE STUDY 5.4 (*continued*)

documented. During our review, all 25 of these programs were either deleted or moved to a more appropriate library.

11. For performance or other reasons, the mainframe was designed to allow certain programs to bypass standard MVS security and control mechanisms. The base Program Properties Table contains the names of several programs that are not used at the service organization. These program names are authorized to bypass certain functions, such as dataset integrity or MVS passwords, and to access main storage owned by other programs. Since these programs do not exist at the service organization, it would be possible for someone to create an unauthorized program, assign it the name of one of the programs not being used in the Program Properties Table, and then run it without being subject to standard security controls.

12. No policy existed to require users to periodically change their passwords.

13. ACF2 has the capability to protect tape files from unauthorized access. However, this feature was not being utilized by the service organization. Thus, it is possible for a programmer to read a production tape, create a copy of it with certain records changed, and substitute it for the production tape.

Deficiencies Noted in 1991 Report

1. The service organization does not have a consistently applied formal systems development methodology in place. Furthermore, written user approval of systems prior to implementation is not always obtained by the service organization, program documentation is not routinely prepared, and program modifications are sometimes placed into production without supervisory review or user approval. As a result, there is an increased risk that areas of user concern could be bypassed, important control features could be overlooked, and programs may not be properly tested or designed to meet user specifications.

2. Programmer documentation describing file layouts, record layouts, subroutine calls, and other data are not routinely prepared. As a result, after a system is developed, program modifications or enhancements are more difficult to perform, and such changes are more likely to contain errors.

3. Programmers are able to write and authorize their own program changes to be placed into production without consistent review or approval. Once a program is assigned to a programmer for modification, the completion of testing is generally at the programmer's discretion. Test plans are not consistently prepared, and test results are not always reviewed by supervisory personnel. These weaknesses increase the risk that source code could be accidentally deleted or otherwise improperly modified.

4. Application programmers have write access to a variety of production source, parameter, cataloged procedure, and macro libraries. This access is not logged by ACF2. Thus, programmers could make unauthorized changes to the source code, which might be placed into production at a later time.

5. The service organization's disaster recovery plan has been developed to address only the destruction of the main data center and the IBM mainframe computers. Network recovery procedures are not addressed, nor are procedures defined in the Card Production Department and Statement Production Department. Also, the existing plan was not tested for a 20-month period.

When a service auditor's report does not express an opinion as to the operating effectiveness of the policies and procedures in place at a service organization, an internal auditor should recommend to the process owner at the client organization that they ask the service organization why the service auditor did not perform tests of operating effectiveness. The most common reason is that the service organization was avoiding the additional fee that would be charged by the service auditor to perform additional testing. If this is the case, the internal auditor should assess the level of risk associated with the process being audited. If the risk is considered high, the auditor should recommend that the process owner submit a request to the service organization that the service auditor perform tests of the operating effectiveness of the policies and procedures in place at the service organization. If the service organization refuses, the internal auditor should work with the process owner at the client organization to determine whether the risk is significant enough to consider utilizing the service of an alternative service organization.

Another option is for the client organization to send its own auditors to the service organization's processing facilities to perform an audit of applicable general controls. While this type of audit will not be as detailed and will not be able to test for a six-month period, it will provide a limited amount of assurance that at least basic controls are being exercised by the service organization. Case study 5.5 describes how a client organization performed a brief on-site audit of a privately held service organization that did not have a SAS 70 audit performed.

CASE STUDY 5.5

Service Organization without a SAS 70

A large, privately held service organization prepared monthly statements, notices, and various promotional mailings for several of the largest banking organizations in the region. This amounted to tens of millions of mailings each month. Since the large name and address databases are extremely valuable to commercial marketing firms, the statements contain confidential personal information, and the monthly postage costs reach into the millions, the risks

(continued)

CASE STUDY 5.5 (*continued*)

pertaining to the service organization's internal controls were significant. The service organization had been in business for about 20 years and was experiencing significant growth.

The internal auditors at one of the client banking organizations were performing an audit of their statement preparation process. One step was to assess the adequacy of controls at request and examine a SAS 70 from the service organization. The auditors learned that the service organization had an independent audit of its financial statements but had no SAS 70 performed. The auditors decided to perform a brief on-site audit since the service organization was located in the same geographical area. The service organization contact representative (the servicer) was very willing to host the client auditors for a brief on-site visit and to provide as much documentation and information as he could to assist in the audit. Surprisingly, none of the other banking organizations had ever requested a SAS 70 or performed an on-site audit.

The client auditors scheduled an initial two-hour meeting with the servicer, the data processing manager, and a systems analyst. In advance of the meeting, the auditors provided the servicer with a list of required information including:

- Most recent audited financial statements
- Current insurance certificate for commercial general liability, fidelity bond, and commercial vehicle insurance
- IS Security Policy and Standards
- Business Resumption/Disaster Recovery Plan
- Postage Control Procedures

The meeting began with a review of the above documents. All were current and their contents considered adequate, although the servicer would only allow visual inspection of its audited financial statements since it is privately held. They did provide the auditors with a copy of the CPA opinion letter.

The auditors asked the data processing manager and systems analyst about the information systems environment (hardware and application systems) used in the preparation of the various mailings and the associated logical security controls. The auditors were also given a brief demonstration of the existence of some of the controls on the production systems. No exceptions were observed.

Last, the auditors were given a tour of the high-speed data processing and printing area where all statements and other mailings are printed. Physical security controls included electronic access badge access to restricted areas and surveillance cameras at all entrances and warehouse delivery bays. The servicer did not employ any external couriers or truck drivers, thereby helping to ensure complete internal control over the preparation and mailing of all documents from the time the electronic downloads are received from clients until the mailings are delivered to the U.S. Post Office.

All postage costs were charged to a unique post office meter number assigned to each client organization. The meter could be replenished only by the post office using funds provided by the servicer. The servicer notifies each client of the estimated postage at the beginning of each month. Clients are required to wire the estimated postage amount to the servicer so that a small reserve remains at the end of the month. Postage internal controls included various balancing and segregation of duties procedures in the IS, statement preparation, and accounting areas.

Based on the limited tests performed and resolution of a few follow-up questions, the client auditors concluded that internal controls at the service organization were adequate. However, two significant internal control deficiencies existed in the internal accounting procedures for prepaid postage at the client organization.

First, the client had been wiring the requested amounts to the servicer each month. The accounting department would debit a prepaid postage asset account and credit cash at the beginning of the month. At the end of the month, accounting would make an accrual entry to debit postage expense and credit prepaid postage for estimated postage costs incurred. The servicer sent a monthly invoice for labor and material costs associated with the preparation of the mailings (these amounts were expensed as incurred). The invoice indicated the amount of postage used for the applicable mailings but did not indicate what amount remained in the prepaid postage meter at the servicer.

The problem was that the monthly expense accrual entry to debit expense and credit prepaid postage had not been adjusted recently to reflect increased postage costs due to steady increases in the number of mailings and postage rates as the organization grew. As a result, the amount in the prepaid postage asset account had been increasing while accrued postage expenses were relatively unchanged. An adjusting entry to debit postage expense and credit prepaid postage for about $120,000 was necessary to reduce the amount in the prepaid postage account to what the accounting department estimated was remaining on the postage meter at the servicer. Also, the monthly expense accrual amount had to be increased by about $10,000.

A second problem was that the accounting department had never attempted to reconcile the amount of prepaid postage in its general ledger to the amount of prepaid postage in the meter at the servicer. Thus, if the servicer was overcharging postage to the client meter, processing mail of other clients or itself to the client organization's meter, embezzling part of the funds out of the client postage wired before the meter was replenished, or having processing problems that depleted the meter amount without stamping any actual envelopes, the client organization would not be able to detect it easily, especially in an environment where the amount wired to the servicer was steadily increasing. The auditors recommended that the accounting department implement reconciliation procedures. This required the service organization to begin providing a remaining postage meter balance amount on the monthly invoices for labor and materials. After the initial reconciliation, an additional $10,000 in postage expense was incurred by the client organization to reduce the amount in the prepaid postage account to what was actually on the postage meter at the servicer. The auditors also recommended that the accounting department implement a control to recalculate the average postage cost per envelope on each invoice.

DESCRIPTION OF RELEVANT POLICIES AND PROCEDURES AND OTHER INFORMATION

It is important for internal auditors to read this section of a service auditor's report to gain a better understanding of the service organization and its control environment. Quite often this information can provide more complete information about the service organization and its applications than the process owner at the client organization. This section commonly includes a general description of operations, a description of control environment elements, and a description of the flow of transactions.

The general description of operations usually consists of a narrative overview of the corporate structure of the service organization, an overview of corporate operations, and a general description of each applicable application. An organization chart is often included, or it may be provided in an appendix.

Control environment elements are those that should be in place at the service organization to provide reasonable assurance that client organization transactions and data are processed in a timely, accurate, and secure manner. Some service auditor reports provide a description of the functions of key departments supporting the overall control environment. Examples of such key departments include Human Resources, Internal Audit, Client Support, Product Delivery, Research and Development, and Product Management. Other service auditor reports instead may describe the policies and procedures surrounding specific control objectives specified by management of the service organization.

The description of the flow of transactions is a high-level narrative of how the application processes transactions and generates output reports and other documents for client organizations. Flow charts may be included in this section or in an appendix.

Application overviews are narrative descriptions of the various services or functions that each application performs. In some cases, complex primary applications are supported by one or more secondary applications. If so, overviews of these secondary applications would also be provided.

Program change procedures at the service organization exist to help ensure that changes have been properly authorized, documented, tested, and placed into production. The procedures may be described in narrative form with an accompanying flow chart or may simply be included as a flow chart in an appendix.

Depending on the industry to which the service organization supplies applications, a description of policies and procedures that help ensure regulatory compliance may be provided. The format will vary with the nature of the laws or regulations being described.

CONTROL OBJECTIVES AS SPECIFIED BY SERVICE ORGANIZATION MANAGEMENT

Control objectives are specified by the service organization's management. However, service auditors play a significant role in consulting with management to ensure that the control objectives specified address the primary risks associated with the service organization's operations. Following each control objective is a detailed description of the policies and procedures purported to be in place to ensure that the control objective is attained. Management of the service organization also provides this information. For service auditor reports that include the auditor's opinion on the operating effectiveness of the policies and procedures placed in operation, the service auditor specifies the tests performed to gain reasonable, but not absolute, assurance as to their effectiveness. These tests typically include inquiries with management and staff of the service organization, sample tests of individual transactions, examinations of system access controls, assessment of segregation of duties, observation of service organization operations, and so on.

Exhibits 5.1 to 5.4 depict some types of control objectives that can be specified within service auditor reports in various industries. Although many unique risks exist within each industry, some of the control objectives are very similar, even though the service organizations serve different industries. This is because many of the risks associated with information systems are not dependent on the type of information being processed or the hardware on which it is processed. Therefore, the controls to mitigate those risks are very similar.

EXHIBIT 5.1   CONTROL OBJECTIVES FOR A CREDIT CARD PROCESSING SERVICE ORGANIZATION

1. The data center and client functions should be structured to maintain adequate segregation of duties.
2. The data center should be organized to provide adequate segregation of duties and functions.
3. Internal audit should provide a review and verification of electronic data processing operations.
4. Appropriate administrative policies and procedures should be documented.
5. A quality assurance function should exist to ensure the quality of service provided to clients.
6. New programs being developed and changes to existing programs should be authorized, tested, approved, properly implemented, and documented.
7. Changes to existing software should be authorized, tested, approved, and implemented properly.
8. Physical access to computer equipment and storage media should be limited to properly authorized individuals.
9. Logical access to production programs and data in the mainframe environment should be granted only to appropriately authorized individuals.
10. Processing should be scheduled appropriately, and deviations should be identified and resolved.

(continued)

EXHIBIT 5.1 *(continued)*

---

11. Data transmissions between the service organization and clients should be complete, accurate, and secure.
12. Data transmissions between the service organization's data centers should be complete, accurate, and secure.
13. Credit card application information should be accepted from authorized sources.
14. Credit card application information should be recorded completely, accurately, and in compliance with client specifications.
15. Output information should be complete, accurate, and distributed in accordance with client specifications.
16. Online input should be received from authorized sources.
17. Appropriate client specifications should be used for programmed calculations.
18. Card-holder activity should be completely and accurately posted to the appropriate accounts.
19. Card-holder statement information should be complete, accurate, and distributed in accordance with client specifications.
20. Personal identification numbers and post mailer notification information should be complete, accurate, and distributed in accordance with client specifications.
21. Management reports and data files should be complete, accurate, and distributed in accordance with client specifications.
22. Output information to other application systems should be complete and accurate.
23. Card production requests should be accepted from authorized sources.
24. Cards should be produced completely and accurately.
25. Access to blank cards should be limited to authorized personnel, and inventory should be accounted for properly.
26. Card production output should be distributed in accordance with client specifications.
27. Input should be completely and accurately received from authorized sources.
28. Interchange transactions should be completely and accurately processed in accordance with client and association specifications.
29. Net settlement amounts should be accurate.
30. Merchant transaction reports should be complete and accurate.
31. Output to other application systems at the service organization should be complete and accurate.
32. Merchant transactions should be received completely and accurately from the merchant system.
33. Merchant information should be processed completely, accurately, and in accordance with client specifications.
34. Output information should be complete, accurate, and distributed in accordance with client specifications.
35. Administrative and operational procedures should be established within the service organization data center to reasonably assure protection of physical assets and continuity of operations.

**EXHIBIT 5.2   CONTROL OBJECTIVES FOR A PAYROLL PROCESSING
SERVICE ORGANIZATION**

---

1. New applications being developed and changes to existing application software are authorized, tested, approved, properly implemented, and documented.
2. Changes to existing system software and implementation of new system software is authorized, tested, approved, properly implemented, and documented.
3. Physical access to computer equipment, storage media, negotiable instruments, and program documentation is limited to properly authorized individuals.
4. Logical access to programs and data is limited to properly authorized individuals.
5. Processing is scheduled appropriately and deviations are identified and resolved.
6. Payroll data transmissions between the service organization headquarters and regional data centers are secure, complete, and accurate.
7. Payroll data transmissions between the service organization and client organizations are secure, complete, and accurate.
8. Payroll data is received from authorized sources.
9. Payroll data is initially recorded completely and accurately.
10. Appropriate statutory specifications are used to process payroll deduction and tax withholding calculations.
11. Output tapes, checks, reports, and transmissions are complete, accurate, and distributed in accordance with client specifications.
12. Access to digitized signatures of authorized client signatures is restricted to authorized individuals, and digitized images are accessed by the appropriate company's payroll process.
13. Disbursements of direct deposit funds are authorized, complete, and accurate.
14. Output reports are complete, accurate, and distributed in accordance with client specifications.
15. Administrative and operational procedures are established within regional data centers to reasonably assure continuity of operations and ensure protection of physical assets (e.g., in the event of disasters).

**EXHIBIT 5.3   CONTROL OBJECTIVES FOR AN ATM NETWORK SERVICE
ORGANIZATION**

---

1. Member institutions are in conformity with the service organization's operating rules to provide adequate end-to-end protection.
2. Senior management should provide for a segregation of duties within the organization, such as between system development and operations, qual-

(continued)

EXHIBIT 5.3   *(continued)*

---

ity control and operations, and customer service and systems development.

3. An internal audit function exists to act as a controlling mechanism through independent inspections and evaluation of security issues and management controls.

4. Employees of the service organization are of the highest integrity and competency to ensure the confidentiality and security of user institution data throughout the network.

5. Card-holder information is adequately protected against unauthorized disclosure.

6. Transactions processed by the service organization are properly accounted for and reconciled among member institutions and other switching networks.

7. Processing is scheduled appropriately, and deviations from scheduling are identified and resolved.

8. Administrative and operational procedures are established within the data center to reasonably ensure avoidance of interrupted service and continuity of operations in the event of an extended disruption of processing ability.

9. Physical access to computer encryption equipment, storage media, and program documentation are limited to properly authorized individuals.

10. Physical access to card production equipment, mailers, cards, and card information media is limited to properly authorized individuals.

11. Logical access to production network systems is limited to properly authorized individuals.

12. Card-holder personal identification numbers and encryption keys are never received, processed, and transmitted in clear text.

13. Changes to existing mainframe and microcomputer applications are authorized, tested, approved, properly implemented, and documented.

14. All database changes to user institution parameters are authorized and controlled to protect data integrity and accuracy.

15. System resources are adequate to provide continuous processing to users.

EXHIBIT 5.4   **CONTROL OBJECTIVES FOR A SERVICE ORGANIZATION THAT PROVIDES MULTIPURPOSE APPLICATIONS FOR FINANCIAL INSTITUTIONS**

Control policies and procedures provide reasonable assurance as to the operating effectiveness of the following:

1. Changes to the application system are authorized, tested, approved, properly implemented, and documented.

EXHIBIT 5.4 *(continued)*

---

2. Changes to existing system software and implementation of new system software are authorized, tested, approved, properly implemented, and documented.
3. Physical access to computer equipment, storage media, and program documentation is limited to properly authorized individuals.
4. Logical access to programs and data is limited to properly authorized individuals.
5. Deposit account transactions are properly authorized.
6. Deposit account transactions are processed completely and accurately.
7. Deposit account balances are calculated correctly.
8. Loan transactions are properly authorized.
9. Loan transactions are processed completely and accurately.
10. Loan balances are calculated correctly.

CLIENT CONTROL CONSIDERATIONS

From the perspective of the client organization, the most important information contained in a service auditor's report are the client control considerations. Client control considerations are procedures that the service organization recommends that each client organization implement. These controls complement the controls at the service organization to enhance the level of control over client organization transactions and data. The controls at the client organization and the service organization comprise the overall control environment for the process being evaluated.

Within a service auditor's report, client control considerations are sometimes described immediately after each description of policies and procedures and tests performed. Client control considerations may also be grouped together in a separate section or in a matrix. Exhibits 5.5, 5.6, 5.7, and 5.8 provide lists of client control considerations corresponding to the service organizations in Exhibits 5.1 through 5.4, respectively. Each control objective does not necessarily require a client control consideration.

When performing an audit of a process that utilizes a service organization, the internal auditor should examine the service auditor's report and confirm that each client control consideration has been implemented at the client organization. If not, the auditor should determine the reason the client control considerations were not implemented, assess the potential risks if the controls continue to be ignored, and then make appropriate recommendations based on the information they have gathered.

ALTERNATIVES TO SAS 70–TYPE AUDITS

With the proliferation of the Internet and e-commerce, the need arose for alternatives to the traditional SAS 70–type audit. Traditional SAS 70–type audits are

---

**EXHIBIT 5.5   CLIENT CONTROL CONSIDERATIONS FOR A CREDIT
CARD PROCESSING SERVICE ORGANIZATION**

1. Procedures should be established to ensure changes to processing parameters are appropriately authorized, implemented, and reviewed.
2. Procedures should be established to ensure transactions are appropriately authorized, complete, and accurate.
3. Procedures should be established to ensure erroneous input data is corrected and resubmitted.
4. Procedures should be established to ensure that output reports are reviewed by appropriate client personnel for completeness and accuracy.
5. Procedures should be established to ensure that output from programs is balanced routinely to relevant control totals.
6. Clients should review online activity log reports generated by the system for all changes made to system parameters and transactions entered online to ensure that all activity is consistent with their requests.
7. The application security should be used to control the functions that client personnel may perform. An individual at each client site should be responsible for maintaining and monitoring access controls, and printouts of the access capabilities of each terminal and operator should be reviewed periodically.
8. Clients are responsible for establishing and maintaining control parameters and for reviewing batch reports to ensure that all data has been received and recorded completely and accurately.
9. The daily credit override report should be reviewed to determine that all overrides were appropriate.
10. Policies and procedures should be established to ensure that credit activity reports are reviewed for completeness, accuracy, and unauthorized activity in a timely manner.
11. Adequate end-of-day procedures should exist to verify transaction volume and dollar amounts reported by the application agree with the client organization's internal accounting records. Out-of-balance conditions and other exceptions should be researched and resolved in a timely manner.
12. Clients should ensure that they have implemented procedures in response to the actions recommended by the service organization in its disaster recovery plan overview.

**EXHIBIT 5.6   CLIENT CONTROL CONSIDERATIONS FOR A PAYROLL
PROCESSING SERVICE ORGANIZATION**

1. Clients should ensure that proper procedures are in place to control the use of user IDs and passwords to access and transmit payroll information.
2. Clients should review the payroll audit report on a timely basis to ensure that all payroll information has been recorded completely and accurately.

EXHIBIT 5.6 (*continued*)

Clients should also review the initial master file setup form prior to the first payroll run to ensure that employee-level and company-level information has been initially recorded completely and accurately.

3. Clients should review the payroll audit report on a timely basis to ensure that all payroll information has been processed completely and accurately.
4. Clients should review the sample payroll check produced by the service organization prior to initial payroll processing to determine that all information is complete and accurate, including company name, codes, logos, and signatures.
5. Clients are responsible for reviewing the completeness and accuracy of all reports produced by the application.
6. Procedures should be established to ensure that access to personal computers and terminals is controlled.
7. Procedures should be established to ensure that transactions are appropriately authorized, complete, and accurate.
8. Procedures should be established to ensure that erroneous input data is corrected and resubmitted.
9. Procedures should be established to ensure that output reports are reviewed by appropriate client personnel for completeness and accuracy.
10. Procedures should be established to ensure that output from programs is balanced routinely to relevant control totals.

EXHIBIT 5.7 CLIENT CONTROL CONSIDERATIONS FOR AN ATM NETWORK SERVICE ORGANIZATION

Client organizations are responsible for:

1. Verifying compliance with operating rules of the service organization and technical requirements.
2. Performing adequate background checks for users having access to service organization systems and processes.
3. Security administration procedures and record maintenance for granting/terminating employee access to the service organization's system.
4. Accuracy and authentication of card production information used as data input to the service organization's card production systems.
5. Verifying and authenticating all card production data output reports generated by and received from the service organization.
6. Ensuring that personal identification numbers (PINs) are delayed appropriately from the mailing of their associated cards.
7. Return mailer practices to ensure appropriate security and control over destruction of returned cards and PINs issued to customers.

(*continued*)

EXHIBIT 5.7   (continued)

8. Reviewing and reconciling their ATM transaction journal activity to that reported by the service organization.
9. Verifying settlement reports and procedures to ensure that adjustments are applied in an appropriate and timely manner.
10. Reviewing and validating net settlement adjustment totals and the debit/credit entries to the settlement account on a timely basis.
11. Timely notification to the service organization Help Desk of operating problems between their institution and the service organization.
12. Maintaining and testing their own business recovery plan.
13. Security administration procedures and record maintenance for granting/terminating employee access to the service organization's system.
14. Verifying compliance with service organization operating rules, technical requirements, and other standards for PIN encryption and key management.
15. Establishing appropriate user authentication procedures to control encryption key management activity (creation, change, deletion).

EXHIBIT 5.8   CLIENT CONTROL CONSIDERATIONS FOR A SERVICE ORGANIZATION THAT PROVIDES MULTIPURPOSE APPLICATIONS FOR FINANCIAL INSTITUTIONS

1. Modems at client financial institution locations should always be deactivated unless remote access is required. Client institutions should regularly review the dial-up report to ensure that remote accesses were authorized and performed by service organization personnel.
2. Client institution procedures should be established to ensure that employees have appropriate application access based on their job responsibilities. In addition, procedures should be established to ensure that changes in staff and/or job responsibilities result in timely security revisions. Authorization change reports should be regularly reviewed to ensure that access is appropriately designated. The authorization system should be restricted to authorized personnel. Passwords should be changed periodically and structured to maintain their integrity. Access to sensitive transaction capabilities should be restricted to authorized personnel. Only authorized personnel should be given the system supervisor password and allowed to perform system administration functions.
3. The daily transaction journal and other system reports should be regularly reviewed.
4. Access to deposit account transactions and file maintenance transactions should be restricted to authorized personnel. System authorization reports should be regularly reviewed to ensure that access is appropriately designated.

EXHIBIT 5.8   *(continued)*

---

5. All necessary documentation for opening new accounts should be obtained, reviewed, and approved by staff other than those who perform teller functions. The new accounts report should be compared on a detail level to all new account documentation to ensure accurate data entry.

6. The interest paid and posted reports should be reviewed to ensure reasonableness of calculations.

7. Supporting documentation of approved loans should also be maintained for comparison to computer-generated reports to ensure that all approved loans have been properly recorded. Details of file maintenance transactions should be compared to source documents. Procedures should be developed to monitor delinquent loans and charge-off transactions, collection and investigation of loan charge-offs, and recovery of charged-off loans. Delinquent loan reports should be periodically reviewed and action initiated to minimize loan losses.

8. Daily manual reconciliations should be performed between loan payment documentation, loan subsidiary records, and teller balances. The system-generated trial balance should also be reconciled to the general ledger.

9. Procedures should be established to monitor delinquency reports, initiate timely investigation of problem loans, and evaluate the adequacy of loan loss reserves. Charged-off loans should also be monitored.

10. The loan interest accrual report should be periodically analyzed for reasonableness. Fee options should be reviewed to ensure that they are consistent with client institution policies.

11. System access to general ledger functions should be restricted to authorized personnel, and general ledger reports should be regularly reviewed.

12. Client institutions should review changes to system tables and parameters to ensure that they are consistent with current policies.

---

typically large in scope, are time consuming, and are more appropriate for large organizations that perform high-volume transaction processing for multiple commercial clients. They are designed to provide detailed information and assurance to auditors of client organizations about controls at the service organization that might affect the financial statements of client organizations. The detailed information includes a description of the IS environment, the testing procedures performed by the service auditor, and the results of the tests.

But many service providers, such as small application service providers or website hosting companies, cannot afford SAS 70–type audits or to hire an internal IS audit staff. In other cases, non–service provider organizations engaged in e-commerce or other Internet-based commercial activities want independent assurance that their own internal systems are reliable and secure, and they want to be able to communicate their secure status to their customers and shareholders to alleviate their security concerns. Some organizations simply want independent assurance that their systems are reliable and secure, beyond what their IS security team or even their internal IS auditors are reporting.

To respond to these needs, several different types of "certifications" have been developed. Most allow the organizations that meet the certification standards to post an electronic certification or seal on their websites. The following sections briefly describe five of the more common certifications: TruSecure, SysTrust, WebTrust, BBBOnline, and TRUSTe.

TruSecure®

TruSecure Corporation (formerly ICSA and originally known as NCSA) is a worldwide leader in security assurance solutions for Internet-connected organizations. TruSecure was one of the first organizations to offer a website certification service. The primary criteria for the TruSecure certification are:

- Use of adequate physical and logical security mechanisms that address the client's desired "security posture." The security mechanisms include: written and implemented access control, antivirus, firewall, backup and redundancy policies and procedures.
- Documented use of standard access controls, encryption mechanisms, and informed consent of data usage that ensure confidentiality of all back-end transactions and session traffic.
- TruSecure-evaluated site documentation, on-site verification, remote testing, and random spot-checking for annual compliance.

One unique aspect of the TruSecure certification is that it provides a small amount of insurance for certified websites in the event of a security breach. For more information about the TruSecure certification, see their website at *www.trusecure.com.*

SysTrust^SM

SysTrust is a service jointly developed by the American Institute of Certified Public Accountants (AICPA) and Canadian Institute of Chartered Accountants (CICA) that enables qualified public accountants with the necessary IS skills to provide assurance that a client's system is in fact reliable. SysTrust Version 1.0 was released in 1999, and Version 2.0 was issued in 2000.

SysTrust has 4 principles and 58 criteria organized:

- *Availability.* The system is available for operation and use at times set forth in service-level statements or agreements. This principle requires testing of 12 detailed criteria that are grouped into 3 categories.
- *Security.* The system is protected against unauthorized physical and logical

access. This principle requires testing of 19 detailed criteria that are grouped into 3 categories.

- *Integrity.* System processing is complete, accurate, timely, and authorized. This principle requires testing of 14 detailed criteria that are grouped into 3 categories.
- *Maintainability.* The system can be updated when required in a manner that continues to provide for system availability, security, and integrity. This principle requires testing of 13 detailed criteria that are grouped into 3 categories.

The SysTrust principles and criteria can be applied to all types of systems. SysTrust defines a system as an infrastructure of hardware, software, people, procedures, and data that produce information in a business context. As with SAS 70–type audits, the auditor issues a SysTrust opinion letter. SysTrust opinions may be unqualified or qualified. Contrary to SAS 70–type audits, client organizations do not receive details about the IS environment, testing procedures, and results of testing.

For more information about the SysTrust service, see the AICPA website (*www.aicpa.org*) or the CICA website (*www.cica.ca*). Also, Boritz et al. have published an excellent article introducing the new SysTrust assurance service.[14]

WebTrust^{SM}

WebTrust is a family of services jointly developed by the AICPA and CICA that enables qualified public accountants with the necessary IS skills to provide assurance that client websites which conduct business-to-consumer and business-to-business electronic commerce transactions meet standards for one or more of various principles. An unqualified opinion letter must be earned from the auditor before the WebTrust seal can be displayed on the client's website.

WebTrust Version 1.0 was released in 1997 with the first website earning the seal in the spring of 1998. Version 2.0 was issued in 1999, and Version 3.0 in 2000. Version 3.0 enables auditors to issue an opinion and corresponding seal on individual principles or combinations of principles.

An entity must be able to demonstrate five WebTrust 3.0 principles. The detailed criteria within each principle are organized into four broad areas: disclosures, policies, procedures, and monitoring.

- *On-line Privacy Principle.* The entity discloses its privacy practices, complies with such privacy practices, and maintains effective controls to provide reasonable assurance that personally identifiable information obtained as a result of electronic commerce is protected in conformity with its disclosed privacy practices.
- *Security Principle.* The entity discloses its key security practices, complies with such security practices, and maintains effective controls to provide

reasonable assurance that access to the electronic commerce system and data is restricted only to authorized individuals in conformity with its disclosed security practices.

* *Business Practices/Transaction Integrity Principle.* The entity discloses its business practices for electronic commerce, executes transactions in conformity with such practices, and maintains effective controls to provide reasonable assurance that electronic commerce transactions are processed completely, accurately, and in conformity with its disclosed business practices.
* *Availability Principle.* The entity discloses its availability practices, complies with such availability practices, and maintains effective controls to provide reasonable assurance that electronic commerce systems and data are available in conformity with its disclosed availability practices.
* *Confidentiality Principle.* The entity discloses its confidentiality practices, complies with such confidentiality practices, and maintains effective controls to provide reasonable assurance that access to information obtained as a result of electronic commerce and designated as confidential is restricted to authorized individuals, groups of individuals, or entities in conformity with its disclosed confidentiality practices.

In addition to these certifications, certification authorities (CAs) can earn a specialized WebTrust seal, which has three principles:

1. *Business Practices Disclosure.* The CA discloses its key and certificate lifecycle management business and information privacy practices and provides its services in accordance with its disclosed practices.
2. *Service Integrity.* The CA maintains effective controls to provide reasonable assurance that subscriber information was properly authenticated (for the registration activities performed by ABC-CA) and the integrity of keys and certificates it manages is established and protected throughout their life cycles.
3. *Environmental Controls.* The CA maintains effective controls to provide reasonable assurance that subscriber and relying party information is restricted to authorized individuals and protected from uses not specified in the CA's business practices disclosure; the continuity of key and certificate management operations is maintained; and CA systems development, maintenance, and operation are properly authorized and performed to maintain CA systems integrity.

For more information about the WebTrust family of services, see the AICPA website (*www.aicpa.org*) or the CICA website (*www.cica.ca*).

BBBOnline®

BBBOnline offers two website certifications, one for reliability and one for privacy. Following are the general requirements of each program:

BBBOnline Reliability Program Requirements

- Become a member of the Better Business Bureau (BBB) where company is headquartered.
- Provide the BBB with information regarding company ownership and management and the street address and telephone number at which it does business, which may be verified by the BBB in a visit to the company's physical premises.
- Be in business a minimum of one year (an exception can be made if a new business is a spinoff or a division of an existing business, which is known to and has a positive track record with the BBB).
- Have a satisfactory complaint-handling record with the BBB.
- Agree to participate in the BBB's advertising self-regulation program and to correct or withdraw online advertising when challenged by the BBB and found not to be substantiated or not in compliance with children's advertising guidelines. (The BBB does not preclear or preapprove online advertising. Its local and national advertising review programs are described on the BBB's website, and complaints about online advertising brought by consumers, competitors, or public officials may be filed online with the BBB.)
- Agree to abide by the BBB Code of Online Business Practices and to co-operate with any BBB request for modification of a website to bring it into accordance with the code.
- Respond promptly to all consumer complaints.
- Agree to dispute resolution, at the consumer's request, for unresolved disputes involving consumer products or services.

BBBOnline Privacy Program Eligibility Requirements

Privacy Program Eligibility Requirements are grouped into seven categories:

1. Threshold: Includes general, eligibility, and contractual requirements
2. Privacy Notice
3. Sharing of Information
4. Choice & Consent
5. Access & Correction
6. Security
7. Kid's Program: There are additional eligibility requirements for websites directed at children under age 13.

For more information about the BBBOnline certifications, see the BBBOnline website at *www.bbbonline.com.*

TRUSTe™

TRUSTe is an independent, nonprofit privacy organization whose mission is to build users' trust and confidence on the Internet and, in doing so, accelerate growth of the Internet industry. It was founded by the Electronic Frontier Foundation (EFF) and the CommerceNet Consortium, which act as independent, unbiased trust entities. The TRUSTe privacy program attempts to bridge the gap between users' concerns over privacy and websites' desire for self-regulated information disclosure standards. TRUSTe issues two different "trustmarks."

TRUSTe (Standard)

Members' websites must adhere to established privacy principles and agree to comply with ongoing TRUSTe oversight and consumer resolution procedures. Privacy principles embody fair information practices approved by the U.S. Department of Commerce, Federal Trade Commission, and prominent industry-represented organizations and associations. The principles include:

- Adoption and implementation of a privacy policy that takes into account consumer anxiety over sharing personal information online.
- Notice and disclosure of information collection and use practices.
- Choice and consent, giving users the opportunity to exercise control over their information.
- Data security, quality, and access measures to help protect the security and accuracy of personally identifiable information

All websites that bear the TRUSTe trustmark must disclose their personal information collection and privacy practices in a straightforward privacy statement, generally a link from the home page. More than one trustmark may be displayed if personal information privacy practices vary within the site.

TRUSTe Children's Privacy Seal Requirements

Websites directed at children under 13 must meet all regular program requirements and must also *not* perform the following:

- Collect online contact information from a child under 13 without prior verifiable parental consent or direct parental notification of the nature and intended use of this information, which shall include an opportunity for the parent to prevent use of the information and participation in the activity. Where prior parental consent is not obtained, online contact information shall be used only to directly respond to the child's request and shall not be used to re-contact the child for other purposes.
- Collect personally identifiable offline contact information from children under 13 without prior verifiable parental consent.
- Distribute to third parties any personally identifiable information collected from a child under 13 without prior verifiable parental consent.
- Give the ability to children under 13 to publicly post or otherwise distribute personally identifiable contact information without prior verifiable pa-

rental consent, and make best efforts to prohibit a child from posting any contact information.

* Entice a child under 13 by the prospect of a special game, prize, or other activity to divulge more information than is needed to participate in such activity.

The site must also place prominent notice where personally identifiable information is collected, requesting the child to ask a parent for permission to answer the questions.

For more information about the TRUSTe certification, see the Electronic Frontier Foundation website at *www.eff.org*.

NOTES

1. American Institute of Certified Public Accountants, *Codification of Statements on Auditing Standards, Service Organizations*, AU Section 324 (March 31, 1993): Paragraph 24(a).
2. *Ibid.*, Paragraph 53.
3. Canadian Institute of Chartered Accountants, *Opinions on Control Procedures at a Service Organization*, Section 5900 (July 1, 1987): Paragraph 6(b).
4. *Ibid.*, Paragraph 7(a)(b).
5. *Ibid.*, Paragraph 13.
6. Faculty of Information Technology of the Institute of Chartered Accountants in England and Wales, *Reports on the Processing of Transactions by Service Organizations*, Technical Release FIT 1/94 (September 1994): Part 1, Paragraph 25.
7. Financial Reporting and Auditing Group of the Institute of Chartered Accountants in England and Wales, *Reports on Internal Controls of Investment Custodians Made Available to Third Parties*, Technical Release FRAG 21/94 (May 1994): Paragraph 14(2)(3).
8. *Ibid.*, Appendix III, 16 (F).
9. Additional information on Australian auditing standards may be requested from the Australian Accounting Research Foundation, Level 10/600 Bourke Street, Melbourne, Victoria 3000, Australia.
10. Auditing Standards Board of the Australian Accounting Research Foundation, Invitation to Comment, "Reporting on Internal Controls" (April 1996): 6–7.
11. Auditing Standards Board of the Australian Accounting Research Foundation, Auditing Guidance Statement 1026 (January 1997): 6.
12. Financial Reporting and Auditing Group of the Institute of Chartered Accountants in England and Wales, Technical Release FRAG 21/94: Appendix III, 16 (F).
13. American Institute of Certified Public Accountants, AU Section 324: Paragraph 53.
14. Efrim Boritz et al., "Reporting on Systems Reliability," *Journal of Accountancy* (November 1999): 75–87.

CHAPTER 6

Assessing the Financial Stability of Vendor Organizations, Examining Vendor Organization Contracts, and Examining Accounting Treatment of Computer Equipment and Software

The first section of this chapter discusses the reasons that organizations should assess the financial stability of the vendor organizations with which they do business and provides a high-level approach to perform such assessments. The second section discusses keys to examining contracts and agreements that organizations may have entered into with vendor organizations. The chapter concludes with a brief section on the examination of the accounting treatment of computer hardware and software.

ASSESSING FINANCIAL STABILITY OF VENDOR ORGANIZATIONS

Service organizations and application vendors provide services that are often critical to the success of their client organizations. Any disruptions in service could significantly impair the ability of client organizations to serve the needs of their customers. If a disruption lasts for an extended period of time, the client organization could begin to lose customers and eventually suffer significant revenue losses. Disruptions in service could be the result of poor operating procedures, outside competition, or poor management decisions at the vendor organization. Eventually these problems will surface in their financial statements. As discussed in Chapter 5, one of the first steps that the project development team at the client organization should perform after the decision has been made to utilize a service organization is to examine a copy of the most recent service auditor's report from each of the bidding service organizations. Such an examination should take place before any contract is entered into with the service organization. Another step the project development team should perform prior to signing a contract with a service organization or application vendor is to analyze the financial statements of each prospective vendor organization to obtain reasonable assurance that it is in sound financial condition for the foreseeable future. Obviously, the project development team will have to employ the services of a qualified individual who is capable of analyzing financial statements. Examples of qualified persons include the chief financial officer (CFO), controller, an appointed subordinate who has sufficient education and experience in accounting and finance, or an independent certified public accountant (CPA).

As is the case with poorly operating internal policies and procedures, poor financial strength and performance could be indicators that the vendor organization may have difficulty providing the level of service and information protection expected by the client organization. It is beyond the scope of this book to discuss the many aspects of financial statements, the types of opinions independent auditors may express on them, and how to analyze them. However, the following discussion provides a general overview of the types of financial statements and independent auditor opinions issued in the United States under generally accepted auditing standards promulgated by the American Institute of Certified Public Accountants (AICPA). Note that there are some differences in financial statements and independent auditor opinions in other countries; however, the purpose and intent of independently audited financial statements is basically the same, regardless of where the vendor organization or its independent auditor reside.

Vendor organizations may submit one of several types of financial statements with their contract proposals. These include audited, reviewed, compiled, or internally prepared financial statements. For *audited* financial statements, an independent auditor expresses a written opinion as to whether the financial statements accurately represent the financial condition of the organization, in all material respects, in conformity with generally accepted accounting principles (GAAP). For reviewed and compiled financial statements, an independent auditor does not express such an opinion. For *reviewed* financial statements, an independent auditor provides only limited assurance that the financial statements are free of material misstatement because the scope of the tests they performed was significantly less than they would perform during an audit. For *compiled* financial statements, an independent auditor states that the information contained in the financial statements are the representation of management and that the auditor does not provide any form of assurance over them. *Internally prepared* financial statements are prepared directly by the management of an organization and have not been examined by an independent external auditor.

The most preferable type of financial statements for the purpose of evaluating the financial strength and performance of a vendor organization would be the *audited* financial statements for the most recently completed fiscal year, along with any interim (e.g., quarterly) financial statements prepared since the vendor organization's fiscal year end. Interim financial statements alone are insufficient since they are usually prepared internally by the vendor organization and are unaudited. They are useful as a supplement to the most recent audited financial statements since they provide a general reference as to the recent financial performance of the vendor organization. Audited financial statements are the most desirable because they include the opinion of an independent auditor as to whether the financial statements are free of material misstatement. An independent auditor can express various opinions in audited financial statements. These include unqualified, qualified, adverse, or disclaimer.

An *unqualified opinion* states that the financial statements present fairly, in all material respects, the financial position, results of operations, and cash flows of the entity in conformity with GAAP.[1] Financial statements on which the independent auditor expressed an unqualified opinion can provide the client organization with a reasonable degree of comfort that there are no material misstatements in the financial information contained in the statements. The project development team can then begin the process of evaluating the financial performance of the vendor organization based on its historical earnings, equity, cash flow, and various other factors. If the client organization suffers a significant loss as a result of relying on audited financial statements with an unqualified opinion, it may have some recourse toward the firm or individual who performed the audit if it can prove that its losses were the result of relying on the independent auditor's opinion. This is why it is also a good idea for the project development team at the client organization to document the review of independent auditor financial statements and include the documentation as part of the permanent project files.

A *qualified opinion* states that, except for the effects of matters to which the qualification relates, the financial statements present fairly, in all material respects, the financial position, results of operations, and cash flows of the entity in conformity with GAAP.[2] Financial statements upon which the auditor has issued a *qualified* opinion indicate that the auditor identified one or more areas in the financial statements where there could be a material misstatement. For example, the auditor may not have been allowed to perform tests to confirm that fixed assets such as computer hardware were accurately reported. If a prospective vendor organization submits audited financial statements containing a qualified opinion, the project development team at the client organization should carefully evaluate the nature of the qualification and determine whether the reasons for the qualified statement are significant enough to warrant disqualifying the prospective vendor organization from further consideration. As with the unqualified opinion, it would be prudent for the project development team to carefully document their analysis of the financial statements and their degree of reliance on the "unqualified portion" of the financial statements.

An *adverse opinion* states that the financial statements do not present fairly the financial position, results of operations, or cash flows of the entity in conformity with GAAP.[3] An adverse opinion could be issued, for example, if revenues at a company were significantly overstated because they were being recognized on a cash basis instead of an accrual basis or because the method of accrual did not conform to GAAP.

A *disclaimer of opinion* states that the auditor does not express an opinion on the financial statements.[4] An auditor usually issues a disclaimer of opinion when circumstances prevent performance of an audit of sufficient scope. This situation can occur, for example, when a company does not make available necessary records, the records have been lost or destroyed, or the auditor was not allowed to perform sufficient tests.

If a prospective vendor organization submits audited financial statements containing an adverse opinion or a disclaimer of opinion, the project development team at the client organization should seriously consider dropping that vendor organization from further consideration. The project development team should give the vendor organization further consideration only if it can provide strong evidence that the issues leading to the adverse or disclaimed opinion have been resolved and the evidence can be corroborated by an independent party.

If a prospective vendor organization submits only reviewed, compiled, or internally prepared financial statements, the project development team at the client organization should also seriously consider dropping that vendor organization from further consideration, especially if the product or service the client organization is developing is mission critical. Although the information in unaudited financial statements may be perfectly accurate, the client organization would be taking a risk that there could be some material misstatement. Such a mistake could critically wound the client organization's ability to successfully launch its product or service.

Another obvious step that the project development team should perform prior to entering into a contract with the vendor organization is to contact a reasonable number of the vendor organization's past and present clients. Each past and present client surveyed should be asked to provide an assessment of the prospective service organization's level of service, product quality, and response to special needs. Candid references from past and present clients can often provide important intangible information about a vendor organization that cannot be gleaned from a service auditor's report or independently audited financial statements.

Once a vendor organization has been contracted and service has been implemented, client organizations should monitor the financial condition of the vendor organization on an annual basis. Audited financial statements should be obtained by the client organization and reviewed by the process owners, the Internal Audit Department, or other designated areas. If the financial statements show a deteriorating financial condition, the client organization should communicate its concerns to management at the vendor organization. If the financial deterioration continues, the client organization should consider formulating one or more contingency plans of action, each depending on the criticality of the vendor organization's financial deterioration. For example, if the vendor organization's independent auditor issues an opinion that states that the service organization's ability to continue as a "going concern" is unlikely due to the outcome of recent litigation, the client organization should immediately develop plans to secure an alternative vendor organization. However, if the vendor organization is experiencing reductions in net income or even negative earnings, the client organization may not necessarily need to begin locating another vendor organization. The core operating earnings of the vendor organization may be sound, while net income was negatively impacted by a one-time charge (e.g., due to costs of corporate restructuring or divestiture of a subsidiary). The degree of concern can be determined only through close communication with management at the vendor organization and a careful analysis of the financial statements by qualified individuals.

Even if a vendor organization has independently audited financial statements that express an unqualified opinion and indicate excellent historical financial performance and, in the case of a service organization, a service auditor's report that does not specify any reservations regarding the operating effectiveness of internal controls, it is still possible that an organization could suddenly experience significant operational and financial difficulties and not be able to provide adequate service to its clients. In some cases, this could cause clients to suffer significant losses. Case study 6.1 describes how one financial institution discovered this firsthand. Case studies 6.2 through 6.4 present a variety of other, less serious types of situations encountered when examining the financial statements of vendor organizations.

CASE STUDY 6.1

A Problem Service Organization

A financial institution decided to enter the mortgage lending market in the early 1990s. The institution wanted to begin offering mortgage loans to its customers as soon as possible, so it decided initially to employ the services of a mortgage loan service provider to supply the staff and expertise to originate the mortgages at the financial institution's facilities and service the loans at the service organization's data center. In about two years, the financial institution planned to begin originating mortgage loans with its own staff. After another two years, the financial institution planned to implement its own loan servicing operation.

The financial institution exercised due diligence by soliciting bids from various mortgage loan service providers. All prospective service providers were asked to include current audited annual financial statements and a recent service auditor's report along with their bids. In addition, the financial institution asked current clients about the reputation and service levels of the various bidding service organizations. The financial institution awarded the

(continued)

CASE STUDY 6.1 (*continued*)

contract to a highly recommended mortgage loan servicing operation out of California. Based on the financial statements and service auditor's report, the mortgage loan service organization appeared to be in excellent financial condition, and its operations were considered to be functioning effectively.

For about the first year, the mortgage loan operation appeared to run fairly smoothly. A few documentation problems were identified, but this was typical for a start-up operation. However, the client organization began noticing an increase in the occurrence of deficiencies in the mortgage loan documentation. These problems led to an increase in the number and frequency of customer complaints about the quality of service. Customers were having to come in and re-sign corrected documents, thus delaying the closing of their mortgage loans. Within a few months after these warning signs surfaced, independent auditors examining the operations at the service organization identified numerous instances of breakdowns in internal controls. After experiencing significant growth for several years prior, the service organization began to lay off staff. Then it was discovered that the CFO had colluded with his wife, who was employed in the Accounts Payable Department, to embezzle several hundred thousand dollars out of the escrow fund that the service organization managed on behalf of the various mortgage loan customers. The wife had prepared a number of unauthorized checks, which were approved by her husband. The checks were not questioned initially since her husband was in a position of authority. Nepotism, especially in smaller organizations, should be a red flag to any auditor. By the time the checks were questioned, the husband and wife had taken a "vacation." After a few weeks, they were located in Alaska and prosecuted. However, there were other problems. Morale at the service organization was understandably low, and many staff members were taking jobs at other companies. The downward spiral was happening rapidly.

The client organization sent its own team of senior managers and auditors to perform their own assessment. By then the service organization was crawling with examiners and auditors. After seeing the poor condition of the operation firsthand, management of the client organization decided to immediately locate a replacement service organization. All mortgage loans that were being serviced for the client organization were to be transferred as soon as possible to a new mortgage loan processing firm. In this case, an immediate solution was necessary. Since the client organization had a sufficiently large mortgage loan servicing portfolio and planned to implement its own servicing operation within two years, it was not looking for a permanent service organization. The replacement firm eventually selected was again based on financial condition, operational effectiveness, and customer reputation.

As a result of the poor internal controls and rapid financial deterioration of the first mortgage loan servicer, the client organization lost several hundred thousand dollars. Some of the loss was due to funds that could not be accounted for by the service organization. Much of the loss was in terms of the thousands of combined hours that management, auditors, and staff had to devote to analyzing the problem, implementing a solution, and improving damaged customer relations. In addition, there was a significant amount of lost business due to poor customer service and the resulting negative word of mouth about the client organization's mortgage loan capabilities.

Fortunately, the client organization was able to recover from the fiasco of its original mortgage loan service organization. It did not sue the independent auditors who issued the unqualified opinion on the service organization's financial statements and issued a service auditor's report that did not identify any significant operational weaknesses. It is difficult to speculate as to the possible outcome of litigation against the independent auditor. However, it is highly unlikely that the internal control structure of the service organization crumbled overnight. Significant internal control weaknesses existed previously but were not detected.

CASE STUDY 6.2

A Vendor with Compiled Financial Statements

A client organization decided to purchase a local-area-network–based mortgage loan origination application. The Internal Audit Department was not involved in the early stages of selection and evaluation of alternative vendors. A postimplementation examination was performed shortly after the new application was placed in service.

One of the steps was to determine whether the project development team evaluated the financial strength of the selected vendor. Management stated that the application vendor had been in business for about 10 years, and the performance of the application was highly regarded in the industry by the major mortgage loan guarantee agencies. Audited financial statements had been examined prior to contracting with the vendor, but management could not locate them. Only faxed copies of a compiled financial statement covering the most recent three-month period following the application vendor's fiscal year end were located. The vendor was subsequently unwilling to provide audited annual financial statements since it was a closely held subchapter-S corporation.

The compiled financial statements were analyzed by the Internal Audit Department, and it was found that the application vendor's anticipated ability to meet current obligations was excellent as evidenced by a current ratio of 2.6 ($2.754 million in current assets divided by $1.061 million in current liabilities) and the fact that the vendor had no long-term debt. It was also noted that $1 million of the $2.2 million in vendor stockholder's equity was accumulated during the most recent three-month period. This meant that if the compiled information was accurate, only $1.2 million in equity had accumulated in the previous 10 years. The lack of retained earnings and profits could be a sign of a well-managed start-up company that invested most of its capital in its infrastructure, thereby sacrificing short-term profits for significant long-term profitability. However, the sudden increase in earnings in financial statements compiled during the bidding period could be an indication that the financial

(*continued*)

CASE STUDY 6.2 (*continued*)

statements were inaccurate, especially since the application vendor was unwilling to supply copies of its most recent annual audited financial statements. Because the contract had already been signed and the application was well into service, it was too late to make a major issue out of the lack of audited financial statements. However, the jury is still out as to the longevity of the application vendor and its ability to support the application. It is hoped that it will not lead to an experience such as the one described in case study 6.1.

CASE STUDY 6.3

A Payroll Processor on the Rebound

A client organization selected a payroll processing service organization to replace its previous payroll processing servicer. The decision to change was made due to the previous processor's inability to provide desired detail information on the pay stubs for client organization employees. As was the case in case study 6.2, the Internal Audit Department was not involved in the early stages of selection and evaluation of alternative vendors. Thus, a postimplementation examination was performed by the Internal Audit Department shortly after the new application was placed in service.

One of the steps performed was to determine whether the project development team evaluated the financial strength of the selected vendor. It was found that the project team had not performed a formal evaluation of the service organization's financial position. They based their decision on the firm's reputation, marketing representations, and the fact that the firm was a large national corporation that had been in business for many years.

A copy of the most recent audited financial statements of the service organization was obtained and reviewed by the Internal Audit Department. The external auditor had issued an unqualified opinion on the financial statements. The service organization was in the process of recovering from significant restructuring, downsizing, and divestiture of unrelated businesses in order to concentrate on its core business of employer payroll services. These efforts negatively impacted earnings to the tune of $393 million two years prior and $30 million one year prior. However, for the most recently completed fiscal year, the company reported a profit of $79 million.

The notes to the financial statements revealed that the service organization was currently in the midst of age-discrimination litigation pertaining to some former employees and had established a $15 million reserve for legal costs and potential damage awards. On the positive side, the service organization had stockholders' equity in the amount of $187 million and total assets of $690 million.

Despite the negative earnings and legal problems of the service organization, it appeared to have taken necessary steps to return to long-term profitability. Therefore, the Internal Audit Department concurred with the decision of the client organization's management to select this service organization for payroll processing services.

CASE STUDY 6.4

A Case of Missing Financial Statements

The Accounting Department of a client organization decided to purchase a local-area-network–based application for the purpose of accounting for term investments (i.e., investments other than overnights). The system received electronic updates of term investments held in safekeeping by the client organization's investment safekeeping service organization. A representative from the Internal Audit Department was not part of the original project development team. However, a preimplementation review was performed.

Copies of audited financials of the application vendor could not be located. The controller and lead financial accountant in charge of the new application project stated that they had examined the audited financials and they were acceptable. However, they could not provide evidence of such review. They also stated that the client organization's external auditor highly recommended the application vendor and that the system was well proven. (These statements are a common theme in case studies 6.2 through 6.4).

A recommendation was not submitted to management of the Accounting Department because the system had already been purchased and the application was a nontransaction processing system. The risks of nontransaction or nonproduction processing systems are usually not as significant as those that process transactions or production information. This system essentially facilitated more customized reporting on information that was readily available at the investment safekeeping organization. (The financial statements and service auditor's reports of the investment safekeeping organization were examined in a separate audit.) Therefore, its risk relative to other systems in the client organization was considered to be low. This is not to say that organizations should not assess the financial and operational health of the small vendors with which they do business. Doing so is sound business practice. If an organization habitually neglects to research the vendors with which it does business, it is only a matter of time before it finds itself wasting significant human and financial resources reimplementing projects because the original vendors failed or were unable to provide the level of service desired.

Case studies 6.1 through 6.4 demonstrate the need for companies that utilize the services of external service organizations and application vendors to assess the financial and operational health of these vendors before and after they have been contracted. Internal auditors and other concerned parties should recommend that their organizations develop formal "new system implementation standards," which should be adhered to by all project development teams when evaluating potential service organizations and application vendors. The new system implementation standards should include steps to examine the most recent audited financial statements and the most recent service auditor's reports (for service organizations) prior to entering into contracts with them. The standards should also include a provision to include an internal information systems auditor on the project development team to advise the team on other significant internal control issues the team should address. The standards should specify that the process owner is responsible for ensuring that the continued financial and operational health of the selected service organization or application vendor is monitored on an annual basis through the acquisition and examination of annual audited financial statements and applicable service auditor reports.

EXAMINING VENDOR ORGANIZATION CONTRACTS

In any significant business transaction, a written contract is usually drafted and signed by authorized representatives of each party. The contract should clearly specify the responsibilities of each party. Even if all parties involved have every intention of completing their end of the bargain as agreed upon in various discussions with each other, a contract helps ensure that there are no misunderstandings as to what actions each party is expected to perform, at what time they are expected to be performed, what services or payments will be received when the actions have been satisfactorily performed, and when the services or payments will be received. As an added incentive, most contracts also include a section specifying the consequences or penalties in the event that one or more of the parties fails to perform as required by the terms of the contract.

The success of the products and services of most organizations is highly dependent on the timely, accurate, and secure functioning of computer systems and related applications, whether they are maintained internally or provided by a vendor. Thus, when a vendor supplies a computer system and/or application to a client organization, a significant business transaction has taken place and thus should be documented by a written contract. The following paragraphs attempt to identify the critical items that all auditors should be cognizant of and that should be specified in contracts between client organizations and vendor organizations.

Many parts of business contracts are included to address local and national laws and regulations. For example, in the United States, the Uniform Commercial Code (UCC) was developed in the mid-1900s to provide consistency among business transactions between parties residing in different states. Each state government has adopted the UCC as a baseline and then added additional provisions based on their interpretations of commercial law. For example, in the State of Washington, businesses operate under the auspices of the Revised Code of Washington (RCW). In addition, each city, county, or other municipality may have its own unique laws or regulations that apply to the client and vendor organizations conducting business there. Although many contracts may appear to be routine in nature, it is a good idea for the client organization to have all contracts reviewed by its legal counsel. Even after an attorney has "blessed" a contract, an internal auditor should still examine it during an audit to assess whether the terms of the contract adequately address the current operational, financial, regulatory, and information systems (IS) security needs of the client organization and whether the provisions of the contract have in fact been carried out.

Most contracts between client organizations and IS vendor organizations include these sections:

- Effective date of the agreement.
- Names of the parties to the agreement (i.e., the client organization and vendor organization).
- Definitions of unique or special terms used in the contract.
- Purchase or lease price of any computer equipment, system software, and application hardware, including delivery, installation, and testing.
- Payment terms, including any down payment or advance, plus any other periodic payments (e.g., monthly, quarterly, or annual).
- Licenses to use the system software and application software. The contract should specify the terms or expiration dates of the licenses (i.e., for what period of time the software may be used), and the number of concurrent users authorized by the licenses.
- Any warranties by the vendors. For example, the vendor should warrant that the equipment will function properly upon completion of installation.
- Costs of training client organization staff on how to operate the new applications and computer equipment.
- Ongoing maintenance services provided (e.g., the normal hours during which service technicians are available, the expected response times, the premiums charged for after-hours response times, and so on) and the costs for such services.
- Maintenance services not provided.
- Requirements of each party in order to terminate the contract (e.g., 30 days' prior written notice must be given by the terminating party).
- Penalties or liabilities to either party for nonperformance of the contract.
- Additional programming and/or support agreements, addenda, and modifications or clarifications often become part of the overall contract, in conjunction with the original contract.
- Approval page.

When performing an audit of a vendor application, an auditor should examine the contract between the client and vendor organizations to ensure that it has been executed by authorized representatives from both organizations. Authorized representatives are typically officers of an organization, such as the president, vice president, and treasurer. The auditor should also determine whether the contract is current (i.e., has not lapsed), addresses current service needs, does not contain wording that could be detrimental to the client organization, and does not omit wording that could pose a risk to the client organization. As mentioned in Chapter 4, IS security standards should require that the contract specify that a copy of the programming source code of the current version of the software be stored in escrow by an independent third party so it is available to the company in the event the vendor goes out of business. Additional sections should be added to tailor each individual contract to the particular process being supported by the application. The number of additional sections is limited only by the imagination of the attorneys for the client and vendor organizations. Case studies 6.5 through 6.9 describe some contract issues encountered in various organizations.

CASE STUDY 6.5

Vendor Application but No Contract

During an audit of the check-clearing process at a financial institution, it was found that the maintenance agreement between the financial institution and the hardware vendor had not been executed. The hardware had been installed for about two years. Fortunately, no significant contractual maintenance issues had arisen. The standard hardware maintenance agreement that the hardware vendor initially provides for clients to review was reportedly in effect during the two years since installation. It was recommended that the manager in charge of the check-clearing process coordinate having the hardware maintenance agreement reviewed and executed by senior management and then executed by an authorized representative of the hardware vendor.

CASE STUDY 6.6

Contract Missing for 12 Years

During an audit of a data processing operation, a copy of the original contract with the vendor of the primary software application was examined. The application vendor marketed its software in conjunction with a major computer hardware manufacturing firm. The client organization had been using the vendor's application and associated hardware for over 12 years. A single contract specified the responsibilities of both the application vendor and hardware manufacturer. The data processing manager could produce only a copy of a contract that was stamped "Preliminary and tentative, for discussion purposes only." A final copy of the actual contract reportedly existed "somewhere." However, the data processing manager was still unable to locate a copy of it.

Some of the terms of the original contract were no longer valid since the client organization had installed numerous software and hardware upgrades during the 12 years that had elapsed since the original installation. However, some of the requirements set out in the original contract were still in effect. Therefore, it was recommended that the data processing manager contact the vendor and request a copy of the original contract for reference purposes. This proved somewhat embarrassing to the data processing manager after 12 years of operation.

CASE STUDY 6.7

No Software Support Contract

A postimplementation review was performed for a new software application that enabled a financial institution's customers to access their accounts remotely by dialing in to the financial institution's host computer, using their personal computer (PC). The application had been placed in service about two months earlier. The project development team had been working on the project for about a year prior to implementation. The Internal Audit Department was not included in the project development team. Examination of the software support contract with the application vendor was planned to assess whether it addressed the service needs of the client organization. When the time came to examine the contract, however, the process owner stated that she was unable to locate a copy of it.

Because the service was new and since the terms of software support were unclear, it was recommended that the process owner at the financial institution obtain a copy of the final software support contract for reference or, if one had not been drafted, that a software support contract be drafted, reviewed by senior management, and executed by authorized representatives of the client and vendor organizations.

CASE STUDY 6.8

An Outdated Software License Agreement

During an audit of a financial institution's PC-based traveler's check application, it was found that the software license agreement with the traveler's check vendor was not current. The license agreement was executed about six years earlier and authorized the use of the software at one location. The financial institution had purchased and installed another copy at a second location. However, a new license agreement specifying the right of the financial institution to use the software at the second location was never drafted.

Although the financial institution did not appear to be violating any software license copyright laws, management at the financial institution was completely unaware of the need to have a license for the software it was using. It was recommended that a current software license agreement be drafted, reviewed by senior management, and executed by authorized representatives of the client and vendor organizations. In all fairness to the financial institution, the traveler's check vendor, which operates internationally, was guilty of not ensuring that the software it issued was properly licensed.

CASE STUDY 6.9

More Unlicensed Software

During an examination of software loaded on a stand-alone microcomputer located in an open area of the department being audited, two unlicensed software programs were identified. Since the PC was authorized for use by sev-

(*continued*)

CASE STUDY 6.9 (*continued*)

eral other departments, it could not be determined who was accountable for the existence of the unlicensed software. Management of the department being audited was aware of the software but reportedly did not remove it because the attributes of some of the files were set to read only, and they did not know how to remove the files. The Internal Audit Department assisted the audited department in deleting the unauthorized software. Unfortunately, this condition was "unofficially" known to be prevalent throughout the organization. There were many stand-alone PCs shared by multiple departments in various buildings. The company did not have a means of tracking the purchase of PC software and thus had no idea how many authorized copies of standard software applications even existed. The company also did not have an effective means of educating users on software copyright laws and penalties or for identifying and disciplining employees who violated the laws. Before the situation could be officially resolved, the company was purchased by another larger corporation.

It is hard to imagine how the acquiring corporation was able to determine the amount of licensed software it had just purchased. It is possible that much of the PC software was simply deleted, resulting in the need for the acquiring corporation to purchase all new software. This would mean that the old company had wasted hundreds of thousands of dollars on software because it could not prove whether any of it was licensed. At least with a centralized tracking mechanism, reduced-price upgrade packages, especially for network licenses, could have been purchased.

EXAMINING ACCOUNTING TREATMENT OF COMPUTER HARDWARE AND SOFTWARE

Internal auditors should examine the proper accounting for computer hardware, software, maintenance, and other costs to determine whether such costs have been properly recorded on the financial statements. For example, computer equipment and software should be capitalized and amortized over their estimated useful lives. Prepaid maintenance costs should be classified as assets and expensed only when the costs applicable to the period in question have been realized. If equipment and/ or maintenance is billed on a monthly basis, the costs should be expensed as incurred.

The audit steps described in this section are not necessarily the type of steps a specialized information systems auditor would perform. If an organization is small and has only one or two internal auditors, those persons will likely have a background in accounting, finance, or industry operations. This type of internal auditor will be more likely to audit the accounting treatment of costs associated with computer equipment and software than would a specialized IS auditor.

If an organization has a large Internal Audit Department, these steps would likely be performed by one or more financial or operational auditors. If the organization uses an integrated audit approach whereby a team of auditors with expertise in various disciplines perform an audit of an entire process, examination of the accounting treatment of computer equipment and software may be performed within the overall scope of the integrated audit. If an integrated audit approach is not used, the accounting treatment of computer equipment and software may be examined completely independently of an audit of the IS-related controls of the same computer equipment and software.

In any event, management of the client organization, whether it is in the Accounting Department or in the user department, is responsible for ensuring that the costs associated with the computer equipment and applications are properly accounted for, in accordance with promulgated accounting standards of the country in which the client organization resides. Case study 6.10 depicts a situation in which the monthly accruals for hardware maintenance in one organization were understated.

See the "Financial Statement Risks" section in Chapter 15 for a discussion about accounting for costs of computer software developed or obtained for internal use.

CASE STUDY 6.10

A Case of Underaccrual

During an audit of the same data processing operation referred to in case study 6.6, it was found that the accruals for hardware maintenance expense on leased pieces of computer equipment were understated by about $5,000 per month for the second half of the year. The reason for the understatement was that the hardware vendor performed a site audit in June and identified numerous hardware items that were being serviced but were not being included in the previous monthly maintenance assessments. The hardware vendor billed its customers for each individual hardware component leased from it. In this case, the billing records of the hardware vendor did not include all of the hardware items residing at the client organization. (This is a separate internal control issue for the vendor to address within its own organization.) After the vendor completed the site audit, the monthly maintenance expense to the client organization increased by $5,000. The data processing manager was obviously unhappy with the sudden, unannounced increase and had delayed paying the maintenance costs in the hope of negotiating a reduced maintenance rate. This meant that the invoices were not approved and forwarded to the Accounting Department for payment. The Accounting Department was told that there would be a delay in the approval of the invoices but was not informed of the increased maintenance cost. As a result, the Accounting Department continued to accrue the monthly hardware maintenance expense at the old rate.

It was recommended that the data processing manager provide the Accounting Department with an estimate of the adjusted annual maintenance cost so that it could post appropriate adjusting journal entries prior to year end. The hardware maintenance payable account was increasing because the data pro-

(continued)

CASE STUDY 6.10 (*continued*)

cessing manager was delaying payment to the vendor by not approving the invoices. However, it was not recommended that the data processing manager approve the invoices because they provided her with some leverage in negotiations with the hardware vendor to possibly reduce the monthly maintenance rate. Since the client organization was a longtime customer of the hardware vendor, the risk of the vendor exercising its leverage by removing the hardware or withholding maintenance was considered remote. Eventually, a lower maintenance rate was agreed upon, and new invoices were received and approved for payment.

NOTES

1. American Institute of Certified Public Accountants, *Codification of Statements on Auditing Standards*, AU Section 508 (January 1, 1989): Paragraph 10.
2. Id.
3. Id.
4. Id.

CHAPTER 7

Physical Security

Physical security controls over computer hardware form the foundation of an organization's information systems (IS) control environment (see Exhibits 1.1 and 1.2). Damage to central processing units (CPUs) and peripheral devices in any organization can be the result of a multitude of natural and human hazards. Earthquakes are a common occurrence along the West Coast of the United States, especially in California. Hurricanes are so common along the southeastern coast of the United States that they are assigned personal first names. Tornadoes tear through the central plains of the United States on a regular basis, especially during the summer months. Floods caused by heavy rains can happen anywhere but are a fact of life in the fall and winter along many river basins in the Midwest, central plains, and northwest regions of the United States. Severe rainfall can also cause mudslides as the water undermines the soil supporting hills and cliffs. Every winter, blizzards and severe cold paralyze the north-central and northeastern United States, often resulting in the need to shut down business activity to minimize human casualties. Wildfires caused by lightning (and humans) have been all too frequent in California. They ravaged Colorado and Arizona in the summer of 2002. Volcanic eruptions are less common but can result in horrific destruction. The 1980 eruption of Mount Saint Helens in Washington state created such an enormous blast that some of its volcanic ash settled on the other side of the world. Trees in the blast zone were flattened like toothpicks, river basins surrounding the volcano were flooded within minutes, and the cloud of ash over eastern Washington state turned day into night. There are hundreds of dormant volcanoes along the entire Pacific Ocean rim that could erupt at any time. Kilauea and Mauna Loa are active volcanoes in Hawaii. Mount Pinatubo in the Philippines erupted fiercely in 1991 after being dormant for six centuries.

Human hazards can be just as destructive as natural disasters. Bombings are unfortunately a common occurrence in many countries. The 1995 bombing that leveled the Federal Building in Oklahoma City was the most devastating in U.S. history. In 1993, a massive explosion ripped apart the World Trade Center in New York City, causing significant destruction. These events both paled in comparison to the destruction caused by the September 11, 2001, jet-plane-turned-missile attacks on the World Trade Center and the Pentagon. Theft is another human hazard that is becoming more significant because computers are becoming smaller and more portable, while the amount and criticality of data they are capable of storing is increasing.

In fall 1996, a desktop computer was stolen from VISA International's San Mateo, California, data processing center. This was no ordinary desktop computer. Information on over 300,000 credit card accounts from VISA, MasterCard, American Express, and Diners Club was stored, unencrypted, on the hard drive. Some issuers, like Citibank, canceled the cards in question and issued new ones. Others elected to keep the theft quiet so as not to inconvenience cardholders. These issuers chose to monitor the accounts in question for unusual activity. VISA agreed to reimburse affected card issuers for the costs of replacing the cards. This theft could cost VISA an estimated $6 million.[1]

The insurance industry reported that over 200,000 laptop computers were stolen in 1995, an alarming 39 percent increase over 1994. One of the reasons for their attractiveness is that thieves can render laptops virtually anonymous by simply reformatting their hard drives. (See Chapter 12 for a discussion on the use of computer forensics to identify stolen computers.) As a result, stolen laptops can command up to 50 percent of their retail price on the black market.[2] Case Study 7.1 provides details of a situation regarding a stolen laptop.

CASE STUDY 7.1

Stolen Laptop

A new laptop computer was issued for use by a select few staff members in a department within a large organization. The laptop was stored in a locked overhead file cabinet on an unsecured floor of the organization's main office building. The key to the cabinet was stored in a cup on the primary user's desk, and a lid was placed over the top of the cup. One day, about a week after the laptop had been delivered, it was stolen from the locked overhead storage cabinet.

The Internal Audit Department was notified of the situation and performed the investigation. The two people who were working with the laptop were the local-area-network (LAN) security administrator of the department and a microcomputer specialist from the Network Services Department. Both had been employed with the organization for less than three months. The job histories and police background checks of both individuals were examined to determine whether their profiles might identify them as candidates for laptop thefts. Also, the employees in question were interviewed. However, without any "hard" evidence, it was impossible to determine whether the laptop was stolen by one of the two primary user employees, some other employee in the building, a customer who was in the building, a vendor, or a custodian. The organization did not incur a direct financial loss because the laptop was insured. However, a significant amount of staff time was spent reconfiguring a new laptop, and the expected productivity increases in the user department were delayed by several weeks.

As a result of this theft, all laptops in the organization were fitted with cable locking devices. The moral of the story: Do not rely on locking overhead storage cabinets, file cabinets, or closets for security of expensive computer equipment unless the keys and spares have been properly secured.

On the positive side, this laptop theft resulted in a recovery of sorts. During the search for the missing laptop, an Internal Audit Department laptop that had been missing for a few weeks was located. Fortunately, the auditor inadvertently left it in the main office warehouse, and it was being "stored" by the warehouse manager since he did not know to whom the laptop belonged.

Arson and vandalism are other commonly visible crimes that could result in damage to an organization's computer resources. Unlike Mother Nature, some destructive human hazards may not always be visible. For example, electrical power surges can instantly fry the circuits of computers and peripherals, and malicious tampering can result in internal damage to computer hardware as well as lost, damaged, or compromised data.

No part of the world is immune to natural and human hazards. Therefore, all organizations should have internal controls in place that help reduce the impact of these disasters on continuing operations. However, physical security controls within many organizations are frightfully inadequate. It is the role of all auditors, including those in charge of examining information systems, to identify significant physical security control weaknesses and to submit recommendations to management to resolve these weaknesses.

One of the most obvious, but often overlooked, preventive controls is to locate key computer equipment somewhere above the first floor of a facility. A few years ago, a data center for a major insurance company in the Midwest installed its computer equipment in the basement of an office building. During unexpected flooding, the basement quickly filled with water and the equipment was rendered useless. (Fortunately, the company had adequate business resumption procedures in place to minimize the disruption of service.) In this case, because of the severity of the flooding, the computer equipment would have been severely damaged even if it had been located on the first floor. However, had the equipment been installed on the second floor or higher, it would not have been damaged at all. Granted, service would have still been disrupted since the power supply, electrical wiring, and telecommunications equipment were not functioning, but the equipment itself would not have required repair or replacement. In addition to location, a number of key types of physical security controls should be deployed within an organization, including:

- Various types of physical locks, including conventional key locks, electronic access badge locks, cipher locks, combination locks, and biometric locks
- Security guards
- Video surveillance cameras
- General emergency and detection procedures
- Heating, ventilation, and cooling (HVAC) systems
- Insurance coverage over hardware and the costs to re-create data

- Procedures to perform periodic backups of system software, application programs, and data as well as storage and rotation of the backup media to a secure off-site location
- Emergency power and uninterruptible power supply (UPS) systems
- Current and tested business resumption program (BRP), including key aspects of an information systems BRP
- Adequately trained backup system security administrators

PHYSICAL LOCKS

The first line of defense in physical security is usually accomplished through the deployment of various types of locks on doors to any rooms that house computer and telecommunications equipment. These rooms include the main computer room, wiring closets, and rooms where file servers, gateways, routers, and other devices are located.

Conventional keys can still be one of the most effective means of controlling access to restricted rooms. It is imperative that a highly trusted member of management, preferably the organization's security officer or designated subordinate, be responsible for issuing all keys, contracting with vendors to install new and replacement locks and make replacement keys, maintaining an inventory of all keys and the individuals to whom the keys are issued, and ensuring that all spare keys are properly secured. If keys are not properly controlled, conventional locks can provide only a false sense of security. For example, unauthorized access to computer equipment could be gained by custodians, former employees, transferred employees who no longer require access as part of their normal duties, and former security guards.

Vendors can manufacture various types of keys. In many buildings, vendors create separate keys for each door. They are also able to make "master" keys that can open all the doors in a certain area, floor, or building, even though each door lock requires a unique "regular" key. In cases in which there are multiple locations, vendors are sometimes contracted to make "grand master" keys that can open all the locks in all facilities. Obviously, it is very important to have an inventory of who has been assigned the master and grand master keys and to ensure that the people who possess such keys are highly trusted. Case study 7.2 describes what happened in one organization when someone who possessed a grand master key was unexpectedly terminated.

CASE STUDY 7.2

Termination of a Grand Master Key Holder

The person in charge of physical security over all facilities in an organization, including the data center, resigned suddenly under difficult circumstances. The termination was not friendly. Because of his position, he possessed a grand master key to all facilities of the organization. Due to the nature of the termination, the possibility existed that one or more duplicate grand master keys could have been made prior to the original's being returned. Ensuring absolute protection against unauthorized key access by the former physical security coordinator would require all door locks to be rekeyed and all new keys to be distributed. This was an expensive proposition. Rekeying all the locks would also be a source of significant inconvenience because there were several other high-level staff members with grand master keys and another group of high-ranking staff who possessed master keys for their respective facilities. In addition, master keys were placed in locked boxes strategically located on the outside of each facility for use by local fire departments.

In this incident, senior management appropriately decided to incur the cost and inconvenience of rekeying all the doors in all facilities and reissuing new keys to all staff to ensure that all facilities were adequately secured. When personnel who possess keys to critical areas terminate on a friendly basis, it is up to senior management to determine whether sufficient risk exists to warrant rekeying all locks. The situation in this example is a good incentive to keep the number of personnel with master and grand master keys to a minimum and to maintain an inventory of individuals who have been issued the keys to each area. If key control is associated with highly risky situations, it may be necessary to implement dual custody procedures to issue, return, or replace keys. Dual custody could be achieved by locking all keys in a vault or locker that requires two keys to open. Each required key would be issued to a separate person, neither of whom have access to the other key or spares.

Electronic access badge systems provide two distinct advantages over conventional keys. First, electronic access badges eliminate the need to have to issue conventional keys to all employees. Rather they can be issued electronic access badges that provide them with the access they need. Whenever someone terminates, transfers, or loses his or her badge, it is simply deactivated on the electronic access badge system, thereby preventing any further access to previously authorized doors. Even if the badge is not returned, there is no need to consider rekeying all the locks in a facility. In addition, when use of previously lost or stolen badges is attempted, their activity can be recorded, possibly leading to the recovery of the badges. The second advantage is that electronic badge access can be restricted to certain times of the day or night. Certain door locks can be programmed to remain locked during specified hours (e.g., after normal business hours). If after-hours access is allowed, such access by employees can be monitored and recorded. The following discussion is a brief description of how a typical electronic badge access application functions. Electronic access badge locks are activated when the holder of an electronic access badge places it on or near a badge reader plate. The badge reader "reads" the authorization information electronically encoded on a computer chip inside the badge and transmits it to the electronic badge access application program, which usually resides on a microcomputer or file server in a centrally controlled location. If the badge information is included in the table of authorized badges in the application program, a command is returned to open the electronic access badge lock. With this type of application, each lock, badge reader plate, central microcomputer or file server, and, in some cases, multiple remote microcomputers or file servers are usually connected via a network of dedicated electrical wiring within facilities and dedicated phone lines between facilities.

Despite their advantages over conventional key locks, electronic access badge locks can sometimes be circumvented with relative ease. Often overlooked is the fact that many doors to rooms housing computer equipment have both an electronic access badge lock and a conventional key lock. Persons holding the keys can simply unlock the door manually and walk in, thus avoiding the audit trail that is available with the electronic access badge system. For this reason it is important to examine the key inventory in conjunction with the electronic access badge system (and any other types of physical locks) when assessing the adequacy of physical security at a data center.

Another way to bypass electronic access badge system controls is when people lend their cards to others. The badge borrower could access areas that only the badge lender should be accessing. A third potential control concern is that electronic access badges can be mistakenly programmed by the system security administrator to provide access that was not authorized or intended. A fourth risk is that the electronic access badge application could contain a programming flaw that unintentionally allows unauthorized access. Case study 7.3 describes such a flaw in an electronic access badge application.

CASE STUDY 7.3

Electronic Access Badge System with Two Halves

Access to the data center of a large organization was controlled primarily through the deployment of an electronic access badge application. No vendor-supplied documentation pertaining to the operation and security of the application existed.

A few days before an audit, a manager lost his electronic access badge and reported it to the system security administrator. The system security administrator blocked the lost badge and issued a replacement. One of the audit tests performed was to examine a printout of all authorized badge holders and to assess the reasonableness of the access capabilities of a sample of badge holders. The manager who had lost his card was asked to provide his electronic access badge number so that it could be confirmed that his new access capabilities had been properly entered on the application. Surprisingly, the number he gave was not on the list of authorized badges. He was asked to use the badge, and it functioned perfectly. The manager stated that after the audit had started, he had found the lost badge and notified the system security administrator so it could be reactivated. How the badge could work but not show on the list of authorized badges was a mystery.

On further investigation, it was found that the vendor's disk-operating-system- (DOS)–based application was designed and programmed to grant access to badge holders according to a database that contained all the authorized badge numbers. The database containing the names of the badge holders was completely separate within the application. The names corresponding to each card number had to be manually entered into the badge holder database and had no effect on the other database, which actually controlled the access capabilities of each badge. In other words, the list of authorized badge holders had nothing to do with who could access what doors in the data center. In the case of the manager who had lost his badge, the system security administrator had reactivated his lost badge number but had forgotten to update the badge holder name database.

A control weakness had been identified—it was possible for active badges to exist without corresponding names in the badge holder name database. A further problem was that the system was not designed to identify authorized badge numbers that lacked a corresponding name in the badge holder name database, despite the fact that both databases contained a common field—the badge number—which could easily have been used as a cross reference. The only way to identify nonmatched badge numbers and names was to manually compare the two printouts. When the situation was discussed further with the system security administrator, he agreed and complained that this had been an efficiency problem and that the vendor was not enthusiastic about developing a better system. The system security administrator further stated that there were very few alternative vendors with competitive systems.

Unfortunately, this application had numerous other physical and logical security control deficiencies. For example, the CPU containing the electronic badge access application was located on an upper floor of the data center. Most updates to the badge holder access database were performed on this floor. However, the badge holder access database could also be updated from the security guard station on the first floor, using a master control unit (MCU). In addition to being a terminal, the MCU had rows of toggle switches on it, each of which controlled different doors throughout the data center. If the toggle switches were manually set to the center position, all the doors of the building would become unlocked. Therefore, anyone wishing to commandeer the entire data center would need only to take over the guard station and then set all the toggle switches to the center position. A disgruntled security guard could easily expose the data center.

The logical security control weaknesses of the electronic badge access application included an unencrypted password file and lack of password expiration and minimum-password-length features. The password file was viewable within the application by anyone with system administration access capabilities and from the operating system level by anyone, without the need to access the application.

To improve the controls and efficiency of the area responsible for administering physical security at the data center, it was recommended that man-

(*continued*)

CASE STUDY 7.3 (*continued*)

agement submit a written request to the electronic badge access application vendor to make the following enhancements:

- Design a graphical user interface (GUI) electronic badge access application that is user friendly and does not allow the use of an MCU with toggle switches on it. It should be controlled exclusively from the console terminal connected to the CPU containing the application software.
- Reprogram the electronic badge access application so that there is just one badge access control database. This database should contain the badge number, badge holder name, and access capabilities.
- Until the new application becomes available, design and program a report that identifies active badge numbers lacking a corresponding entry in the badge holder name database. This would save hours of manual reconciliation time.
- Design and prepare a user manual for the new application.
- Design and program the new application so that the password file is encrypted, using a secure algorithm so that it cannot be viewed by anyone from within the application or from the operating system.
- Design and program the new application with minimum-password-length and password expiration features.

In addition to the application control weaknesses just noted, several weaknesses with the internal security administration procedures over the electronic badge access application were identified. For example, examination of the databases of active badge numbers and badge names revealed that access badges for four former employees were still active, extra badges were issued to seven employees who did not require them, and incorrect names were entered on the application for six badge holders. It was recommended that the system security administrator implement procedures to ensure that transferred and terminated employees were removed from the electronic badge access application in a timely manner, that proper written authorization be obtained prior to issuing extra badges, and that the accuracy of the names entered on the application be confirmed.

Another security administration weakness was that employees from temporary agencies were being issued badges but were not returning them each day. Instead, they kept them until their term of duty had expired. Since temporary agency employees were not subject to the same background checks as other company employees, it was recommended that procedures be implemented whereby each employee of a temporary agency be required to sign in at the guard station to receive his or her access badge at the beginning of each shift and return the badge at the end of each shift.

A third security administration control weakness pertained to the fact that the electronic log of badge access attempts was stored for only 90 days before being overwritten. Since the identification and research of unauthorized access activity may not occur for several months or longer, it was recommended that the electronic log be archived for at least one year.

Despite all of these anticipated corrections to the electronic access badge application and surrounding administrative procedures, numerous senior management and security personnel were issued grand master and master door keys, which allowed access to various rooms without the need for an electronic access badge. Unfortunately, all that could be done was to assess the reasonableness of those to whom the keys were issued, examine the key inventory, and hope that the master keys were properly secured each time someone who possessed one transferred or terminated.

A *cipher lock* is simply a lock that is opened by entering a secret set of numbers and/or characters on a keypad next to the door. If the secret code is correct, the lock is electronically opened. An obvious problem is that each time someone transfers or terminates, the cipher code must be changed and, more important, communicated to all individuals who require access. In a large organization, this can be a challenging task for building security staff and frustrating to those who need to access cipher-locked doors.

A *combination lock* requires that a secret set of combination numbers be spun on a dial in the appropriate sequence. (Some new combination locks have digital key pads.) Although not typically used to control access to doors in a building, combination locks are commonly used to secure passwords, keys, and other information necessary in the event the primary system security administrator or control person is not available and changes need to be performed. It is important to be sure that one person cannot access the combination lock alone. Dual custody over a combination is sometimes accomplished using a four-number combination, with one person knowing the first two numbers and the second person knowing the third and fourth numbers. The problem with this method is that the person knowing the third and fourth numbers can see the second number where the first person stopped spinning the combination dial. Thus, the second person could easily determine the full combination by systematically trying a combination beginning with each number on the dial and ending with the last three known numbers.

A more effective means of achieving dual control over a combination lock is to allow key people to know the full combination but to ensure that they cannot access the room containing the lock. Obviously, the people who let these key people into the room should not know the combination. If this method is chosen, a log should be maintained. The log should show the date and time of each access, the signatures of each person accessing the lock, and the purpose of the access. A difficulty with combination locks is that each time a person who knows it transfers or terminates, a locksmith must change the combination. Fees for this service can be high, so the number of persons who know the combination should be kept to a minimum.

A *biometric lock* is one that authenticates a person by recognizing one or more unique physical features of the accessing individual. Such features include fingerprints, handprints, iris images, retinal images, facial images, voice recognition, or some other unique biological feature. Because of the relatively high cost of biometric systems, they are typically used to control access to only those facilities containing highly sensitive equipment and information. However, after the

September 11, 2001, terrorist attacks, interest in biometric identification and authorization systems has significantly increased. In fact, the U.S. Congress is considering requiring states to include biometric data on encrypted microchips in driver's licenses and state-issued identification cars.[3]

The cost of some biometric systems has decreased enough in recent years to where commercial applications are beginning to be deployed. For example, San Antonio City Employees Federal Credit Union and Security Services Federal Credit Union have each installed a biometric access device at the safe deposit entrance in one of their branches. The devices use a hand-image verification in conjunction with a personal identification number to grant unescorted access to the safe deposit box vault. Conventional keys are still required to open the box, but no credit union employees are required to be present, thereby freeing them to perform other duties.[4] To help deter fraud by more accurately identifying members, Naval Weapons Credit Union spent about $100,000 to install fingerprint readers at each of its teller windows. The system requires that, upon completion of a transaction, the member also signs a digitized pad that electronically captures the signature.[5]

With demand on the increase, one biometric consulting group estimates that biometric sales will grow from $58 million in 1999 to $594 million in 2003, with the U.S. making up 65 percent of the market.[6] After the recent terrorist attacks, the amount and percentage purchased by the U.S. will undoubtedly increase.

However, as with any system, biometric controls are not without their flaws. A Japanese researcher named Tsumtomu Matsumoto created fake fingerprint images with the permission of a volunteer using the same gelatin ingredients found in Gummi Bears candy. He also lifted a volunteer's fingerprint off a surface, digitally enhanced it on a computer, and printed it on a transparent sheet. The imprint was then etched to create a fingerprint impression, which was later filled with gelatin. Both methods fooled 11 different detectors 70 to 90 percent of the time.[7] Mr. Matsumoto highlighted the fact that while fingerprint recognition is one of the least expensive and least invasive types of biometrics upon which to base controls, it is relatively easy to circumvent, because the average fingerprint has between 25 and 40 points of measure. Contrast this with iris identification, which has between 250 and 266 points of measure. According to one expert, the iris is the most feature-rich and stable part of the anatomy because it is formed by a natural tearing process of the tissue in the colored portion of the eye that creates a random, totally chaotic structure that is different in each eye.[8] The cost and perceived invasiveness of iris identification controls makes it less practical in commercial applications than fingerprint identification. But top-secret military and other highly sensitive applications are likely candidates for iris identification systems.

Each of the aforementioned physical lock controls can be circumvented using the "piggyback" method. Piggybacking is a method in which an authorized person unlocks a door and then allows another person to follow him or her through the door without using that person's personal access method. This is often done for convenience and courtesy. Piggybacking can lead to unauthorized access, however, especially in large companies in which all employees do not know each other and in cases in which one employee may not know that another employee has been terminated and is no longer authorized to access the facility. In the case of electronic access badges and biometric locks, piggybacking circumvents the individual audit trail that would have been created if one of these access methods was used. Piggybacking can be controlled through strict enforcement of single-file access by a security guard. Some companies have installed steel floor-to-ceiling turnstiles at entrances to help ensure that each employee uses his or her own badge. The turnstiles are constructed so that it would be difficult for two people to enter at the same time. Another way to discourage piggybacking is to install videotape surveillance cameras at entrances to rooms containing computer equipment. In sensitive facilities, timely review of the tapes and strict enforcement of persons allowing piggybacking should be enforced. "Deadman" entries are also used in sensitive facilities to reduce the incidence of piggybacking. Deadman entries require the accessing person to pass through a "trap" or holding area that has a door at both ends and is visible by a security guard and/or video surveillance camera. The doors can be secured by any of the physical locking mechanisms (key, cipher, combination, electronic access, biometric).

Inadequate deployment of available physical lock controls is probably one of the most common physical security control weaknesses. In many cases, physical lock controls are readily available throughout an organization but are inadequately deployed in obvious high-risk situations. Case studies 7.4 through 7.6 summarize three such situations.

CASE STUDY 7.4

Inadequate Deployment of Physical Security Controls over a Wire Transfer/ACH CPU

A financial institution processed billions of dollars of wire transfer and automated clearing house (ACH) transactions each month through a special application that directly interfaced with the Federal Reserve's host application. The CPU for the wire transfer/ACH application was located on a semisecured floor that was accessible by employees, vendors, and guests of employees. Unfortunately, the CPU was located on a desk that was situated along a well-traveled path near the elevators. Telecommunications wires through which the transactions traveled were simply hanging out the back of the CPU, facing the heavily used walkway. Anyone walking by could easily damage the CPU, potentially disrupting operations for hours or even days. Furthermore, during off hours, anyone with access to the floor could walk up and attempt to access the wire transfer application. Although the risk of unauthorized access was adequately controllable through the proper deployment of available logi-

(continued)

CASE STUDY 7.4 (*continued*)

cal security controls programmed into the wire transfer/ACH application, the ACH data residing on the hard drive was not adequately protected.

Automated clearing house is a process whereby debit and credit transactions initiated by various vendors (e.g., utilities, businesses) and government agencies (e.g., Social Security Administration) are electronically transmitted by originating financial institutions to accounts at other financial institutions. The account holders must have previously authorized the transactions. It was noted that each morning between 3:00 A.M. and 6:00 A.M., the Federal Reserve automatically downloaded an electronic ACH transaction file to the hard drive of the wire transfer/ACH CPU at the financial institution. No staff were required at the financial institution to perform the download. The ACH file included debit and credit control totals of all dollars transacted. These totals were used for balancing to the amounts to be posted by the mainframe, using the downloaded ACH file. At about 6:00 A.M., a data processing operations person would upload the ACH file to the mainframe for posting to customer accounts. The staff member would then balance the total dollars posted to those from the original data file. The Accounting Department also balanced the total amounts posted to the debits and credits posted to the Federal Reserve account of the financial institution. Thus, if the amounts of debits or credits were manipulated, an out-of-balance condition would be detected.

This process was relatively effective. However, while the downloaded data file resided on the hard drive of the wire transfer/ACH CPU, it could be viewed and edited, using a common utility software (i.e., the file was not encrypted) that was conveniently installed on the CPU to assist microcomputer support personnel during maintenance. It was easy to determine which fields were dates, account numbers, amounts, and so on. If a destination account number for an incoming ACH credit (e.g., monthly Social Security or retirement deposit) were changed to an unauthorized account number, the control totals would not be affected. The customer would have to notice the unauthorized transaction. Identifying the unauthorized transaction within the data file would require examination of each transaction with the amount that the customer did not receive. If the amount was common, it could be a tedious and time-consuming proposition. Meanwhile, the unauthorized amount could be withdrawn in cash or wired out of the financial institution.

As far as physical security is concerned, it was recommended that the wire transfer/ACH CPU and staff be relocated to a separate room, accessible only by authorized personnel. Removing the utility software from the hard drive of the CPU to make it more difficult to tamper with the downloaded ACH data file was also recommended.

There were also opportunities to improve other controls. For example, the Federal Reserve could design the ACH data file to include hash totals along with the dollar control totals. Then, if an alteration was made to the data file, the hash totals would not match and the fact that there was an alteration would be identified. Unfortunately, the record or records that were altered would be difficult to identify. A replacement download would probably need to be requested. A better control enhancement would be for the Federal Reserve to encrypt the ACH data file using a secure algorithm. This would make it much more difficult to alter the ACH data in a meaningful manner. The best an un-authorized person could do would be to delete or damage the data file. Since these two control options would have to be coordinated with the federal government, such challenging recommendations were deferred until a later audit.

CASE STUDY 7.5

Inadequate Physical Security over Audio Response CPUs

A financial institution provided an audio response transaction processing service for its customers. The application was loaded on three separate microcomputers, each of which serviced a designated number of incoming phone lines. The microcomputers were located just inside the entrance to the main computer room and thus were accessible to all who had access to the computer room. Since the computer room housed the primary computers of several different platforms, it was recommended that the keyboards to the audio response microcomputers be locked, using the available keys on the CPUs. Many microcomputers manufactured today do not have keys that enable the keyboard to be locked. If this situation is encountered in an organization, keyboard-locking software should be installed on each CPU. Such software should require a password to be entered prior to enabling any commands to be entered, and it should reside in the random access memory (RAM) of the microcomputer, thereby making it more difficult to circumvent.

CASE STUDY 7.6

Inadequate Physical Security over System Console

Some commercial computers have what is called a system console. The console is a special terminal connected to the CPU from which the computer operator executes various operating system commands to control the computer (e.g., to run production jobs, copy and print output, perform backup procedures). A major risk with systems that have a system console is that anyone with physical access to the console could shut down the entire system, thereby erasing all previous user IDs and passwords and resetting all system access parameters, including the initializing user ID and password, to the factory default settings. The person could then restart the system from scratch. If so, the system would recognize the initial user ID and password, which are often printed in the system documentation, thus enabling the perpetrator to sign on as if he or she were the system security administrator.

(continued)

CASE STUDY 7.6 (*continued*)

Some systems are more secure in that they do not have a specific system console that must be physically secured. In these systems, the system security administrator is able to execute operating system commands from any terminal, so long as he or she has properly signed on.

Sometimes a system shutdown can be performed by someone who simply has physical access to the CPU's on/off switch or power supply cord. As with the system console, turning off the power could erase all previous user IDs and passwords and reset all system access parameters, including the initializing user ID and password, to the factory default settings. In these types of systems, access to the system console may not be a requirement to take over the system, so long as the system recognizes the initial user ID and password from any terminal connected to the CPU.

The CPU of an IBM AS/400 has several key settings that, if properly deployed, can reduce the risk of unauthorized access in the event of a system shutdown. If the key setting on the CPU is in the "secure" position, the system cannot be restarted (unless, of course, the key was left in the keyhole and the person restarting the system turned it to a less secure position). During an audit of an IBM AS/400 installation at one organization, the CPU key was turned to a vulnerable setting ("normal") instead of the secure setting. Since the AS/400 CPU was located in the main computer room of the data center along with other unrelated types of large CPUs, anyone with access to the console in the computer room could have shut the system down, restarted it, and then accessed it as the system security administrator. Further compounding the insecurity of the situation was the fact that the system security administrator left the key in the keyhole on the CPU. As a result, there was an increased risk of accidental or unauthorized system shutdowns. Also, an unauthorized user could turn the key to the "manual" setting and bypass certain security settings by restarting the system or using other special system commands. These control weaknesses were the result of inadequate training of the system security administrator, who did not have a technical background and was unaware of the potential security risks. Because there were physical keys associated with the AS/400 CPU, additional tests of the security over the keys and any spares had to be performed (see previous discussion in this chapter on controls over keys).

SECURITY GUARDS

Security guards are an important component of an organization's overall physical security program. Although the guards are not police, they are a deterrent to theft, danger in the workplace, and other illegal and unauthorized activity. They can also assist in reducing the incidence of piggybacking into data centers and in the monitoring of controls such as video cameras. Furthermore, the incident reports they prepare can be crucial evidence in cases of criminal prosecution and employee misconduct.

For organizations that utilize the services of an outside security guard company, the responsibilities of the security guard company should be clearly specified in a contract with the organization being protected. The contract should specify these key items:

- Term (e.g., from January 1, 20XX to December 31, 20XX) and cost.
- Security guard company shall subject all guards to police background checks.
- Training and performance requirements of security officers, including excellent skills in observation and writing. Attention to detail in observations is particularly important because security guards are often required to complete incident logs and incident reports. This is where writing (and spelling) come into play. Incident logs are used to record routine events that guards observe while making their normal rounds. The events are recorded as to time and location on the premises. Individually, the events recorded may not seem to be very important, but collectively, accurately recorded events can provide a glimpse of how a more significant event began to unfold. Incident reports are for significant events. If these events are poorly described, their credibility can be more easily questioned. If the description is difficult to understand, poor spelling can make incident reports even more difficult to read, thereby compounding their lack of credibility. For safety reasons, many security guards are required to be certified in first aid and cardiopulmonary resuscitation (CPR).
- Contract should refer to a separate procedures manual. Day-to-day responsibilities should not be specified in the contract. This would result in a situation in which each time there was a change in procedure, an officer of the organization and the security guard company would need to review, approve, and sign a new contract. Instead, a separate procedures manual should be developed by the manager in charge of security at the particular facility and agreed on by the first-line manager of the guard service company. The contract should refer to the fact that the procedures in the manual will be followed. Routine changes to procedures should be approved by the organization's security manager and the first-line manager of the security company. The contract should be revised only in cases in which there are significant revisions or the liability of the organization or security guard company has changed significantly.
- Liability of the security guard company and indemnification to the organization in the event that damages are caused by security guards. For example, the contract could specify that the security guard company will maintain a certain amount of liability insurance and name the organization as the beneficiary. Proof of such insurance should be obtained from the security guard company's insurance company.
- Termination requirements, including the number of days required for written notice to be given to either party prior to terminating the contract.
- Signatures of the president or other designated officer of the organization and of the security guard company.

This list is by no means comprehensive. It highlights some of the minimum requirements of a contract between an organization and a security guard company. Additional items that tailor the contract to the unique needs of the organization and the security guard company should be included.

If the security guards are employees of the organization, the procedures manual would effectively constitute the contract between the security department and the rest of the organization. Internal security guards should still be held to the same, if not higher, performance standards as external guards. Again, minimum job requirements should include excellent observation and writing skills.

VIDEO SURVEILLANCE CAMERAS

Video surveillance cameras are an additional control that can act as an effective deterrent to unauthorized activities and provide critical evidence in criminal prosecution and employee misconduct. Video surveillance cameras are usually positioned in strategic locations that afford full views of the doors and/or equipment they are designed to protect. The video system should be designed so that the day, date, and time appear on the recording. In addition, monitors should be installed in the guard station. One monitor for each video camera would be optimal. However, in many facilities, there are more video cameras than there is space available for monitors in the guard station. These systems are designed so that the views appearing in the monitors rotate among the various video cameras periodically (e.g., every 30 seconds). Security guard procedures should specify that they are to observe the activity in the monitors on a regular basis. For video tape systems, procedures should also be included in the security guard manual to ensure that videotapes are replaced before they run out. Full tapes should be stored for a reasonable time period in a secure off-site location.

Newer digital video surveillance systems should be programmed to save the data images on the hard drive. Nightly backups of the hard drive should be performed, and the backup tapes, CD-RWs, or other digital storage devices should be stored at a secure off-site storage facility for a predetermined, operationally practical time period commensurate with the risk of the areas being monitored. In some more sophisticated systems, data images can be electronically transmitted to the remote storage facility in real-time mode so that nightly backup procedures are not necessary.

GENERAL EMERGENCY AND DETECTION CONTROLS

Alarms can be triggered by smoke, fire, or a number of other specific actions (e.g., forcibly opening a restricted door). Alarms should be installed at strategic locations throughout a facility for both safety and security reasons. They should be electronically monitored on a continuous basis. Fire alarms are typically monitored by both security guards and the local fire department. Physical access alarms are normally monitored by security guards and, depending on the application, the local law enforcement agency. Alarms should also notify security management within the organization. The security guard procedures manual should specify whom the guards should notify, depending on the nature and type of alarm.

Heat-activated overhead sprinkler systems are required in most facilities. In the case of data centers, they may or may not be located above computer equipment, depending on the local fire code and the wishes of management. Overhead sprinkler systems should be installed even in areas where CPUs and other equipment are located for four reasons:

1. Employee safety would be maximized.
2. Fire damage can be contained in one area rather than being allowed to grow and spread, thereby risking the loss of the entire facility.
3. Most equipment should be insured (see the Insurance Coverage section for more details), so losses from water damage should not be a major concern.
4. If the organization has an effective business resumption plan, business operations should be able to be restored within a reasonable time period despite water damage to computer equipment at the original data center or other location.

Many data centers used to be equipped with fire prevention systems that released pressurized halon gas in the event of a fire. Halon gas rapidly removes oxygen from the air, thus suppressing a fire. Halon dissipates quickly, leaves no residue, and is "nontoxic." Because of its inert properties, it does not damage equipment. Unfortunately, halon has some significant side effects. Halon damages the ozone layer of the atmosphere. Also, prolonged exposure can be hazardous to humans. For these reasons, halon gas is heavily taxed in some cities and jurisdictions. Therefore, installation and maintenance of halon fire prevention systems is being phased out.

Fire extinguishers are a simple but necessary component of the overall fire prevention control environment. They should be strategically located around the facility, especially in areas where the risk of fire is greatest. Alarms, sprinkler systems, and fire extinguishers are periodically inspected by local fire departments to ensure compliance with fire codes.

A master key to all the doors in a facility is commonly located in a locking key box on the outside of a facility. The key box should be accessible only by the fire department. Building blueprints should be on file with the local fire department and/or located in a restricted area that is accessible by the fire department.

HEATING, VENTILATION, AND COOLING SYSTEMS

Computers survive best in a cool, dry, dust-free environment. Many computers do not require special HVAC equipment. For example, laptop and desktop computers function very well in a typical office or household room. These small computers are cooled by internal fans and do not require any special dust filters. The larger the computer, the more likely it is to require special cooling and dust removal equipment. Large mainframe computers generate significant amounts of heat, thus requiring special air-conditioning systems to maintain temperatures within manufacturer-specified ranges. Many mainframes also require special dust removal equipment due to the significant amount of air turbulence they create.

The comfort requirements of the people operating the equipment must not be forgotten. Computer rooms should not be so cold that staff members can see their breath and must wear arctic clothing to be able to function. This type of atmosphere can lead to other hazards, for example, space heaters placed on the floor underneath computer consoles to warm the toes of the operators. Unless designed to supply power to a space heater for extended periods of time, the electrical wiring could short circuit and start a fire.

Faulty or poorly maintained ventilation systems can lead to poor health of the staff. Failure to perform routine maintenance of ventilation systems is one of the most commonly overlooked procedures in many companies. Companies that do not routinely maintain their ventilation systems may save a few dollars on paper, but they pay much more in terms of lost productivity when employees are sick and must miss work. As with household heating filters, the filters of commercial facilities should be changed on a regular basis. The ducting should also be inspected and cleaned if necessary. If there are overhead vents with significant amounts of soot around them or with dust protruding from the grates, one should inquire as to when the last time the ventilation system was cleaned. The response might be surprising.

The role of an information systems auditor should be to ensure that the HVAC systems receive maintenance on a regular basis as required by the manufacturers. The person or persons in charge of the computer facility and equipment should maintain a log of all equipment and facility vendors, the types of maintenance that are required, and the approximate times during the year that such maintenance is to occur. The auditor should confirm that the log has been updated periodically during the year as the various maintenance procedures are completed. The auditor should also examine the contracts with each vendor to ensure that they are current and that they specify the types of maintenance that are to be performed, the frequency of such maintenance, and the cost. The auditor should then confirm that the maintenance procedures are included on the maintenance log.

INSURANCE COVERAGE

Insurance should be maintained to cover computer hardware and software at replacement cost and the costs to re-create lost data. Some policies may even cover lost revenues that are directly attributable to computer hardware or software failures. However, coverage for lost revenues may be costly and can be difficult to prove. Most insurance policies specify that coverage applies so long as certain procedures are implemented. For example, the policy may require that the company implement daily, weekly, or monthly backup procedures for software and data and that the data should be stored at a secure off-site location. The policy may also specify that all covered equipment must have routine maintenance procedures performed according to manufacturer's specifications. Neither of these conditions should be a problem since the company should already have these procedures in place. Deductibles should be set at reasonable levels so that premiums are not excessive.

The insurance policy should be examined to ensure that it is current and that it covers all computer hardware, software, and data at replacement cost. It should also be confirmed that the amount of coverage is adequate so that the company is not paying for too much or too little insurance. This can be accomplished by examining the procedures used by the insurance manager to determine the amount of coverage necessary and then testing the sources of the information. For example, the insurance manager may receive inventory listings of capitalized computer equipment and software costs from the Accounting Department. Using this historical cost information, the insurance manager can then adjust the required coverage upward to arrive at an anticipated replacement cost. A member of the audit staff should test the reliability of the inventory listings, because the acquisition and disposal of some equipment may not be recorded or may be improperly recorded. Case study 7.7 describes a situation in which computer equipment was improperly removed from the fixed assets listing of a company.

CASE STUDY 7.7

Improper Removal of Computer Equipment from Fixed Assets

During a review of the fixed assets inventory by the Internal Audit Department of an organization, it was noted that six microcomputers with original costs totaling $40,000 were removed from the listing and written off because they could not be located. Since the computers were a few years old and had been fully depreciated, no loss was recognized and the disposal of the equipment went relatively unnoticed. There was some concern that the equipment may have been stolen, so these items were selected for testing. Within a short period of time, each of the six computers were located in the building. Three were still being used in their respective departments, and three were located in a locked storage room in the Microcomputer Support Department. Further investigation revealed several control weaknesses that resulted in the improper write-off of computer and other equipment.

First, temporary agency personnel were hired to perform the inventory. They were unfamiliar with the facility and all possible locations of equipment. Also, since they were strangers in the workplace, some employees did not allow

(continued)

them full access to all possible equipment locations. Allowing temporary agency personnel to enter all areas of a facility increases the risk of theft of company assets and personal belongings of employees. It also increases the risk that confidential customer and company information could be divulged. Furthermore, the agency personnel were improperly trained in follow-up procedures when large equipment items could not be located. Overall, the use of temporary agency personnel to perform the inventory was found to be highly inefficient due to the number of fixed asset items that were not accounted for during their initial attempt to scan the bar codes of all equipment. Another problem was that the Accounting Department had inadequate follow-up procedures to confirm that expensive equipment items were in fact missing prior to writing them off.

It was recommended that procedures be implemented whereby the Microcomputer Support Department had to approve all disposals of microcomputer equipment prior to the Accounting Department's writing them off from the fixed assets inventory and that all items over a predetermined dollar threshold be reviewed by management prior to write-off. It was also recommended that regular employees perform the fixed assets inventory instead of using temporary agency personnel.

Fixed assets inventories are always one of the most difficult procedures facing an organization. The larger the company, the more difficult it becomes. Large, complex computer systems can be one of the most difficult types of items to inventory because they have numerous expensive components, many of which are purchased and installed at different times. Often they are installed within a CPU, so they are not visible. Most companies assign a fixed asset identification number to each item purchased over a certain dollar amount (e.g., $1,000). Thus, when an inventory is performed, the components appear to be missing, and the Accounting Department has to follow up with management of the computer facility, only to find that the items are installed inside of hardware covers. To simplify the process for the Accounting Department, it is recommended that the inventory for complex computer systems be performed by knowledgeable staff who operate and maintain the equipment. The inventory should then be approved by the management of the area and returned to the Accounting Department. This procedure would save a significant amount of time by eliminating the need for an Accounting Department employee to attempt to locate all computer components and then question the management of the computer facility regarding the whereabouts of each component that could not be located.

Another procedure that auditors should perform when examining insurance coverage is to confirm that all required procedures are being performed by the company. Case study 7.8 describes how procedures in a financial institution did not conform to insurance policy requirements and thus placed the institution at significant risk.

CASE STUDY 7.8

Noncompliance with Insurance Requirements

During an audit of the wire transfer process at a financial institution, the company's insurance policy was examined to ensure that potential losses from large fraudulent wire transfers were covered. The policy required, among other things, that the financial institution record voice-initiated wires, that the recordings be retained for 90 days, and that commercial customers who requested wires over $5 million be called back to confirm that the wire instructions were correct.

The auditors found that voice recordings were being retained for only 60 days and call-back procedures were being performed only for voice-initiated wires exceeding $10 million. These deficiencies placed the financial institution at significant risk in the event of a wire transfer loss. The insurance company may not cover the loss if it was due to the failure of the financial institution to comply with procedures specified in the policy.

PERIODIC BACKUPS

As mentioned in the Insurance Coverage section, procedures should be in place to perform periodic (daily, weekly, monthly) backups of system software, application programs, and data as well as storage and rotation of the backup media (e.g., magnetic tapes, disks, compact disks [CDs]) to a secure off-site location. Daily backups are usually necessary only for data since the application programs and system software do not change significantly. Full backups of the entire system, including system software, application programs, and data should be performed weekly or monthly, depending on the number and types of changes that have been made. Full system backups should also be performed on completion of a major upgrade or significant changes to the operational and security parameters of a system.

Logs should be maintained to document that backups have been performed and that the backup media have been transported to the off-site location. The auditor should visit the off-site storage facility to evaluate the adequacy of its physical security controls. If the off-site storage facility is a vendor, the contract should be examined to ensure that the vendor agrees to reimburse the client organization for any losses or damages that occur as a result of the backup media's being lost or stolen while under the control of the vendor.

Most off-site storage vendors require each client organization to supply a list of authorized individuals who are allowed access to the organization's storage containers. The auditor should examine the list to ensure that listed personnel are correct and that transferred or terminated employees have been removed.

Case studies 7.9 and 7.10 describe a situation in which periodic backups were performed but had never been tested. Case studies 7.11 and 7.12 describe situations in which backups of critical information were not performed.

CASE STUDY 7.9

Failure to Perform a Test Restore from Backup Media

During an audit of a check-processing area in a financial institution, the backup and recovery procedures were examined. Procedures were in place to perform daily data backups. Complete system backups were performed on a monthly basis. Backup tapes were appropriately sent to a secure off-site storage facility as part of the organization's overall backup and recovery program. Since the processing of checks was critical to the financial institution, the manager was asked whether a test restore had ever been performed using the full-system backup tape. She stated that a test restore had never been attempted. It was recommended that the manager schedule a time to perform a test restore over a weekend, using the backup tape.

The lesson here is to confirm that restoration from the backup media can actually be performed. Assuming that system restoration from the backup tape will work without testing it could waste valuable time and could prove very costly in the event of an actual system failure, disaster, or other business interruption.

CASE STUDY 7.10

Backup Was Not Really a Backup

During an audit of a microcomputer-based electronic access badge system for a secured telephone call center accessible by approximately 400 card holders, the IS auditor asked the security officer about system backup procedures. The security officer had a physical security background, but his duties also included administering the electronic badge access system. The security officer stated that the system had a menu option to create a backup file on a 1.4 megabyte diskette and that procedures existed for him to run the backup process each business night. The diskette was sent to a secure off-site data storage facility on a five-day rotation cycle as part of the organization's business resumption plan (BRP). Given these seemingly adequate procedures, the IS auditor asked the security officer to run the backup procedure. The IS auditor observed that the procedure finished rapidly. Examination of the backup diskette revealed that the only information that was backed up was the door accesses since the last backup. No other critical information was backed up, including the card holder database, application system software, and application system parameter settings. In the event of a CPU failure or physical damage to the CPU hard drive, the application system would need to be reloaded in vanilla format; all parameter settings would have to be reestablished. Furthermore, the entire card holder database for all 400 card holders would have to be re-created from scratch.

In this case, the security officer was going through the motions of performing what he thought was a backup procedure, and his entire chain of command had incorporated the backup procedure into the organization's BRP. The key flaw was that no one had thought to examine the output from the backup process or attempted a test restore using the backup diskette. As a result, the backup procedure was almost a complete waste of time.

The IS auditor recommended that the security officer's manager contact the IS department to install, as soon as possible, an independent program that creates a daily backup of the entire hard drive, including card holder database, application system parameter settings, all door accesses since the last backup, the application software, and the operating system to a rewritable CD or high-capacity tape. The IS auditor also recommended that the security manager ensure that a test restore was performed using the new backup process and storage media. Once it was determined that the new process was working, the security manager should discontinue the application system backup procedure, notify the application system software vendor of the program's deficiencies, and request that the vendor reprogram the next version of the software to have options for weekly full-system backups and daily backups of all data.

CASE STUDY 7.11

Failure to Back Up Critical Data and Software

A process was being audited in which the Federal Reserve Bank electronically transmitted ACH transaction data each day to a desktop computer residing at a financial institution. A special software application designed to receive the ACH transmission was loaded on the desktop computer. The application also enabled an operator at the financial institution to upload the ACH data to the mainframe computer for posting to customer accounts. There was reportedly one week of ACH data stored on the hard drive of the desktop computer. The following week, as each day's ACH transmission was received, the data from the corresponding day of the previous week would be overwritten. There were no procedures to back up the data download to an external diskette or tape. Furthermore, the backup application software diskettes were stored in the same room as the ACH desktop computer.

The ACH operation had never experienced a problem in which ACH data had to be restored. However, if the ACH desktop computer were to fail, or if data more than five days old had to be re-created due to posting or data integrity problems, the financial institution would have to rely solely on the Federal Reserve Bank to re-create the download. The Federal Reserve Bank provides numerous services to thousands of financial institutions each day. Therefore, it could take several days for it to provide a replacement download. Also, if the ACH application software were to fail, a new copy would have to be ordered from the Federal Reserve Bank. It would take at least one day to receive and install the software.

Since there were millions of dollars in ACH transactions being downloaded to the financial institution each day, it was recommended that the ACH data

(*continued*)

CASE STUDY 7.11 (*continued*)

be backed up to an external storage medium each day and that backup data for at least 30 days be stored at the organization's secure off-site storage facility. It was also recommended that the backup application software diskettes be stored at the secure off-site storage facility.

At least this ACH operation possessed backup diskettes for the application software. Several instances have been encountered in which process owners did not have a backup copy of the primary application software. These process owners failed to recognize the need to create a backup copy for use in the event of a system failure, disaster, or other business interruption.

CASE STUDY 7.12

Failure to Perform Weekly Backups in a Record Storage and Retrieval Application

The Records Department of a financial institution utilized a semiautomated record storage and retrieval application to archive new account documents, loan documents, incoming and outgoing checks, and other critical documents. Within this process, images of the documents were recorded on reels of film. On receipt of the developed film, a user in the Records Department would sign on to the record storage application and enter referencing information such as the date, type of records being stored, and the account number range of the records. The application would provide a unique index number, which the user recorded on the film box. When a filmed document needed to be located, the user would enter the account number and then locate the index number of the desired document by the date and record description. From the index number, the specific box containing the filmed image of the document could be located. Procedures in the Records Department required the indexing database in the record storage and retrieval system to be backed up on a weekly basis. Duplicate copies of the film reels were housed at a secure off-site location.

During an audit of the record storage application and related procedures, it was noted that weekly backups had not been performed for 3 of the 22 weeks sampled, or 13.6 percent of the time. If a data loss had occurred during one of the weeks when no backup was performed, all documents since the previous backup would need to be reindexed. In addition, any requests to view recently filmed documents would have to be delayed until the reference information could be reentered or the boxes containing the paper originals could be located in the warehouse. Both of these conditions could cause significant delays in internal and external customer service and cause the Records Department to fall behind in recording and indexing newly filmed documents. It was recommended that management implement controls to ensure that weekly backups were consistently performed.

Although the semiautomated storage and retrieval system was later replaced by a fully automated CD-ROM imaging system, the need to perform periodic backups of the indexing information and to store updated copies of the image bearing CDs at a secure off-site location is equally as critical.

EMERGENCY POWER AND UNINTERRUPTIBLE POWER SUPPLY SYSTEMS

An *emergency power system* and an *uninterruptible power supply system* should be designed into every information processing facility. An emergency power system consists of a generator and the necessary hardware to provide limited electrical power to critical operational areas within a facility. In the event of a power loss, the emergency power system should activate automatically. A UPS system consists of an arrangement of batteries and supporting hardware components that are configured to provide smooth, continuous power to computer equipment. The UPS system acts as a buffer between the outside power source and the computer equipment, so that power surges and spikes are minimized. Also, in the event of primary power loss, a UPS system continues to supply electricity to the computer equipment until the emergency power system can fully activate.

During an audit of physical security at one information processing center, a description of the emergency power system and UPS system was prepared, and key aspects of the systems were tested. They were well designed and supplied with modern, reliable equipment. Excerpts of the description are provided in case study 7.13, as they may be a useful reference as to what types of equipment should be included in the emergency power and UPS systems within an organization. The case study also describes an incident in which the described emergency power and UPS systems were relied on during an actual event.

CASE STUDY 7.13

Emergency Power and UPS Systems

The emergency power system at an information processing center consisted of an on-site diesel engine generator capable of producing 350 kilowatts of electric power. In the event of a power failure, the generator automatically activates and achieves full power within 10 seconds. A 650-gallon fuel tank enables the generator to run for approximately 24 hours before refueling. The generator is equipped with a timer device that automatically starts it and runs it for 30 minutes each Wednesday morning. This keeps the generator in good working condition. The generator supplies power only to electrical circuits within the building that management has designated as critical to ongoing operations. Other areas, such as office workstations and hallway lights, would not receive power from the generator in the event of a power loss. The orga-

(continued)

nization contracts with the diesel generator vendor to service the generator on a semiannual basis.

To reduce the risk of data loss during a power failure, key data processing equipment receive electric power directly from a UPS system. The UPS system consists of a power-filtering system and a set of batteries capable of producing 100 kilowatts of electric power. Power from the street is fed to the main power control panel for the building and to the UPS system. This provides continuous charging of the batteries during normal operation and eliminates power fluctuations to the computer equipment. In the event of power loss, the UPS system acts as an interim power source for key data processing equipment until the diesel power generator reaches full power (within 10 seconds). If the diesel generator fails, the UPS system can power the computer equipment for up to 45 minutes. The organization contracts with an electronics and battery vendor to service the UPS system quarterly.

One day, the system was put to a live, unplanned test. For unknown reasons, the main power control panel shortcircuited, leaving the entire information processing center without power. The diesel generator and UPS system functioned flawlessly. However, this was not a short-term situation. A spare main power control panel was not immediately available. A new one had to be fabricated, a process expected to take at least one week. Since the company could not afford to have the information processing center operating at minimal capacity for an entire week or more with only one diesel generator, management decided to lease two special generators, each capable of producing one megawatt of electricity. These large generators had to be flown in from another city, trucked to the information processing center, and hooked into the power supply grid. The total costs resulting from the failed power control panel amounted to $500,000. Fortunately, the loss was covered under the organization's insurance policy. An organization's insurance policy should be checked to make sure it covers this type of loss. An organization also should make sure that spare main power control panels are readily available at each information processing center. In the case of leased office buildings, one should ask the building management company whether adequate procedures are in place to deal with this type of situation.

BUSINESS RESUMPTION PROGRAMS

Every organization should have a current and tested business resumption program (BRP). Such plans are sometimes referred to as disaster recovery programs, but this phraseology infers that the program applies only to disasters. Since some BRP procedures may be implemented in events less severe than a disaster, the phrase *business resumption program* is more appropriate. Before describing the contents of a BRP, it is important to note that a BRP does not have to be the size of an encyclopedia. If it is too large, it can be difficult to maintain and management may let it collect dust. The BRP should be as brief, concise, and easy to read as possible, while still retaining the key procedures necessary to ensure that all steps are carried out in a timely and appropriate manner. A BRP should include, at a minimum:

- List of key contact personnel throughout the organization, including contact phone numbers (home, work, cell phone, pager) and home addresses.
- Primary and secondary headquarters sites where key management are to convene in the event that a disaster has rendered the main headquarters location inoperable.
- Identify and rank operational areas in terms of criticality and risk. The high-risk processes should be the first ones to be made functional in the event of a disaster. Data processing areas are usually at or near the top of the list of critical operational areas since so many other areas rely on data processing resources. Key aspects of a data processing BRP are discussed later in this section.
- Brief description of events that should trigger the BRP. This section should include initial BRP procedures as well as procedures for escalating the BRP, depending on the severity of the situation.
- Concise descriptions of the actions that will take place in each of the operational areas. These narrative descriptions may also include drawings and schematics of the facility.
- Often forgotten in the planning for disasters is the potential psychological impact of the disaster on the ability of employees to perform their duties. The September 11, 2001, terrorist attacks were a clear example of the devastating psychological impact of this type of disaster. During disaster recovery training, it should be clearly communicated to all staff that their first priority is to be sure that their family members are safe. If employees fear for the safety of their families, they will be mostly ineffective at performing their job duties. In addition, if employees have witnessed or experienced severe trauma during a disaster, some are going to be in need of counseling and other assistance. The BRP should provide for these needs.

Once the BRP has been established, the organization must provide training for management and key personnel in charge of each operational area to ensure that they understand their roles and the sequence in which they are to carry out their business resumption duties. On completion of training, periodic tests of the BRP should be conducted. Initially the organization should conduct limited walk-through tests to identify and resolve any inconsistencies or administrative difficulties. Next, the organization should plan limited tests of the BRP, beginning with the previously identified high-risk areas. At some point, the organization should be proactive and schedule a full mock disaster. Many companies do not perform such trials because of the inconvenience to employees and customers and the cost. Although full mock disasters can be very costly, committing the resources to stage them periodically (e.g., annually) should be viewed as paying an insurance premium for an event that, it is hoped, will never happen. In the event of a disaster, the organization's potential exposure will have been minimized. After completing training and testing, the organization must be committed to maintaining the plan. This means that the plan should be updated on an annual basis or more often when significant changes have occurred in operational areas.

The recent terrorist attacks have taught us some additional lessons for BRPs. Alternatives must be provided for each key BRP assumption. For example, most of us take for granted that backup storage tapes and key personnel could be quickly flown to an alternative processing site. If all airplanes are grounded, this assumption is invalid. Even the assumption that ground transportation could be used was invalid in the immediate vicinity of New York City shortly after the terrorist attacks. Many BRPs also assume that cell phones will be the primary mode of communication during a disaster. Shortly after the Nisqually earthquake in Washington state on February 28, 2001, cell phones were virtually useless as frequencies were jammed with people trying to call loved ones. Traffic became gridlocked within hours. Therefore, as part of the annual BRP maintenance process, all key assumptions should be questioned and at least one if not two alternative sets of processes should be developed for each key assumption, including transportation, communications, staffing, and processing facilities.

KEY ASPECTS OF AN INFORMATION SYSTEMS BUSINESS RESUMPTION PROGRAM

For full-blown information processing disasters, an organization's BRP should provide for alternate information processing sites. Hot sites, cold sites, vendor sites, and reciprocal sites are four commonly deployed alternative information processing sites. The type of site selected depends on the type of computing system platform (i.e., computer hardware and operating system), available financial resources, and desired time to full information processing capability at the alternative site. For each type of site, computer equipment must be compatible with the primary computer system, and backup tapes must be readily available so that the computers have the most current system software, application programs, and data. Most organizations have multiple IS platforms. Thus, they will likely have separate IS BRPs. Each BRP may utilize a hot site, cold site, third-party site, reciprocal site, or some variation of these sites in the event of a business interruption.

A *hot site* is an information processing facility that is fully equipped and configured with lights, electricity, air-conditioning equipment, computer equipment, and supplies such that it can be fully operational in less than 24 hours. The primary advantage of a hot site is its fast start-up time. This can be especially critical to large companies whose customers require immediate service. Each day that a data processing center is not functioning can cost a large organization millions of dollars in lost revenues. A hot site's primary disadvantage is cost. Maintaining a hot site requires the organization to lease or purchase a building, pay for maintenance of the facility (including property taxes if the facility is purchased), and continuously upgrade and test computer equipment to ensure that it will function properly if it needs to be placed in service.

A *cold site* is a facility that is equipped only with the basic infrastructure necessary to operate the primary information processing system. The infrastructure includes lights, electrical wiring, air conditioning, and supplies but does not include the computer equipment. A cold-site plan provides for the organization to receive the necessary computer equipment from a vendor or alternative supplier within a predetermined period. Because the equipment must to be transported from the vendor, installed, and tested before being placed in operation, a cold site can take several weeks to become operational. The main advantage of a cold site over a hot site is that it is cheaper to maintain. There is no computer equipment to continuously upgrade and test. The disadvantages include a relatively slow return to operations and the costs of leasing or purchasing the facility.

A *vendor site* is an information processing facility that is provided by a vendor that specializes in providing such facilities. Advantages include fast return to operations and elimination of the need to acquire and maintain a facility and related equipment. Disadvantages include a relatively high cost that the vendor may charge and the potential risk that the vendor's site is not maintained at full compatibility with the client organization's information processing system. As with any vendor, the contract should be specific regarding the responsibilities of the vendor and the client organization. It should also specify the vendor's liability if information processing capacity is not restored within the required time frame.

A *reciprocal site* is an information processing facility located within another organization. Two organizations form an agreement in which each agrees to allow the other to utilize its IS resources if one or the other experiences a business interruption. The agreement should be documented in writing. The agreement should specify the rights and responsibilities of each organization and should provide for periodic testing by both organizations. It is very important that reciprocal sites not be located in the same geographic area. Otherwise, in the event of a regional catastrophe, both sites may be rendered inoperative. The primary advantage of a reciprocal site is that there is little or no cost. One disadvantage is the risk of the two organizations not keeping their computing platforms compatible. Another disadvantage is the potential difficulty in enforcing the agreement if one organization cannot grant the other full IS processing resources. The organization called on to provide alternative IS processing resources could claim that doing so would prevent it from being able to meet its own information processing needs. This is why it is important that the written agreement specify the rights and responsibilities of each organization and that management of each organization fully understand the implications of the agreement.

Case studies 7.14 and 7.15 describe instances in which BRPs were inadequate.

CASE STUDY 7.14

Failure to Update a Business Resumption Plan

During an audit of a consumer loan servicing center for a financial institution, the manager in charge of the operation was asked for a copy of the BRP. He looked a little nervous and stated that he would have to look for it. The next day, he presented the BRP and qualified it by saying that it needed to be up-

(continued)

CASE STUDY 7.14 (*continued*)

dated. On further examination of the document, it was found that the drawings of the facility looked nothing like the building in which the consumer loan servicing center currently resided. There were no dates in the document, so it could not be determined when it had last been updated. The manager was asked why the drawings looked so different from the existing building. He stated that the drawings were for the previous building where the loan servicing center had been located. In fact, he stated that the BRP had not been updated for over three years. Obviously, it was recommended that the BRP be updated, that key management and staff be trained in the updated BRP procedures, and that the BRP be tested.

This scenario is typical of situations encountered regarding BRPs. In fact, many operations likely will have no BRP at all. In some cases, this can expose the organization to significant potential regulatory damages. For example, the Federal Financial Institutions Examination Council (FFIEC) requires that the board of directors and senior management of federally insured financial institutions develop comprehensive contingency plans and review them at least annually.[9]

CASE STUDY 7.15

Failure to Consider a Service Organization's Business Resumption Plan

The Internal Audit Department at a financial institution received a memo from a credit card service organization announcing that it had implemented several changes and enhancements to its BRP. The memo specified certain procedures that the credit card and data processing departments at the client organization needed to implement in the event of a business interruption at the service organization. The memo also requested that certain pieces of information be provided to the service organization for use during a business interruption at the service organization. It was found that management at the credit card and data processing departments had not received a copy of the memo and thus were not even aware of the necessary BRP procedures and information. The internal auditors provided a copy of the memo to each area and recommended that they implement the necessary procedures, supply the required information to the service organization, and request that the service organization add both departments to their distribution list for BRP updates.

BACKUP SYSTEM SECURITY ADMINISTRATOR

The movie *Jurassic Park*, based on the novel by Michael Crichton, provides an excellent example of how not to administer security over a high-risk system.[10] In the movie, Jurassic Park is a giant, computer-controlled tropical theme park with Tyrannosaurus rexes, velociraptors, and numerous other live dinosaurs as its main attractions.

Any IS auditor who saw the movie should remember the part where the system programmer was bribed into stealing several dinosaur embryos. To facilitate his theft and getaway, he had programmed the system to unlock secured doors to the research facility where the embryos were located while the primary console terminal for the system displayed what appeared to be typical processing. The system was actually locked to prevent anyone from accessing the system without the appropriate password. To complicate matters further, a severe tropical storm was battering the park. The resulting power outages enabled some of the predatory dinosaurs to escape and attack the humans.

The embryo theft and escape of dinosaurs were possible because the data processing facility suffered from a severe lack of internal controls. Complete control over tens of millions of dollars' worth of research facilities and dinosaurs was granted to a single individual—a classic example of inadequate segregation of duties. There was no trained backup system security administrator, no BRP, and no procedures to back up software and data to enable the system to be restored in the event of a system restart. After the system lockout was discovered, the system supervisor did not know how to resolve the situation other than to completely turn off the power to the system and then restart it from scratch. As a result, all of the customized system parameter settings were wiped out. Fortunately, the young granddaughter of Jurassic Park's owner was able to operate the system and get it functioning, albeit at a less-than-optimal level of performance. The theft of the embryos and all of the problems that followed could have been avoided had the owner of the park and the system security administrator implemented many of the IS security controls described in this book.

Unfortunately, situations like the one just described are not restricted to the movies. Granting complete control over a computer system to one individual is one of the most common control weaknesses in the real world. Management of many organizations fail to recognize the need and urgency to designate and adequately train a backup system security administrator. As a result, they are subjecting their organizations to the risk that one person can perform unauthorized activities as well as the risk that a system may experience problems that cannot be resolved. For example, the system security administrator could be involved in an accident, have to leave work unexpectedly, or may be at a location where he or she cannot be reached. Thus, the organization might not be able to restore operations adequately in a timely manner. Case study 7.16 describes a situation in which an inappropriate person was designated as the backup system security administrator. Case study 7.17 describes three real-world examples in which organizations failed to designate and train backup system security administrators.

CASE STUDY 7.16

Carefully Select a Backup System Security Administrator

During an audit of a wire transfer system at a financial institution, it was found that a backup system security administrator had not been designated and

(continued)

CASE STUDY 7.16 (*continued*)

trained. The wire transfer supervisor was the only person with system administration capabilities. It was recommended that a backup system security administrator be designated and trained so that the system could be kept operational in the absence of the primary system security administrator. The wire transfer department manager was subsequently appointed as the backup system security administrator.

During a follow-up review, the auditors assessed whether the manager was an appropriate person to designate as the backup system security administrator. It was noted that the manager was also the financial institution's designated "security contact" with the Federal Reserve Bank. One of the roles of the security contact is to send written instructions to the Federal Reserve to add and delete users who are authorized to transmit verified wire transfers from the financial institution's local wire transfer application to the Federal Reserve's host wire transfer system. As a system security administrator, the wire transfer manager could defeat the local application controls at the financial institution that required two separate user IDs to initiate and verify a wire transfer. All a system security administrator needed to do was create two phony user IDs, one of which could initiate an unauthorized wire and one that could verify the wire. Another way to defeat the dual user ID requirement would be to change the system parameter setting from requiring two user IDs to initiate and verify a wire to requiring only one user ID. To complete a wire transaction after it has been verified, however, a user must be authorized to sign on to the Federal Reserve's host wire transfer system and transmit the wire. As the security contact, the wire transfer manager was in a position to be able to instruct the Federal Reserve to set up a user that it does not know is fictitious. Therefore, the auditors found that the wire transfer manager had the capability to initiate, verify, and transmit an unauthorized wire transfer all by herself. As a result, it was recommended that someone other than the security contact and other than one of the wire transfer operators be designated as the backup wire transfer system security administrator.

This example illustrates an important point: *The backup system security administrator must be carefully selected so that adequate segregation of duties is maintained.*

Because of their significant risk, other issues pertaining to wire transfers are discussed in various parts of this book.[11]

CASE STUDY 7.17

No Backup System Security Administrators—Three Cases

During an audit of an incoming check-processing operation at a financial institution, it was discovered that a backup system security administrator had not been designated and trained. The system had been in existence for over four years. The current system security administrator was the department supervisor. She did not come from a technical background and had very little experience in administering controls over a complex computing system. She had been in her position for only a few months and was struggling just to operate the system, let alone adequately deploy system access controls. The previous supervisor was available because she had transferred within the company. However, she also was not very familiar with administering controls over the system and could not be considered an adequately trained backup system security administrator. During her three-and-a-half-year tenure, the previous supervisor also did not designate and train a backup system security administrator. As a result of the audit, a backup system security administrator was designated and both the primary and backup system security administrators attended training on how to operate the system proficiently and administer security over it.

During an audit of a marketing database application at another organization, it was found that a backup system security administrator had not been designated and trained. Like the check-processing application, this application had also been in operation for several years. The marketing application database was updated monthly from a magnetic tape containing a copy of a data extract file from the mainframe computer. The system security administrator not only had to know how to operate the system and administer security, he had to balance the database to the source application to ensure that the extract total was correct. It was recommended that a backup system administer be designated and trained in the necessary procedures.

During a postimplementation review of a relatively new application used to account for investments in one organization, it was found that a backup system security administrator had not been designated and trained. The system had been in operation for four months. Similarly, during a postimplementation review of a new mortgage loan origination system at a financial institution, it was found that a backup system security administrator had not been designated and trained. This system was placed in service two months prior to our review. In both cases, backup system security administrators were later designated and trained based on recommendations from the Internal Audit Department.

NOTES

1. "Credit Card Computer Stolen," *Kiro Radio News Fax* (November 19, 1996): National Business Page; and "Stolen PC May Cost Visa $6 Million," *Infosecurity News* (January/February 1997): 7.
2. "Protect That Laptop!" *Armed Forces Insurance Newsletter* (Fall 1996): 5.
3. P. J. Heller, "Texas CUs Install Latest Biometrics Safe Deposit Technology," *Credit Union Times* (May 15, 2002): 25.
4. Ibid.
5. Paul Gentile, "Naval Weapons CU Installs Biometrics Identification System," *Credit Union Times* (August 12, 1998): 15.
6. Myriam Bourjolly, "Real-Time Kiosks, SAFLINK Bring Biometrics to Credit Unions," *Credit Union Times* (March 7, 2001): 14.
7. "Biometrics Fail Sticky Test," *Security Wire Digest* (May 20, 2002).

8. "Iris ID: A Panacea for Bankers?" *Bank Fraud, Bulletin of Fraud and Risk Management* (July 1998): 6–7.

9. Federal Financial Institutions Examination Council, Supervision Policy #5, "Interagency Policy on Contingency Planning for Financial Institutions" (July 1989).

10. Universal City Studios, Universal City, CA (1993).

11. For a complete discussion of internal controls over wire transfer systems, see Jack Champlain, "Is Your Wire Transfer System Secure?" *Internal Auditor Journal* (June 1995): 56–59.

CHAPTER 8

Logical Security

The initial key to protecting an information system from unauthorized access lies in the design and programming of logical security controls into the system, whether it is an operating system, a database management system (DBMS), or an application program. Before logical security controls can be designed, the project design team must first be aware of the significant risks to which the system may be exposed. The degree of risk will have an impact on the types of logical security controls that need to be designed into the system as well as the number of controls and their relative strength. High-risk systems would obviously warrant the time and resources to design a greater number of robust logical security controls than a low-risk system.

LOGICAL SECURITY DESIGN

Identification of the significant risks facing a system can best be accomplished through a formal risk assessment process. Because many internal and external auditors prepare risk assessment documents as a standard part of their audit process, they can be an excellent resource to a system design team for assistance in performing a formal risk assessment. Since members of a design team usually include representatives from all significantly impacted areas of the organization who are experts in their respective fields, the team will likely be able to identify most of the significant business risks. However, auditors are often aware of risks that a design team may not have considered.

For example, one of the most difficult risks to control is the performance of unauthorized activities by a system security administrator. By definition, a system security administrator needs to be able to add, delete, and change users and their access capabilities, monitor and regulate system activities, control system security parameters, review system security and operational logs, and perform various other unrestricted tasks. (*Note*: In large organizations, some of these tasks may be segregated.) To accomplish these tasks, a system security administrator requires virtually unrestricted access within the system. Most design team members do not think twice about the fact that the system security administrator essentially will have free rein of the system. In these cases, it is the responsibility of the auditor to make the rest of the design team aware of the risks posed by the system security administrator. The challenge facing the design team is whether the risk of a system security administrator performing unrestricted activities outweighs the costs of designing controls to limit what functions a system security administrator can perform.[1] Two techniques can be designed into a system to control system security administrator activities:

1. Program the system to require a second system security administrator to confirm any additions, changes, and deletions of user IDs and their access capabilities and to make changes to system operating and security parameters. This control would effectively prevent one system security administrator from performing unauthorized activities. However, the disadvantage of this control is that requiring two system security administrators to bless every security-related change to the system could cause significant operational delays if two system security administrators are not available when a situation requiring immediate action arises.

2. Program the system to log all potential system security related events and implement procedures whereby the log is reviewed regularly for unusual or unauthorized activity, preferably by the manager of the system security administrator. Loggable events include additions, deletions, and changes to user IDs and their access capabilities (including changes to the system user ID), system reinitializations, changes to system operating and security parameters, software upgrades, unsuccessful sign-on attempts, resetting of user IDs when users forget their password, and any other activity that could affect system security. Logging these events would provide an audit trail of the activities of system security administrators, other users, and hackers who are attempting to infiltrate a system.

The system should also be programmed so that a system security administrator cannot delete or change the log file (i.e., the log file should be read-only), even at the operating system level. In this way, the system security administrator cannot remove audit trail evidence of unauthorized activities from the log. The system should be further programmed to automatically archive the log file on a periodic basis (e.g., monthly) and then purge the archived files after a reasonable time (e.g., annually or less often, depending on the criticality of the information). Alternatively, log files can be recorded on permanent storage devices such as compact disks (CDs) via a WORM (write-once-read-many) drive. System security administrators should not have physical access to the CDs in the WORM drive. If system security administrators know that their activities are being automatically recorded and then reviewed by their superiors, they are much less likely to perform unauthorized activities.

Although logging can be a deterrent to performing unauthorized activities, it is not a preventive control. Rather, logging is a detective control that will identify a potential violation after it has already taken place. Another consequence of logging of system security related activities is that it requires a certain amount of system processing capacity and disk storage space. If the volume of activity is very high, this "overhead" can degrade system performance. To circumvent this problem, the system could be designed with parameters that enable the system security administrator to reduce, but not eliminate, the period of time that log files are archived. Additionally, the system could be programmed so that the log records only the riskiest types of system-security-related events (e.g., adding users with system administration capabilities, reinitialization of the system). A third problem with logging is that it is difficult to prevent a system security administrator from being able to access and delete a log file, or any other file, at the operating system level. It might be possible to disguise the log file or files so that they are difficult to locate, but an experienced system security administrator might still be able to locate them. See case study 8.1 for a case of how a log file helped identify a deceptive action by a system security administrator. Also, see case study 15.3, which describes some of the difficulties that can be encountered in the security design of a complex information systems project.

CASE STUDY 8.1

Deceptive Action Identified by Logging

During an audit of the primary loan and deposit application at a financial institution, the data processing (DP) manager was asked to print a list of all users and their access capabilities. From the printout, those users who had system security administrator capabilities were identified. In this particular shop, the DP operations staff and DP manager performed security administration duties.[a] Therefore, when the printout of all users and access capabilities was examined, it was found that the DP operations staff and DP manager had system security administrator capabilities, as expected.

Two system software analysts from the DP Department were expected to be found on the printout. These analysts did not require system administration capability as part of their normal duties. However, through informal discussions and through prior dealings with the DP Department, it was found that they routinely performed such duties to assist the DP operations area and to expedite their own work in both the live and test databases. Review of the printout showing the access capabilities of these two analysts revealed that they did not have system security administration capability.

---

[a] I was well aware that combining the duties of data processing operations and data security administration was undesirable since an operator could perform unauthorized transactions and mask them as being performed by an authorized user. The external auditors and I had recommended to management that the duties be segregated. However, management believed that this risk was minimal and their staff could be trusted. Thus, management decided not to segregate the functions. Since management was advised of the risk, they assumed at least some liability in the event one of the operators was to perform an unauthorized transaction.

(continued)

CASE STUDY 8.1 (*continued*)

The system security administration manual was then referred to, and it was noted that the application automatically logged all system security-related changes, including changes to the access capabilities of users. A printout of this log for the entire month was requested from the unsuspecting DP manager. The log showed changes listed in chronological order. For each change, the log showed the date, time, change made, and the user ID of the person making the change. The log was examined for the date and time immediately prior to the run date and time of the list of users and access capabilities received from the DP manager. It was noted that the DP manager had removed system security administrator capabilities from the two system software analysts immediately prior to printing the list of users and access capabilities.

I discussed the matter with my manager. For three reasons, we decided not to confront the DP manager about the deceptive change.

1. By removing system security administration capabilities from the system software analysts, the DP manager had already carried out what would have been our recommendation anyway.
2. The DP manager could change the access capabilities of the system software analysts back to system security administration capabilities at any time.
3. Most important, we wanted to strengthen our relationship with the DP department. We felt that confronting the manager about the change would hinder rather than help our efforts. Since the DP manager was a well-respected employee, the issue was documented only in the audit workpapers but not the management report.

Depending on the potential risk of a system, the design team may wish to incorporate one or both of the aforementioned control techniques, as well as others, into their final design requirements. On completion of the risk analysis, the design team can focus on what types of logical security controls should be incorporated into the system they are developing. To illustrate other common forms of logical security which may need to be designed into a system, let us examine how a new system is brought to life.

BRINGING A NEW SYSTEM TO LIFE

After programming and installation have been completed, a system security administrator or installation technician initializes an execution program to activate the system for the first time. The system should be programmed to recognize a *system user ID* and *maiden password*. The system user ID and maiden password should be specified in the system documentation in the event the system needs to be reinitialized at a later date. The system should be programmed such that, on entering the system user ID and maiden password, the system security administrator is required to enter a new password comprised of *eight or more alpha-nu-*

meric, case-sensitive characters. By allowing combinations of numbers and case-sensitive letters to be used in a password, the number of possible character combinations is significantly increased. A longer minimum password length requirement for the system user ID should be programmed into high-risk systems.

Password characters should not appear on the terminal screen as they are entered by the system security administrator. This control is called *password masking.* Password masking makes it difficult for a passerby or observer to steal another user's password and then perform unauthorized activities.

The system should also be programmed so that passwords cannot be viewed by the system security administrator from within the application, database management system (if applicable), or at the operating system level. To accomplish this, the password file should be encrypted, using a relatively secure encryption algorithm. Adequately encrypted files are much more difficult to examine and change as compared to the unencrypted files. User IDs and passwords should remain in their encrypted state as they are transmitted through any telecommunication networks. (*Note*: See discussion on cryptography in Chapter 11.)

The system user ID should be programmed to have system security administration capabilities to enable the system security administrator to enter customizable operations and security parameters and to create user IDs for other users of the system. When additional user IDs are created, the system should grant them read-only access capabilities as a default, as opposed to granting universal access capability. This design control ensures that additional effort must be performed before a new user ID can be dangerous.

The system should be programmed to enable the system security administrator to assign a maiden password of at least eight characters to each new user ID. When the user signs on for the first time, the system should prompt the user to change his or her password. In this way, the system security administrator is prevented from knowing the passwords of other users (assuming that the password file has been adequately encrypted).

The number and types of customizable operations parameters will vary greatly, depending on the type of application and the user requirements specified during the design stage. The number and types of customizable system security parameters will also vary by application, depending on the risk of the applications and the financial and human resources available during system design and development. System security parameters should be customizable on a system-wide basis and on an individual user basis. Five common customizable system-wide security parameters include:

1. *Minimum password length.* The system should reject any user attempts to enter passwords with fewer characters than the parameter setting. For most commercial business systems, a minimum password length of eight characters is sufficient. However, if the system in question supports a highly risky process, more characters will be warranted, even into the 20-plus range. With long passwords, passphrases are usually necessary. A *passphrase* is simply a statement that is typed instead of just a single word. Passphrases can be highly effective because they require an unauthorized

user to guess a concept statement rather just a single word. They are also effective against dictionary "cracking" software. Some systems have a parameter that enables system security administrators to require users to include one or more numbers or special characters in their passwords.

2. *Password expiration period.* When the password expiration period has elapsed, the system should prompt each user to enter the old password as well as a new password two consecutive times. For most commercial applications, a password expiration period of 60 days is sufficient. Again, in the case of a highly risky system, more frequent changes of passwords may be necessary. Keep in mind that if the system enables users to enter a new password, then immediately change their password back to their old password, the effectiveness of frequent password changes is eliminated.

3. *Number of consecutive unsuccessful sign-on attempts allowed before suspending a user ID.* If the number of unsuccessful consecutive sign-on attempts has been reached, the system should suspend the user ID. Suspension means that the user ID is unusable until a system security administrator resets the user ID back to an active status. This is an excellent control to prevent a hacker or hacking system from trying to sign on an unlimited number of times. In most cases, suspending user IDs after three consecutive unsuccessful sign-on attempts is sufficient for operational and security purposes.

4. *Time of day and day of week that users can sign on.* The system should reject any user attempts to access the system during times of the day or days of the week that are outside the parameter settings. This control helps prevent unauthorized access attempts during nonbusiness hours by persons who have physical access to a facility (e.g., a custodian or security guard).

5. *Period of inactivity allowed before a user is automatically signed off.* When a user ID has been inactive for the period specified in the parameters, the system should automatically save and close any files that are still active, terminate the application, and sign off the user. This control reduces the risk of unauthorized access when users leave their workstations and forget or choose not to sign off. The most appropriate session time-out period must be determined based on a balance between operational and security needs. Initially, a session time-out period of 10 minutes or less should be recommended.

The system should be programmed to allow these same system security parameters to be separately specified on an individual user ID basis by the system security administrator. If no separate system security parameters are designated for a particular user ID, the default system security parameters should apply. The system should apply any individual user ID parameters in preference over the system default parameters. This logic enables the system security administrator to accommodate users who have unique access requirements without changing the access restrictions of all users. For example, in the case of a user who wishes to work over a weekend on a special project, the system security administrator would assign an individual user ID access parameter for this person. Another example would be when a backup system security administrator's user ID is created. The primary system security administrator may wish to set the minimum password length for this user ID at a higher minimum number of characters than the standard for other nonsystem security administrator user IDs. The five system security parameters should apply to all nonsystem security administrator user IDs. Parameters, 1, 3, and 4 however, should not apply to the system user ID.

The system should be programmed so that the system-wide and individual minimum-password-length parameters do not apply to the system user ID. The reason is that a new system security administrator who is unfamiliar with the need for minimum-password-length controls could intentionally or inadvertently set the parameter to an undesirably low minimum, such as three characters. The password for the system user ID could then be changed to only three characters, thus exposing the system to a significantly higher risk of unauthorized access. This could also happen in the case of a lazy system security administrator. Having a separate, unchangeable programming requirement that the password for the system user ID be at least eight mixed alphanumeric characters long eliminates the possibility of a password that is too short or simple being assigned to the system user ID and thus considerably reduces the risk of unauthorized access.

The parameter concerning the number of consecutive unsuccessful sign-on attempts allowed before suspending a user ID should also not apply to the system user ID. If it did, then someone who attempted to hack at the password for the system user ID could cause it to become suspended after only a few tries. This would be a highly undesirable situation in the event the system security administrator had not created a backup system user ID and needed to perform functions that no other user ID could perform. If the system is programmed so that the system user ID is not protected by the automatic suspension control, the need to program the system with an unchangeable minimum password length for the system user ID of eight or more mixed alphanumeric characters becomes even more critical.

The time-of-day and day-of-week parameters should not apply to the system user ID because the system security administrator could require access at any time of the day or week. If a critical problem were to arise during a time when the system user ID was restricted, the organization could suffer significant damage to system programs and data. This could be similar to having a time lock on a bank vault and then having a fire break out inside the vault. One would not be able to open the time lock and would have to hope that the oxygen ran out before the money was burned up.

Parameters 1, 3, and 4 should still apply to backup system security administrator user IDs that were created using the system user ID. Although backup system security administrator user IDs are usually granted access equivalent to the system user ID, they are nonetheless created user IDs, which can be erased by the system user ID or a different backup system security administrator's user ID, and which could be deleted in the event the system is reinitialized. This brings up another key design issue.

The system should be programmed so that the system user ID cannot be deleted. For instance, one of the backup system security administrators could inadvertently or intentionally attempt to delete the system user ID. If such a request were allowed, critical operation of the system would be dependent on the system access parameters applicable to backup system security administrator user IDs. If the parameters were improperly conceived, as in the case of time-of-day and day-of-week parameters, the system may not be accessible in the event of a problem during off hours.

Granularity of system access controls refers to the degree of specificity with which system access parameters can be controlled. In the design stage of a system, the granularity should be clearly determined. Keep in mind that there is a trade-off between granularity and cost, in terms of increased dollars and programming time and in system overhead once the system has been implemented. In addition to the above typical types of logical security controls, other, more detailed controls may be designed into a system. These four logical security controls would add to the granularity of control provided to the system security administrator:

1. Passwords could be screened to prevent users from entering easily guessed passwords. For example, the system could be programmed with a changeable parameter as to the maximum number of consecutive characters that would be allowed. Thus, passwords such as "aaaaaa" or "111111" could be prevented.
2. The system could be programmed to require a minimum of two numbers and two non-alphabetic characters in the password, thus making passwords more difficult to guess.
3. The system could be programmed to prevent a user from entering a password that he or she had recently used. To accomplish this control, the system would need to record, in encrypted format, a predetermined number of previous passwords of all user IDs (e.g., 10). A parameter could then be created that allows the system security administrator the flexibility to set the number of previous "generations" of passwords the system will not allow users to reuse.
4. The system could be programmed to allow only certain user IDs to sign on from specific workstations. For example, user IDs assigned to computer operations personnel could not sign on from workstations in the programming department, and vice versa. Each device (workstation, terminal, printer, gateway, etc.) on the system is assigned a unique "node" number by which the system can identify it. To implement workstation restrictions, the system security administrator would assign specific sign on nodes or node ranges to each user ID. An attempt by a user to sign on to a node number different from his or her authorized node number or outside the authorized range would be rejected.

The system should be programmed to apply granularity controls 1, 2, and 3 to all user IDs, including the system user ID. However, granularity control 4 should apply to all user IDs except the system user ID, which should be allowed to sign on from any workstation in order to troubleshoot and maintain system security in an efficient and effective manner.

An additional granularity control programmed into some systems is a system access parameter that can be set to allow concurrent sign-on sessions by users. A *concurrent sign-on session* is when the same user ID is allowed to be signed on from two or more workstations simultaneously. From an operational viewpoint, this feature can be very useful. For example, a system security administrator may be signed on at his or her normal workstation and may be in the middle of performing a lengthy interactive database query. An emergency problem may arise, thereby requiring the system security administrator to perform some sort of immediate action (e.g., the company president forgot his or her password and it needs to be reset immediately). Rather than terminating a lengthy interactive job and then having to restart it from the beginning, it is obviously more efficient for the system security administrator to go to another workstation to perform the reset operation. However, this type of activity can present significant control weaknesses. In this example, the system security administrator may need to use a workstation in another room or location within the facility. While the system security administrator is away, the interactive job could finish, thereby freeing the system security administrator's sign-on session at the the original workstation. An unauthorized user could then proceed to access the system and perform unauthorized system security administration functions (e.g., create an unauthorized user ID with system security administrator capabilities for use at a later time). If three or more concurrent sessions are allowed, the potential for this type of unauthorized access increases drastically.

Therefore, end users should not be granted concurrent sign-on capabilities because of the number of potential security weaknesses that could arise in the end-user environment. If warranted by operational need, only system security administrators and possibly a very select few other users may need concurrent sign-on capability. If so, no more than two concurrent sessions should be allowed, and their activities should be logged and reviewed. The most secure situation would be to design and program a system so that concurrent sign-on sessions are not allowed and are not even an optional system security parameter. To address the problem of having to terminate an interactive program or query that takes many minutes to complete, the system security administrator or user in question should submit his or her job for "batch" processing. A *batch program* is one that is submitted by the user and executed by the system when data processing resources are available. Submitting jobs in batches frees the user ID to perform other interactive functions without having to wait for the job to complete.

Even if a system is designed so that concurrent sign-on sessions are not even an option, system security administrators can circumvent the design control by simply creating multiple user IDs for the same user. The risks of one user having two or more user IDs are the same as for the same user having concurrent sign-on capability. Therefore, this practice should be strongly discouraged.

The logical security controls just described pertain to an optimal system design situation. However, in the real world, some of the controls will not have been designed into systems. It is likely that some of the controls exist, but they affect the system user ID in a manner that could result in an increased risk of unauthorized access via the system user ID. For example, the minimum-password-length parameter may be set to a low level and may apply to the system user ID as well as all other users. Additional granularity controls that may or may not affect the system user ID will likely be encountered. In each case, assess the overall risk of the process affected by the system and then determine whether the lack of certain controls, or the manner in which they have been designed, is significant enough to warrant a recommendation to reprogram the applicable part of the system. In some cases, the identified weaknesses can be overcome partly or completely by proper deployment of system security related controls.

USER IDs AND PASSWORDS

As can be seen from the preceding illustration of logical security controls in a newly installed system, *user IDs in conjunction with passwords form one of the most common and critical types of logical security control.* Hence, user IDs and passwords are deployed in virtually every computer system requiring at least some form of security. Without them, almost anyone could access an information system and perform unauthorized transactions; gain unauthorized access to information; damage data and programs; release viruses; add, change, and delete users and user access capabilities; make unauthorized changes to system operations and security parameters; and perform a myriad of other undesirable activities. Unfortunately, the mere presence of user IDs and passwords does not ensure that an information system is adequately secure. All logical security controls, including those over user IDs and passwords, must be carefully designed and properly administered to be effective.

REMOTE ACCESS CONTROLS

In the early days of computing, system security administrators were typically the only users who required the ability to sign on to a system remotely. Computer processing was centralized, and users typically signed on using dumb terminals. Today more and more users are requiring the ability to sign on remotely using laptops, personal digital assistants (PDAs), and some kinds of cell phones. They typically require access to the organization network and, from there, access to various applications. Remote access facilitates numerous efficiencies and enables more timely communications and completion of work, but it also significantly increases the risk to an organization's network of computing systems to unauthorized access, viruses, and other operational challenges. To help mitigate these risks, a number of remote access control technologies have been developed. The most common remote access controls include dedicated leased lines, automatic dial-back, secure sockets layer (SSL) sessions, multifactor authentication, and virtual private networks (VPNs). In some situations, a combination of one or more of these controls is deployed. Each of these controls is discussed briefly here. Most rely on some sort of encryption technology. Please refer to Chapter 11 for a detailed discussion of encryption and cryptography.

Dedicated leased lines are telephone connections that are private in the sense that the leasing telecommunications company does not allow external parties to access them. Data transported between computers across a dedicated leased line is not encrypted by default because there is less risk of interception. Depending on the nature of the information being exchanged, a separate encryption control may need to be implemented. Dedicated leased lines are expensive but provide enhanced performance since there is less external traffic and there is a reduced need to encrypt all internal traffic. A remote user should still be required to authenticate to the network using a user ID and password at a minimum.

Automatic dial-back is a control in which the remote user's computer modem dials a phone number dedicated to remote network sign-on. The remote computer provides enough identification information such that the authenticating system can automatically terminate the original call and dial the authorized phone number in its database for that remote computer. This control helps prevent unauthorized users from attempting to access the organization's network, even if they know the remote network sign-on phone number. The authenticating computer will dial only preauthorized phone numbers in its database. After successful dial-back, a remote user should still be required to authenticate to the network using a user ID and password at a minimum. Depending on the nature of the sign-on session, data traffic may or may not need to be encrypted.

Secure sockets layer is a protocol used to provide encrypted Internet sessions between remote computers and the network server. It normally runs on port 443 of the network server and uses public key encryption to establish a trusted connection. Once the connection has been established, all data exchanged between the remote computer and the network server is symmetrically encrypted. The strength of the encryption depends on the symmetric key length (typically 128 bits) supported by the remote computer's browser and the network server. The constant data encryption utilizes enough central processing unit (CPU) processing capacity to degrade the performance of the remote computer and the network server. While SSL encrypts data between the remote computer and the network, it does not provide proof that an authorized remote user initiated the session. A remote user should still be required to authenticate to the network using a user ID and password at a minimum.

Multifactor authentication is the implementation of two or more controls prior to granting access to a user. *Two-factor authentication* is typically applied to remote users. It requires the user first to authenticate to a challenge-response server and then to authenticate to the network server with their network user ID and password. To authenticate to the challenge-response server, a user must possess a token device. During the authentication process, the user is challenged to enter a single-use randomly generated number. The number is obtained from the token device, which is synchronized with the challenge-response server upon issuance. To access the token, the user must first enter a PIN. Three common products providing this type of internal information technology control include SecurID® by RSA Security Corporation, Defender® by Symantec Corporation, and CRYPTOCard® by CRYPTOCard Corporation. An example of three-factor authentication would be to require the user to present a biometric possession (e.g., finger, palm, retina, iris, voice, etc.) in addition to the two-factor authentication process. Obviously, applicable hardware and software would need to be implemented at both the client end and on the network server.

Virtual private networks enable secure Internet sessions between remote computers and the network server, much like SSL. Unlike SSL, VPNs typically require special hardware and software. A VPN gateway server commonly protects the network server, and the remote computer must have the corresponding VPN client application to establish a secure channel (sometimes referred to as a tunnel) for the purpose of electronic data interchange or exchange. Internet Protocol Security (IPSec) has emerged as the dominant protocol standard for implementing VPNs. Internet Protocol Security was developed by the Internet Engineering Task Force (IETF), which is a group of scientists and other technical experts who provide support on technical issues related to the Internet and who help develop Internet standards. The three security goals of IPSec are to provide:

1. Mechanisms for authentication, in order to reliably verify the identity of the sender
2. Mechanisms for integrity, in order to reliably determine that data has not been modified during transit from its source to its destination
3. Mechanisms for confidentiality, in order to transmit data that can be used only by its intended recipient and not by any unauthorized interceptor[2]

These goals are achieved primarily through the use of encryption and digital certificates. By taking advantage of the existing Internet infrastructure throughout the world, properly deployed VPNs can provide significant cost savings, efficiencies, and other benefits for organizations. For example:

- Remote users can access their organizational networks without the costs of long-distance phone calls or the need for the organization to pay for an 800 number.
- Site-to-site connections no longer require expensive dedicated leased telephone lines.
- Access connections can be made virtually anywhere in the world.
- VPNs can be constructed and dismantled in a relatively short period of time.
- VPNs can be designed with complex proprietary encryption and authentication controls so that the look and feel of each organization's internal network is presented to remote individual users and users at each organization or commercial partner site.
- VPNs are more secure than applications that rely on the secure sockets layer protocol for security.[3]

These benefits can be summarized and quantified in this way: "Using the Internet as a backbone, a VPN can securely and cost-effectively connect all of a company's offices, telecommuters, mobile workers, customers, partners and suppliers. Forester Research estimates that companies can achieve savings of up to 60 percent using Internet-based VPN's instead of private networks and corporate modem banks."[4]

But VPNs also present a number of challenges. Christopher King has identified eight challenges:

1. VPN devices must possess a mutually agreeable method of securing data (typically digital certificates). The challenge is that there is currently not a standard protocol for requesting, validating, and cross-certifying digital certificates.
2. VPNs must be designed so they provide high availability to users.
3. VPNs must be designed to handle the computationally intensive modern encryption products while also providing high-speed data processing.
4. VPNs must be able to quickly transport high volumes of data among users via the Internet. The challenge is that sometimes the Internet contains bottlenecks that prevent or delay data from reaching its destination.
5. The organization's internal network must be configured so that the VPN gateway device does not compromise other security mechanisms, such as the firewall.
6. The electronic addressing and routing of VPN devices must be carefully designed to ensure that the same private address number sequences are not assigned to two or more different networks.
7. Vendor software for VPNs often is difficult to administer and manage.
8. Different VPN software products that are labeled IPSec compliant may not necessarily work together.[5]

SYSTEM SECURITY ADMINISTRATION

System security administration is the process through which an information system is protected against unauthorized access and accidental or intentional destruction or alteration. How the available logical security controls are administered after the system has been implemented is equally as critical as the design of the logical security controls. Very likely the majority of systems encountered in the real world have less-than-optimal logical security design, thereby elevating the urgency to strengthen other available controls. In some cases, weaknesses in the logical security design of a system can be controlled sufficiently through proper deployment of other available logical security controls. In other cases, the weaknesses cannot be adequately controlled. If not, then monitoring controls and procedures should be implemented to identify potential system violations in a timely manner until the system can be redesigned and programmed to prevent such weaknesses. Essential security-related functions performed by a system security administrator include the creation of user IDs and assignment of their associated system access capabilities, the deployment of system security parameters, and monitoring of the system to help prevent and detect potential instances of unauthorized system usage.

When a user ID is first created on a system, the system security administrator should grant the user only those access capabilities authorized by the data owner, system owner, or other appropriate management person. The system security administrator should perform this action only on receipt of authorization in writing or via a secure electronic communication message.

Sometimes a vendor technician enters the system user ID and maiden password during installation. Since the installation technician usually does not have any ongoing purpose for accessing a system after installation has been completed successfully, the system security administrator should make sure to change the password of the system user ID so that no one else knows it. If the technician still requires access for specific purposes, the system security administrator should create a separate user ID for the technician but grant only the necessary access capabilities, excluding any system administration access capabilities. No outside vendor user IDs should be granted system security administrator access capabilities.

Department managers should be responsible for training users not to share or divulge their passwords to anyone, write them down, post them in their workstations, store them in an electronic file, or perform any other act that could potentially result in their password's being divulged. However, all areas of the organization should stress the importance of exercising confidentiality over passwords to protect information systems. There should be a company policy statement and specific standards pertaining to such confidentiality. (See Chapter 4 for a discussion on information systems [IS] security policies and standards.) System security administrators should carry out the policy and standards. Internal auditors should help ensure that the policy and standards have been adequately implemented. The policy and standards should be communicated to employees as part of a new employee training program. In addition, quick reference reminder cards and periodic reminders in company newsletters and electronic mail should be prepared and distributed by the system security administration department. These communication media should be updated on a regular basis (e.g., quarterly or semiannually).

A procedure should be implemented whereby the access capabilities of users are reviewed on a periodic basis (e.g., annually). In theory, management should perform periodic access capability reviews in the user areas. In reality, implementation of this procedure is very difficult. The main reason that the effectiveness of a periodic review is limited is that, in a majority of cases, management personnel called upon to review and approve the staff system access capabilities do not understand what all of the access capabilities mean. Management must be educated in what the complex system access security matrices, tables, specific functions, rights, and attributes enable the users to do on the system. Such education could be accomplished through formal training courses performed by system security administrators or IS auditors familiar with system access security over the platforms in question. Further complicating the matter is the fact that there are numerous computer systems accessible by staff within a department. For example, when a typical user comes to work in the morning, he may check his voice mail box, sign on to the network and check electronic mail, check his Internet e-mail, sign on to the mainframe to check the status of reports or other work, and then sign on to several restricted access network applications to perform various business and audit tasks. By the end of the day, the user may have accessed 10 or more independently administered computer systems. Other users with the same manager may also sign on to 10 or more systems during the day, but they may not be the same 10 systems that the other user accessed. In a department of 15 or 20 employees, the combined number of different systems accessed during the day could be 50 or more. Thus, training of management to understand system access capabilities in all systems becomes an enormous undertaking.

Should the department manager be expected to understand and approve the system access capabilities of all department employees to all systems? This is a question whose answer will vary by organization. It will depend on the nature of the systems being accessed, the degree of control exercised by the system security administrators of each system, by the system and/or data owners of each system, and by end-user management. The organization's size and corporate culture will also play a role in determining the degree to which access to various information systems is administered and monitored. The realistic answer to this dilemma is that monitoring of system access capabilities is a joint organization-wide effort. Management is ultimately responsible for the activities of their staff. However, system security administrators are responsible for protecting system resources from unauthorized access and damage. Therefore, they must advise management as to why certain access capabilities should not be granted. Internal auditors must also assist in the overall process by evaluating the reasoning behind the system access capabilities granted, including the abilities of the system security administrators themselves.

Another procedure that system security administrators should perform is to immediately remove the user IDs of terminated or transferred users. Procedures should be established that require department managers and/or the Human Resources Department to notify all applicable system security administrators when employees terminate or transfer. Such notification should take place within one day or less of the transfer or termination to reduce the risk of unauthorized actions by the terminated or transferred employee prior to having his or her system access revoked. Telephone calls are the quickest way to notify system security administrators of terminations and transfers. Telephone notification usually must be followed up with a written memo. An alternative notification means is e-mail. E-mail is very timely, and, if the e-mail system and originating user ID are properly secured, the e-mail message can serve as the documented authorization mechanism.

Case studies 8.2 through 8.19 are real-world situations that emphasize the fact that the strength of the design and deployment of logical security controls within many organizations varies across the spectrum from excellent to almost nonexistent. Because of the importance of logical security controls in the overall control environment, a large number of case studies have been included. In many of these case studies, the problems could have been avoided or at least reduced by effective system security administration and monitoring procedures. The many instances in which user IDs of transferred and terminated employees were not removed demonstrates that this is one of the most common internal control weaknesses. In many cases, the control weaknesses were a combination of both poor system security design and poor implementation of internal control procedures.

CASE STUDY 8.2

Check Processing Control Weaknesses

During an audit of an incoming check processing operation at a financial institution, the following control weaknesses were discovered:

- The "audit journal" feature was not activated. The platform in question was an IBM AS/400, and the department manager was also the system security administrator. The AS/400 audit journal could be set to record key types of system activities such as user authorization failures (i.e., invalid sign-on attempts); system restore operations; delete operations; program failures; user profile additions, changes, and deletes; and other system security-related activities.
- In order to provide an efficient and secure method of reviewing system activity for authorized transactions, it was recommended that the audit journal be activated and procedures be implemented whereby the department manager periodically reviews and approves activity indicated in the journal. It was also recommended that the department manager work with the IBM support technician to develop the most efficient and effective archiving schedule for the log so that it would not fill up too fast and thus degrade system performance.
- Seven users had system security administration capabilities when they should not have. One was used by the vendor that installed the business application; the other six were training user IDs used to run system operator tutorials. The existence of these user IDs increased the risk of unauthorized access.
- Maiden passwords of five of the six original system user IDs had not been changed since the system was originally installed four years earlier. Since the maiden passwords were well documented in the vendor manuals, there was an increased risk of unauthorized access and changes to security settings. It would have been preferable if the vendor had designed and programmed the system to require the user IDs of all users, including the system security administrators, to change their maiden passwords during initial sign-on. It was recommended that the system security administrator submit this request to the vendor for programming consideration in future releases of the software. If users do not inform vendors that they want better system security features, vendors are less likely to expend the resources to provide them.

- Three system access control weaknesses were identified:
  1. Users were allowed to have concurrent sign-on sessions (i.e., they could be signed on to more than one workstation at the same time).
  2. Normal sign-on controls were not required of remote users who accessed the system via modem. These remote users were usually the application vendors.
  3. The automatic session time-out feature was available but was not activated.

To provide increased protection against unauthorized access, it was recommended that sign-on sessions be limited to only one workstation at a time; the remote sign-on setting be changed to require sign-on for all users, including those signing on remotely; and the automatic session time-out be set to 10 minutes (5 minutes would have been more desirable, but 10 was agreed on for reasons of operational efficiency and effectiveness).

CASE STUDY 8.3

Temporary Employee User IDs Control Weaknesses

During an audit of a mainframe based e-mail system, a list of all authorized user IDs on the e-mail system was examined. There were 77 user IDs with the temporary employee indicator code (the company's naming convention for temporary employees was to use the letter "Y" as the last letter in the user ID). However, it was found that there were only 51 active temporary employees at the time the list was printed. Thus, there were 26 former temporary employees who could theoretically still access the e-mail system. Internal controls were obviously lacking to consistently notify e-mail system security administrators when temporary employees terminated their assignments so that their access capabilities could be removed. The immediate supervisors and managers were responsible for notifying the e-mail system security administrators of temporary staff turnover.

Tracking of the current employment status of temporary employees is a difficult task in many organizations. The Human Resources Department is usually responsible for organization-wide tracking of the status of temporary employees. In this particular organization, the process was primarily a manual effort whereby Human Resources sent e-mail solicitations to each department as to the names of all temporary employees they were utilizing. Human Resources compiled the information and included it as part of the total number of "full-time-equivalent" employees working at the financial institution that was reported to the board of directors.

It was recommended that the Human Resources Department send a copy of the monthly report of active temporary employees to the e-mail system security administrators so that any user IDs of terminated temporary employees

(continued)

CASE STUDY 8.3 (*continued*)

that were previously overlooked could be deleted. This monitoring control would at least reduce the time period during which terminated temporary employees could potentially access the e-mail system. Also, at a meeting of the organization's management team, supervisors and managers were verbally reminded of the need to immediately notify the e-mail system administrators and any other applicable system administrators of any changes in the status of temporary employees working in their respective areas.

This example demonstrates how in many firms temporary employees are often afforded a lower degree of system access control scrutiny than regular employees. If these firms frequently utilize the services of temporary employees, then the assets and information residing on their systems could be at considerable risk of loss or unauthorized access.

These weaknesses were not limited to just temporary employees. During the same e-mail audit, it was found that eight terminated employees still had valid user IDs, six current employees had two or more user IDs, one user ID had an unidentifiable name, and four user IDs were identified by first names only.

It was recommended that a procedure be established whereby e-mail system security administrators periodically (e.g., monthly) compare user IDs on their systems to a list of current employees supplied by the Human Resources Department. As with the terminated temporary employee user ID issue, this monitoring control would at least reduce the time period during which terminated employees could potentially access the e-mail system.

CASE STUDY 8.4

Credit Card Processing Control Weaknesses

During an audit of a credit card processing application, six logical security control weaknesses were identified:

1. User IDs existed for eight former employees, two transferred employees, and two former temporary employees.
2. Seven users each had two user IDs.
3. Forty-seven users had the system access capability to perform some system security administration functions, such as resetting user IDs after they were suspended because of three invalid sign-on attempts. Therefore, these users could repeatedly attempt to hack the passwords of other users. Each time the user IDs were suspended due to consecutive unsuccessful sign-on attempts, the hacker could simply reset the user ID to active and continue the hacking assault. This issue was further compounded by item 6 below.
4. The password expiration feature was not activated.
5. The automatic session time-out feature was not activated.
6. The logs of system security related events were not being reviewed by the system security administrators for unusual activity.

In addition to the preceding logical security weaknesses, two instances in which system access capabilities resulted in inadequate segregation of duties were noted. In the first case, two supervisors who approved new credit card accounts possessed system security administrator access capabilities and also routinely performed system security administration duties. With both of these capabilities, either supervisor could have approved a fraudulent credit card application and also entered it on the system. In most lending operations, the loan approval process should be segregated from the process of setting up (also referred to as booking) loans. The loan officers should review reports of all new loans to confirm that they were properly approved and booked on the system. This procedure is designed to ensure that no one in the booking area creates an unauthorized loan. Conversely, the loan booking area is a control to help reduce the risk of loan officers creating fictitious loans. In the second case, a senior collector had system security administrator access capability. This collector could have entered unauthorized extensions on repayment amounts and terms, waived late fees, and performed a myriad of other unauthorized changes. We recommended that the system access capabilities of the two new credit card account supervisors and the senior collector be reduced from system security administration to only those functions necessary to perform their normal duties.

Needless to say, the audit report for the credit card service process was quite lengthy.

CASE STUDY 8.5

Teller Fraud Due to Poor Password Security

Early one morning, two tellers were working in the drive-up area of a financial institution branch. One of the tellers left her workstation to attend a staff meeting in the lobby while the other remained in the drive-up area. The drive-up teller attending the meeting either left without signing off her terminal, or the other drive-up teller knew her password through observation. A control existed to automatically sign off terminals after 10 minutes of inactivity. However, 10 minutes was ample time for what subsequently transpired. If the password was observed by the other teller, then the violated teller had not exercised proper protection over her password.

In either case, the teller who remained in the drive-up area used the other teller's user ID and password to perform a fraudulent $9,600 withdrawal from a customer's savings account. (Operational controls to identify the fraudulent withdrawal in a timely manner were also lacking, but that was a separate issue.) When the customer noticed the withdrawal after a few days and called the financial institution, an investigation began. All evidence seemed to point to the innocent teller as the perpetrator because her user ID was used to perform the transaction. Fortunately, a surveillance camera videotape captured all the staff who were sitting in the staff meeting at the time of the fraudulent

(continued)

CASE STUDY 8.5 (*continued*)

transaction, including the innocent teller. The only staff member who was not in attendance at the meeting was the guilty drive-up teller. This and other evidence eventually led to the conviction of the guilty drive-up teller.

The message that can be extracted from this incident is that users of all systems can safeguard themselves and their organizations against malicious activities by exercising strict protection of their passwords. Simply put, users should sign off their workstations when they leave an area, and they should be certain that co-workers and customers are not watching when they enter their passwords.

CASE STUDY 8.6

ATM Parameter-setting Weaknesses

During an audit of the automated teller machine (ATM) process at a financial institution, the daily cash withdrawal limit parameters that were programmed at the institution and at the switching service vendor were examined. It was found that the switching service vendor had appropriately set the daily withdrawal limit at $300. However, the daily withdrawal limit setting on the financial institution's mainframe application was $999,999 for 98 card holders. These exceptions were identified by requesting a special report of all accounts with daily withdrawal limits exceeding $300. Unfortunately, the limit in effect most of the time was the financial institution's $999,999 limit, so long as its mainframe application was online. Only when the financial institution's mainframe application was offline would the $300 limit at the switching service vendor take effect. Thus, most of the time, the ATM cards of each of the 98 card holders could have been used to withdraw the entire amount available in the customer's accounts, or the entire amount of cash remaining in the ATM, whichever was less.

After bringing this control weakness to the attention of management, the parameter settings for the 98 card holders at the financial institution were reduced to $300. From a design perspective, the exposure could have been reduced by designing a more reasonable maximum daily withdrawal limit of, say, $10,000 into the ATM application so that $999,999 would not even have been a valid parameter option.

CASE STUDY 8.7

Incoming Wire Transfer Operations Control Weakness

During an audit of a newly implemented wire transfer system at a financial institution, controls over incoming wires were evaluated. For an incoming wire, the system was designed to automatically credit funds to a customers' account so long as the account number was valid. If the account number was invalid, the wire transfer instructions were stored in an invalid account queue. A wire transfer operator would then perform the necessary research to determine the proper account number. Once identified, the wire transfer operator would sign on to the wire transfer system and enter the correct account number that was to be credited. To help protect against diversion of an unposted deposit into an unauthorized account, the system transferred the resubmitted wire instructions to a confirmation queue in which the wire transfer system required a different wire transfer operator to reenter the correct account number. The wire transfer system would authorize each wire transfer operator by his or her unique user ID and authenticate the operator from his or her secret password. If the resubmitted account numbers did not agree, the transaction would be denied and the process would have to be repeated.

The system access capabilities of the wire transfer operators were derived from an access control matrix. The matrix was examined to confirm that wire transfer operators could not enter the initial account number to be credited and also perform the confirmation for the same transaction. However, it appeared that wire transfer operators may have been able to perform both parts of the same transaction. It seemed that it must be a misunderstanding of the way the access controls were implemented, so they were tested with a live transaction.

To test the incoming wire transfer system controls, I asked the wire transfer manager to accompany me and instruct a wire transfer operator to show me the current invalid account queue for incoming wires. I selected a wire of about $150,000 (one of the smaller ones of the day) and observed the wire transfer operator enter my personal account number as the corrected destination account. The wire transfer system performed as expected and transferred the resubmitted wire transfer instructions to the confirmation queue. I then asked the same wire transfer operator to attempt to reenter my account number as the corrected destination account. We fully expected the wire transfer system to reject the transaction and require a different wire transfer operator to sign on and perform the confirmation. To the surprise of the manager, operator, and myself, the system accepted the transaction and credited my account. Of course, I was not able to keep the $150,000.

Further investigation revealed that all wire transfer operators had the capability to redirect unposted incoming wires all by themselves. In her defense, the wire transfer manager, who was fairly new, stated that the wire transfer system access controls were modeled after the regional parent bank's wire transfer system access matrix located in another state. On investigation, it was found that the regional parent banks wire transfer system contained the same weakness. Furthermore, subsidiary banks in three other states had also modeled their wire transfer system access matrices after the regional parent bank. In fact, the bank had the same incoming wire transfer exposure in multiple states for several years before it was even aware that it existed. Fortunately, no losses were known to have occurred before the control weakness was elimi-

(*continued*)

CASE STUDY 8.7 (*continued*)

nated. We were required to put this statement in the audit report prior to issuing it to senior management.

An interesting side note is that the project leader for the new wire transfer system development team was previously the IS audit manager. Why she did not closely evaluate the access controls assigned to individual users is still a mystery.

CASE STUDY 8.8

Traveler's Check System

During an audit of the logical security controls over a traveler's check application at a financial institution, a user ID named "ANONYMOUS" was identified that had system security administrator capabilities. The two system security administrators reported that this user ID was used by the traveler's check vendor technicians when maintenance was required. Since the maintenance provided by the vendor technicians did not include adding, changing, and deleting users and their access capabilities, nor changing system security parameter settings, it was recommended that the system security administrator capabilities of the ANONYMOUS user ID be removed and only those capabilities required for maintenance be assigned.

CASE STUDY 8.9

Remote Vendor Terminal

Poor system security design and procedural issues can sometimes be found within client systems that organizations access for data entry or other business purposes. For example, during an audit of the IS controls pertaining to a payroll process performed by a financial institution for a corporate client, it was found that user IDs existed for two former financial institution employees on the corporation's own payroll system. One user had terminated 11 months earlier, and the other had terminated 2 months earlier. In this particular application, the financial institution users signed on to the corporation's payroll system to perform certain loan payment information changes for employees of the corporation who had loan payments automatically deducted from their payroll checks. The system security administrators of the corporation's payroll system were responsible for adding, changing, and deleting users of the system, including those at the financial institution. Three procedural weaknesses existed:

1. Procedures were lacking at the financial institution to ensure that the corporation's payroll system security administrators were notified when financial institution users transferred or terminated.

2. Procedures were lacking at the corporation to require written authorization from financial institution management to assign user IDs to financial institution employees. (Copies of authorized payroll system access request forms for each of the financial institution users could not be located.)

3. Procedures were lacking at the corporation to require financial institution management to periodically review a list of financial institution users to confirm that they were still authorized.

The implementation of each of these procedures was recommended.

However, the procedural weaknesses did not stop there. A list of users of the corporate payroll system was tacked to the wall next to the workstation at the financial institution. The list indicated the user ID and password of each user. Obviously, it was recommended that the list be removed and that no other lists be posted. It was also recommended that all users change their passwords, although doing so is not completely secure, as discussed in the next paragraph.

The design of the corporation's payroll system had these control design weaknesses:

- No password expiration
- No automatic session time-out period
- Maximum password length of only four characters
- No online password change capability (In other words, a user must request that the corporation's payroll system security administrator change his or her password. As a result, the system security administrator could memorize or record the passwords of each user.)

These control design weaknesses were communicated to management of the corporation so that future updates of its payroll system could be designed to eliminate them.

CASE STUDY 8.10

Automated Clearing House Users Share Passwords

Written procedures for an automated clearing house (ACH) department at a financial institution included the user ID and password of a user. The reason was that this particular user ID and password were shared as staff rotated jobs within the department. Sharing of user IDs eliminates the ability to enforce individual accountability for unauthorized or erroneous transactions. The system security administrator was the department supervisor. She was from an operational background and was not given any formal training in the administration of system security controls.

It was recommended that the written procedures be revised to exclude any specific user IDs and passwords. It was also recommended that the system security administrator assign unique user IDs for each user, that the users enter unique passwords, and that the user IDs of any transferred or terminated employees be deleted immediately.

Logical Security Design and Control Weaknesses of a Vendor Deposit and Loan Application

During an audit of a vendor application licensed for use by numerous financial institution clients for their primary deposit and loan processing, a significant design flaw was noted in that the password file was not encrypted at the application level. Therefore, user passwords could be viewed by anyone with system security administration capabilities.[a] To compound the control weakness, the application was designed so that system security administration functions could be performed by users who also performed data processing operational functions. In fact, this lack of segregation of duties was part of the routine procedures within this particular shop. There were eight users who, at the time of the audit, were responsible for both system security administration duties as well as running daily production jobs. Any one of these eight users could look up the passwords of any other users of the system including their own. This control weakness could subject any of the vendor's client financial institutions to significant loss exposures.

For example, suppose a teller were to perform an unauthorized transaction from a depositor's account. The financial institution would be relying on the audit trail, which clearly shows which teller ID performed the unauthorized transaction. Normally this evidence would be sufficient to contribute to the conviction of the accused teller. However, if the teller's attorney were to find out about the control weakness whereby any one of eight other users could have looked up the accused teller's password, and then present this evidence to a court, the court would find that a reasonable doubt existed as to whether the accused teller performed the transaction or whether one of the other eight persons did. A stronger system design would provide the ability for the data processing area of a financial institution to segregate operational functions from system security administration functions.

Management in the data processing area used the defense that this design was useful when a user, such as the company president, forgot his or her password. All the system administrator had to do was look up the current password and remind the user to change it. This view is obviously flawed for the reasons stated in the previous paragraph.

A second significant design flaw existed with the log of system security related events for this vendor application. The log not only identified unsuccessful sign-on attempts, but it also showed the characters that were unsuccessfully entered. Therefore, even if the password file were encrypted, this report would enable anyone with access to it in paper form or while it was still in the print spool to note the theme of password that a user was attempting to enter. Using this theme, an unauthorized user could easily guess the real password. For example, suppose my real password were "aprilmay" but

---

[a]The lack of an encrypted password file was also not identified in the service auditors' report issued by the vendors' independent external auditors. Refer to case study 5.2 for further details on the service auditor report lacking this information.

I typed in "aprlmay" on my first attempt and then typed the correct password on my second attempt. My first attempt would show on the system security log. Anyone viewing the log could fairly easily deduce that my password was "aprilmay" and access the system with my user ID. Furthermore, the unauthorized user could deduce that some of my future passwords might be "mayjune," "junejuly," "julyaugust," and so on. Therefore, the system should have been designed so that the log of system security related events would show only that an unsuccessful sign-on attempt occurred, but not show the actual characters that were entered.

A third design flaw was that the log of system security-related events could not record activity of specific users or access to sensitive data files or system resources. Therefore, a mechanism was lacking to monitor the activities of particular users (e.g., vendors or employees suspected of misconduct).

A fourth design flaw in the same vendor application was that when a user happened to enter a password that had already been selected by another user, the system would notify the user that the password was already in use and prompt the user to enter a different password. Users receiving this message would know that they had discovered someone else's password. They could then systematically test the known password on various other user IDs until a match was found. User IDs were readily determinable by the naming convention used in the financial institution. In this case, the user ID consisted of the first letter of the first name, first letter of the last name, and first letter of the user's department. A more secure system design would allow the same password to be used by two different users, but would never inform the users of this occurrence.

A fifth design flaw in this vendor application was that user passwords could be reused every other time the password was changed. In other words, the application did not retain prior generations of passwords. A more securely designed system would retain several generations of passwords (e.g., five or more) in encrypted form and not allow any of the prior generations to be reused. The more generations retained, the more secure an application will be against users who reuse only a few passwords, thus reducing the risk that their passwords could be easily guessed.

A sixth design flaw was that user IDs were not suspended after several consecutive unsuccessful sign-on attempts, despite the existence of a parameter that purported to provide this control. Instead, the system expelled the user to the local prompt, where he or she could try to sign on again. Thus, anyone, including an unauthorized user, could repeatedly try to guess the password of another user without the user's knowledge since the user ID would never become suspended. At least a partially compensating control existed in that the invalid sign-on attempts were being recorded in a log of system security-related events. However, procedures to review the log on a regular basis were not being followed. The system should have been designed to suspend the user ID after the allowed number of consecutive unsuccessful sign-on attempts had been exceeded. In addition, this type of design should require that a system security administrator reset any suspended user IDs.

(continued)

Yet a seventh control design flaw existed. The application had an automatic session time-out feature, but it did not function when a user was more than two "layers" deep into a process. Therefore, a system security administrator, system software programmer, or even a teller could be performing highly secure processes or financial transactions, forget to sign off, leave his or her workstation, and then subject the organization to the major risk of unauthorized access. At least with a fully functioning automatic session time-out feature designed into a system, the window of opportunity for such access is reduced considerably.

Flaw number eight was one for which the cause could not be determined. Nineteen user IDs that lacked password expiration dates were identified. Each of the several hundred other users of this system had passwords that expired according to the system security parameter feature. For some reason, the passwords of these users did not expire. This problem obviously made the effectiveness of the password expiration feature suspect, thereby increasing the risk of unauthorized access.

It was recommended that management in the data processing area submit a list of these control design flaws to the application vendor and request that enhancements be developed and included in future releases of the application. The astonishing reality is that the preceding design weaknesses were inherent in the vendor's application and therefore existed within each of the vendor's several hundred client financial institutions.

The control weaknesses of this vendor application were not limited to just the architectural design. Examination of system user IDs and other procedures during this same audit also revealed several issues of poor system security administration. For example, a user ID called "USR" existed for use by vendor maintenance and support technicians. Unfortunately, this user ID had system security administrator capabilities. This control weakness subjected the organization to the risk that a vendor technician could create unauthorized user IDs, change or delete access capabilities of other users, and potentially perform a multitude of other unauthorized functions. As with any user, the access capabilities of vendor user IDs should be limited to only those required to perform their normal duties. Granted, vendor technicians could damage information to which they had access, but the extent of the potential damage they could inflict would be limited to their realm of access.

Another system security administration issue was that the user IDs of seven former temporary employees and three terminated employees had not been deleted. The temporary agency employees had not worked in over 6 weeks, while the regular employees had been terminated for 10 months, 9 months, and 2 months, respectively. It was recommended that procedures be implemented whereby the system security administrators deleted user IDs of former employees, both regular and temporary, on the day of termination.

A third system security administration control weakness was that four individuals were assigned two user IDs each. This situation increases the risk of unauthorized access via one of the "spare" user IDs. For example, suppose one of these individuals was signed on to the system simultaneously from two different workstations using the two assigned user IDs. If one of the workstations were out of the user's view or if the user forgot to sign off one of the workstations, there exists a much greater risk of unauthorized access than if the user were only assigned one user ID. It was recommended that the spare user IDs be deleted.

A fourth system security administration control weakness existed in that procedures were lacking for the system security administrators to review the log of system security-related events on a timely basis. The logs were printed and then stacked against a wall in the back of the printer room until they were discarded. It was recommended that procedures be developed whereby a system security administrator would review the log for evidence of potential unauthorized access attempts or activity and then initial and date the log. It was also recommended that the logs be retained for a reasonable time, such as one year.

System security administration control weakness number 5 pertained to the fact that several users possessed access capabilities that were not necessary for normal duties. Most significant among these weaknesses was a loan officer who had the capability to disburse loans. Although procedurally this individual was not supposed to perform loan disbursements, there were no system access controls to prevent him from doing so. This situation was part of a larger issue in that a system access profile of users was not reviewed and approved by user management on a periodic basis (e.g., annually or semiannually). As a result, many users possessed access capabilities of which their supervisors had no comprehension or that they did not require as part of their normal duties. Periodic review of the system access capabilities of each user by management would help reduce the potential for unauthorized system access resulting from unnecessary system access capabilities. It is important to note that this solution will be effective only if management is trained and knowledgeable regarding the ramifications of the system access capabilities granted to their employees.

Believe it or not, despite all of the aforementioned system security design flaws and system security administration weaknesses, the organization in question was financially healthy and had been functioning effectively for many years.

CASE STUDY 8.12

Outgoing Wire Transfer Control Weaknesses

During an audit of the logical security controls over a wire transfer application at a large financial institution, numerous weaknesses in operational and system security administration procedures that resulted in significant exposure were discovered.

(continued)

CASE STUDY 8.12 (*continued*)

Operational Procedures

The most critical operational flaw pertained to inadequate segregation of duties. Financial institutions process enormous dollar amounts through their wire transfer systems. According to the National Organization of Clearing Houses, in 1996 the average wire transfer transaction size was $3 million on Fedwire, the Federal Reserve Bank's national wire transfer system, and $6 million on CHIPS (Clearing House Interbank Payment System). In 1996, daily turnover was 5 times bank capital for Fedwire and 76 times reserve accounts for CHIPS. In total, daily turnover for wire transfer systems exceeded bank reserves by $600 billion. [a] Because of the tremendous financial volume of wire transfers, the goal of wire transfer controls at each financial institution should be to ensure that no one person can perform a wire transfer alone. In other words, wire transfer controls should enforce segregation of duties. Without such segregation, financial institutions are subjecting themselves to the largest risk of loss among all the activities they perform. A single unauthorized wire can wipe out a financial institution's earnings for an entire year. Each day, financial institutions wire funds among themselves that can exceed the total amount of all their assets.

In the financial institution being audited, the wire transfer application was called Fedline II. Fedline II was supplied by the U.S. Federal Reserve Bank. It is a microcomputer-based application that is installed at thousands of financial institutions throughout the United States. The application was designed to perform two of the three steps necessary to transact an outgoing wire. The three steps of a wire transfer are initiation, verification, and transmission. *Initiation* is when a wire operator enters wire information (routing number of the destination financial institution, the recipient's accounts number, the dollar amount, and so on) into Fedline II. *Verification* is when a second wire transfer operator with a different user ID from the initiating user ID confirms that the initiated wire instructions were accurately entered into Fedline II. *Transmission* is when the wire instructions are electronically transmitted to Fedwire, the Federal Reserve's host wire transfer system. Fedwire debits the sending financial institution's account at the Federal Reserve and credits the receiving financial institution's account at the Federal Reserve. The receiving financial institution then credits the beneficiary's account.

Fedline II enables initiation and verification to take place at a financial institution. However, transmission of a wire transfer requires a user at the financial institution to be signed on to Fedline II and then to sign on to the Federal Reserve's host wire transfer system, Fedwire. Then and only then can transmission of the wire take place. The fact that a user must be authorized on two systems is the key to ensuring that one person cannot perform a wire alone. Unfortunately, if operational and logical security controls are not properly implemented, one person could easily perform an unauthorized wire. In fact, during the audit in question, it was found that two users had the system access capability to perform unauthorized wires alone. Furthermore, this problem was not unique to the financial institution being audited. A Federal Re-

---

[a]"What's the Risk? Look First at Wire Transfer!" *Bank Fraud, Bulletin of Fraud and Risk Management* (November 1996):1.

serve system security administrator stated that this condition existed at almost all of the over 10,000 U.S. financial institutions with Fedline II.

Ensuring adequate segregation of duties within a wire process that utilizes Fedline II requires three controls:

1. The Fedline II verification parameter must be set to require verification by a user other than the one who initiated the wire.
2. Any Fedline II users with system security administrator access capabilities should not be authorized users on Fedwire. In other words, they should not be able to transmit wires.
3. Any Fedline II users with system security administrator access capabilities should not be designated as the authorized "security contact" with the Federal Reserve Bank. The security contact is the person who notifies the Fedwire system security administrator to add and delete users. The security contact is authorized in writing by the financial institution's treasurer, assistant treasurer, or other authorized signer on the financial institution's account at the Federal Reserve.

Control 1 is critical to ensure that wire transfer operators cannot initiate and verify a wire alone. It is acceptable for wire operators to transmit alone because they cannot do so until Fedline II has confirmed that the wire instructions were verified by a different user. Controls 2 and 3 are critical in that they prevent one-person wires even if the Fedline II system security administrators have circumvented the Fedline II verification controls. Fedline II system security administrators could circumvent the verification controls in two ways. First, they could simply change the verification rule to not require a different user ID to verify any initiated wire instructions. Alternatively, Fedline II system administrators could create one or more phony user IDs. One could be used to initiate a wire, and the other could be used to verify the falsely initiated wire.

The financial institution in question did not have control 2 or 3 in place. Two users had system security administration capabilities and were also authorized users on Fedwire. In addition, one of the two system security administrators was the financial institution's designated security contact. Based on inquiries with the Federal Reserve system security administrator, it was found that the Federal Reserve does not require that the financial institution's security contact be someone other than the Fedline II system security administrator. Furthermore, no such recommendation by the Federal Reserve was located in the Fedline II system documentation.

When auditing a wire transfer system, remember to evaluate the procedures that segregate duties as well as the people who have system security administrator access capabilities, regardless of whether they use them. A user may procedurally not be a system security administrator or designated backup, but could have the same system access capabilities. If that person is also authorized to transmit wires via Fedwire, then he or she could perform an unauthorized wire alone.[b]

(continued)

---

[b]For additional information on internal controls over wire transfer systems, see Jack Champlain, "Is Your Wire Transfer System Secure?" *Internal Auditor Journal* (June 1995): 56–59.

CASE STUDY 8.12 (*continued*)

System Security Administration

Fedline II was designed with logical security controls, which, if properly deployed, could provide reasonable assurance that outgoing wire transfers were entered by one person. Unfortunately, it was found that logical security controls were not properly deployed. Some of the control weaknesses noted include:

- A Fedwire user ID and password for transmitting wire information to the Federal Reserve was shared by various users in the department. In addition, terminated personnel knew the user ID and password because they had not been changed for several months. Furthermore, the user ID and password had been included in the written procedures of the department.
- Fedline II user IDs existed for four transferred users and two users who no longer required access as part of their normal duties. One user never changed her password after her initial sign-on. She was still using the standard initial password of "pass1234" (the system obviously did not force password change). Seven users shared the same Fedwire user ID and password. Seven users were assigned various access capabilities that were not required as part of their normal duties.

WIRE TRANSFER FRAUD

The lack of segregation of duties and inadequate system security administration procedures in case study 8.12 should not be taken lightly, especially because of the potential risk that is associated with any wire transfer process. Many types of fraud, such as loan fraud, can be costly to financial institutions. Some loan fraud schemes take months or years to reach significant proportions, while others require the perpetrator to expend a great deal of effort in preparing false documents to prevent detection while trying to carry on their normal duties. Even when a fraudulent loan has been executed, the task of withdrawing the funds by cash or check is difficult to accomplish without being noticed. Losses from wire transfer fraud, on the other hand, can occur instantaneously. Sometimes wire fraud can occur with little or no advance planning. For example, a wire fraud can occur from an opportunistic wire transfer operator who notices that another operator has left his or her workstation without signing off. What makes wires so risky is that, to the delight of perpetrators, the funds are immediately available for withdrawal.

Numerous recent cases of wire transfer fraud have resulted in significant losses and embarrassment. This list illustrates the importance of the need for adequate internal controls in a wire transfer environment:

- A large bank in the Eastern United States incurred a $1.5 million loss to a former manager at a large international public accounting firm. When the manager learned that the bank had eliminated its information security function during downsizing, he resigned from the public accounting firm and started his own consulting firm, specializing in data security and integrity.

Using social engineering, the consultant obtained secret computer codes directly from a senior management information systems (MIS) officer. Using these codes, he initiated a $4.3 million wire transfer from a commercial customer's concentration account to an account he opened in Switzerland. By the time the fraud was discovered the next day, the consultant had already flown to Switzerland and withdrawn the equivalent of $4 million ($300,000 in currency, $2 million in bearer bonds, and $1.7 million in manager's checks). After nearly a year on the run outside the United States, the consultant was apprehended by customs agents as he tried to return to the United States. By then he had spent $1.3 million but still had $2.7 million in his possession. Through a plea bargain, the consultant confessed to one count of wire fraud, which was punishable by a fine of $1,000 and/or five years in prison. In exchange for consulting with authorities as to how he perpetrated the scheme, the courts did not fine the consultant and he was sentenced to only 30 months in a minimum security prison.[6]

This article points out the need for employees at all levels of an organization to be adequately trained not to share sensitive information with anyone unless they are absolutely certain that the requesting party is authorized.

• A Bloomberg news release reported that a Russian computer expert and his wife were charged in the United States with breaking into Citibank's cash management system and, from June to October 1994, transferring $10 million to accounts he and at least four others had set up in Finland, Russia, Germany, the Netherlands, the United States, Israel, and Switzerland. Citibank's cash management system is used by customers to shift funds from their Citibank accounts to their accounts at other banks. According to a Citibank official, all but $400,000 of the money the ring withdrew was recovered and client funds were never at risk (in other words, Citibank absorbed the loss). The ring breached Citibank's internal control system by using the identification numbers and passwords of employees of the three Citibank customers that were victimized. The customers were themselves banks, two from Argentina and one from Indonesia. The charges did not specify how the passwords and identification numbers were compromised by the ring. Security analysts not involved in the case speculated that the ring could have gotten help from "renegade" employees at Citibank or the victimized banks. One security analyst revealed that bank frauds often involve people who have access to secret passwords or confidential information and that the amount of crime committed by insiders is far greater than that from outsiders.[7]

According to a Wall Street Journal report covering the same wire transfer fraud story, the Russian "hacker" exploited a method by which employees of Citicorp corporate clients can access accounts and transfer funds from them. This type of access is guarded by multitiered authentication. Some have suggested that knowing the system well enough to penetrate its security may have been impossible without information coming from a Citicorp employee.[8]

The fact that this fraud was believed to have been perpetrated with the assistance of one or more bank employees demonstrates the need for information systems to be designed so that employees cannot access customer passwords. Readers should note that fraud in all types of organizations, not just banks, can occur from employees who have access to secret passwords and confidential information. Therefore, systems should be designed so that passwords are encrypted and no one, including a system security administrator, can view them. The design should also include an unalterable audit trail so that if a system security administrator were to reset a customer's password and perform unauthorized transactions, the action could be irrefutably traced to the offending system security administrator, thereby incriminating him or her.

- Bloomberg reported yet another wire transfer breach at a financial institution. United States authorities charged a former employee of Amsterdam-based ABN Amro Bank NV with 11 counts of embezzling a total of $1.9 million between March 1991 and September 1993. The former employee, who was an assistant vice president at the bank's San Francisco office, stole the money by arranging wire transfers of funds from ABN Amro Bank accounts in San Francisco to an ABN Amro Bank account in New York and then on to an account she controlled at another bank in San Francisco.[9]

  A different article reported that a former office manager of a small Washington, D.C., credit union pleaded guilty to a an embezzlement scheme in which she stole approximately $412,000 over a period of three years by, among other methods, electronically transferring member funds into her own account. Since the credit union had assets of only $1.7 million, it was forced into bankruptcy and had to be liquidated by the National Credit Union Administration.[10]

  Both of these situations appear to be the result of a "trusted" employee's ability to circumvent an established system of internal control by virtue of their position of authority. The lesson that can be learned is that internal control systems should be designed so that even senior management personnel would have an extremely difficult time breaching them. Such internal control systems are highly desirable but are also very difficult to implement effectively, especially in small companies in which segregation of duties can be prohibitively restrictive to routine operations. In many large organizations, there exist senior executives who can be so intimidating and demanding that even the best-conceived internal control systems could be easily circumvented if the executives so desired.

- The *Credit Union Times* reported that a number of credit union losses were due to sloppy wire transfer controls. One credit union suffered a $70,000 loss when it transferred that amount into the wrong account at the receiving bank. The account holder who requested the wire mistakenly provided an incorrect destination account number to the credit union. The incorrect account holder at the receiving bank could not resist the temptation to spend the mysterious "gift." The account holder who requested the wire transfer was not liable because the credit union had failed to notify the member in advance of any potential liability. Furthermore, there was no insurance bond coverage since there had been no fraud on premises and no forgery. Therefore, the credit union absorbed the entire loss.[11]

The same article described a $250,000 loss that a credit union suffered when it wired funds to an unauthorized account after receiving a faxed wire request on which the perpetrator had apparently pasted a forged signature of the account holder. The credit union made the common mistake of failing to call the account holder to verify the request. To prevent these types of losses, most financial institutions have implemented a procedure whereby account holders who request wires exceeding a predetermined amount ($5,000, for example) by phone, fax, or other remote means are called back to confirm that the account holder, in fact, requested the wire transfer.

Although these two wire transfer losses were not the result of IS control weaknesses, they illustrate the fact that even complex computing systems are still reliant on effective operational controls as well as organization's ability to keep abreast of pertinent laws and regulations. An internal control system includes all forms of internal control, including logical security, physical security, policies, procedures, operational controls, and organizational controls. The internal control system is only as strong as its weakest point. Therefore, all internal controls associated with a particular process must work in harmony in order to function effectively and provide adequate protection. Information systems controls cannot be conceived and implemented in a vacuum. They must be viewed as a component of the overall internal control environment.

CASE STUDY 8.13

Poor Design of System Access Parameters in a Vendor Payroll Application

During research of the logical security controls of a vendor payroll application, it was found that it was programmed to allow the system security administrator to change one security parameter setting—that of minimum password length. All other logical security control parameters were not changeable. In addition, the unchangeable parameters that were preprogrammed by the vendor were weak. For example, after three consecutive invalid password entries, the application kicked the user out to the Windows Program Manager but did not suspend the user ID. As a result, someone attempting to gain unauthorized access could make an unlimited number of attempts to break into the system. Furthermore, there was no feature to enable logging of system security-related events, such as unsuccessful sign-on attempts. This lack of control would benefit someone who was attempting to gain unauthorized access because the person could make multiple access attempts without detection. The application was also not designed with a password expiration feature or a feature allowing users to change their passwords on their own. The only way for users to change their passwords was to have the system security administrator initiate the change on the system. To make matters more difficult, they had to

(continued)

CASE STUDY 8.13 (*continued*)

be at the system security administrator's workstation so they could enter their password. Otherwise, the system security administrator would have to assign a password, thereby causing the user to lose password confidentiality. Even the minimum-password-length feature was poorly conceived. It allowed passwords to be anywhere from 1 to 22 characters. The design flaw lies in the fact that a system would even give the system security administrator the option of assigning a password with fewer than eight characters. A one-character password is hardly better than having no password at all.

Fortunately, the system in question was a nontransaction processing system, and there were only a few users to administer. The only recommendation submitted to management for internal change was to implement procedures whereby the system security administrator was required to force users to change their passwords at least every 60 days. The other internal control weaknesses would need to be corrected by the vendor. It was recommended that management communicate the control design weaknesses to the vendor so that they could be resolved in a future release of the payroll application.

The payroll application vendor had thousands of client organizations nationwide. Thus, each of them possessed the same internal control weaknesses. When vendor processing firms provide software that is fraught with internal control design weaknesses, client organizations should unify and jointly notify the vendor of their displeasure with the internal control design. For example, if the vendor sponsors an annual user group conference, client organizations could voice their concerns in force directly to the vendor representatives.

Another interesting fact is that a service auditor's report was prepared on the policies and procedures placed in operation with regard to the vendor's payroll application, but not on the operating effectiveness of the policies and procedures. The service auditor's report issued an unqualified opinion on the policies and procedures. For unknown reasons, that report did not mention any of the identified design control weaknesses.

CASE STUDY 8.14

E-mail System Design Weakness

During an audit of an electronic mail application, it was found that a password expiration feature had not been designed into the application, the system did not have a minimum password length and thus did not require passwords, internal procedures were lacking to require users to change their passwords, and users were able to use one or more of over 100 shared department user IDs. We also found that 35 of the shared department user IDs had blank passwords, and over 50 individual users had blank passwords.

It was recommended that management request that the vendor program future releases of the e-mail application with a required password and password expiration feature. It was recognized that the change may be slow since the e-mail application was just one module within a very large application. Thus, programming resources would more likely be focused on other, possibly more significant problems. It was also recommended that procedures be implemented whereby the system security administrator required users to enter passwords and to change their passwords at least every 60 days. As a matter of note: About one year after the audit, a derogatory e-mail was sent to all staff by an unknown user via a shared department user ID. The message was signed "The Management." The perpetrator could not be identified conclusively due to the lack of individual accountability afforded by the shared department user IDs.

CASE STUDY 8.15

Multistate Local-Area-Network Access Control Weaknesses

Within one large multistate banking organization, an audit of local-area-network (LAN) security in subsidiaries located in three states was performed. The network operating systems within each subsidiary were Novell NetWare, and network security was administered separately within each subsidiary. One subsidiary had 10 file servers and 150 workstations; the second state had 28 file servers and 650 workstations; and the third had 8 file servers and 200 workstations. Many of the control weaknesses identified below existed in the LANs of the subsidiaries in each state. Following is a combined summary of each of the types of logical security control weaknesses identified in the LAN security environments of all three subsidiaries. The pervasiveness of the weaknesses exemplifies what can result with inconsistent deployment of logical security controls. Corporate-wide system security standards existed but had not been applied in this region of the organization. It is hoped that this list of control weaknesses will provide ideas for assessing the adequacy of controls of the LANs within organizations.

- A formal process for reviewing the status of LAN system security control parameters did not exist. If these parameters (e.g., default account restrictions, time restrictions, intruder lockout settings, disk space allocations) were altered or were no longer adequate, the weaknesses would not be detected and corrected in a timely manner.

  It was recommended that management implement a periodic (e.g., quarterly) network security review. The review should be centrally administered by the Network Security Department. Items to include in the review include: running the security utility and resolving any potential security weaknesses; documenting and assessing the adequacy of system security control parameters applicable to each user; reviewing the network supervisor error log for intruder log-in attempts and other improper activity; verifying that the system configuration and application files have read-only and hidden file attributes to help protect them from deletion or alteration; and searching for unauthorized software, using newly established procedures.

(continued)

CASE STUDY 8.15 (*continued*)

- Running the "security" utility on each file server revealed numerous instances of insecure user IDs. For example, unique passwords were not required for some user IDs; an unlimited number of grace log-ins were allowed for various user IDs, including the "supervisor" user ID on one server; and password change was not required. These weak system access security settings increased the risk of unauthorized access. For example, a hacker could make multiple unauthorized access attempts without suspending the user ID. If unauthorized access were successful with the "supervisor" user ID, the hacker would have system security administrator capabilities.

  It was recommended that unique passwords be required for all user IDs, the number of grace log-ins for all user IDs be reduced to three, and passwords be set to expire after a predetermined time period (e.g., 60 days).

- The "intruder lockout" period was set at only 15 minutes on one server and 4 hours on another server. These system access security settings increased the risk of unauthorized access by allowing an unauthorized user to repeatedly guess the password of a network user. Although the "intruder lockout" parameter was set to suspend a user ID after three consecutive unsuccessful sign on attempts, the suspension was only temporary. Instead of suspending the user ID until a system security administrator could unlock it, the system would reenable the user ID after 15 minutes on one server and 4 hours on the other. After a user ID had been reenabled by the system, the unauthorized user could resume making additional attempts to sign on.

  It was recommended that the intruder lockout times on all file servers be set to a minimum of three days to ensure coverage during holiday weekends, so long as the log of system security-related events was reviewed by a network system security administrator on a daily basis. This would allow time for a network system security administrator to identify possible unauthorized access attempts. It would also significantly slow the progress of an unauthorized user's trying to impersonate an authorized user. We concurred that procedures would need to exist whereby locked out users could be unlocked by network system security administrators prior to the end of the lockout period so long as the identity of the user could be accurately determined.

- Users of each file server were allowed 24-hour sign on access. This increased the risk of unauthorized access during nonbusiness hours.

  It was recommended that the default sign on access time period be restricted to certain hours for most users (e.g., from 5:00 A.M. to 10:00 P.M.). Some users would require access during other hours; therefore, it was also recommended that written management approval be obtained prior to granting access during other hours.

- The minimum password length on all file servers was five characters, although the corporate standard called for a six-character minimum password length to reduce the risk of unauthorized access.

  It was recommended that the minimum password length be increased to eight characters on all file servers. The longer the password, the more difficult it becomes to guess the password of an authorized user.

- Two concurrent sign-on sessions were allowed for the same user ID, thereby increasing the risk of unauthorized user access and user ID sharing. For example, a user could be simultaneously signed on at two workstations in different rooms. Since the user could not physically be located at both workstations at the same time, an unauthorized user could perform unauthorized functions without the knowledge of the authorized user. User ID sharing can result in the loss of accountability in the event an unauthorized function is performed. If two or more users share the same user ID, the guilty party could accuse any one of the other users of performing the unauthorized function.

  It was recommended that users be allowed only one LAN connection at any one time. In rare cases in which some users may require multiple concurrent sign-on sessions, written management approval should be obtained.

- The password encryption feature was not being used. This increased the risk of unauthorized password disclosure during the sign on process. It was recommended that the password encryption feature be activated.

- The network operating systems were lacking the capability to automatically suspend user IDs after a predetermined period of inactivity. As a result, there was an increased risk of unauthorized access if a user forgot to sign off or left his or her workstation without signing off.

  It was recommended that management search for a cost-effective solution in order to conform to the corporate IS security standard, requiring automatic session time-out or password reverification after a predetermined period of inactivity. At least three vendor products could provide the necessary security.

- A formal procedure to identify unauthorized software did not exist. This increased the risk that unauthorized software could be loaded on the file servers and workstations, thereby subjecting the organization to potential software copyright violation penalties.

  It was recommended that management implement procedures whereby system security administrators examine the storage media on all workstations and file servers on a periodic basis (e.g., quarterly) and document the results of their examinations.

- There were no standards limiting the amount of disk space allocated to each user. This created an excessive amount of wasted disk storage space and increased the risk of unauthorized software being loaded on workstations. In one state, 184 of 378 users (49 percent) had disk space allocations exceeding 5 gigabytes. Essentially, each of these users had unlimited disk space allocation.

  Establishment and implementation of a standard user disk storage space allocation (e.g., 100 megabytes) was recommended. Some users may have required more than the standard allocation. Therefore, it was recommended that management approval be obtained for any users requiring more than the standard disk space allocation.

- Formal procedures for requesting and approving new LAN users did not

(*continued*)

CASE STUDY 8.15 (*continued*)

exist. Users were frequently authorized verbally. As a result, unauthorized users could be granted access to the networks.

It was recommended that formal LAN user authorization procedures be established. Such procedures should require written management authorization for each new user and a mechanism to ensure that terminated and transferred users are removed in a timely manner.

- In one state subsidiary, 1,802 executable application and configuration files were reviewed, and it was found that 1,527 (85 percent) did not have the read-only file attribute and 100 percent did not have the hidden file attribute. Therefore, the files were susceptible to unauthorized deletion, alteration, and copying.

  It was recommended that all application and configuration file attributes be changed to read-only and hidden.

- Physical access controls over one file server were inadequate. The server and console were located in a restricted access room. However, the room was accessible by individuals who were not network supervisors. Thus, these people could perform unauthorized functions on the file server (e.g., load unauthorized software, delete or alter software and data, system restarts, and so on).

  It was recommended that the file server consoles be physically key locked or that the "secure console" or "monitor" features be utilized to help prevent unauthorized access to the file server consoles.

- A method of monitoring network system security administrator activities had not been implemented. Therefore, there was no control to identify unauthorized activities of network system security administrators.

  It was recommended that management consider a vendor application that was capable of logging the file accesses of selected users, including network system security administrators. If adopted, a member of management or other designated person who is not a network system security administrator would be responsible for examining the report for unauthorized activities by network system security administrators.

  This particular control weakness is one of the most difficult to rectify with any system because system security administrators can often delete or modify such monitoring software by virtue of their almost unlimited system access capabilities.

CASE STUDY 8.16

Logical Security Design and Control Weaknesses for a Variety of Applications

Following is a compilation of logical security control weaknesses existing in a variety of IS environments in a number of different organizations over the years. Although many of the control weaknesses may seem redundant, they are included to demonstrate that auditors must be on the alert during every audit. Auditors must maintain a constant awareness that many systems are not designed with adequate logical security features and that system security is often inadequately administered. These weaknesses could be found in virtually any IS environment in any organization. Even if no logical security control weaknesses were identified during a previous audit, multiple weaknesses could materialize within a relatively short time, especially if the system security administrator were to transfer or terminate. These examples also demonstrate the sad state of system security design in many systems in existence today.

- During an audit of an investments management, reporting, and accounting application, it was found that user passwords were set to expire in a minimum of 6 months and a maximum of 30 years. The 30-year password belonged to the system user ID called ADMIN. The ADMIN password also had not been changed since the system was installed (four months before the audit tests were performed). This is yet another example of poor system security design. A system should not be designed to even allow the possibility of setting a password to expire in more than 90 days.
- During a review of a recently implemented mortgage loan origination system, it was noted that the system lacked a password expiration feature. Also, the original password of the system user ID had not been changed since the system was installed three months earlier.
- During an audit of a marketing database application, it was found that the passwords of all user IDs were set to expire in more than one year. One password was set to expire in 11 years.
- During an audit of a traveler's check application, it was found that the application lacked a password expiration feature and that procedures were lacking for system security administrators to change their passwords at least every 60 days. In addition, passwords of some users were less than five characters, user IDs existed for three employees who had transferred to other positions and no longer required access, a user ID existed for one terminated employee, and one user had two user IDs. To complicate matters, some user IDs were created with only the first names of the users. This made it difficult to determine which user ID belonged to which user.
- During an audit of a records indexing application, it was found that five users had passwords less than five characters. Numerous system security design weaknesses were also identified. For example: the password file was unencrypted so that passwords could be viewed by the system security administrator; there was no password expiration feature; there was no feature to automatically suspend a user session after a specified period of user inactivity; user IDs could not be suspended after consecutive unsuccessful sign-on attempts; and there was no mechanism to log system security-related events.
- An audit of a home equity real estate loan document preparation application revealed that the password of the system security administrator was only four characters long and had not been changed for over one year. These weaknesses were the result of poor logical access control design as well as poor implementation of system security administration procedures.
- An audit of a wire transfer system at a major financial institution revealed

(continued)

that five consecutive unsuccessful sign-on attempts were allowed before disabling user IDs. Setting the available system security parameter to allow only three consecutive unsuccessful sign-on attempts would have provided a more secure environment. Another example of poor system security administration procedures was the fact that the password for the system user ID had not been changed since its inception, over six years earlier.

- During an audit of a vendor payroll application, it was found that the initial system user ID and two other user IDs that were used only during the system installation process were still active on the system. However, since the system security administrator had a separate personal user ID with system security administrator access and a backup system security administrator had been designated and trained, there was no need to retain the three initial user IDs. Based on our recommendation, the three user IDs in question were deleted. The new system had been implemented about one year prior to the examination. Some systems may not allow the initial system user ID to be deleted. Others, like this system, allow the initial system user ID to be deleted but will recognize it again if the application is reinstalled.

- During yet another audit of a wire transfer application at a financial institution, it was noted that the central processing unit (CPU) supported two modems, which allowed unprotected remote dial-up access. Weaknesses were also identified in the program change control process whereby some application programmers had the ability to run certain programs in the production environment that could potentially allow posting of unauthorized transactions. It was also found that application-level logical security controls could be circumvented at the operating system level because the native operating system did not have comprehensive security features designed into it and alternative internal control procedures were not adequately implemented to help mitigate the design deficiencies.

Three alternatives for the remote access modems were recommended: remove them completely; install password-protected modems; or install dial-back devices so that access can take place only from predetermined phone numbers. It was also recommended that the access capabilities of the application programmers in question be restricted so that they could only execute programs in the test environment. A third recommendation was that the operating system vendor be notified of the logical security design deficiencies so that they could be resolved in future releases and that the system security administrators implement logging procedures to enable system security related activity to be monitored.

Credit Bureau Audit Trails Lacking

Case study 2.3 illustrates one type of situation that can arise if internal controls over the acquisition of credit reports are inadequate. Although the offending party in this particular example was identified, such identification was not the result of good internal controls. Rather, it was proper interviewing techniques and guilt on the part of the offending party that solved the case. Although this was an isolated occurrence, the financial institution was fortunate that it was not sued by the violated party or fined under the Fair Credit Reporting Act. The whole situation could have been prevented had adequate logical security controls been designed into the credit reporting information systems environment.

The unauthorized credit report was obtained via a stand-alone terminal that was directly linked to the credit bureau vendor. The terminal was located in an unrestricted area of the facility. The terminal was not designed with any logical security controls such as user IDs, passwords, or logging. Anyone who knew how to operate the terminal could have requested an unauthorized credit report. There was a second unprotected credit report terminal located elsewhere in the same building. These terminals were supposed to be used only by the centralized lending operation in the event the primary application system was inoperable and by the Collections Department for certain types of credit inquiries. All other requests were to be performed by signing on to a mainframe application that was programmed with a direct interface to the credit bureau database. However, the mainframe application lacked any sort of audit trail to associate credit inquiry requests with the user IDs. The mainframe application afforded better control than the stand-alone credit report terminals in that the requesting party had to be an authorized user. However, it was impossible to determine which mainframe users performed credit report requests.

It was recommended that management contact the credit bureau vendors to determine whether the credit report terminals could be programmed to require user IDs and passwords. If not, the terminals should either be removed or placed in locked rooms that were accessible only to authorized personnel. It was also recommended that the mainframe application be programmed to create an audit trail that associates the requesting user ID with each credit report request.

CASE STUDY 8.18

Inquiry Access Lacking

During an audit of a vendor's multipurpose banking application, which was installed at numerous financial institutions, it was noted that the application was not programmed to allow inquiry-only access to be assigned to users for most of the access functions that were designed into the system. In other words, when users were assigned access functions, they had the capability to change and update information, even though their duties may have required them only to view information. The application designers failed to design the two basic levels of access capabilities (inquiry-only and update) into the individual functions within the application, thereby making it significantly more difficult to administer system security.

(continued)

CASE STUDY 8.18 (*continued*)

For example, tellers who post transactions to customer accounts at a financial institution also typically require the ability to examine the names and addresses of customers for identification and servicing purposes. However, to properly segregate duties, tellers should not have the ability to change customer names and addresses. Name and address changes should normally be performed by staff members who do not have the ability to post monetary transactions. The reason for this segregation of duties is to reduce the risk of a teller's changing the name and address on an account and then performing an unauthorized transaction such as the creation of a cashier's check with the changed customer's name and address printed on it. (See case study 9.6 for a description of an actual fraud that occurred due to failure to enforce segregation of duties by properly administering system access capabilities.) Due to the poor design of this particular banking application, system security administrators had no choice but to assign name and address change capability to tellers because they could not assign view-only capability. At least the application was designed with audit trails to record the user ID of each person who changed customer information. However, it is more effective to prevent a problem from happening than to try to correct it after the fact.

It was recommended that a special programming request be submitted to the vendor to add the ability to provide view-only capabilities for key functions at a minimum (e.g., for viewing names and addresses and for viewing loan information). The vendor provided a customized *patch* to the application for the particular financial institution that was being audited, but the patch was not provided to other financial institutions unless they specifically requested and paid for it.

CASE STUDY 8.19

ATM Vendor Applications

During an audit of an ATM process, the adequacy of the logical security controls of three different applications, each of which served a different aspect of the ATM back office process, was assessed. The applications were supplied by the local ATM switching service vendor. System security was administered by the manager of the ATM Department at the financial institution.

ATM Vendor's Adjustment Request Application

Several design flaws and system security administration weaknesses were identified in this application, which resulted in an increased risk of unauthorized access. The design flaws were that passwords could be as short as two characters, the system security administrator could view user passwords from within the application, and a password expiration feature was lacking. The system security administration weaknesses included two employees who had transferred to other areas of the company but still had valid user IDs on the system; one user had three different valid user IDs, one of which had system security administrator access capabilities even though such access was not part of his normal duties; and one valid user ID existed for an employee who had been terminated several months earlier.

ATM Vendor's Replacement Card/PIN Application

As with the previous application, weaknesses were found in both system security design and administration. The design issues were that passwords could be as short as four characters and a password expiration feature was not available. The system security administration control weaknesses included the fact that five users were granted system access capability, which enabled them to purge the audit log file of system security-related events and to perform application screen design functions. In addition, the original system diskettes were stored in the user documentation manual instead of in a locked location.

ATM Vendor's Hotcarding Application

System security design flaws and administration weaknesses were also evident in this system. The design flaws included passwords that could be as short as zero characters and the lack of a password expiration feature. Control weaknesses that could have been avoided with proper system security administration procedures included the fact that one user had system security administrator access capabilities that were not required as part of her normal duties, the system security administrator had a 20-minute session time-out parameter setting instead of 5 minutes like the other users, and all user IDs were named after department positions rather than user names. This last control weakness was operationally workable so long as the position names were unique and passwords were not shared by multiple users. But the practice of assigning the user's actual name to user IDs provides a better audit trail.

Summary of ATM Vendor Applications

Obviously, from the number and types of design flaws described for each of the three applications, system security was not a primary consideration during the design phase of their development. The ATM Department compounded the system security design flaws by failing to implement adequate system security administration procedures.

It was recommended that management of the ATM Department send a letter to the ATM switching service vendor, requesting that each of the identified security design flaws be corrected in future releases of the ATM applications. It was also recommended that ATM Department management resolve the identified control weaknesses and implement procedures to help ensure that similar control weaknesses do not occur again.

NOTES

1. See the discussion and examples on backup system security administrators in Chapter 7 for some examples of why their activities need to be limited.
2. Pete Loshin, "IP: The Next Generation," *Information Security* (October 1998): 21.
3. The technical reason is that VPN security occurs at a lower level in the ISO (International Organization for Standardization) OSI (Open Systems Interconnect) model.

The ISO model has seven layers that are commonly referred to as a "stack." Starting from highest to lowest, the layers are: Application, Presentation, Session, Transport, Network, Data Link, Physical. VPN security occurs at the network layer while SSL security occurs at the transport layer.

4. Christopher M. King, CISSP, "The 8 Hurdles to VPN Deployment," *Information Security* (March 1999): 23.
5. Ibid.
6. "Lax Security Leads to Wire Transfer Loss," *Bank Fraud, Bulletin of Fraud and Risk Management* (April 1996): 2–3.
7. "Russian Computer Expert Charged with Citibank Security Breach," *Bloomberg News Service* (August 21, 1995).
8. "Citibank Hit by Fraudulent Transfers," *Infosecurity News* (November/December 1995): 12.
9. "Former ABN Amro Employee Charged with Embezzling $1.9 Million," *Bloomberg News Service* (May 31, 1995).
10. "Office Manager Pleads Guilty to Massive Embezzlement," *The Credit Union Accountant* (September 13, 1993): 5.
11. Martha Woodcock, "Costly Crimes Could Be Thwarted by Simple Measures," *Credit Union Times* (March 15, 1995): 19.

CHAPTER 9

Information Systems Operations

This chapter briefly discusses how to audit information systems (IS) operations from a broad perspective. It also includes examples of a variety of real-world internal control weaknesses and inefficiencies pertaining to IS operations. Some of the computer operation controls discussed in this chapter are closely related to physical security controls, which are discussed in greater detail in Chapter 7.

Information systems operations include internal controls at data processing facilities as well as those in place in end-user environments, which are designed to help an organization's operational processes function as efficiently and effectively as possible within the constraints imposed by the economic, financial, political, legal, and regulatory environments. Because all operations throughout an organization are interdependent, auditors should not view IS operations as completely separate functions from the other operations within an organization. They are all essentially part of the same large "information system." They form one comprehensive input, processing, and output engine working toward achieving the organization's long-range strategic objectives. Therefore, when examining IS operations, auditors should consider the overall impacts of inefficiencies and ineffective procedures on the organization's ability to achieve its long-term objectives.

With the proliferation of distributed data processing systems in recent years, IS operations of various scales have materialized at multiple locations within most organizations. Computers and related peripheral hardware devices can exist centrally, as at a large data center, as well as at every physical location in a company, as in the case of a wide-area-network (WAN) that enables all processes within an organization to electronically exchange information. Within these IS operations, each functional area is responsible for conducting its processes in a responsibly controlled manner. Because of how widespread IS operations are, all auditors should be familiar with the approaches that are necessary to assess their adequacy. To provide a high-level approach, IS operations within an organization can be divided into two interrelated components: computer operations and business operations.

COMPUTER OPERATIONS

Computer operations consist of those IS processes that ensure that input data is processed in an efficient and effective manner to support the strategic objectives and business operations of an organization. A typical computer operations audit should include assessments of internal controls that ensure that:

- Production jobs are completed in a timely manner and production capacity is sufficient to meet short- and long-range processing needs
- Output media are distributed in a timely, accurate, and secure manner
- Backup and recovery procedures adequately protect data and programs against accidental or intentional loss or destruction
- Maintenance procedures adequately protect computer hardware against failure
- Computer hardware, software, and data are insured at replacement cost
- Problem management procedures ensure that system problems are documented and resolved in a timely and effective manner

Production Job Scheduling and Monitoring

Automated job-scheduling and initiation software can significantly enhance operational efficiency by automatically initiating the next scheduled production program immediately on completion of the previous program. Each job should be assigned a priority number (e.g., one through nine, with one having the highest priority), which enables the job-scheduling software to initiate programs with the highest priorities first. While computer operators still need to monitor the program queue for abnormal program failures and may occasionally need to alter the sequence of program initiation, this kind of software significantly reduces the need for computer operators to manually initiate each program, thereby freeing them to perform other duties. Automated job-scheduling software also reduces the risk that a computer operator may run a program out of sequence or forget to run one altogether. When a program is run out of sequence or not run at all, subsequent data output may not be correct because it is dependent on updated data from the program that should have been completed previously.

To monitor the effectiveness of the automated job-scheduling software, management of the computer operations area should receive a system-generated daily production report indicating the start and end times of each job, preferably with a comparison to the planned production schedule, and any job that abnormally terminated. This information provides management with a tool to independently assess whether jobs are being completed in a timely manner and in accordance with the preapproved schedule. Problems may identify a need to alter the sequence in which jobs are scheduled in order to more efficiently utilize system processing capabilities. Management can also observe whether a large number of jobs are abnormally terminating. Such activity could indicate a system programming problem or the need to expand the production capacity of the system hardware.

Other monitoring controls that should exist include periodically examining the amount of available disk storage and the dynamic system capacity utilization. Examining the amount of available disk storage space is similar to checking the amount of disk space available on the hard drive of a personal computer. Dynamic system capacity utilization is more difficult to determine. This monitoring control involves tracking the percentage of total system processing capacity that is used over a specific time period, such as one day, one week, one month, or one year. It is preferable for a system to automatically log this information and generate management reports for the desired periods. This information can assist management in scheduling system maintenance, planning production schedules, and identifying when the system is reaching a capacity utilization level that requires upgrading of the system to accommodate higher volumes of data processing. Some more sophisticated systems can be programmed to page or e-mail a system administrator if a predetermined processing capacity or data storage threshold is exceeded.

Case study 9.1 depicts some internal control weaknesses related to job scheduling and monitoring in the computer operations area of one organization. It includes CS 9.1 which is a 10-hour snapshot of the kind of report that management could use to monitor the data storage and dynamic processing capacities of a specific network central processing unit (CPU). Note that CPU capacity began to rise dramatically after 8 A.M., when workers began logging on to the network and performing various functions. Peak CPU processing occurred between 10 A.M. and noon, when work productivity was at its peak. At noon there was an expected dip as workers went to lunch, with another increase as workers returned from lunch. After 2 P.M. CPU processing dropped significantly as workers began wrapping up their day.

Total data storage capacity fluctuations were generally much flatter than CPU processing fluctuations. Capacity peaked at 10 A.M., presumably as peak worker productivity required the temporary saving of multiple new data files. By 4 P.M. total data storage capacity utilization dropped back down almost to its original 6 A.M. level, as network users purged excess and unnecessary data files prior to the end of their workday. Unfortunately, many systems do not provide the ability to dynamically monitor system capacity utilization.

CASE STUDY 9.1

Lack of Automated Job Scheduling Software and Capacity Utilization Monitoring Controls

During an audit of the Computer Operations Department of an organization, it was noted that programs were being manually executed by computer operators. On completion of a job, the system would remain idle until a computer operator entered the name of the next job. The fact that jobs were not

(continued)

CASE STUDY 9.1 (*continued*)

automatically executed created the risk that an operator could initiate a job out of sequence or could forget to initiate a job entirely. Also, if an operator becomes preoccupied with another problem, he or she may not notice when a job abnormally terminates. This situation can cause serious delays in the production schedule if a large job that takes hours to run were to terminate and the operator did not realize it for an extended period of time. As a result, there were significant opportunities for enhancing the efficiency and effectiveness of job scheduling and initiation.

The system software application was licensed from a vendor, and the vendor reportedly offered a module that would enable automated job scheduling and initiation with the existing application. Therefore, it was recommended that management of the Computer Operations Department contact the vendor to determine whether it would be cost effective to acquire the automated job-scheduling and initiation software.

There also were no reports or other controls to enable the Computer Operations Department to dynamically monitor the system capacity utilization during specified periods. In this particular case, management reported that the vendor, which was also a licensed hardware reseller for the computer being used by the organization, could supply a report of dynamic system capacity

EXHIBIT CS9.1   DAILY CPU AND DATA STORAGE CAPACITY UTILIZATION

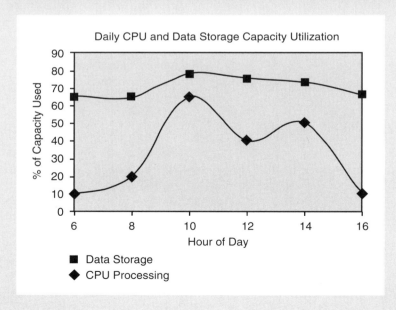

utilization, showing high and low points of computing output during a desired period. Unfortunately, management reported that the vendor could supply the report only on an individual-request basis, not on an ongoing basis. Furthermore, management in the Computer Operations Department did not consider the lack of such a report to be a significant concern. They felt that they were well aware of the system performance and knew when they would need to upgrade. Although we knew that management did not concur with our recommendation, we still recommended that management consider working with the vendor to generate periodic reports showing system capacity utilization over time. In this way, we documented the fact that we had identified this issue and presented a viable recommendation to management, even if they chose not to implement any changes.

A primitive but sometimes effective alternative to monitoring system performance on an exception basis is to examine the number and types of calls to the system help desk. If a system is slow to respond or if it completely shuts down due to overcapacity or other problems, users inevitably call the help desk to inquire when the system will be up and running again or to simply complain. If these calls are accurately logged as to time and classification of problem type, a representative graph of when system performance degrades can be created. However, the graph would not identify periods of low system capacity utilization. Such information helps IS managers identify when certain system activities (e.g., batch programs) could be performed to more optimally utilize system capacity.

Output Media Distribution

Many production jobs result in the creation of electronic output files. These output files are stored in a temporary queue sometimes referred to as a SPOOL, which stands for "simultaneous peripheral operation online." Output files in the SPOOL can be printed, copied to another directory, or both, depending on the requirements of the data owners. These activities should be performed by an output distribution area in a timely manner so that the data owners can effectively utilize the information. Output files should also be purged from the SPOOL on a regular basis, typically within one or two days, in order to free up disk storage space.

Physical output media (paper printouts, microfiche, and microfilm) should be strictly controlled to ensure that unauthorized personnel are not able to view or acquire sensitive information. Similarly, logical access to the SPOOL files should be granted only to necessary computer operations staff and system security administrators. This is an important control because an unauthorized user with access to the SPOOL could quickly view, copy, and possibly alter a wide variety of data files containing sensitive information.

Case study 9.2 illustrates how sensitive information was compromised, much to the embarrassment of an Internal Audit Department.

CASE STUDY 9.2

Unprotected SPOOL File

The Internal Audit Department of a large, multibranch financial institution performed surprise branch audits commencing on Mondays. Certain financial activity reports were generated by the Internal Audit Department during the middle of the previous week so the printouts would be available by the Friday before the audit was to begin.

A user at the data center possessed system access capabilities that enabled her to view the SPOOL containing recently completed production programs, including those of the Internal Audit Department. From her experience, the user knew that certain standard reports were initiated each week by the Internal Audit Department in advance of performing surprise branch audits. Since the user had a friend who was a branch internal auditor, she thought she would flaunt her knowledge by looking in the SPOOL for the internal audit reports to find out which branch was being audited the following week. Then, on Monday morning, before the auditors had arrived for their surprise audit, the woman called the branch and left a message for the branch auditor. This obviously removed any element of surprise from the audit. The auditor received her message shortly after the audit commenced, much to the dismay of the auditor in charge.

The user at the data center was reprimanded for her actions, and controls were put in place whereby internal audit output files were automatically moved to a restricted directory upon completion of the programs to prevent similar occurrences.

Backup and Recovery Procedures

As discussed in Chapter 7, every organization should have a business resumption plan. As part of the plan, procedures should exist to adequately protect data and programs against accidental or intentional loss or destruction. The primary controls to provide this protection are to perform periodic (daily, weekly, monthly) backups of system software, application programs, and data as well as storage and rotation of the backup media such as magnetic tapes, disks, and compact disks (CDs) to a secure off-site location. Daily backups are usually necessary only for data since the application programs and system software do not change significantly. Full backups of the entire system, including system software, application programs, and data, should be performed weekly or monthly, depending on the number and types of changes that have been made. Full system backups should also be performed on completion of a major upgrade or significant changes to the operational and security parameters of a system. Furthermore, management should ensure that tests are performed to confirm that system operations can in fact be fully restored using the backup media. This is one test that is often overlooked. See Chapter 7 for additional information and examples on the topics of periodic backups and business resumption programs.

Maintenance Procedures

All computer hardware should be serviced according to the manufacturer's recommendations as specified in the contract with the hardware vendor. Maintenance procedures should adequately protect computer hardware against failure over the expected useful life of the equipment. In most instances, proper maintenance is also a requirement in order for manufacturer's warranties on the equipment performance to remain in effect. For this reason, it is important that every organization maintain accurate records of all maintenance performed. Depending on the type of equipment deployed in an organization, vendor technicians or subcontractors may need to perform the necessary maintenance services. If so, the costs and availability of routine and nonroutine maintenance procedures should be documented in the contract with the vendor or subcontractor. Before allowing maintenance services to be performed by in-house technicians, management should review the contract terms to ensure that any warranties will not be invalidated if nonvendor technicians perform the maintenance. The contract may allow nonvendor technicians to perform the maintenance but require them to be a certified expert in the technology being maintained for the warranty to remain in effect.

Insurance

As discussed in Chapter 7, every organization should purchase insurance in an amount that adequately covers all computer hardware and software at replacement cost, the costs to re-create any lost data, and possibly the value of lost revenues that are the direct result of computer hardware or software failures. The insurance policy may require that routine maintenance procedures specified by the computer manufacturers be performed in order for coverage to remain in effect. The policy may also specify that daily, weekly, and monthly software and data backups be created and stored at a secure off-site location. Deductibles should be set at levels that provide a reasonable balance between annual premiums and the overall coverage amount. See Chapter 7 for additional information and examples on insurance coverage.

Problem Management

The number and types of system problems that arise should be carefully logged to help ensure that system problems are documented and resolved in a timely and effective manner. Some organizations maintain a central Help Desk Department that fields various user telephone inquiries, including those pertaining to system problems. Other organizations may require the process owners of each system to field and resolve their own system problems. In either case, all system problems should be logged, preferably in an electronic format that facilitates management review and that can be provided to system vendors for use in troubleshooting the causes of any problems. Types of information that should be logged include the date and time the problem was reported; a description of the problem; the name, title, department, e-mail address, and telephone number of the individual reporting the problem; and the action steps taken by the person fielding the report. Actions may include resolving the problem over the phone, referring the problem to a technician, or escalating the problem to a manager. Follow-up procedures should exist whereby a designated person in the problem resolution area or help desk tracks each action step taken after the initial report and records it in the log until the problem has been resolved. Even minor system problems should be noted in the log since a high incidence of minor problems may be a precursor to more serious problems. If a particular problem cannot be resolved, the reason should be recorded in the log.

On a periodic basis, (e.g., weekly), a management report of system problems should be prepared. The report should classify problems as to type and severity to enable management to determine the frequency and urgency of the problems that occurred over the period under review. Unresolved problems should be highlighted, especially those that have not been corrected for an extended period of time. The report should be reviewed by management in affected areas. Significant problem trends and other related system performance issues should be communicated to vendors, technicians, and other appropriate parties.

BUSINESS OPERATIONS

Business operations consist of all other functions within an organization besides those in the computer operations area. Business operations areas typically provide input data to the computer operations area and utilize the resulting output in their daily processes. Business operations audits should include assessments of the adequacy of internal controls pertaining to all significant aspects of the particular process under consideration. Obviously, the number and types of internal controls in a business operation will vary greatly depending on the type of business or process being audited. In the operating environments of almost every organization, there are many end-user IS controls. These controls must function in tandem with traditional centralized computer operations controls to adequately protect the organization against unauthorized system access and to help ensure that business operations are being carried out in an efficient and effective manner. In other words, internal controls in centralized computer operations areas complement those in business operating units, and vice versa. Neither can function effectively without the other. As mentioned at the beginning of this chapter, computer operations and business operations together comprise the IS operations of an organization. It is true that an organization's internal control environment is only as strong as its weakest component.

Information systems controls existing in business operating environments can pertain to each of the three basic electronic data processing categories: input, processing, and output. But there are other controls impacting information systems that are critical to the effective functioning of business operations. Several examples of business operations controls likely to be encountered are presented next.

Edit and Reasonableness Checks

To help prevent invalid data from being entered into a system, many systems are programmed with automated *edit and reasonableness checks.* For example, edit checks can prevent letters from being entered into a field that should only have numbers, or vice versa. Edit checks can also prevent invalid codes from being entered into a particular field and can prevent dates or amounts outside of predetermined ranges from being entered. Some systems require a second data entry person to rekey some or all of the data that was key-entered by the original data entry person and will accept the data only if both sets of data are exactly the same.

Alternatively, edit checks can be detective in nature. In other words, edit controls can be manual or after the fact. For example, a system may generate a data entry report that must be compared to the original input documents to identify any errors, or a system may accept and attempt to process all the data originally entered and generate exception reports in which key-entered data did not meet prescribed standards or filters. The recipient of the exception reports must then enter the necessary corrections to the original data. Detective IS controls are usually less efficient and effective than preventive controls because they require additional action and thus slow down the overall process.

Integrity/Completeness Checks

When large volumes of data are electronically imported from or exported to other systems, data integrity and completeness controls can provide reasonable assurance that the recipient has received all the data intact, without any alterations or missing information. *Control totals* are the most common form of integrity/completeness check. The sender provides the recipient with control totals, such as the total number of records in the data file and the total dollar amount of the records. When the recipient processes the data, the total number and dollar amount of items received can be compared with those provided by the sender to determine whether there could be missing or altered records. However, control totals may not identify instances in which records have been altered in a field other than the amount. For example, a destination account number or customer name may be changed to that of an unauthorized account. In this case, the total number and dollar amount of the original records would not be changed and thus would not be identified by basic control totals.

Hash Totals

Hash totals are a common form of integrity/completeness control that can reduce the exposure to altered records. A hash total is simply a number that is calculated based on a key field that does not normally have numeric calculations performed on it. For example, a simple hash total formula may add the account numbers or invoice numbers of every record in a data file. An alteration to even one of the account or invoice numbers would cause the hash total to change. When the recipient rehashes the data received, the total would not agree with the hash total supplied by the sender, thus alerting the recipient to a possible unauthorized change or unintentional scrambling of data during the transmission process. More complex hash totals that utilize arithmetic algorithms to calculate variations and combinations of multiple fields can be designed. The results may even be encrypted prior to transmission or transport. The basic objective is the same as with simple hash totals.

Segregation of Duties

When examining a business operation or traditional centralized IS processes such as computer operations, systems development, and program change control, one of the most critical internal control objectives is segregation of duties. Duties must be properly segregated to adequately protect an organization from unauthorized access to information, loss of physical or financial assets, and a myriad of other potential risks. Segregation of duties can therefore exist in data entry areas, data processing areas, and in business operating areas in which processing output is utilized. Segregation of duties can be most effectively enforced through the proper deployment and administration of system access capabilities. (See Chapter 8 for a complete discussion of system access controls.) Implementation of strong procedural controls is equally as critical but more difficult to enforce because of the increased possibility of human error or distraction. As will be seen in some of the examples later in this chapter, segregation of duties is where business operations often falter.

Efficiency/Effectiveness Controls

Within any business operation, there are almost always opportunities to enhance efficiency and effectiveness by automating manual procedures. Management may often overlook obvious opportunities because they are preoccupied with meeting ongoing deadlines and dealing with day-to-day operational issues. Ironically, if management were to automate some of their most difficult and time-consuming processes, they would enhance their ability to meet deadlines and reduce the severity of the operational difficulties that are causing them the most grief.

Internal Database Balancing and Monitoring

Management reports and other information that are derived from internally generated databases are only as reliable as the data from which they originate. Many organizations create *extract databases* for use in preparing various types of specialized reports. Extract databases, which are essentially copies of original production databases, enable multiple end-user areas to prepare customized reports and perform various database analyses and other operations without impacting the production operations. Extract databases thus make the information available to a greater number of users within an organization who, through their analyses, can help their organization more effectively attain its objectives. Security over the information must obviously be tight to ensure that the information is not compromised. An additional, perhaps more critical concern is that the extract program creates an accurate database. Otherwise, information and analysis results derived from the extract database may be incomplete or meaningless, possibly resulting in material misstatements of information or poor strategic decisions.

Inadequate Support of End-User Applications

Customized computer application programs are being developed at an alarming rate in end-user areas. Many of these applications are created by individuals who have a limited amount of technical training. As a result, documentation as to the logic and design of the applications is usually limited or nonexistent. Then, when the developer transfers or terminates, so does all the knowledge about how to support the application. Some end-user applications are relatively simple and can easily be re-created and even improved when the developer leaves. There are also many highly complex applications upon which end-user organizations have become highly dependent. If the developer transferred or terminated and a problem arose, management could be seen frantically trying to contact the previous developer. The resulting impacts on the business operations could have been avoided had management required the developer to take the time to clearly document the application from the very beginning so that another person with reasonable knowledge about the development language or software could support the application.

Case studies 9.3 through 9.7 illustrate some of the many types of IS internal control weaknesses and inefficiencies that may be encountered within the business operations of an organization. For auditors, it is important to look for these types of opportunities to demonstrate their value to management as business consultants who can contribute to the achievement of strategic objectives.

CASE STUDY 9.3

Erroneous Automated Clearing House Effective Entry Date Posting Using Electronic Batch Header Information

During an examination of the automated clearing house (ACH) process within a financial institution, it was noted that some ACH transactions were incorrectly being posted to customer accounts as of the "effective entry dates" supplied by the merchants rather than the "settlement dates," which are the dates that the sending and receiving financial institutions exchange funds to settle the net totals of all debit and credit ACH transactions. Each day ACH transactions are received by the financial institution via an electronic data download from the Federal Reserve's host computer system (Fedwire). Merchants that

(continued)

CASE STUDY 9.3 (*continued*)

originate ACH transactions (e.g., Social Security Administration, various pension plans, utilities, insurance companies, health clubs) supply effective entry dates in the electronic ACH batch header information. Other information included in the electronic ACH record for each transaction includes customer name, customer account number, transaction amount, merchant name, and other pertinent information.[a] No flaws in the format or content of the ACH data received from the Federal Reserve were identified.

However, at the receiving institution that was being audited, it was found that the ACH posting application program was incorrectly designed to post ACH transactions to customer accounts using vendor effective entry dates instead of financial institution settlement dates. This method of posting is in violation of National Automated Clearing House (NACHA) operating rules and regulations. In some cases, the effective entry dates were 30 to 45 days prior to the settlement dates. Thus, the ACH posting application "backdated" ACH transactions. For debits to interest-bearing checking and savings accounts, customers were being paid 30 to 45 days' less interest than they were entitled to receive. Conversely, for credits to interest-bearing checking and savings accounts, customers were being paid too much interest, although this second situation is less common because customers tend to complain when large ACH deposits are not processed immediately. Backdating of ACH transactions also provides inaccurate information to customers by making it appear on their statements that transactions should have been posted earlier when in fact they were being posted on the proper dates (i.e., the settlement dates). Analysis of backdated ACH transactions during the month of the audit revealed that 8,718 debits totaling over $2.8 million were backdated as many as 40 days while 868 credits totaling over $723,000 were backdated up to 14 days. The financial institution had been incorrectly backdating ACH transactions for years.

It was recommended that a programming change be made to the ACH posting application so that transactions are posted using the settlement date instead of merchant effective entry dates. A postaudit follow-up with management of the ACH Department was performed to confirm that the recommendation had been implemented. Management stated that the change had been implemented, and no further testing was performed.

During a subsequent audit three years later, it was expected that the ACH batch header control weakness identified in the previous audit had, in fact, been corrected so that ACH transactions were being posted as of the settlement dates. Unfortunately, the original batch header control weakness still existed. In other words, there had been absolutely no change in ACH programming or procedures related to the batch header problem. The current manager speculated that the original weakness had been corrected shortly after the first audit but that a subsequent oversight had occurred that resulted in the original control weakness rematerializing. However, the manager could not provide any evidence of such an occurrence. The original control weak-

---

[a]The exact record layout is determined by the National Automated Clearing House Association (NACHA), which establishes ACH operating rules and regulations.

ness had in fact never been resolved—apparently because the manager during the first audit had transferred to another area. The incoming manager had limited ACH knowledge and experience at the time and was preoccupied with understanding the operations. The new manager was not able to reliably determine whether the ACH batch header control weakness had been resolved.

In this particular situation, the Internal Audit Department erred by considering a verbal follow-up to the original recommendation to be adequate. Since the method of resolution was straightforward and since there were no financial penalties for failure to comply with ACH operating rules and regulations, the risk of the recommendation's not being adequately implemented was considered low. However, spending the time to visually confirm just one day's ACH transaction posting history could have identified the failure to implement the recommendation more than two years earlier.

This case study illustrates the need for internal audit departments to evaluate their methods of confirming whether recommendations have been implemented. For low-risk, less significant recommendations, verbal confirmations are usually adequate. Recommendations to resolve medium- and high-risk control weaknesses should be confirmed through limited testing. This situation was more of a moderate-risk situation, which obviously should have had more than just a verbal confirmation performed.

CASE STUDY 9.4

Mergers Resulting in Oversights in Business Operations

During the many mergers and acquisitions that occurred during the 1980s and 1990s, the opportunity for IS operation oversights to occur were many. Often one merger was followed by another and then another. Information systems managers were hard-pressed to keep up with the acquisitions and subsequent conversions, let alone to adequately perform the conversions. This case study is a typical example of how mergers can negatively affect the IS operations of various organizations.

Corporation B is in the middle of absorbing the data processing operations of a recently acquired subsidiary, Corporation A, when it itself is acquired by another organization, Corporation C. Understandably, the staff members in Corporation B who are responsible for absorbing the IS operations of Corporation A become more concerned with self-preservation and salvaging their own jobs and careers than performing a thorough conversion of Corporation A's systems. They perform only limited testing while searching for new jobs in other departments and companies. Inevitably, significant IS testing and related operational issues are overlooked. Then Corporation C's IS operations have to absorb the IS operations of Corporation B, including the inadequately absorbed IS operations of Corporation A. The situation is further complicated when a fourth organization, Corporation D, begins proceedings to acquire Corporation C.

(continued)

CASE STUDY 9.4 (*continued*)

Although seemingly far-fetched, this is exactly the situation I observed during the 1980s. Many of my colleagues were working for a now-extinct bank called Rainier Bancorporation. Rainier was a highly profitable regional bank holding company headquartered in the State of Washington with assets of over $9 billion. Rainier had been actively acquiring small banks in the region and converting their banking application systems to its own. In 1987, Rainier was purchased by Security Pacific Bancorporation of Los Angeles. Security Pacific, which had assets of over $60 billion prior to the acquisition, began the arduous task of swallowing the information systems of Rainier Bancorporation. Then, in the early 1990s, Security Pacific Bancorporation, with assets of over $90 billion at the time, was itself acquired by Bank of America. Bank of America is now one of the largest and most successful bank holding companies in the United States.[a]

On the surface, the end result appears to be a highly profitable bank holding company that was able to successfully absorb the IS operations of all of the previously merged companies. Due to the sheer dollar size of these acquisitions, the previous statement is true. However, millions of dollars in immaterial operational losses slipped through the cracks virtually unnoticed. Executives of these corporations may have expected large "merger losses" to occur and probably considered them to be an acceptable cost of doing business, so long as their impact was not *material* to the financial statements. However, what constitutes a *few* million dollars to management of megacorporations end up as lost potential dividends and reduced stock value to shareholders. There is also ample opportunity for dishonest acts to go undetected. On the positive side, some of these losses ended up benefiting small consumers who were customers of the acquired banks. Many of the losses may not have been preventable during the acquisitions as management and staff scrambled to keep systems running while making any difficulties as transparent to customers as possible. However, many of the losses could have been readily detected after the fact using relatively simple computer-assisted audit tests, including various database queries. Recovery procedures could then have been implemented. Two examples of operational losses that occurred as a direct result of oversights during the aforementioned merger and acquisition process are presented:

1. *Former employees with current employee rates on credit cards.* Many people were laid off during the mergers in the 1980s. While employed at their existing banks, they were granted reduced interest rates and annual fees on their credit cards. Many of these people were still receiving the employee rates and annual fees on their credit cards, even though they had not been employed with these banks for over 10 years. The number of former employees who are benefiting from this oversight is unknown. However, there are tens of thousands of former employees of the banks mentioned, many of whom were laid off during the mergers.

2. *401(k) retirement savings plan fiasco.* Each of the corporations previously discussed provided a 401(k) supplemental retirement savings plan to em-

---

[a]Bank of America and Nations Bank merged in 1998.

ployees. Each plan was independently administered by separate organizations with different information systems prior to the mergers. Through each merger, the 401(k) assets of the acquired corporations had to be absorbed into the 401(k) assets of the acquiring organization or distributed to former employees. Complicating the process was the delay that occurs during the settlement of 401(k) activity that employees were initiating (sometimes up to six months), collection of 401(k) loan payments and related activity, and settlement and collection of 401(k) investment earnings. In short, consolidating multiple 401(k) plans is no simple task.

In several instances, 401(k) distributions were granted to laid-off employees of the corporations that exceeded the amounts due to them, in some cases by over 30 percent. As with the employee fee situation described above, none of these differences has ever been detected and the total number of people who benefited from this weakness is unknown.

These types of business operational losses bring into question the adequacy of the internal controls over the 401(k) plans and how well they were managed. The losses were more than likely borne by the other 401(k) participants, not the corporations themselves.

Situations similar to those described in case studies 9.3 and 9.4 exist in the IS environments of companies all over the world, both large and small, that actively acquire other organizations. Business operations losses like these are the types of low-hanging fruit that auditors can identify by using computer-assisted audit techniques. For example, database queries of all former employee accounts could identify cases like those just described. Identification of just a few significant IS weaknesses that affected thousands of employees could recover substantial sums for their organizations and reemphasize the value of internal audits to senior management.

CASE STUDY 9.5

Credit Bureau Update Tapes Created at Wrong Time

During an audit of the process by which credit report information was updated by a financial institution, it was noted that the Data Processing (DP) Department was creating monthly credit bureau update tapes on the weekend *prior* to the 15th of each month. Since many loans had a payment date of the 15th, this procedure caused loans on which payments were made after the tape creation date but prior to the 16th of the month to be reported to credit bureaus as delinquent, even though they were current. This procedure consequently resulted in unnecessary credit bureau disputes between customers and the financial institution.

(continued)

CASE STUDY 9.5 (*continued*)

A simple timing change was recommended, whereby the DP Department began creating the credit bureau update tapes on the first Sunday after the 15th of each month. This procedure was implemented during the audit and had no significant effect on resources in the DP Department. In addition, the credit bureau resolution area of the financial institution and many of its customers were relieved of a significant amount of potential grief.

CASE STUDY 9.6

Combination Loan/Automated Teller Machine Fraud Resulting from Inadequate Segregation of Duties

Two fraudulent loans totaling over $30,000 were perpetrated by a former employee of a financial institution, who will be referred to as Susie. Susie was responsible for disbursing funds for approved consumer loans and was granted various system access capabilities commensurate with her duties. Susie was also granted system access capabilities that enabled her to change customer addresses in the financial institution's customer information database. This access capability was commonly granted to most employees of the financial institution. In fact, at one time, over 90 percent of the financial institution's employees could change customer addresses. Furthermore, Susie had the system access capability to view confidential customer information necessary to order replacement automated teller machine (ATM) cards and personal identification numbers (PINs) for customers as well as the capability to perform deposits to inactive accounts. With such a wide variety of system access capabilities, it was only a matter of time before someone perpetrated a fraud in the financial institution. This particular scheme was very ingenious.

Susie disbursed two fraudulent loans totaling over $30,000 to two different inactive accounts. The inactive accounts previously had minimal balances of under $10. The financial institution did not have the classic control to monitor inactive account activity. Susie set up the loans so that automatic payments would come from the accounts to which the principal amounts had been credited. She prepared loan files containing a limited number of falsified documents for the two fraudulent loans, being careful to limit the amount of handwriting. Due to the large volume of loans being disbursed from the financial institution's centralized loan operation, the classic internal control whereby loan officers review all consumer loans disbursed for accuracy and propriety were lacking. In fact, not even a sample of the loans was being independently reviewed. Thus, Susie's disbursement of two unauthorized loans to the inactive customer accounts went unnoticed. Susie then changed the addresses of the two inactive accounts on the customer information database to that of post office boxes that she had previously opened under the names of the inactive accountholders. Since the inactive account customers had so little funds, they did not notice that they were no longer receiving their monthly statements. The final step in Susie's scheme was to call the Customer Service

Department and order replacement ATM cards and PINs. The cards and PINs were conveniently mailed to the fraudulent post office boxes. As you can probably surmise, Susie used the cards and PINs to acquire cash from ATMs. Since she was an employee, Susie knew which ATMs had cameras and which did not. She therefore obtained maximum daily cash withdrawals from various cameraless ATMs, going back nearly every day for several weeks. The financial institution also lacked the classic ATM fraud prevention control of monitoring accounts for maximum daily withdrawal activity.

But Susie was not an overly greedy thief. After withdrawing slightly more than half of the $30,000 in fraudulent loans, she discontinued making ATM withdrawals and left the financial institution. This enabled the remaining balances in the previously inactive accounts to pay the monthly loan payments, thereby making the loans appear to be current and active. After about two more years, the funds in the accounts ran out and the loans became delinquent. When the Collections Department contacted the actual customers of the inactive accounts, neither one knew to what loans the collectors were referring. The customers stated that they never applied for any loans at the financial institution. The fraud had finally been discovered.

By this time, much of the incriminating evidence was cold. For example, visual identification by the postal clerks who opened the post office boxes or persons using the ATMs before or after any of the fraudulent withdrawals was impossible. The loan documents had insufficient handwriting to draw any conclusions. There were no ATM camera pictures. All that could be proven was that Susie had credited the two inactive accounts with loan disbursements. Since disbursing funds was her job, she could have countered that she was just doing what she was told and that someone else had falsified the documents. Susie was never prosecuted and her whereabouts are now unknown.

Needless to say, the *classic internal controls* mentioned above are now strongly in place at the victimized financial institution.

CASE STUDY 9.7

Unsupported End-User Application

A financial institution's primary mainframe-based loan application was designed only to accommodate open-end loan applications, which comprised a vast majority of the loans approved at the institution. Since the institution approved a relatively low number of closed-end loans, it contracted with a small local vendor to develop a microcomputer-based software application that generated disclosure statements for closed-end loans. The user would need only to enter certain information and the application would print disclosure information onto standard disclosure forms that were manually fed into the printer. As the financial institution grew and legal requirements for disclosure statements changed, so did the need to revise the application because the software was inflexible and inefficient. For example, it was not Windows

(continued)

> **CASE STUDY 9.7 (*continued*)**
>
> based, the only way to exit the program was to reboot the microcomputer, there was no user help function, and the software could be updated only by the vendor. Furthermore, there was no user or instruction manual. Unfortunately, the vendor was no longer in business and was not available to make changes to the application. The financial institution also did not own the source code and therefore had to rely on the developer to change it.
>
> It was recommended that management solicit bids for a replacement disclosure software application from at least three reputable and qualified vendors with proven track records in the industry. Contracts with these vendors should specify that the source code be held in escrow so that, in the event the vendor goes out of business or otherwise violates a significant aspect of the contract, the financial institution is awarded the original source code. Alternatively, it was recommended that management assess the feasibility and timeliness of having the software programmed internally, depending on internal resource availability.

EFFICIENCY AND EFFECTIVENESS OF INFORMATION SYSTEMS IN BUSINESS OPERATIONS

Auditors should always be on the lookout for opportunities to recommend automation of previously manual procedures to increase operational efficiency. Management is often so concerned with day-to-day operations that they overlook automation opportunities. In some cases, management may not be aware of new technologies that would enable an operation to be automated with relative ease. In other cases, management in business units may look to the Internal Audit Department to assist in being heard by management of the IS development process. Internal auditors can reinforce a business operation's justification for a programming request to automate a procedure. This is not to say that an operation should automate simply for the sake of automating. There must be concrete evidence that the benefits of automation will outweigh the costs of designing and programming the system.

The same arguments can be made for effectiveness opportunities. Sometimes a process may already be automated or a system may be providing automated information, but the quality of the service or end product could be enhanced through a change in the automation process. For example, customers may be receiving automated transaction statements or invoices, but the information on the documents may be unclear or confusing. In this case, a change in the type or clarity of information provided would make the statements and invoices more effective for customers.

Quite often, efficiency improvements concurrently provide enhancements to the effectiveness of an operation. Case studies 9.8 through 9.13 present examples where opportunities to enhance the efficiency and/or effectiveness of business operations by implementing automated solutions were identified during internal audits.

CASE STUDY 9.8

Wire Transfer Automation

During an audit of a wire transfer operation at a financial institution, it was noted that incoming wires were being manually posted to customer accounts. The incoming wire information was electronically transmitted from the Federal Reserve to the financial institution's personal computer (PC)–based wire transfer application. An analysis of recent incoming wire transfer volume revealed that the Wire Transfer Department was manually posting an average of about 200 wires per day. This volume extrapolates to about 1,000 wires per week or approximately 50,000 manually posted wires annually. As the financial institution continued to grow, the volume of incoming wire transfers was also expected to grow.

It was recommended that the Wire Transfer Department work with the data processing systems development group to create an application that could take the electronically downloaded incoming wire transfer data from the Federal Reserve and automatically post the transactions to customer accounts. In this way, only incoming wires that had invalid account numbers would need to be processed manually.

This case study illustrates how an operation in a fast-growing company can grow so much that automation becomes cost effective, but the operation is preoccupied with simply keeping up with the day-to-day volume. In this case, management had not recognized that a significant amount of manual effort could be saved by automating the posting of incoming wire transfers.

CASE STUDY 9.9

Confusing Information on an Interactive Online Banking Application

During a review of a newly implemented interactive online banking application, it was noted that loan transaction history detail incorrectly listed *principal* as the column heading above the transaction amounts column. Although this information did not affect the mainframe history, it led to confusion on the part of loan customers.

The obvious recommendation was to simply change the column headings, but this did not prove to be an easy task. Two vendors had originally codeveloped the software several years earlier and marketed it as an off-the-shelf product. The financial institution had purchased the software application about one year in advance and completed installation of it about one month prior to our tests. Unfortunately, the vendor firms had divorced subsequent to the software purchase, and neither one provided programming support for the software. Furthermore, the financial institution's contract failed to specify that the source code was to be held in escrow by an independent third party so that it could be released to the financial institution in the event the

(continued)

CASE STUDY 9.9 (*continued*)

vendors could not or would not support the software, or the vendors otherwise violated a significant term of the contract.

Fortunately, the financial institution employed the services of one of the two vendors for other software applications. As a result, the financial institution was able to leverage the vendor into correcting the software program by threatening to withhold future business if it did not. Sometimes shrewd business practices are necessary to accomplish simple tasks. This situation could have been avoided had adequate testing been performed on the system early in the project and had the contract been properly written.

CASE STUDY 9.10

Automation of Manual Check Preparation and Other Manual Processes in an Individual Retirement Account Operation

During an audit of the individual retirement account (IRA) and related operations of a financial institution, five opportunities were identified to enhance efficiency and effectiveness through automation of what were previously manual procedures or enhancement of existing automated procedures.

The first efficiency opportunity was that the Accounting Department was manually creating and mailing checks twice each week for the remittance of withheld income taxes to the federal government. It was recommended that the funds be electronically remitted utilizing an existing application that was already being used to remit other funds to the government. Our recommendation resulted in three benefits:

1. It eliminated the use of paper checks and the associated processing and mailing costs.
2. It reduced the amount of time required to prepare and transmit the remittances as compared to the amount of time required to prepare and mail the paper checks.
3. The company could more effectively manage its cash. Previously, the company had to estimate the number of days it would take for the remittance checks to clear and would make its short-term investments based on these estimates. However, the company had to mail the checks early enough so as not to incur any late penalties. As a result, the government usually received the checks and cashed them prior to the due date. By electronically remitting tax collections on the due date, the company could invest the funds in short-term securities until the last possible day, thereby maximizing the investment income from these funds.

The second efficiency/effectiveness opportunity pertained to the fact that the primary IRA application at the financial institution could not calculate automatic IRA distribution information. Instead, the IRA Department was using a microcomputer-based vendor application to perform these calculations, but the IRA application did not communicate with the vendor application. In other words, the information necessary to calculate IRA distributions was being manually keyed into the vendor application by IRA Department staff. It was recommended that the IRA Department submit a request to the IS Department to develop a system that could electronically transfer the necessary information from the primary IRA application to the vendor application (e.g., in ASCII [American Standard Code for Information Interchange] format). The labor cost savings were significant, especially since the number of IRA accounts requiring automatic IRA distribution calculations had been steadily increasing each year, and the growth rate was projected to continue.

A third inefficiency was the fact that neither the primary IRA application nor the microcomputer-based vendor application could perform interest-only automatic distributions. As a result, these calculations had to be performed manually. In this case, it was recommended that IRA Department management locate a more effective IRA payment calculation software package that meets all of its needs. If the decision was made to purchase a replacement application, then the previous recommendation to program a data transfer module would be deferred until the new application is installed.

The fourth inefficiency resulted from the fact that the IRA Department was manually key entering data into 11 independent databases, each of which was used for tracking historical information not otherwise available in the primary IRA application. Examination of these databases revealed numerous instances of data redundancy and, in two cases, unnecessary databases. It was recommended that management eliminate the unnecessary databases and consolidate the others so that only seven databases remained. This resulted in a significant reduction in the amount of time necessary to enter information into the databases and enabled the IRA Department to more effectively generate IRA database reports.

The fifth issue pertained to the effectiveness of management reporting. A report that could identify the actual number of active IRA accounts could not be prepared from the primary IRA application. The closest information the IRA application could provide was the number of new accounts opened and the number of existing accounts that were closed. From this information, the total number of active IRA accounts was calculated, using a running total. In other words, the number of new IRA accounts opened was manually added to the ending total from the previous month, and then the number of closed IRA accounts was subtracted. The resulting totals were provided to senior management in various IRA reports as the total number of active IRA accounts. This method had been in place for several years, and the total number of active accounts had never been compared to the system totals. During the audit, a special report from the IRA database was requested to confirm the accuracy of the running totals being reported to management. Based on the number of accounts identified from the special report, the number of IRA accounts reported to management during the most recent month was overstated by 3.4 percent. It was therefore recommended that IRA Department management submit a request to management of the IS Department to receive a report generated from the primary IRA application, showing the total number of active IRA accounts, and that the IRA Department use that information in its management reports (after explaining to senior management how the number of accounts could be so far overstated).

CASE STUDY 9.11

Failure to Automate the Deactivation of a Large Issuance of Debit Cards

This is a case in which Internal Audit was not included on the development team for a financial institution's planned introduction of a new debit card product. The new debit cards provided card holders with the ability to use a single card for PIN-based ATM and point-of-sale transactions as well as signature-based debit card transactions. Therefore, the old ATM cards were to be replaced by the new debit cards. Since the project was not considered to be of high risk, the Internal Audit Department monitored the progress of the project through inquiries of the project leader and limited written correspondence.

After the product development had been completed, new debit cards were initially issued to over 150,000 card holders. On receipt, each card holder was to activate his or her other debit card by performing a PIN-based transaction. The Debit Card Department then received a daily report of activated debit cards and had to manually deactivate the corresponding ATM card for each card holder. With the large number of debit cards issued, deactivation of old ATM cards was a highly labor-intensive proposition. In fact, the Debit Card Department had to hire three temporary employees to do nothing but deactivate old ATM cards. The obvious flaw in the debit card project was that during planning, an automated procedure for deactivation of the old cards was not conceived. Prior to the next issuance of debit cards, an automated deactivation program should be developed.

Although it was too late to implement this recommendation for the first issuance, this is a good lesson for auditors to be alert to identify these kinds of efficiency opportunities early in a project, even if a member of the Internal Audit Department is not a formal part of a project team. Informing the project team about potentially significant inefficiencies before it is too late to correct them can significantly enhance the attraction of including internal auditors on future project teams, especially as favorable word is communicated within the organization.

CASE STUDY 9.12

Failure to Balance a Marketing Extract Database

During an audit of a marketing database application in a financial institution, it was noted that procedures were lacking to balance the number of accounts and total account balances in the application database to the source data on a regular basis. Each month an extract program copied deposit and loan account balances, demographic information, and other selected marketing data from the mainframe database to a magnetic tape. The data on the tape was then copied into the marketing database application. Data from magnetic tapes containing marketing information from other applications were also copied into the marketing database. After the update process was completed, the

Marketing Department would perform various queries and other customer analyses for use in planning and evaluating the success of marketing promotions and product development efforts.

The total dollars and number of accounts were balanced after the first downloads had been completed for this system and then only once at the end of each year. Since downloads were performed on a monthly basis, if the data contained errors due to problems in the programs used to extract data or in the database update process, they may not be detected in a timely manner. As a result, monthly marketing and demographic reports that were prepared throughout the year could have contained inaccurate information, which in turn could have affected the success of the company's marketing promotions and its ability to accurately evaluate the success of promotions. Failure to balance extract database totals to source data is a common but often significant oversight with many end-user databases.

CASE STUDY 9.13

Inadequate Documentation and Testing of Critical FOCUS Database Programs

A large financial institution utilized FOCUS[a] databases extensively to create various types of financial, affirmative action, banking regulatory compliance, and ad hoc reports for all levels of management. FOCUS databases are a source of data that enables end users to obtain information relatively quickly without having to request it through a centralized data processing report request process. FOCUS databases are created through a process in which records from the production application files are extracted by a program that subsequently copies them in a FOCUS readable format to a designated electronic storage address.

Within the scope of the audit at this particular financial institution, there were approximately 820 authorized FOCUS users, many of whom used FOCUS on a daily basis. The FOCUS databases within the audit scope included information on demand deposit accounts, savings accounts, certificates of deposit, human resources information, commercial and consumer loan information, and general ledger financial information. To reduce the risk of poor strategic decisions by management and fines and/or lawsuits resulting from inaccurately reported legal and regulatory activity, the FOCUS databases were balanced to the production database totals on a daily basis by an automated program. Any out-of-balance conditions would appear on reports that were sent to the FOCUS database owners.

During the audit, it was found that many departments had written sophisticated FOCUS programs to extract information from the FOCUS databases.

---

[a]FOCUS was created by Information Builders, Inc. of New York, NY, USA.

(*continued*)

CASE STUDY 9.13 (*continued*)

These programs were developed independently of the centralized Systems Development Department, sometimes by end-user technical staff and sometimes by contract programmers. Many of the FOCUS programs contained little or no documentation as to their purpose, logic, field definitions, external data sources, and other types of descriptive information that could help in the daily operations and maintenance of the programs and if the programs needed to be corrected. In addition, testing of the programs was not documented prior to their production implementation in the end-user departments. In many cases, the programmers had transferred to other departments or terminated altogether, thereby causing difficulty in maintaining and troubleshooting the programs when problems were encountered.

It was recommended that management in end-user departments request that complex FOCUS programs be developed in conjunction with the centralized Systems Development Department to help ensure that the programs are properly designed, documented, and tested in accordance with previously established company systems development and programming standards. As part of this recommendation, end-user management would have to work with Systems Development Management to define complex programs. It was also recommended that all other FOCUS programs developed in the end-user departments adhere to established company systems development and programming standards.

PART THREE

Contemporary Information Systems Auditing Concepts

CHAPTER 10

Control Self-Assessment and an Application in an Information Systems Environment

The first part of this chapter provides a definition and overview of Control Self-Assessment (CSA), followed by a brief history of CSA. The next three parts discuss the various CSA approaches, keys to a successful CSA program, and CSA program benefits. The chapter concludes with an analysis of a real-world application of control self-assessment in an information systems (IS) environment within one organization.

DEFINITION AND OVERVIEW

Following is my definition of control self-assessment:

> Control Self-Assessment (CSA) is a leading edge process in which *auditors* facilitate a group of *staff members* who have expertise in a specific process, with the objective of identifying opportunities for internal control enhancement pertaining to critical operating areas designated by *management*.

The CSA process is usually accomplished during *workshops*. Note in the definition that the words *auditors*, *staff members*, and *management* have been *italicized*. The reason is to emphasize that a CSA workshop can be successful only through the combined positive efforts of each of these three groups of individuals, or *players*. If any one of the players does not adequately perform his or her role, constructive ideas to enhance the internal control environment will not be as effective as they otherwise could have been.

Other key words in the CSA definition are *facilitate*, *identifying*, and *critical*. Each key word relates to the role that each of the three groups of CSA players must perform. Successful CSA depends on auditors effectively facilitating a lively, open, honest, and constructive session. Without effective facilitation, a CSA workshop can easily wander into irrelevant topics or negative discussions about problems with other individuals or departments that do not pertain to the objectives of the workshop. This can result in wasting valuable time and resources.

Staff members are also essential to the success of a CSA workshop because they have the detailed working knowledge of the process being evaluated. With their detailed knowledge, they are in the best position to identify which internal controls are working well, which ones are not working well, and how internal controls could be most effectively improved.

Management's role is to designate those operating areas that are critical to the success of the process being evaluated, whether it is a department, operating unit, or higher-level organization. Management is also instrumental in the implementation of the internal control enhancements identified by their staff members.

HISTORY

The CSA concept was originated in the late 1980s by Bruce McCuaig, then at Gulf Canada Resources, a subsidiary of Gulf Corporation. Another CSA pioneer at Gulf, Paul Makosz, assisted McCuaig in developing CSA into a process that could be used to measure soft controls, which traditional audit techniques could not measure. These soft controls include things like management's integrity, honesty, trust, willingness to circumvent controls, and overall employee morale. Collectively, these attributes comprise an organization's corporate culture, which is often derived from the tone at the top. This phrase refers to the fact that unwritten accepted corporate standards of conduct take their cue from the behavior and actions of the leaders of an organization; key officers such as the chairman, chief executive office (CEO), president, and other senior executives. The reason for wanting to measure soft controls is that soft control failure has often been attributed to the demise of many failed organizations. In fact, soft control failure coupled with a rapidly increasing interest rate environment were almost entirely responsible for the near extinction of the savings and loan industry in the United States. Because of his early experimentation and continuing enhancements to CSA approaches, as well as his efforts to promote CSA, Makosz is now considered by many to be "the father of CSA."[1] Both McCuaig and Makosz have left Gulf Canada Resources and established successful consulting practices that specialize in CSA.

By the early 1990s, a few other organizations began implementing CSA. For example, in 1991, Jim Mitchell, the general auditor of MAPCO, Inc., a Fortune 500 energy corporation headquartered in Tulsa, Oklahoma, became interested in CSA and put it into practice in 1992. By 1996, CSA was one of MAPCO's three major audit methods, and about 30 percent of MAPCO's audit resources were devoted to CSA. MAPCO was so successful with its CSA program that two of its former CSA managers published an article that described their approach.[2]

During the mid-1990s, interest in CSA began taking the auditing world by storm. The Institute of Internal Auditors (IIA) hosted its first CSA conference in Orlando in 1995. This conference was so successful, the IIA hosted a second CSA conference in Toronto in 1996 and a third in Las Vegas in 1997. Based on the enormous popularity of CSA, the IIA now hosts annual CSA conferences and training seminars.

By 1996, all of the Big Six (now Big Four) accounting firms had begun to offer CSA consulting services, although their degrees of commitment varied. Deloitte & Touche, LLP, had been the most aggressive CSA proponent among the Big Six in terms of the number of CSA consultants they hired and their visibility and participation at CSA conferences. Deloitte & Touche also invested significant financial resources in hiring CSA experts and marketing CSA services. In fact, some of their experts were hired directly from firms like MAPCO, Inc., which pioneered CSA. Deloitte & Touche was also the most visible at the 1996 CSA conference. Other Big Six firms represented at the conference included Ernst & Young, LLP; KPMG, LLP; and Arthur Andersen, LLP. The remaining Big Six firms, Coopers & Lybrand, LLP, and Price Waterhouse had also begun to offer CSA services.[3]

In January 1997, the IIA launched its Control Self-Assessment Center. The objective of the center is to offer guidance and training opportunities to individuals engaged in the practice of CSA. Some of the services provided by the center include *The CSA Sentinel*, a triannual electronic newsletter; professional guidance on CSA implementation; a series of CSA seminars culminating in CSA qualification; reduced prices on IIA products related to CSA; and an annual directory of CSA Center participants.[4]

By 1997, many major organizations around the world had implemented CSA programs to varying degrees (see Exhibit 10.1). However, these CSA pioneering organizations represented a vast minority of all the organizations in the world. Many organizations had been considering implementing CSA, but relatively few had actually implemented CSA, even to a limited extent. The reason was that implementing CSA requires a major commitment from all parts of the organization, including the Internal Audit Department as well as all levels of management. The next two paragraphs describe the results of two informal verbal surveys regarding how many organizations had implemented CSA.

In December 1996, the local chapters of the Information Systems Audit and Control Association (ISACA) and IIA in Seattle, Washington, held a joint meeting at which the featured speaker from a Big Six accounting firm discussed CSA. Of the 70-plus people in attendance, representing over 30 organizations, only 2 persons stated that their companies had implemented CSA, but only on a limited scale. However, many organizations were still thinking about CSA, and some were still researching what approach would be best for them.

In March 1997, the Association of Credit Union Internal Auditors (ACUIA) held a regional meeting in Seattle, Washington. This meeting produced verbal CSA survey results similar to the joint ISACA/IIA meeting. Many credit unions in Washington and Oregon were considering CSA, but none had implemented it other than Boeing Employees' Credit Union (BECU).

Interest in CSA is widespread, but implementation has been spotty. The limited implementation is evidenced by the fact that there have been relatively few articles written about CSA and even fewer regarding CSA as applied to IS pro-

---

EXHIBIT 10.1   EARLY ADOPTERS OF CONTROL SELF-ASSESSMENT[a]

AgAmerica, FCB (Spokane, WA, USA)
Alliance Blue Cross–Blue Shield (St. Louis, MO, USA)
American Electric Power (Columbus, OH, USA)
Arizona Department of Transportation (Phoenix, AZ, USA)
ARCO Alaska, Inc. (Anchorage, AK, USA)
Bank of Canada (Ottawa, Ontario, Canada)
Bell Canada (Toronto, Ontario, Canada)
BellSouth Corp. (Atlanta, GA, USA)
Boeing Company (Seattle, WA, USA)
Boeing Employees' Credit Union (Seattle, WA, USA)
Boise Cascade Corporation (Boise, ID, USA)
Bremer Financial Services (St. Paul, MN, USA)
Cornell University (Ithaca, NY, USA)
Department of Employee Trust Funds (Madison, WI, USA)
Excel Communications, Inc. (Dallas, TX, USA)
First USA, Inc. (Dallas, TX, USA)
Johnson & Johnson (New Brunswick, NJ, USA)
MAPCO, Inc. (Tulsa, OK, USA)
The Mutual Group (Waterloo, ON, Canada)
Nike Corporation (Beaverton, OR, USA)
Northeast Utilities (Hartford, CT, USA)
Pacific Bell (San Francisco, CA, USA)
Praxair, Inc. (Danbury, CT, USA)
Sun Microsystems, Inc. (Mountain View, CA, USA)
Telemalta Corp. (Marsa, Malta)
Transamerica Corp. (San Francisco, CA, USA)
University of Tennessee (Knoxville, TN, USA)
University of Texas (Austin, TX, USA)
Washington Metropolitan Area Transit Authority (Columbia, MD, USA)
World Bank (Washington, DC, USA)
Zurich Canada (Toronto, ON, Canada)

---

[a]This list is not intended to be all-encompassing.

cesses. The *Information Systems Audit and Control Journal* dedicated a large part of its Volume I, 1997, issue to the subject of CSA.[5] One of the articles described an approach referred to as Control and Risk Self-Assessment (CRSA), which is essentially a spinoff of CSA.[6] The author, Tim Leech, uses this approach in training and implementation engagement services offered by his firm. The bimonthly *Internal Auditor Journal* has also published several articles pertaining to CSA. The IIA's *CSA Sentinel*, which was first published in January 1997, in conjunction with the opening of its CSA Center, fills some of the void. As of 2002, the IIA has been the most progressive organization with regard to CSA. In addition to the aforementioned CSA Center, educational seminars, and conferences, and the *CSA Sen-*

tinel, the IIA sponsors the Certification in Control Self-Assessment (CCSA) specialty professional designation.

Perhaps the most comprehensive CSA reference source is the IIA Research Foundation's 1996 study entitled *Control Self-Assessment: Experience, Current Thinking, and Best Practices*. This project was commissioned by the Ottawa Chapter of the IIA and conducted by Arthur Andersen, LLP. The study discusses the CSA experiences of nearly 100 professionals from 80 organizations.[7] With such a broad base of CSA experiences, the study can be an excellent benchmark for many organizations. I hope that this chapter of the book also motivates some auditors who are "on the fence" to at least attempt to implement CSA to assess its potential value within their organizations.

KEYS TO A SUCCESSFUL PROGRAM

Control Self-Assessment is still in an early growth stage in its evolution. Relatively few organizations have taken the plunge and made the commitment of time and resources necessary to develop and implement an effective CSA process. As with any new business venture, there are risks involved with the implementation of CSA. The purpose of this section is to help reduce those risks so that the CSA program can be successful and to identify six key elements of a successful CSA program.

The most important part of any CSA program is the need to obtain the encouragement and support of senior management. Without their backing, lower levels of management will not be anywhere near as likely to take the process seriously. Without serious participation, a CSA program could be viewed as a waste of time. Senior executives and others who support and promote CSA are fondly referred to as "champions" by those in the CSA arena. Senior management support must be earned through effective demonstrations of the potential for significant gains in operational efficiency and effectiveness, and reductions in exposure to financial, regulatory, and other significant risks. These demonstrations can be supported by success stories at various companies that have implemented successful CSA programs (e.g., MAPCO, Inc.). Articles written about CSA (see previous section) may need to be referred to, and senior management may have to be better educated on the objectives of internal controls. This brings up the second key to a successful CSA program.

To effectively sell CSA to senior management and to effectively facilitate a CSA workshop, auditors must be intimately familiar with the objectives of internal controls. There are several contemporary national and international models, or frameworks, of internal control. Six of the most well-known frameworks include COSO (United States, 1992); CoCo (Canada,1995); Cadbury (Great Britain,1994); COBIT (ISACA, 1996, 1998, 2000); SAC (IIA, 1977, 1991, 1994) and eSAC (IIA, 2001); and SASs 55/78/94 (AICPA, effective 1990, 1997, 2001). A detailed understanding of these frameworks is pertinent to audits of all processes, including IS processes, in every country in the world. A brief discussion of each of these models follows.

Internal Control Frameworks

COSO

The formal name of this report is *Internal Control—Integrated Framework*. It was published by the Committee of Sponsoring Organizations of the Treadway Commission (COSO) in September 1992. The official name of the Treadway Commission was the National Commission on Fraudulent Financial Reporting, which was established in 1985 through the joint sponsorship of five U.S. organizations: American Institute of Certified Public Accountants, American Accounting Association, Financial Executives Institute, Institute of Internal Auditors, and Institute of Management Accountants (formerly the National Association of Accountants). The Treadway Commission, which was named after its first chairman, James Treadway, was charged with identifying the primary causes of fraudulent financial reporting, which had been proliferating in the United States during the 1970s and 1980s. The Commission was also responsible for providing recommendations to reduce the incidence of such fraud.

The Treadway Commission's 1987 report recognized that weak internal controls were the primary contributing factor to many fraudulent financial reporting cases. The report stressed the importance of the control environment, codes of conduct, audit committee oversight, an active and objective internal audit function, management reports on the effectiveness of internal control, and the need to develop a common definition and framework of internal control. The evolutionary process of developing a generally accepted definition and framework of internal control was finally realized in 1992 with the publication of the COSO report.

COSO defines internal control as

A process, effected by an entity's board of directors, management, and other personnel, designed to provide reasonable assurance regarding the achievement of objectives in the following categories:

- Effectiveness and efficiency of operations
- Reliability of financial reporting
- Compliance with applicable laws and regulations[8]

One of the key aspects of this definition is that internal control can provide only reasonable, but not absolute, assurance as to the achievement of the objectives. The report goes on to state that each of the above internal control objectives consists of five interrelated components, which are derived from the way management runs a business:

1. Control environment
2. Risk assessment
3. Control activities
4. Information and communication
5. Monitoring

Exhibit 10.2 depicts the relationship of internal control objectives and components as presented in the COSO report.[9]

EXHIBIT 10.2 COSO RELATIONSHIP BETWEEN OBJECTIVES AND COMPONENTS OF INTERNAL CONTROL

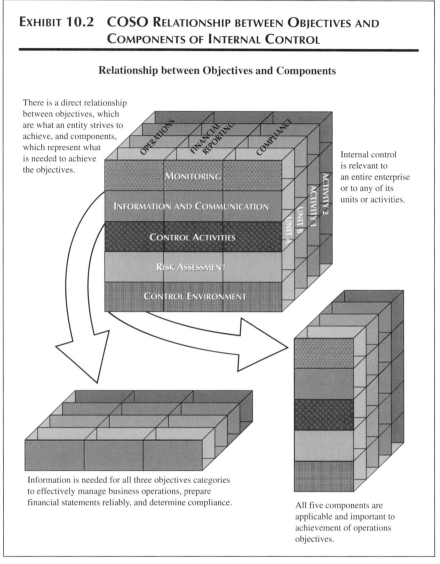

Relationship between Objectives and Components

There is a direct relationship between objectives, which are what an entity strives to achieve, and components, which represent what is needed to achieve the objectives.

Internal control is relevant to an entire enterprise or to any of its units or activities.

Information is needed for all three objectives categories to effectively manage business operations, prepare financial statements reliably, and determine compliance.

All five components are applicable and important to achievement of operations objectives.

Source: Reprinted with permission from Internal Control-Integrated Framework, copyright © 1992 by the American Institute of Certified Public Accountants, Inc.

Another key concept of COSO is that management is responsible for an entity's internal control system, and the CEO should assume ownership of the control system. This concept is further supported by the fact that U.S. federal sentencing guidelines complement the COSO framework. Whereas COSO defines what constitutes effective internal controls, the U.S. federal sentencing guidelines specify penalties for failure to maintain an effective system of internal controls.

Senior management of organizations subjected to these penalties are ultimately responsible. A 1997 article provides an excellent comparison between COSO and the United States federal sentencing guidelines.[10]

For more details about COSO, please refer to the complete four-volume COSO report, which is available from the American Institute of Certified Public Accountants. The four volumes are: *Executive Summary, Framework, Reporting to External Parties*, and *Evaluation Tools*.

CoCo

The formal name of this report is *Guidance on Control*. It was published by the Criteria of Control Board (CoCo) of the Canadian Institute of Chartered Accountants (CICA) in November 1995. CoCo is responsible for issuing guidance on designing, assessing, and reporting on the control systems of organizations. The CoCo guidance builds on the understanding of control set out in COSO. Like COSO, it defines control and specifies criteria for effective control. The CoCo control framework is intended to be used by people throughout an organization to develop, assess, and change control.

CoCo defines control as "those elements of an organization (including its resources, systems, processes, culture, structure and tasks) that, taken together, support people in the achievement of the organization's objectives." It defines three categories of objectives:

1. Effectiveness and efficiency of operations
2. Reliability of internal and external reporting
3. Compliance with applicable laws and regulations and internal policies[11]

This definition is very similar to COSO, but the CoCo *Guidance on Control* presents additional concepts not contained in the COSO framework. Appendix 1 of the *Guidance on Control* provides an excellent comparison of COSO versus CoCo. Some of the key differences specified in that appendix are:

- Within the scope of control, CoCo includes objective setting, strategic planning, risk management, and corrective actions, while it excludes decision making.
- CoCo explicitly states that control includes the identification and mitigation of the risks of failure to maintain an organization's ability to identify and exploit opportunities, and failure to maintain the organization's resilience.
- CoCo includes control criteria pertaining to mutual trust between people and the periodic challenge of assumptions.
- CoCo's concept of monitoring includes monitoring of the operating performance of the organization.
- CoCo judges the effectiveness of an internal control system in relation to specific objectives (such as customer service levels), not a category of objectives (such as efficiency and effectiveness of operations).

- CoCo assesses control effectiveness against 20 criteria (see Exhibit 10.3) that are somewhat different from COSO's 15 control "cubes" depicted in Exhibit 10.2. To assure users that CoCo is COSO compliant, Appendix 1 of CoCo regroups the 20 criteria of control into the 5 COSO components of internal control.[12]

EXHIBIT 10.3 COCO CRITERIA OF CONTROL REGROUPED INTO COSO COMPONENTS

Control Environment

B1   Shared ethical values, including integrity, should be established, communicated and practised throughout the organization.

B2   Human resource policies and practices should be consistent with an organization's ethical values and with the achievement of its objectives.

B3   Authority, responsibility and accountability should be clearly defined and consistent with an organization's objectives so that decisions and actions are taken by the appropriate people.

B4   An atmosphere of mutual trust should be fostered to support the flow of information between people and their effective performance toward achieving the organization's objectives.

C1   People should have the necessary knowledge, skills and tools to support the achievement of the organization's objectives.

Risk Assessment

A1   Objectives should be established and communicated.

A2   The significant internal and external risks faced by an organization in the achievement of its objectives should be identified and assessed.

A5   Objectives and related plans should include measurable performance targets and indicators.

D1   External and internal environments should be monitored to obtain information that may signal a need to re-evaluate the organization's objectives or control.

Control Activities

A3   Policies designed to support the achievement of an organization's objectives and the management of its risks should be established, communicated and practised so that people understand what is expected of them and the scope of their freedom to act.

C4   The decisions and actions of different parts of the organization should be coordinated.

C5   Control activities should be designed as an integral part of the organization, taking into consideration its objectives, the risks to their achievement, and the inter-relatedness of control elements.

Information and Communication

C2   Communication processes should support the organization's values and the achievement of its objectives.

C3   Sufficient and relevant information should be identified and communicated in a timely manner to enable people to perform their assigned responsibilities.

A4   Plans to guide efforts in achieving the organization's objectives should be established and communicated.

D4   Information needs and related information systems should be reassessed as objectives change or as reporting deficiencies are identified.

Monitoring

D2   Performance should be monitored against the targets and indicators identified in the organization's objectives and plans.

D3   The assumptions behind an organization's objectives should be periodically challenged.

D5   Follow-up procedures should be established and performed to ensure appropriate change or action occurs.

D6   Management should periodically assess the effectiveness of control in its organization and communicate the results to those to whom it is accountable.

Source: Reprinted with permission from *Guidance on Control: Control and Governance*, Volume 1, The Canadian Institute of Chartered Accountants, Toronto, Canada. © 1995, page 30.

- CoCo specifies that control is effective to the extent that it provides reasonable assurance that the organization will achieve its objectives (i.e., control is effective to the extent that the remaining risks of the organization failing to meet its objectives are deemed acceptable).[13]

For more details about CoCo, please refer to the complete *Guidance on Control* report which is available from the CICA.

Cadbury

The formal name of this report is *Internal Control and Financial Reporting*. It was published in December 1994 by the Committee of the Financial Aspects of Corporate Governance (Cadbury Committee) of the Institute of Chartered Accountants in England and Wales (ICAEW). Like CoCo, the Cadbury report builds on the understanding of internal control set out in COSO.

Cadbury initially defines internal control as:

The whole system of controls, financial and otherwise, established in order to provide reasonable assurance of:

- effective and efficient operations
- internal financial control
- compliance with laws and regulations[14]

Cadbury goes on to define internal *financial* control as:

The internal controls established in order to provide reasonable assurance of:

- the safeguarding of assets against unauthorized use of disposition; and
- the maintenance of proper accounting records and the reliability of financial information used within the business or for publication.[15]

The reason for the more specific internal financial control definition is that Cadbury requires that the board of directors of every company incorporated in the United Kingdom publish a statement about their system of internal *financial* control. The statement must, at a minimum:

- Acknowledge that the directors are responsible for internal financial control.
- Provide an explanation that the system can provide only reasonable, not absolute, assurance against material misstatement or loss.
- Describe key procedures that the directors have established to help ensure effective internal financial control.
- Confirm that the directors have reviewed the effectiveness of the system of internal financial control.

Cadbury encourages, but does not require, directors to state their opinion on the effectiveness of the system of internal financial control.

Cadbury's criteria for assessing the effectiveness of internal financial control fall into the five COSO-derived categories:

1. Control environment
2. Identification and evaluation of risks and control objectives
3. Information and communication
4. Control procedures
5. Monitoring and corrective action

For more details about the Cadbury framework, please refer to the complete *Internal Control and Financial Reporting* report, available from the Institute of Chartered Accountants in England and Wales.

COBIT

COBIT, which stands for Control Objectives for Information and Related Technology, was published by the Information Systems Audit and Control Foundation in 1996 and updated in 1998 and 2000. COBIT is a comprehensive internal control framework specifically pertaining to internal control issues associated with information technology (IT). COBIT's mission is to "research, develop, publicize, and promote an authoritative, up-to-date, international set of generally accepted information technology control objectives for day-to-day use by business managers and auditors."[16] COBIT consists of six volumes: *Executive Summary, Framework, Control Objectives, Audit Guidelines, Management Guidelines*, and *Implementation Tool Set*. The COBIT package also comes with a diskette of the six volumes in ASCII format and a CD-Rom of the powerpoint slides in the *Implementation Tool Set*.

COBIT is an internationally developed, comprehensive IT evaluation tool that envelops virtually every major generally accepted standard in the world pertaining to controls and IT. Included for consideration during its development were standards from numerous organizations, including the International Organization for Standardization (ISO); Electronic Data Interchange for Administration, Commerce, and Trade (EDIFACT); Council of Europe; Organization for Economic Cooperation and Development (OECD); ISACA; Information Technology Security Evaluation Criteria (ITSEC); Trusted Computer Security Evaluation Criteria (TCSEC); COSO; United States General Accounting Office (GAO); International Federation of Accountants (IFAC); IIA; American Institute of Certified Public Accountants (AICPA); CICA; European Security Forum (ESF); Infosec Business Advisory Group (IBAG); National Institute of Standards and Technology (NIST); and the Department of Trade and Industry (DTI) of the United Kingdom.

COBIT defines control as "the policies, procedures, practices, and organizational structures designed to provide reasonable assurance that business objectives will be achieved and that undesired events will be prevented or detected and corrected."[17] This definition is very similar to the other frameworks previously discussed. Contrary to what some readers may have thought, the objectives of IS auditing are essentially the same as financial, operational, and other branches of auditing. The difference lies in the body of knowledge and the tools necessary to accomplish the objectives.

Exhibit 10.4 presents the principles of the COBIT framework. Within the framework, there are seven business information requirements, or criteria: effectiveness, efficiency, confidentiality, integrity, availability, compliance, and reliability. COBIT goes on to specify that IT resources provide the information needed by business processes. Thus, the framework identifies five types of IT resources: people, application systems, technology, facilities, and data.

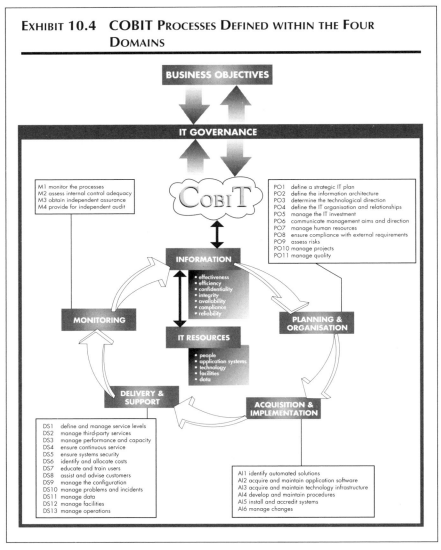

EXHIBIT 10.4 COBIT PROCESSES DEFINED WITHIN THE FOUR DOMAINS

Reprinted with permission. COBIT: Control Objectives for Information and Related Technology. Copyright 1996, 1998, 2000, The IT Governance Institute™ (ITGI™), Rolling Meadows, IL USA 60008.

COBIT groups individual activities within an IT environment into processes and then groups processes into domains. As can be seen in Exhibit 10.4, there are four high-level COBIT domains.The exhibit also details 34 processes that comprise the four domains as follows: planning and organization (11 processes), acquisition and implementation (6 processes), delivery and support (13 processes), and monitoring (4 processes). The third edition of COBIT cross-references each of the 34 processes to a total of 318 control objectives.

COBIT further identifies to which of the seven information criteria each of the 34 IT processes apply and to what degree (primary or secondary). Additionally, COBIT identifies which of the five IT resources are applicable to each IT process. Exhibit 10.5 is the COBIT summary table, showing the relationships among the domains, processes, information criteria, and IT resources.

EXHIBIT 10.5   CONTROL OBJECTIVES SUMMARY TABLE

The following chart provides an indication, by IT process and domain, of which information criteria are impacted by the high-level control objectives, as well as an indication of which IT resources are applicable.

DOMAIN		PROCESS	effectiveness	efficiency	confidentiality	integrity	availability	compliance	reliability	people	applications	technology	facilities	data
Planning & Organisation	PO1	Define a strategic IT plan	P	S						✓	✓	✓	✓	✓
	PO2	Define the information architecture	P	S	S	S					✓			✓
	PO3	Determine technological direction	P	S								✓	✓	
	PO4	Define the IT organisation and relationships	P	S						✓				
	PO5	Manage the IT investment	P	P					S	✓	✓	✓	✓	
	PO6	Communicate management aims and direction	P					S		✓				
	PO7	Manage human resources	P	P						✓				
	PO8	Ensure compliance with external requirements	P					P	S	✓	✓			✓
	PO9	Assess risks	P	S	P	P	P	S	S	✓	✓	✓	✓	✓
	PO10	Manage projects	P	P						✓	✓	✓	✓	
	PO11	Manage quality	P	P		P			S	✓	✓	✓	✓	
Acquisition & Implementation	AI1	Identify automated solutions	P	S							✓	✓	✓	
	AI2	Acquire and maintain application software	P	P		S		S	S	✓				
	AI3	Acquire and maintain technology infrastructure	P	P		S						✓		
	AI4	Develop and maintain procedures	P	P		S		S	S	✓	✓	✓	✓	
	AI5	Install and accredit systems	P			S	S			✓	✓	✓	✓	✓
	AI6	Manage changes	P	P		P	P		S	✓	✓	✓	✓	✓
Delivery & Support	DS1	Define and manage service levels	P	P	S	S	S	S	S	✓	✓	✓	✓	✓
	DS2	Manage third-party services	P	P	S	S	S	S	S	✓	✓	✓	✓	✓
	DS3	Manage performance and capacity	P	P		S					✓	✓	✓	
	DS4	Ensure continuous service	P	S		P				✓	✓	✓	✓	✓
	DS5	Ensure systems security			P	P	S	S	S	✓	✓	✓	✓	✓
	DS6	Identify and allocate costs		P					P	✓	✓	✓	✓	✓
	DS7	Educate and train users	P	S						✓				
	DS8	Assist and advise customers	P	P						✓	✓			
	DS9	Manage the configuration	P			S		S		✓	✓	✓		
	DS10	Manage problems and incidents	P	P		S				✓	✓	✓	✓	✓
	DS11	Manage data			P				P					✓
	DS12	Manage facilities			P	P							✓	
	DS13	Manage operations	P	P		S	S			✓	✓		✓	✓
Monitoring	M1	Monitor the processes	P	P	S	S	S	S	S	✓	✓	✓	✓	✓
	M2	Assess internal control adequacy	P	P	S	S	S	P	S	✓	✓	✓	✓	✓
	M3	Obtain independent assurance	P	P	S	S	S	P	S	✓	✓	✓	✓	✓
	M4	Provide for independent audit	P	P	S	S	S	P	S	✓	✓	✓	✓	✓

Information Criteria   IT Resources

(P) primary (S) secondary   (✓) applicable to

COBIT goes on to provide a generic audit guideline template to assist in the evaluation and testing of the control objectives. The generic approach is to obtain an understanding of the process, evaluate controls, assess compliance, and substantiate the risk of control objectives not being met. The template is applied to each of the 34 processes, with specific audit guidelines detailed within each process.

COBIT was designed to be broad enough to apply to existing technologies as well as to technologies not yet developed. It is specific enough to provide guidance for conducting IT audits, while it is general enough that it does not have to be updated or revised every time a new type of technology is developed. John Lainhart IV, a member of the COBIT Steering Committee, described COBIT and the impact it is having on the IS audit and control profession in a 1996 article.[18] For additional details about COBIT, please refer to the complete COBIT document, which is available from the Information Systems Audit and Control Foundation (ISACF).

SAC and eSAC

The Systems Auditability and Control (SAC) report is intended to provide "sound guidance on control and audit of information systems and technology. The report focuses on the business perspective of information technology and the risks associated with planning, implementing, and using automation."[19] SAC emphasizes management's responsibility to identify, understand, and assess the risks associated with the integration of technology in an organization and to oversee and control the organization's use of technology. The SAC report was originally published by the IIA in 1977. It was the first internal control framework pertaining to IT. Due to the enormous changes in IT since 1977, an updated and extended SAC report was published in 1991 and was then further revised in 1994.

SAC defines the system of internal control as those processes, functions, activities, subsystems, procedures, and organization of human resources that provide reasonable assurance that the goals and objectives of the organization are achieved and ensure that risk is reduced to an acceptable level.[20]

The SAC report consists of 14 modules: Executive Summary, Audit and Control Environment, Using Information Technology in Auditing, Managing Computer Resources, Managing Information and Developing Systems, Business Systems, End-User and Departmental Computing, Telecommunications, Security, Contingency Planning, Emerging Technologies, Index, Advanced Technology Supplement, and a case study.

The conceptual model of the SAC report is presented in Exhibit 10.6.[21] Each area of the structure represents a different SAC module. In the exhibit, the SAC report also describes certain key elements of the system of internal control: control environment, manual and automated systems, and control procedures. For more details about the SAC report, please refer to the complete 14 module set, which is available from the Institute of Internal Auditors Research Foundation (IIARF).

EXHIBIT 10.6   OVERVIEW OF THE SAC REPORT

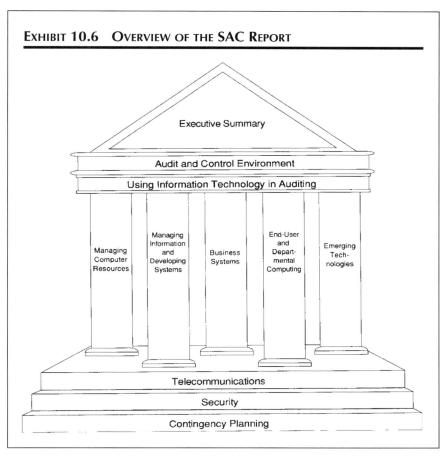

Source: From *Systems Audibility and Control,* Module I, Executive Summary, pp. 1–18, by The Institute of Internal Auditors Research Foundation. Copyright ©1991 by The Institute of Internal Auditors, Inc., 249 Maitland Avenue, Altamonte Springs, Florida 32701. Reprinted with permission.

In 2001 the IIA published a more contemporary IS control model called *Electronic Systems Assurance and Control (eSAC).* eSAC brings executive management, corporate governance entities, and auditors new information to understand, monitor, assess, and mitigate technology risks. *Electronic* was added to the title to emphasize both the e-business impact and electronic delivery of the new material. The title was further enhanced by changing "Auditability" to "Assurance," to recognize the important perspectives of governance and the alliances, internal and external, needed to ensure effective security, auditability, and control of information.

The centerpiece of the eSAC model couples the four COSO internal control objectives (operating, reporting, compliance, safeguarding) with five e-business assurance objectives (availability, capability, functionality, protectability, accountability) and five infrastructure building blocks (people, technology, processes, investment, communication). The organization's mission, values, strategies, and objectives drive the centerpiece to three outcomes: results, reputation, and learning. Feeding into the top of the centerpiece are five external market forces (customers, competition, regulators, community, owners) and speed of change (velocity). The bottom of the centerpiece has three external interdependencies (providers, alliances, agents). Exhibit 10.7 presents the eSAC conceptual model.

Within the five e-business assurance objectives, *availability* means being able to receive, accept, process, and support transactions at all times; *capability* means there is end-to-end reliability along with timely completion and fulfillment of all transactions; *functionality* means the system provides necessary facilities, responsiveness, and ease of use to meet user needs and expectations; *protectability* means logical and physical security controls ensure authorized access, and deny unauthorized access, to servers, applications, and information assets; and *accountability* means transaction processing is accurate, complete, and nonrefutable.[22]

Additional details about the eSAC model including a free downloadable seven-page PDF file with an overview of eSAC are available at the IIA website (*www.theiia.org*). To access various eSAC products and services, including the original SAC model and modules, interested parties must register and pay a subscription fee.

Exhibit 10. 7 eSAC Model

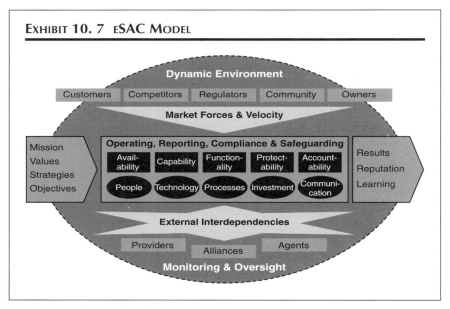

Source: Copyright 2001 by The IIA Research Foundation, 249 Maitland Avenue, Altamonte Springs, Florida 32710-4201, USA. Reprinted with permission.

SASs 55/78/94

The AICPA's Statements on Auditing Standards (SAS) 55, 78, and 94 pertain to the independent auditor's consideration of internal control in an audit of financial statements in accordance with generally accepted auditing standards. SAS 55, which was effective for audits of financial statements for periods beginning on or after January 1, 1990, used a non-COSO definition of internal control. SAS 78, which was effective for audits of financial statements for periods beginning on or after January 1, 1997, amended SAS 55 to include the COSO internal control definition and model of internal control. SAS 94, which was effective for audits of financial statements for periods beginning on or after June 1, 2001, added significant new sections regarding the effect of information technology on internal control.

SAS 94 specifies that an entity's use of IT may affect any of the five COSO components of internal control; that IT affects the fundamental manner in which transactions are initiated, recorded, processed, and reported; that IT provides potential benefits of effectiveness and efficiency for an entity's internal control; and that IT poses specific risks to an entity's internal control such as:

- Reliance on systems or programs that are inaccurately processing data, processing inaccurate data, or both
- Unauthorized access to data that may result in destruction of data or improper changes to data, including the recording of unauthorized or nonexistent transactions or inaccurate recording of transactions
- Unauthorized changes to systems, programs, or data in master files
- Failure to make necessary changes to systems or programs
- Inappropriate manual intervention
- Potential loss of data[23]

SAS 94 goes on to recommend that the auditor should consider whether specialized skills are needed to determine the effect of IT on the audit, to understand the IT controls, or to design and perform tests of IT controls or substantive tests. A professional possessing IT skills may be either on the auditor's staff or an outside professional. But the auditor should have sufficient IT-related knowledge to communicate the audit objectives to the professional, to evaluate whether the specified procedures will meet the auditor's objectives, and to evaluate the results of the procedures as they relate to the nature, timing, and extent of other planned audit procedures.[24]

Other key new statements in SAS 94 address the effects on the five COSO components of internal control. For example, SAS 94 recognizes that the *control environment* sets the tone of an organization and that management's failure to commit sufficient resources to address security risks presented by IT may adversely affect internal control by allowing improper changes to be made to computer programs or data, or by allowing unauthorized transactions to be processed; the use of IT may be an important element in an entity's *risk assessment* process; the use of IT affects the way that *control activities* are implemented; the auditor should understand the automated and manual procedures an entity uses to prepare and *communicate* financial statements and related disclosures, and how misstatements may occur; if management assumes that data used for *monitoring* are accurate without having a basis for that assumption, errors may exist in the information, potentially leading management to incorrect conclusions from its monitoring activities.[25]

Summary of the Six Major Internal Control Frameworks

Each of the six internal control framework models just presented conclude that the boards of directors, officers, and other managers within every organization are primarily responsible for ensuring that effective control and risk management systems are in place. As an internal control expert, the role of an internal or external auditor is to consult with these key management personnel to help them better achieve their internal control objectives and responsibilities. This role is especially important in the information systems arena due to the rapidly changing environment that does not appear to have an end.

ADDITIONAL KEYS TO A SUCCESSFUL PROGRAM

The third key to a successful CSA program is proper training of auditors in the skills necessary to facilitate CSA. Historically, auditors have interacted with client staff and management on a one-on-one basis or in small group meetings. Auditors were not typically required to facilitate discussion by other groups. However, as CSA becomes more and more the norm in leading-edge companies, the demand for IS auditors as well as non-IS auditors who possess CSA facilitation skills will be significantly enhanced.

As a result, many firms are finding it necessary to send some of their staff to attend facilitation training in order to hone their facilitation skills. Because facilitation skills are often used by many course instructors, the training department within an organization should be able to assist in finding facilitation courses. Other possible sources would be conferences and seminars sponsored by local chapters and international headquarters of internal auditing professional associations such as the IIA and the ISACA. The IIA also sponsors the Certificate in Control Self Assessment (CCSA) designation.

Auditors must also be highly knowledgeable about the particular internal control framework(s) adopted by an organization's audit department. Therefore, training of both IS and non-IS auditors on the details of the applicable internal control framework(s) is also critical. Again, conferences and seminars can be an important source of training on internal control frameworks.

The fourth key to facilitating successful CSA workshops is that the group being assessed should consist of staff members in the area being assessed but no supervisors or managers. If a management group is being facilitated, higher levels of management should be excluded from the CSA group. A manager insisted on attending one CSA workshop. When she excused herself to answer a pager call and stepped out of the room, there was a marked difference in the willingness of staff members to share their ideas and to participate in the general discussion. When the manager returned, she was oblivious to staff members' return to their subservient role of looking to her before answering. Since management identifies the control objectives to be discussed in the workshop, they should not be concerned about what their staff might be saying. Instead, they should be optimistic that their people can develop workable solutions to the specified control objectives. Severe resistance to being omitted from a CSA workshop may even be a red flag that there could be some internal control environment weaknesses.

A fifth key to CSA success is having the proper tools. These tools include a private conference room or training room with flipcharts, marking pens, whiteboards or chalkboards, and other typical training materials, in addition to automated tools such as a laptop computer with a visual projection device for recording CSA successes, failures, and action items. For electronically tallying voting results, groupware products such as Option Finder can expedite the voting process, summarize and analyze the results, and make the process more enjoyable. If the organization is on a low budget, scratch paper and a calculator can be effectively utilized. Be careful not to get carried away with automated tools. In fact, they can act as barriers between the groups, as in the case of a training room in which classroom participants each sit in front of their own workstation. Such an arrangement is definitely not conducive to an interactive CSA workshop. A bag of miscellaneous toys or other amusements can prove effective at lightening the atmosphere of a CSA workshop and energizing the group when they get complacent.

Key number six to a successful CSA workshop is to avoid the pitfall of excessive time usage. In many CSA workshops, the need for better communication between management and staff, or between the operation being assessed and the outside departments or areas they deal with, is identified as an obstacle to effective job performance. CSA facilitators should be cognizant of this fact because, although communication among these areas is very important, an entire CSA workshop can be completely consumed by this one issue, often without any deployable internal control enhancements being developed. Ideas for enhancing inter- and intradepartmental communication should be discussed, but the CSA group should not be allowed to dwell on this one issue. During planning for the CSA workshop, the facilitator should accept this issue as a given and plan to spend only about 30 to 60 minutes discussing it.

VARIOUS APPROACHES

CSA can be implemented in a variety of ways within an organization. Each approach has positive and negative factors. Therefore, the methodology adopted by an organization should be tailored to meet the specific needs of its management. It might even be necessary to apply one CSA approach for one set of operating units and a different CSA variation to another set of operating units. Four general types of CSA approaches can be utilized: pure CSA, centralized CSA, targeted CSA, and hybrid CSA.

Pure CSA

Pure CSA is a method in which operating units within an organization are responsible for conducting CSA workshops on an ongoing basis as part of their normal operating procedures. The Internal Audit Department or an external consultant usually designs and develops the CSA program to ensure consistent application throughout the organization. Also, internal auditors or consultants usually conduct the initial CSA workshop for each operating unit and provide training to the designated CSA facilitators within the operating unit. After the initial CSA workshop has been completed, management of the operating unit becomes responsible for ensuring that identified action items are appropriately addressed, future CSA workshops are conducted on a periodic basis (e.g., annually), and the results of the future CSA workshops are reported to appropriate areas within the organization.

Under pure CSA, a central department receives a copy of the report of the results of each CSA workshop. This department then assumes the role of monitoring the progress of the implementation of any solutions and can act as consultants and mediators on issues that span multiple operating units. This central department can be within the Internal Audit Department, or it can be a separate control-monitoring department.

Advantages to pure CSA include complete ownership by operating units, increased awareness of internal controls and who is responsible for ensuring that they are adequately deployed, and more effective solutions because they come directly from the experts within the operating unit. Disadvantages include loss of continuity as turnover occurs within operating units, failure of operating unit management to consider the CSA process as important and thus failure to perform CSA workshops on a regular basis, poor CSA facilitation within operating units, and stifling of new ideas by management of the operating units.

The World Bank, headquartered in Washington, D.C., has implemented a pure CSA approach. At the 1996 CSA Conference in Toronto, Blanshard Marke, senior controls specialist at the World Bank, described in detail the approach used in his organization. Marke shared the idea that management wanted to remove the notion that the Internal Audit Department was responsible for internal control. Therefore, the World Bank established a separate Controls Department and charged it with implementing CSA in various work areas. The main elements of the World Bank methodology are:

- CSA is implemented by management.
- The Controls Department provides intellectual leadership, counsel, and advice.
- The Internal Audit Department and external auditors are actively involved.
- Business units take over the CSA process after the first year. Designated "COSO Champions" are trained to perform future CSA workshops.
- Implementation of action plans are monitored by the Controls Department.

Marke identified the advantages of the World Bank approach as reinforcing the fact that people are critical factors in the success of controls, providing documentary evidence for COSO attestation, providing flexibility to accommodate a diversity of business processes, and providing adaptability to changing world and economic environments.

Centralized CSA

Centralized CSA is a method in which the Internal Audit Department or other designated department within an organization performs the CSA workshops and issues reports on the results to management of the operating units. The operating units do not assume ongoing CSA workshop facilitation duties. As a result, the department responsible for performing the CSA workshops must devote significant resources to maintaining an effective CSA process. Thus, CSA becomes one of the available audit tools while still enabling traditional audit testing of controls in areas of significant risk to be performed.

Centralized CSA is perhaps the most common approach since it enables an Internal Audit Department to gradually develop and implement CSA without the shock of attempting full implementation and the risk of complete failure. Another advantage of the centralized CSA approach is that by performing traditional auditing techniques as well as some CSA workshops, the Internal Audit Department is able to diversify its audit approaches. Diversification enables internal auditors to tailor the approach most appropriate for each operating unit.

Centralized CSA is also the most practical in highly regulated and highly risky industries. Pure CSA may not be an option because a certain amount of compliance testing is required by various laws and regulations. Furthermore, relying on the operating unit to fully report on the effectiveness of controls in high-risk processes may not always be wise. For example, neither management nor staff may be aware of how to effectively implement adequate segregation of duties in a particular process. This situation has been seen in several audits in wire transfer departments in various financial institutions.

Potential disadvantages of centralized CSA are confusion by operating units over who is responsible for internal controls, inconsistent evaluation of internal controls throughout the organization, and ineffective solutions in areas where CSA was not applied.

Because a centralized CSA approach is easier to implement than pure CSA, the degree of audit resources devoted to centralized CSA implementation varies by organization, but it typically falls somewhere between 10 and 50 percent.

Targeted CSA

Targeted CSA is a method in which the Internal Audit Department performs CSA on a limited basis and does not devote a significant amount of resources to facilitate CSA workshops. Targeted CSA is an approach that is best applied by organizations that have researched CSA and have reached a point where they are ready to attempt to facilitate a few CSA workshops. Although the success of targeted CSA obviously cannot be expected to be extensive, targeted CSA can be effective if deployed in high-risk areas, usually in conjunction with traditional audit methods. Targeted CSA can also be useful in organizations where acceptance of CSA by management is spotty. If there are a few innovative managers willing to try it, internal auditors should take advantage of the opportunity. If they find value in the process, auditors will have a much easier time selling the process to other managers. Almost all firms that are just beginning to implement CSA are essentially at the targeted CSA stage.

The advantages of targeted CSA are low cost in terms of resources required, and minimal risk if the process fails. The disadvantages are reduced effectiveness at identifying opportunities to improve operations, failure by management to see the benefits of CSA, and lack of enthusiasm within the Internal Audit Department due to limited use of the process.

Hybrid CSA

Hybrid CSA is a method in which CSA is applied centrally in some areas of an organization and in its pure form in other areas. For example, some organizations have limited audit resources and multiple remote operating units. In these cases, it may be more practical to apply pure CSA to the remote operating units and centralized CSA to common functional areas in the organization such as accounting, data processing, payroll, human resources, accounts payable, or customer service. A hybrid form of CSA may also be necessary if an organization has limited audit resources and also operates in a highly regulated industry.

I received an inquiry about CSA from an internal auditor of a nonpublic, multistate holding company with various subsidiaries, each of which comprises an independent operating unit in a different industry. The Internal Audit Department in this private conglomerate had only a handful of auditors to cover a large territory. For this reason, they felt that pure CSA would be very practical in the remote operating units. For centralized operations, they planned to perform centralized CSA.

BENEFITS OF A SUCCESSFUL PROGRAM

The benefits of a successful CSA program are many. They encompass the entire organization, including individual staff members, management, internal and external auditors, and the owners of the organization.

Staff members benefit by having their creative ideas for improving operations and controls implemented, or at least considered. They participate in the process of identifying internal control weaknesses and formulating solutions. Thus, they are more likely to take ownership of the solutions since they contributed to their development. This employee empowerment enhances worker morale while helping to improve operational effectiveness. Without CSA, they might believe that their ideas are not valuable, thereby leading to job dissatisfaction and higher turnover.

Management benefits by gaining the opportunity to enhance their ability to meet their business objectives with the direct help of their staff. Management has input into the process by identifying the critical business objectives to be addressed by the CSA workshop participants. This can sometimes directly improve their financial incentives. Also, increased employee morale reduces the incidence of employee disgruntlement and the related difficulties of counseling and other disciplinary actions. Management also learns that they are responsible for internal control, not the internal auditors.

Internal auditors benefit by being perceived as helping to add value to the organization. This results from the fact that they are consulting with operating units to address the key business objectives of the operating unit. As facilitators, auditors are also in a position to focus the direction of CSA workshops on the other objectives of internal controls, including reliability of financial reporting and compliance with laws and regulations, thereby helping to ensure internal control compliance.

Another major benefit to internal auditors is that performing a CSA workshop as one of the early steps in an audit serves as an icebreaker between the staff participants and the auditors. The participants have an opportunity to see the facilitating auditor in a role other than the traditional auditor who comes into their realm and points out flaws in their processes. Instead, participants interact openly with the auditors in a fun and constructive manner. Then, in cases in which CSA workshops are followed by the performance of audit testing, the participants are much more comfortable working with the auditors.

External auditors can benefit because are able to observe internal control compliance, which includes accuracy and reliability of financial reporting. They also have the opportunity to secure contracts to perform CSA workshops. This is particularly important for external auditing firms because their largest market for future growth lies in increased revenues from consulting services such as CSA.

Organization owners benefit because many control enhancements arising from CSA workshops pertain to improving operational efficiency and effectiveness. As a result, firms can maximize their profitability and effectiveness, thereby increasing the value of the organization to its owners, whether it is a publicly traded corporation, a governmental entity, or a privately held business.

The beauty of CSA is that it can be applied in IS areas as well as nontechnical operating areas within virtually any organization. It can even be performed on a mid- or upper-level management group. In such cases, if any potentially significant internal control weaknesses are identified during a CSA workshop, auditors can perform "drill-down" CSA workshops on lower levels of the organization pertaining to the potential internal control weaknesses. Drilling down can help determine the extent of the potential weaknesses.

Detractors have argued that CSA is nothing more than a quality control process molded to fit the needs of auditors. In fact, quality control departments in some firms feel as if they need to compete with auditors who perform CSA. It is true that improved quality and service can result from CSA since quality and service may be one of the key business objectives identified by management. However, CSA goes far beyond just quality control in that it can identify ways to address risks within the generally accepted internal control framework models. For example, CSA can identify ways to increase the accuracy of financial reporting, compliance with laws and regulations, and safeguarding of assets.

CSA has been well received by management within organizations that have properly applied it. However, CSA is not a panacea. It must be diligently applied and constantly reexamined to ensure that it is meeting the current needs of the organization. As organizations adapt to changes in their environments, CSA must also adapt to organizational changes. Case study 10.1 describes the CSA approach developed at the Boeing Employees' Credit Union in Tukwila, Washington, and demonstrates how the approach was applied in a telecommunications environment. Case study 10.2 demonstrates why CSA cannot be substituted for tests of key internal controls.

CASE STUDY 10.1

Development of CSA at Boeing Employees' Credit Union

The Internal Audit Department of Boeing Employees' Credit Union (BECU) planned and developed its CSA and related internal control training curriculum over the course of approximately one year and performed its first CSA workshop in the fall of 1996. A second CSA workshop was performed in December 1996. Then, in 1997, the Audit Department began performing CSA workshops as a standard audit step in every major audit. At one point, due to scheduling conflicts, three CSA workshops and internal control training classes were performed over a one-week period. This proved to be a little overwhelming to the department since the process was still relatively new. As with any new process, the format of overheads, flip charts, computer aids, class materials, and final reports was evolving and improving after each workshop. Because three workshops were performed in such a short period, there was little time to discuss and communicate potential improvements within the department. As a result, we had to do the best we could and debrief as a department afterward to discuss the best techniques and training aids and to reach agreement as to the generally accepted approach to be used by the department. My advice would be to never schedule more than one CSA workshop in a week. This would allow some time for any questions and potential improvements to be discussed. Each new process and group of participants evaluated through CSA seems to identify new questions and observations that can lead to the continuous enhancement of the CSA process.

Boeing Employees' Credit Union Methodology

The BECU utilizes a centralized CSA approach. The methodology for applying CSA at the BECU is as follows:

- Meet with management of the process being evaluated to identify the four most important primary business objectives, answer questions about internal controls and CSA, and schedule internal control training class and CSA workshop.

- Conduct a two-hour internal control training class with six to eight staff members who are going to be present in the CSA workshop. Supervisors, managers, and higher levels of management are encouraged to attend this class.
- Facilitate a half-day CSA workshop with staff members to identify successes and obstacles to the primary business objectives and to identify action plan items for resolving obstacles.
- Summarize results in a report to management. The action plan items for operational and control improvement are treated as if they were typical audit recommendations. In other words, management is expected to respond to the CSA recommendations regarding the actions, if any, they expect to take to address the issues identified.
- Track the action plan items to ensure that the agreed-on actions are implemented.

Control Self-Assessment Applied in a Telecommunications Environment

CSA was applied as the first step in a major audit of a telecommunications process. Exhibit CS 10.1 provides excerpts of the CSA report that accompanied the final audit report issued to management.

EXHIBIT CS 10.1 CONTROL SELF-ASSESSMENT MANAGEMENT REPORT: TELECOMMUNICATIONS PROCESS

Internal Audit performed a control self-assessment (CSA) workshop with the Telecommunications Department on Month xx, 20xx. The objective of the workshop was to assess the effectiveness of four supporting objectives that were identified by the telecommunications director as critical to the telecommunications process, and to facilitate the identification of opportunities to improve the effectiveness of the objectives. The four objectives were:

1. Security against unauthorized access
2. Customer service, both internal and external
3. Planning and directing telecommunications needs of the organization
4. Keeping current on new technologies

The CSA workshop consisted of these steps, which were performed in conjunction with the Telecommunications Department staff:

- Discussing and recording successes and obstacles pertaining to the implementation level of each objective.
- Conducting anonymous voting with the staff to rate the actual (current) effectiveness of each objective and the desired (how effective should it be) effectiveness of each objective. The difference between the two ratings was considered to be the opportunity for improvement.
- Identifying action plans to address the opportunities for improvement.

(continued)

EXHIBIT CS 10.1   *(continued)*

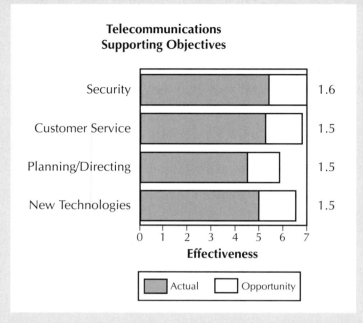

The items listed below are provided in the following pages for review:
* Graph of voting results showing opportunities for improvement
* Analysis of voting results
* Significant successes
* Significant obstacles and action plan ideas
* Detailed CSA worksheets

CSA Analysis of Voting Results

Although there was little variation in the effectiveness ratings and improvement opportunities among any of the four supporting Telecommunications objectives, the participants identified the Security and Customer Service objectives as having the highest desired effectiveness. They rated the *actual* effectiveness of the Security objective at 5.4, with the highest possible rating being 7.0. The *desired* effectiveness was rated at 7.0. The difference of 1.6 was considered the opportunity for improvement in the Security objective. They rated the *actual* effectiveness of the Customer Service objective at 5.3 and the *desired* effectiveness at 6.8. The difference of 1.5 was considered the opportunity for improvement in the Customer Service objective.

The participants identified the Planning/Directing and New Technologies objectives as having slightly lower desired effectiveness levels. They rated the *actual* effectiveness of the Planning/Directing objective at 4.5 and the *desired* effectiveness at 6.0. The difference of 1.5 was considered the opportunity for improvement in the Planning/Directing objective. They rated the *actual* effectiveness of the Customer Service objective at 5.0 and the *desired* effectiveness at 6.5. The difference of 1.5 was considered the opportunity for improvement in the Customer Service objective.

These ratings and the lists of successes on the accompanying CSA worksheets indicate that Telecommunications staff believe that the supporting objectives of the Telecommunications process are being carried out with a reasonable degree of effectiveness. They also indicate that there is about the same amount of room for improvement in each objective. We noted that the participants had more difficulty identifying action plan items to help increase the effectiveness of the Telecommunications process in the Planning/Directing and New Technologies categories.

CSA Significant Successes

Following are the significant successes identified by the participants during the CSA workshop. The accompanying detailed CSA worksheets list the other successes identified by the participants.

Objective: Security Against Unauthorized Access

1. The organization has never been successfully hacked.
2. Fraud detection software notifies Telecommunications staff of abnormal call destinations, volumes, and lengths based on custom settings.
3. The organization received a high score on the risk assessment performed by the outside consulting firm 18 months ago.
4. To enhance security, the automatic circuit assurance feature of the PBX (private branch exchange) system monitors phone traffic for abnormally long calls or rapid repetitive short calls.

Objective: Customer Service—Internal and External

5. All phones are now on one system. The PBX provides more effective and efficient service, and allows for future expansion and flexibility.
6. Positive customer satisfaction.

Objective: Planning and Directing Telecommunication Needs of the Organization

7. Participate in the operating plan process and facility move meetings.

Objective: Keeping Current on New Technologies

8. Attend various types of training, seminars, and conferences.

CSA Significant Obstacles and Action Plan Ideas

Following are the significant obstacles identified by the participants during the CSA workshop and the action plan ideas they developed to address the obstacles. The accompanying detailed CSA worksheets list the other obstacles identified by the participants.

(*continued*)

Exhibit CS 10.1   *(continued)*

Objective: Security Against Unauthorized Access

1. If the personal computer (PC) containing fraud-detection software crashes or runs out of paper, Telecommunications staff will not be notified of problems identified by the fraud detection software.

   Action Plan Ideas
   a. Reorganize reports to reduce risk of paper running out.
   b. Submit new request for replacement printer.
   c. Determine when the Windows NT version of the fraud-detection software is available (call beta site users).

2. Organization staff lack knowledge and awareness of security and passwords.

   Action Plan Ideas
   a. Develop separate training course on telecommunications security for all employees to attend.
   b. Finalize the "Security Statement of Responsibility," which is to be signed by each staff member after completing telecommunications training and stored in their Human Resources file.

3. Getting complacent or overconfident. For example, a backup system security administrator has not been fully trained.

   Action Plan Ideas
   a. Have technicians give security updates to Telecommunications staff at weekly department meetings.
   b. Update Telecommunications Department procedures manual and train department staff on fraud detection software and related procedures.

4. Not enough attention paid to Automatic Circuit Assurance (ACA) feature of the PBX.

   Action Plan Idea
   a. Have experienced technicians train other Telecommunications staff on ACA.

Objective: Customer Service—Internal and External

5. During preparation of the internal phone list, management often supplies incorrect information. Also, the spreadsheet is inefficient for creating the phone list.

   Action Plan Ideas
   a. All available software is PC based. Telecommunications will continue to research software that can better automate creation of the phone list.
   b. Eliminate the need to rely solely on managers to notify Telecommunications of staff changes. Will rely more on e-mail from Human Resources regarding changes, additions, and terminations.

6. The Microcomputer Department could provide a higher level of service

and support to meet the needs of the Telecommunications Department. This issue affects department efficiencies as well as the Planning/Directing and New Technologies objectives.

Action Plan Ideas

a. Acquire a separate file server for Telecommunications to add telephony applications to LAN, AUDIX, and Conversant.

b. Have Telecommunications hire a technical support analyst to add telephony applications to the LAN and maintain them. Alternatively, the Microcomputer Department could appoint a designated Telecommunications support person/system administrator to team with Telecommunications on applications.

c. Need clarification of Microcomputer Department's span of responsibility. Is it too broad?

Objective: Planning and Directing Telecommunication Needs of Organization

7. Lack of communication from other departments and unreasonable service level expectations by other departments. For example, if customers do not give ample notice when service is required, Telecommunications has a difficult time meeting their needs.

Action Plan Ideas

a. Conduct surveys and one-on-one meetings with each department.

b. Conduct presentations about the Telecommunications Department to management.

Objective: Keeping Current on New Technologies

8. Lack of time to keep current

Action Plan Ideas

a. Schedule two hours each week to read and study literature on new technologies.

b. Spend more time researching telecommunications-related information on the Internet.

CSA Worksheet

Supporting Objective 1: Security Against Unauthorized Access

	Actual	Desired	Opportunity
Effectiveness Rating: Low–1, High–7	5.4	7.0	1.6

Successes	Obstacles/Risks
1. Never been hacked.	1. Social engineers.
2. Good password controls (lockout after six tries, expiration, minimum length).	2. If Fraud Fighter PC crashes or runs out of paper, it won't notify of problems from Fraud Fighter software.

(continued)

Exhibit CS 10.1 *(continued)*

Supporting Objective 1: Security Against Unauthorized Access (*continued*)

	Actual	Desired	Opportunity
Effectiveness Rating: Low–1, High–7	5.4	7.0	1.6

Successes	Obstacles/Risks
3. Electronic lock devices attached to maintenance ports. Only Telecommunication laptop and Lucent have the key device.	3. Staff abusing long-distance calls (e.g., incoming 800# calls from relatives, outgoing long-distance calls).
4. Fraud detection software notifies Telecommunication of abnormal call destinations, volumes, lengths, etc. based on custom settings.	4. Organization staff lack knowledge and awareness of security, passwords.
5. Remote access (DISA) removed from software.	5. Getting complacent, backup system administrator not fully trained.
6. Entry Plus security to switch room.	6. Not all employees get phone training.
7. Training—Lucent book of scams, user groups, magazines (e.g., 2600).	7. Numerous people have access to wiring closets (Telecommunications, DP, Microcomputers, electrician vendor all hold master keys).
8. Organization got highest score on vendor risk assessment 18 months ago.	8. Automatic Circuit Assurance (ACA) feature not paid enough attention.
9. Lucent performs quarterly scan of organization passwords and notifies if any are set to default.	9. Fraud Fighter vendor slow with delivery of upgraded software.
10. Monthly review of phone invoices.	10. Cell phone cloning.
11. Can't transfer from outside to outside (e.g., extension 9011).	11. Fraud detection software notifies Telecommunication only upon completion of call (i.e., after the fact). The software won't report hung circuits.
12. Video on telecommunication fraud shown in training.	12. Calling card shoulder surfers steal access codes.
13. Cell phone activity monitored by AT&T Wireless.	
14. Calling card spending limit ($500).	

Supporting Objective 2: Customer Service, both Internal and External

	Actual	*Desired*	*Opportunity*
Effectiveness Rating: Low–1, High–7	*5.3*	*6.8*	*1.5*

Successes	*Obstacles/Risks*
1. All one system now (Lucent PBX), no more Aspect. Allows for future expansion and flexibility. 2. No complaints. 3. Good survey responses to AUDIX training and facilities moves. 4. Positive communications within the organization. 5. Positive feedback on call service level reports sent to management (daily, weekly, monthly, quarterly). 6. Phone lists. 7. AUDIX available to all staff with management approval. External 1. Line monitoring to ensure adequate phone line availability (traffic engineering). 2. Rate/fax lines. 3. Employment information line.	1. Tracking service levels on clientele. 2. Phone list: get incorrect data from management; also Lotus spreadsheet is inefficient. 3. Staff resistance to change. 4. Other Organization departments reluctant to turn over processes (e.g., jobline from HR). 5. LAN control: PC Department swamped so not timely in implementing new services (e.g., new paging software). 6. Interdepartment communications and teamwork. External 1. Need skill-based call-routing system in certain areas like Member Services (management resistant to menu phone system; want members to get a real person). 2. Updating/educating members (e.g., on new area codes). Members resistance to change/ automation. 3. Disasters or system crashes.

Supporting Objective 3: Planning and Directing Telecommunications Needs of the Organization

	Actual	*Desired*	*Opportunity*
Effectiveness Rating: Low–1, High–7	*4.5*	*6.0*	*1.5*

Successes	*Obstacles/Risks*
1. Internal department meetings to discuss telecommunication needs. 2. Participate in operating plan process.	1. Lack of communication and teamwork from other departments. 2. Inadequate service and cooperation in teaming from Microcomputer Department.

(*continued*)

EXHIBIT CS 10.1 *(continued)*

Supporting Objective 3: Planning and Directing Telecommunications Needs of the Organization (*continued*)

	Actual	Desired	Opportunity
Effectiveness Rating: Low–1, High–7	*4.5*	*6.0*	*1.5*

Successes	Obstacles/Risks
3. Participate in facility move meetings. 4. Internal timelines for project completion.	3. Unreasonable service-level expectations by other departments (e.g., not enough lead time given, same/next day requests can be challenging).

Supporting Objective 4: Keeping Current on New Technologies

	Actual	Desired	Opportunity
Effectiveness Rating: Low–1, High–7	*5.0*	*6.5*	*1.5*

Successes	Obstacles/Risks

1. Attend training by user groups.
   • *International DEFINITY Users Group (IDUG)*
   • *VTEL User Group (VUGA) for videoconferencing users*
2. Attend seminars/conferences.
   • *Telecommunication Association (TCA)*
   • *Call center*
3. Read periodicals:
   • *Telecommunication Network Security*
   • *411*
   • *Call Center*
   • *2600 (hacker magazine)*
   • *Telecommunication Alert Bulletin*
   • *Business Communication Review (BCR)*
4. Get Lucent training.
5. Read newspapers.
6. Read vendor information, network with vendors.
7. Form strong committees within users groups.
	1. Previously short staffed/ trained.
	2. Some vendors slow about product releases and information (e.g., Fraud Fighter).
	3. Lack of time.

CASE STUDY 10.2

Why CSA Should Not Be Considered a Substitute for Tests of Key Internal Controls

Although CSA was applied to the telecommunications process within one client organization, compliance tests of critical internal controls were also performed. The reason was that CSA can identify whether critical internal controls have been implemented, but it cannot assess whether those controls are actually functioning or whether they have been properly implemented. This can be a problem if the staff members think the controls are functioning when, in fact, they are not.

For example, during the audit, the phone numbers of the maintenance ports of each of several private branch exchanges (PBXs) and other telecommunications central processing units (CPUs) were dialed to test whether the electronic lock devices attached to the ports would prevent unauthorized access. For those ports that were properly locked, an intermittent beeping sound could be heard on the phone receiver. However, a normal dial tone could be heard from the maintenance port of the primary PBX. The technician checked the port and found that the electronic lock device had somehow worked its way loose and was therefore not blocking the port as required. This finding was not included in the report because it appeared to be an isolated occurrence, and an independent examination of the PBX controls by an outside vendor about 18 months earlier did not reveal any similar weaknesses. The technician was thankful because, according to the head of telecommunications for the organization, the number-one business objective of the Telecommunications Department was security.

Another internal control weakness identified was the fact that procedures for monitoring long-distance call activity had not been performed for almost four months. Each month, an electronic database of all phone calls was received from the long-distance service provider. A technician was supposed to query the database for selected criteria that could identify patterns of potential long-distance call abuse by employees. For various reasons, the analyses had been delayed.

A third control weakness pertained to the ineffective deployment of some reports designed to identify the 15 longest long-distance calls made each week. These reports were rendered ineffective because the routine, extended long-distance phone connections between the mainframe CPU and the vendor were not excluded from the report. These calls were known to occur on a routine basis for various reasons. However, they were often the only calls appearing on the fifteen-longest-calls report. The same report for a different location was also ineffective because it did not exclude the phone connections between the remote location and the centralized video camera monitoring system. It was recommended that the routine long-distance phone numbers be suppressed from the reports and that the number of calls appearing on the reports be increased from 15 to 30.

Another interesting check was to check conference rooms and other publicly accessible telephones to ensure that long-distance calls could not be

(continued)

> **CASE STUDY 10.2 (*continued*)**
>
> performed. Of the phones tested, only one exception was found. That exception happened to be the conference room utilized by external auditors and regulatory examiners, which had long distance enabled. This oversight occurred when the Telecommunications Department was not properly notified of the conclusion of the most recent audit.
>
> A physical security issue was also identified. Access to the PBX and other telecommunications CPUs was restricted by an electronic access badge locking device on the door to the room where the CPUs were located. Only the telecommunications staff had access to the room. Because of this security, the telecommunications CPUs were left signed on 24 hours a day, even though staff were not present. By leaving the CPUs signed on, a step was saved when they had to be accessed remotely for maintenance or other monitoring purposes. However, the room was accessible with conventional master door keys, which were possessed by various individuals, including the security guard, electrician vendor, facilities manager, and several other managers. The CPUs are now signed off when the telecommunications technicians are not present.

As can be seen from the above results, CSA by itself does not constitute an audit. In fact, an organization could be placing itself at significant risk of financial loss if it rests its future solely on CSA as a substitute for internal auditing. CSA can produce effective results, but it must be coupled with effective tests of internal controls in high-risk areas.

NOTES

1. "Paul Makosz, Serious About CSA," *CSA Sentinel* (January 1997): 1.
2. Larry L. Baker and Roger D. Graham, "Control Self-Assessment," *Internal Auditor* (April 1996): 52–57.
3. Coopers & Lybrand LLP and Price Waterhouse LLP merged in 1998.
4. "CSA Sentinel Debuts," *Internal Auditor* (December 1996): 9; and CSA Sentinel (January 1997): 12.
5. *Information Systems Audit and Control Journal* (Volume I, 1997): 4, 8–10, 20–23, 30–33 (Part I).
6. *Information Systems Audit and Control Journal* (Volume II, 1997): 58–62 (Part II).
7. "Control Self-Assessment—Here to Stay," *Internal Auditor* (December 1996): 9.
8. *Internal Control–Integrated Framework* (September 1992): 9.
9. Id. at 15.
10. Paul E. Fiorelli and Cynthia J. Rooney, "COSO and the Federal Sentencing Guidelines," *Internal Auditor* (April 1997): 57–60.
11. *Guidance on Control* (November 1995): 2.
12. Id. at 27–29.
13. Id. at 30.
14. *Internal Control and Financial Reporting* (London: ICAEW, December 1994): 1.
15. *Internal Financial Control* (December 1994): 1.

16. *COBIT Framework,* First Release (December 1995): iv.
17. *COBIT Framework* (2000): 12.
18. John W. Lainhart IV, "Arrival of COBIT Helps Refine the Valuable Role of IS Audit and Control in the Enterprise," *IS Audit and Control Journal* (Volume IV, 1996): 20–23.
19. *SAC Report, Executive Summary* (1991): 1–5.
20. Id. at 1–17.
21. Id. at 1–18.
22. *www.theiia.org* (July 5, 2002).
23. American Institute of Certified Public Accountants, Codification of Statements on Auditing Standards, Consideration of Internal Control in a Financial Statement Audit, AU Section 319 (January 2002): Paragraphs 16–19.
24. Id. at Paragraphs 31–32.
25. Id. at Paragraphs 34, 36, 39, 46, 51, 54.

CHAPTER 11

Encryption and Cryptography

> Encryption is the ultimate means of information asset protection. If properly implemented, encryption will foil almost any attack short of a nationally sponsored effort. Encryption can be used to protect any information asset, whether stored on tape or disk, or while in transit on a communications link.[1]

Prior to the 1990s, national governments, government contractors, and private banking systems were the primary users of encryption technology. With the proliferation of the Internet and electronic commerce, however, the need for secure exchanges of electronic information has now also become of significant importance to commercial entities and the consumer public in general. There appears to be global concurrence that cryptography is the strongest means for securing electronic information against theft or compromise. However, cryptography can be both an ally and an adversary of secure electronic information exchange. On one hand, encryption technology can protect information from unauthorized viewing or attack. On the other hand, dishonest or devious persons can employ cryptanalysis techniques to divulge, alter, steal, divert, or otherwise disrupt electronic information exchanges. The following discussion provides a series of references and quotes that help put into perspective the need for deployment of strong encryption techniques.

In 1997, Ian Goldberg, a University of California–Berkeley graduate student, linked together 250 idle workstations in a manner that enabled him to test 100 billion possible keys per hour. Using this method, he was able to crack RSA Data Security, Inc.'s 40-bit encryption algorithm in three and a half hours.[2]

> Computer systems in the United States Department of Defense (DOD) may have experienced as many as 250,000 hacker attacks in 1995, according to a report from the United States General Accounting Office (GAO). Such attacks are often successful, granting unknown and unauthorized persons access to highly sensitive information, and they double in number each year due to easier and more widespread use of the Internet and to the increasing sophistication of computer hackers.
>
> According to the GAO, the DOD lacks a uniform policy for assessing risks, protecting systems, responding to incidents, or assessing damages. In addition, training of users and system and network administrators is haphazard and constrained by limited resources. Technical solutions should help, but their success depends on

whether the DOD implements them in tandem with better policy and personnel measures.[3]

Dutch computer hackers stole United States military secrets during the Persian Gulf War and offered them to Iraq. The secrets could have altered the course of the war. But the Iraqis allegedly never used the information, fearing a hoax.[4]

The Internet has made it possible to assemble massive computing resources to crack a key. In 1994, a 129-digit RSA key was broken through the combined efforts of 1,600 computers around the world. The attack, which was coordinated through e-mail and involved finding the prime factors of the 129-digit number, consumed 5,000 MIPS months over an eight-month interval of real time.[5] (*MIPS* stands for machine instructions per second.)

Hiding behind anonymous keyboards, a group of hackers struggled for two weeks to breach United States military and civilian computer networks. They succeeded beyond their wildest dreams. . . The cultprits [were] a special United States national security team that was secretly testing the vulnerability of the nation's computer systems using software found on the Internet. . . [The] hackers gained access to computer systems across the country. . . , including the United States Pacific Command in Hawaii. [They also] gained access to a United States electric power grid system that they could have sabotaged to plunge the nation into darkness.[6]

In August 1999, an international team of scientists in the Netherlands was able to determine the prime factors of a 512-bit number that models the key in the well-known RSA-155 cryptographic algorithm used extensively in hardware and software to protect electronic data traffic (e.g., the international version of secure sockets layer [SSL]). RSA-155 was designed by three scientists (Ronald Rivest, Adi Shamir, Leonard Adelman) at the Massachusetts Institute of Technology in the mid-1970s. It has two parts: a sieving step and a matrix reduction step. For the sieving step, about 300 fast SGI Sun workstations and Pentium personal computers (PCs) ran in parallel mostly on nights and weekends and used about 8,000 MIPS-years. For the matrix reduction step, a Cray C916 supercomputer at the SARA Amsterdam Academic Computer Center was used. The total effort took about seven months. However, the scientists said that using a distributed processing effort over the Internet with thousands of participants, it is possible to reduce the factoring time to one week. This led world-renowned cryptographer Bruce Schneier to recommend using 2,048-bit keys.[7]

But even large keys have their downfall. Typical encryption keys consist of 40 to 2,048 bits of random data, which have to be stored on a PC's hard drive where everything is filed in a very logical, ordered way. According to Adi Shamir (RSA codesigner) and Nicko van Someron, chunks of randomness stand out, making it easy for malicious programs to locate them.[8]

Encryption is arguably the most important aspect of information security. It is a major component in the overall information security infrastructure of any electronic process. Virtually all electronic exchanges of significant or important data employ the use of some form of encryption. Encryption is vital to the exchange of information pertaining to matters of national security, to electronic monetary transactions within all major banking systems, to electronic commerce among merchants and consumers, to electronic data interchange (EDI) among businesses and their customers, and to the security of passwords and other confidential information residing in virtually all computing systems.

Proper cryptographic controls can help ensure the confidentiality, integrity, authenticity, and nonrepudiation of electronic messages transmitted or transported between or among various computing systems. Policies, procedures, physical security over devices, logical security controls, and cryptography all play critical roles in the overall information systems (IS) security environment. Without effective cryptographic controls, the other IS controls are simply supporting a weak infrastructure. Noncryptographic controls are much more susceptible to circumvention because they rely on human education and the ability of humans to carry them out. In modern times, cryptography, while relying on humans for creation and certain aspects of control, is essentially a set of computerized controls, thereby providing the potential for significantly greater speed and reliability than human-based controls. Therefore, if properly designed and implemented, cryptographic controls can be broken only by another computer. Fortunately, humans must direct computers to break encryption algorithms and other cryptographic controls. The thought of *intelligent* computers independently determining when, how, and which cryptographic controls to crack and divulge to the world is far less appealing than knowing that when a hacking attempt is identified, somewhere in the world there is at least one human perpetrating the action. Probably the time will come when computers have to be faced as direct adversaries.

Because of the importance of cryptography in helping to secure electronic information in virtually all computer systems, a basic understanding of this concept is essential for IS auditors to effectively perform their jobs. The remainder of this chapter provides a sufficient amount of information to effectively understand and assess the adequacy of cryptographic controls that auditors are likely to encounter.

TERMINOLOGY

The terms *encryption*, *cryptography*, *cryptanalysis*, and *cryptology* are often used interchangeably. However, differences in these terms warrant including their definitions so that they can be used in the proper context in discussing this already complex and sometimes confusing subject.

- *Encryption* is the act or process of translating a message into hidden form using a secret formula, or algorithm.
- *Decryption* is the act or process of translating a hidden message into its original, readable form. Encrypt and decrypt are synonymous with the terms *encipher* and *decipher*.

- An *algorithm* is a step-by-step procedure for solving a problem in a finite number of steps. As applied to encryption, an algorithm is a secret formula used to encrypt and decrypt messages. Each time the formula is employed to encrypt a message, it calculates a unique random secret key, which must be used to decrypt the message.
- *Cryptography* is the art or science of encrypting and decrypting messages using secret keys or codes. Some of the earliest uses of cryptography can be traced back to early civilizations such as the Egyptians around 2000 B.C. The Roman Empire also employed the use of cryptography about 2000 years later. Since then, the need for and use of cryptography has been documented throughout history. With the advent of computers and the need for secure electronic communications, the use of cryptography has spread extensively throughout the world at an ever-increasing rate.
- *Cryptanalysis* is the art or science of deciphering encrypted messages without the benefit of the secret key or code.
- *Cryptology* is the scientific study of both cryptography and cryptanalysis.

GOAL OF CRYPTOGRAPHIC CONTROLS

The goal of cryptographic controls is to reasonably ensure the confidentiality, integrity, and authenticity of electronic information being transmitted, while providing nonrepudiation by the sender. Encryption, coupled with hashing and digital signatures, has become the most commonly accepted solution to ensure reasonably secure electronic transmissions of information, especially with the need for electronic commerce transactions. Encryption, hashing, and digital signatures can each be thought of as one of three legs supporting a secure electronic message (see Exhibit 11.1). If any of the legs fails, the message is no longer fully secured.

EXHIBIT 11.1   SECURE ELECTRONIC MESSAGES

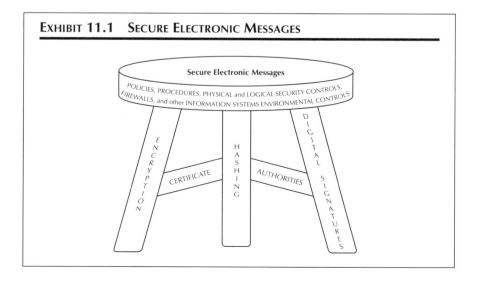

Encryption helps ensure the confidentiality of the information being transmitted. *Confidentiality* is achieved when only the intended recipients of transmitted information can read it. Encryption is also used to protect data stored on electronic media such as disk storage devices, magnetic tapes, and diskettes.

Hashing helps ensure message integrity. *Integrity* is achieved when the transmitted information has not been altered, other information has not been added to the transmission, and information has not been deleted from the transmission.

Digital signatures help ensure the authenticity of electronic transmissions and helps ensure nonrepudiation of the transmissions by their creators. *Authenticity* is achieved when the message recipient can be reasonably certain that the message was originated by the entity that appears to have originated it and not by some other unknown entity. *Nonrepudiation* is achieved when the sender of a message cannot refute the fact that he or she sent it. The concepts of encryption, hashing, and digital signatures will be discussed in the following sections.

ENCRYPTION

Within the computing world, encryption algorithms can be classified into two categories: symmetric or asymmetric. *Symmetric algorithms* use the same key for encrypting and decrypting messages. Perhaps the best-known and extensively implemented symmetric algorithm is the Data Encryption Algorithm (DEA), which was adopted as a Federal Information Processing Standard (FIPS) for sensitive but unclassified information by the U.S. government in 1977. This standard is known as the Data Encryption Standard (DES). DES was developed by IBM under contract with the National Institute of Standards and Technology (NIST), which was formerly known as the National Bureau of Standards. DES utilizes a 56-bit key length. The use of DES by government agencies has led to its general acceptance for commercial encryption. For example, DES is currently deployed by many financial institutions and automated teller machine (ATM) switching services to help ensure secure ATM transactions. In addition, Fedwire, the United States Federal Reserve Bank's wire transfer system, uses DES for transactions among financial institutions.

Advances in technology have eroded the future strength and effectiveness of DES. On June 17, 1997, the DES encryption algorithm was broken by Rocke Verser, a Loveland, Colorado, programmer. He stated, "We have demonstrated that DES can be cracked, and it's not difficult to do it. It means that we need to take a very serious look at how data is encrypted and stored and passed."[9] Verser created a brute-force program that was flexible enough to be downloaded over the Internet and run on Unix, Windows, Macintosh, and OS/2-based computers. The program was designed to test all the mathematically possible keys for RSA's DES-encoded message. A 56-bit key has over 72 quadrillion possible keys (72,057,594,037,972,936 to be exact). Verser employed the assistance of companies, individuals, and scientists around the world by offering to split the $10,000 prize 60/40 with the operator of the computer that finally identified the winning key. Verser's team, which eventually grew to a network of tens of thousands of volunteer computers, began their cracking effort in February 1997. Utilizing idle computer processing resources from the worldwide network, Verser's team was at times testing nearly 7 billion keys per second and 601 trillion keys per day! The winning computer, a 90-MHz Pentium desktop with 16 megabytes of RAM, was operated by Michael Sanders at Salt Lake City–based iNetZ Corporation. The key was identified after testing about 18 quadrillion keys, or about 25 percent of the possible keys. The winning message read, "Strong cryptography makes the world a safer place."[10]

The cracking of DES was in response to a worldwide "RSA Secret-Key Challenge" sponsored by RSA Data Security, Inc., a wholly owned subsidiary of Security Dynamics, Inc. At its January 1997 Data Security Conference, RSA offered amounts ranging from $1,000 to $10,000 for breaking various RC5 variable-length keys of different maximum sizes and offered $10,000 for breaking the fixed-length 56-bit key DES algorithm. RSA, which was founded in 1982 and is headquartered in Redwood City, California, is named after its founders: Ronald Rivest, Adi Shamir, and Leonard Adelman.

RSA announced "DES Challenge II" on January 13, 1998, at its Data Security Conference in San Francisco. The goal of this challenge was to discover the secret DES key used to encrypt a message in less time than it took Rocke Verser's team to win the original RSA Challenge. The winning team, which consisted of programmers and enthusiasts known as Distributed.Net, solved the challenge in only 39 days. The Distributed.Net team coordinated the efforts of 22,000 participants worldwide, connecting over 50,000 central processing units (CPUs). The winning message read, "Many hands make light work." "The team searched more than 61 quadrillion keys at a peak rate of 26 trillion keys per second. The winning key was found by a U.S.-based machine powered by an Alpha CPU after searching 85 percent of the total possible solutions."[11]

On July 17, 1998, the Electronic Frontier Foundation (EFF) reported that a single computer had been used to defeat the 56-bit DES algorithm. The project, which cost about $220,000, used a computer named "Deep Crack" to break a DES-encrypted message in 56 hours. It used brute force to test about 18 quadrillion possible keys. Deep Crack had a total of 36,864 microprocessors, each of which could test 2.5 million possible keys per second. Since there are at most 72 quadrillion possible keys, Deep Crack could crack any DES encrypted message in less than 9 days and 1 hour. As a result, every financial institution that has credit, debit, or ATM cards secured with card verification value, card verification code, or data encryption standard offsets must urgently assess its crytographic security.[12]

Due to increased processing speeds of computers and their lower cost, DES is reaching the end of its useful life. In fact, DES can currently be defeated with the proper knowledge and equipment. The ease with which symmetric algorithms can be defeated is primarily a function of the speed of the computer being used, the key length, and the financial resources available to the hacker. Faster computers are able to test more possibilities in a given time period. Regarding key length, every additional bit added to the length doubles the number of possible combinations.[13] Since fast computers are usually more expensive than slow ones, the amount of cash available to employ the use of fast computers is a constraint to hackers. One article effectively describes this relationship:

Given current technology, approximately 90 million DES key combinations or 5 million RC4 combinations can be processed per second. The cost of the computer hardware to accomplish this is approximately $50,000–$75,000. In other words, for about $50,000, given current technology, it would take only a second or so to break encryption tied to a key length of 26 bits. It would take approximately one hour to break a key length of 38 bits. A 40-bit key could be broken in about 4 hours,[14] a 48-bit key in about 1 month, and a 56-bit key in 30 years or so. Up the price to about $1 million and DES can be broken in about 10 days. Security tied to a 128-bit encryption algorithm is very secure, given the state of technology today and the expected state of technology for the next 30 years.[15] This quote assumes that only one of a few computers are used. The RSA Secret-Key Challenges demonstrated that multiple internetworked computers working together can reduce these time horizons exponentially.

In 1996, as a result of these and other technological advances that threaten the security of DES, NIST began the process of selecting a replacement algorithm, to be known as the Advanced Encryption Standard (AES). The goal of NIST is to replace DES with another algorithm that has a 128-bit block size and a key size of 128, 192, or 256 bits.

By June of 1998, a total of 15 candidates for the AES were submitted to NIST during round 1 of the selection process. The source code and documentation of all the candidates were openly reviewed by the cryptographic community at large for security, efficiency, and randomness. In March 1999, the candidates were subject to further scrutiny among peers at the second AES conference held in Rome, Italy. Revisions and enhancements to the candidate algorithms were allowed during round 1. Round 1 culminated in August 1999 with NIST naming the five AES finalists:

1. **MARS**, developed by IBM, is a shared-key symmetric block cipher, supporting 128-bit blocks and variable key size. MARS offers better security than triple DES while running significantly faster than single DES. The combination of high security, high speed, and flexibility make MARS an excellent choice for the encryption needs of the information world well into the next century.

2. **RC6**, by Ron Rivest in collaboration with RSA Laboratories, is an evolutionary improvement over RC5 and makes essential use of data-dependent rotations. It offers good security and good performance.

3. **Rijndael**, by Joan Daemen and Vincent Rijmen of Belgium, has variable block and key lengths of 128, 192, or 256 bits. Both block and key lengths can be extended very easily to multiples of 32 bits. Rijndael can be implemented very efficiently on a wide range of processors and in hardware.

4. **Serpent**, by Ross Anderson (UK), Eli Biham (Israel), and Lars Knudsen (Norway), is a 128-bit block cipher. It is faster than DES and supports a very efficient bitslice implementation.

5. **Twofish**, by Bruce Schneier, John Kelsey, Doug Whiting, David Wagner, Chris Hall, and Niels Ferguson, utilizes a 128-bit block and variable key

lengths of 128, 192, or 256 bits. It features efficient key setup on large microprocessors, smart cards, and hardware. [16]

Round 2 ended shortly after the third AES conference, which was held in New York City in April 2000. In October 2000, NIST announced that Rijndael had been selected for the proposed new AES. According to NIST, it showed the best combination of security, performance, efficiency, ease of implementation and flexibility. Rijndael was more versatile and can be implemented efficiently on a wide range of platforms using very simple operations.[17] The proposed selection of Rijndael as the AES was announced in the *Federal Register* on February 28, 2001, and was subjected to a 90-day public comment period. Finally, in the December 6, 2001, *Federal Register*, Rijndael was announced by NIST as Federal Information Processing Standard (FIPS) 197, also known as AES. It became effective on May 26, 2002.[18]

It is likely that DES will remain the government's standard for less sensitive applications, with AES specified as a standard when sensitivity of the protected data is higher. If computer processing power continues to increase at the rate of Moore's Law (i.e., doubles every 18 months), AES will likely replace DES in almost all commercial applications. But even AES will not be the panacea of security we might like. Using techniques called "side channel attacks," even AES encrypted messages are at risk. These attacks analyze things like the amount of time that cryptographic operations take, power consumption, radiation emissions, and fault analysis to help determine the secret keys.[19] There will never be such a thing as total security.

Asymmetric algorithms require the use of different but mathematically related keys for encrypting and decrypting messages. These keys are commonly referred to as public and private keys. The public key is provided openly to the public so that entities with which the key creator communicates can send electronic information. The private key is kept secret by the creator of the key. Once a message has been encrypted with one of the keys, only the other key can decrypt it. Also, possession of one key does not enable the holder to determine the other key. Typically, the sender of the message uses the receiver's public key to encrypt a message. Upon receipt, the receiver uses his or her private key to decrypt the message. RSA is a well-known developer of asymmetric algorithms.

Asymmetric algorithms utilize much longer key lengths than symmetric algorithms. To defeat an asymmetric algorithm, one must determine the matching secret key from the public key. In the case of RSA, this is equivalent to factoring a large integer that has two large prime factors.[20] Various mathematical approaches are employed in other cryptosystems. This quote provides a good perspective of the relative security of asymmetric algorithms:

> For an (asymmetric) RSA cryptosystem, a 256-bit modulus is easily factored by a computer user with average experience and resources. Keys with 384 bits can be broken by university research groups or companies; 512-bit keys are within the reach of major governments. Keys with 768 bits are probably not secure in the long term. Keys with 1,024 bits and more should be secure for a number of years unless ma-

jor algorithmic advances are made in factoring; keys of 2,048 bits are considered by many to be secure for decades.[21]

Symmetric or asymmetric encryption algorithms can be defeated in at least two ways. First, the algorithm itself may be weak, or mathematically predictable. For example, in 1995, two first-year graduate students at the University of California–Berkeley, David Wagner and Ian Goldberg (yes, the same Ian Goldberg referred to at the beginning of the chapter) discovered a method to crack the public key encryption scheme deployed within the popular Netscape Navigator World Wide Web browser software. For each encrypted transaction, the software required a new key. To create the key, it needed a starting number, which it generated using the time and date of the transaction and certain information about the user's computer system. All of this information is obtainable by a code-breaker, who would then face a greatly reduced task to crack the code. In fact, according to reports, "Goldberg and Wagner could break Netscape code in less than a minute using a simple workstation."[22] Similarly, Paul Kocher identified the fact that the keys to some encryption systems could be predicted by noting the elapsed time the algorithm required to decrypt a message.[23]

Brute-force attacks can also be used to defeat encryption algorithms. *Brute force attacks* employ the use of a computer or computers to systematically test all possible keys until the correct one is identified. The longer the key, the more difficult it becomes to defeat the encryption algorithm in terms of time and money. However, longer keys have operational drawbacks. The longer the key, the more time consuming and costly it becomes for the intended recipient to decrypt the information. Because many asymmetric cryptosystems have keys that are much longer than keys in most symmetric cryptosystems, they can be many orders of magnitude slower than their symmetric counterparts. In fact, one group of authors recently reported that some of the old private key (symmetric) cryptosystems are about 100 times faster than some public key (asymmetric) cryptosystems.[24] As a result, asymmetric cryptosystems are less practical for encrypting high-volume, real-time, or large information transmissions. For example, most automated teller machine (ATM) networks use symmetric encryption systems such as DES. Some ATMs encrypt just the personal identification number (PIN) as it is being transmitted between the ATM and the host computer at the card holder's financial institution. Other ATMs encrypt the entire transaction message and the PIN. Computers processing speeds have advanced enough where many new ATMs support triple-DES encryption without significantly affecting transaction speeds.

Asymmetric encryption appears to be the generally accepted method of ensuring the confidentiality of most electronic commerce transactions. Exhibit 11.2 demonstrates how asymmetric encryption can be used to provide message confidentiality. The sender encrypts a message using the receiver's public key and then transmits the encrypted message to the receiver. The receiver decrypts the message using his or her private key. Confidentiality is achieved because only the receiver knows his or her private key and is therefore the only one who can decrypt the sender's message. While encryption cannot assure complete confidentiality, with sufficiently long keys, encryption algorithms can provide reasonable degrees of confidentiality assurance. The degree of reasonableness required for a particular application will depend on the importance and/or value of the information being protected.

However, this procedure does not provide assurance that the message has not been altered or has not been sent by an impostor. The next section builds on the example in Exhibit 11.2 by incorporating the concept of hashing to help ensure the integrity of the message being sent.

HASHING

The primary purpose of hashing is to help ensure that electronic information being transmitted to a receiver has not been altered, other information has not been added to the transmission, and information has not been deleted from the transmission. This kind of message integrity can be achieved through the deployment of *one-way hash functions*. A one-way hash function is a mathematical formula that uses an electronic message as its input and creates a block of data called a *message digest*. When both an electronic message and a cryptographic key are processed through a one-way hash function, the resulting block of data is called a *message authentication code* (MAC).

Two common one-way hashing functions are Message Digest 5 (MD-5) and Secure Hash Algorithm 1 (SHA-1). MD-5 is not considered to be as secure as SHA-1. SHA-1 is currently a United States government Federal Information Processing Standard (FIPS) as well as a standard of the American National Standards Institute (ANSI).

One-way hash functions should be designed so that they can be used only to calculate message digests or MACs in a single direction. In other words, someone should not be able to determine the original information from the corresponding message digest or MAC.

Another desirable characteristic of one-way hash functions is that they should not generate the same message digest or MAC for different sets of data. Such assurance is achieved by designing hash functions that create lengthy message digests or MACs. The longer the message digest or MAC, the less risk there is of a "hash clash" from two different originating sets of data.

Exhibit 11.2   Asymmetric Encryption

SENDER PERFORMS THE FOLLOWING:

Encrypt message using receiver's public key ⇒ Encrypted message
Transmit encrypted message ⇒ Receiver

RECEIVER PERFORMS THE FOLLOWING:

Decrypt encrypted message using receiver's private key ⇒ Message

Exhibit 11.3 depicts how hashing can be applied in conjunction with asymmetric (public key) encryption to achieve message confidentiality and integrity. The sender subjects a message to a one-way hashing function to create a message digest. The message and message digest are encrypted, using the receiver's public key, and then the encrypted data file is transmitted to the receiver. The receiver decrypts the message and appended message digest using his or her private key, subjects the decrypted message to the same one-way hashing algorithm used by the sender of the message, and compares the resulting message digest to the one received from the sender. If the integrity of the message is intact, the sender's message digest will agree with the digest computed by the receiver. As in Exhibit 11.2, confidentiality is achieved because only the receiver knows his or her private key and is therefore the only one who can decrypt the sender's message. In addition, integrity is achieved because only the same one-way hashing function used by the sender to create the message digest can create an identical message digest. The next section builds on the example in Exhibit 11.3 by incorporating the concept of digital signatures and digital certificates to help ensure the authenticity of the message being sent.

DIGITAL SIGNATURES AND DIGITAL CERTIFICATES

Digital signatures and digital certificates are used to provide assurance to the message recipient that the message is authentic and that it cannot be repudiated by the sender. To digitally sign a message, the sender subjects a message to a one-way hashing function. The resulting message digest is encrypted, using the sender's private key, thereby resulting in a *digital signature*. The digital signature is appended to a message that has been encrypted with the receiver's public key.

EXHIBIT 11.3   ASYMMETRIC ENCRYPTION WITH HASHING

SENDER PERFORMS THE FOLLOWING:

Hash message using one-way hash function ⇒ digest
Encrypt message and digest using receiver's public key ⇒
                                        Encrypted message and digest
Transmit encrypted message and digest ⇒ Receiver

RECEIVER PERFORMS THE FOLLOWING:

Decrypt message and digest using receiver's private key ⇒
                                        Message and digest
Hash message using same one-way hash function as sender ⇒ digest
Compare digests ⇒   If same, message is intact.
                                        If different, reject transaction.

Prior to receiving a message from the sender, the receiver must independently obtain a *digital certificate* for the sender. A digital certificate is issued by a trusted *certificate authority* (CA). The digital certificate identifies the sender and contains the sender's public key as well as the digital signature of the trusted CA. (See the last paragraph in this section for more details on how the sender obtains a digital certificate.)

On receipt of the message, the receiver decrypts the message with his or her private key. As in Exhibits 11.2 and 11.3, the receiver is now assured of message confidentiality. Next, the receiver subjects the decrypted message to the same one-way hashing function used by the sender to generate a message digest. Then the receiver decrypts the digital signature using the sender's public key contained in the digital certificate obtained from a trusted CA, thereby revealing the message digest. The receiver compares the message digest in the digital signature with the recomputed message digest to ensure that there have not been any changes (integrity). Since the sender's public key contained in the digital certificate successfully decrypted the digital signature, the receiver can be assured of the authenticity of the message. Furthermore, since the digital certificate was obtained independently from a trusted CA, the sender cannot repudiate the message. Exhibit 11.4 summarizes all of these controls.

In Exhibit 11.4, confidentiality is achieved by encrypting the message with the sender's public key. Integrity is achieved by comparing the message digests created by one-way hashing. Authenticity and nonrepudiation are achieved through the use of digital signatures and digital certificates.

EXHIBIT 11.4   ASYMMETRIC ENCRYPTION WITH HASHING AND DIGITAL SIGNATURES

SENDER PERFORMS THE FOLLOWING:

Hash message using one-way hash function $\Rightarrow$ digest
Encrypt digest using sender's private key $\Rightarrow$ Digital signature
Encrypt message using receiver's public key $\Rightarrow$ Encrypted message
Transmit encrypted message and digital signature $\Rightarrow$ Receiver

RECEIVER PERFORMS THE FOLLOWING:

Decrypt message using receiver's private key $\Rightarrow$ Message
Hash message using same one-way hash function as sender $\Rightarrow$ digest
Independently obtain digital certificate of sender $\Rightarrow$ Sender's name and
    public key
Decrypt digital signature using sender's public key $\Rightarrow$ digest and sender's
    public key
Compare digests $\Rightarrow$ If same, message is intact; if different, reject.
Compare sender's public key from digital signature and digital certificate $\Rightarrow$
If same, sender is authentic; if different, reject, possible impostor.

To obtain a digital certificate, an applicant must utilize the services of a certificate authority. *Certificate authorities* are established to help ensure that holders of public keys know who created messages using the corresponding private keys. Certificate authorities are organizations that certify the authenticity of public keys, identify the public/private key creators, and distribute public keys. Certificate authorities that are emerging include financial institutions, security product vendors, and government agencies.[25] Some states, such as Utah and Washington, have drafted legislation to attempt to ensure that certificate authorities meet certain standards before they become licensed and thus legally "trusted." Without CAs, public key holders might think they are sending and receiving encrypted messages with one party when they are actually exchanging messages with an unknown and potentially malicious party. Even with CAs, naïve public key holders could encrypt and send a message, using the public key of a malicious private key holder, if they obtain the digital certificate from the sender rather than a trusted CA. Trusted CAs offer much greater assurance of authenticity because once a CA has satisfactorily identified the applicant, it creates a digital certificate, encrypts the certificate using its private certification key, and transmits the certificate to the owner and any other parties with which the owner wishes to exchange messages. The digital certificate owner and subsequent recipients of the certificate can decrypt it using the CA's public verification key and then use the sender's public key to decrypt the sender's digital signature that has been appended to the sender's message.

KEY MANAGEMENT

Symmetric encryption key management is practical for a relatively limited number of communicating pairs wishing to exchange information. For example, most ATM networks that employ symmetric encryption are able to reasonably manage keys because the number of ATMs with which the host computer must communicate is relatively small (i.e., a few thousand). The encryption keys are usually administered and controlled by a central entity such as a network switching service vendor.

Unfortunately, with electronic commerce, key management becomes a much greater challenge. Consider that every individual in the world who utilizes the Internet could be a potential customer of every business in the world, with each business needing to communicate securely with every individual. Also, every business in the world could be a customer of almost every other business in the world. As a result, the number of potential communicating pairs is staggering. At a conference I attended, one of the speakers provided the mathematical formula for determining the total number of unique keys needed to ensure confidentiality among all communicating pairs.[26] The formula is:

$$K = \frac{n^2 - n}{2}$$

In this formula, K is the number of unique keys and n is the number of communicating entities. Using this formula, a table can be constructed to depict how rapidly the number of unique keys required increases as the number of communicating entities increases:

n	*Formula*	K
10	$\dfrac{10^2 - 10}{2}$	$= 45$
100	$\dfrac{100^2 - 100}{2}$	$= 4,950$
1,000	$\dfrac{1,000^2 - 1,000}{2}$	$= 499,500$
10,000	$\dfrac{10,000^2 - 10,000}{2}$	$= 49,999,500$

As can be seen, with just 10,000 communicating entities, the number of unique keys required is nearly 50 million. Imagine how many keys would be required if the number of communicating entities was 1 billion. In reality, the potential number of communicating entities in the world is several billion. Centralized key management with this many communicating entities would obviously become an unmanageable task. Because public key cryptography does not require centralized key management, it is much more practical for electronic commerce than private key cryptography. Although public key cryptography does require the use of trusted certificate authorities to issue digital certificates, the actual key management is performed by the private key holders, thereby removing the burden of centralized key management.

POLITICAL ASPECTS OF CRYPTOGRAPHY

In the United States, companies that develop encryption products have been precluded from exporting symmetric encryption software greater than 40 bits. The restriction was eased to 56 bits for some firms in 1997.[27] In June 1997, Netscape and Microsoft were granted an exception to the United States export restrictions, which allowed them to sell software protected by 128-bit encryption technology to banking institutions so long as the software was used only for financial transactions.[28]

On July 17, 2000, the Clinton administration announced it would loosen controls on the export of encryption software. U.S. companies no longer need a license to export encryption products to any end users in the 15 nations of the European Union, Australia, Norway, the Czech Republic, Hungary, Poland, Japan, New Zealand, and Switzerland.[29]

The issue of export restriction of encryption products stems from the fact that criminals, including spies from other countries, could employ cryptography to mask their activities. Therefore, the U.S. government believes that it should be able to access key recovery programs for law enforcement purposes and the protection of national security interests.

While these reasons seem appropriate, opponents, including RSA Data Security, Inc., contend that users of cryptographic products have a right to privacy. They believe that U.S. law enforcement agencies may abuse their authority to obtain key recovery software and subsequently violate the privacy rights of various individuals and companies.

Another problem with export restrictions is that they discourage the open market development of cryptographic products by U.S. companies. As a result, U.S. companies are at a competitive disadvantage with some of their counterparts in Europe and other continents that are able to market 128-bit symmetric key encryption software. Furthermore, these "high-bit" encryption products could be purchased for use in the United States by criminals and spies, thereby circumventing the control intended by U.S. export restrictions.

Other countries also restrict the import and use of cryptographic products. Some of these countries have the same criminal concerns as the U.S. government. However, other countries such as China restrict the import and use of cryptographic products so they can retain their ability to censor incoming electronic information. These governments use the guise that they are protecting the people and their homeland. In reality, they are actually censoring some of the incoming electronic transmissions.

The involvement of world governments brings to light the importance of cryptography in the protection of information vital to national security. The next excerpt, from the website of the U.S. National Security Agency (NSA), describes how cryptography has been of concern for decades:

> In 1972, the U.S. President established the Central Security Service (CSS) to provide a more unified cryptologic effort within the Department of Defense. As Chief of the CSS, the Director of the NSA exercises control over the signals intelligence activities of U.S. military services. In 1984, under Presidential directive, the mission of the National Security Agency (NSA) was expanded to encompass information systems security for national security systems. The NSA has two missions: to help design cipher systems that will protect the integrity of United States information systems, and to search for weaknesses in adversaries' codes. The NSA employs the country's premier codemakers and codebreakers, and is one of the largest employers of mathematicians in the U.S. and perhaps the world.[30]

Obviously, cryptography plays a significant role in all aspects of our lives. It affects us as individuals regarding our personal privacy and the security of our financial transactions and other information. It also affects the competitive and private activities of the businesses and organizations that employ us and to which we belong. Finally, it affects the future existence of the countries in which we live. Cryptographic controls benefit us in all three areas, but cryptography can also be used maliciously.

Several books have been written on the subject of malicious use of information. One of the better known books was authored by Winn Schwartau. Schwartau groups *information warfare* into three "classes": Class 1 is personal information warfare, which includes the study of all sources of information about each of us as individuals. Class 2 is corporate information warfare, which pertains to the study of information as it affects business, commercial, or economic interests. Class 3 is global information warfare, which encompasses the study of information concerning national interests.[31] Each of these classes of information warfare affects all of us. Cryptographic controls play a critical role in combating information warfare. When deployed in conjunction with effective policies and procedures, and physical and logical security controls, cryptographic controls can create an IS environment that is resilient and secure against malicious attacks. To remain effective, these IS security controls must continuously evolve and adapt as attackers become more innovative and aggressive.

Case studies 11.1 and 11.2 describe various encryption-related issues.

CASE STUDY 11.1

Weak Password Algorithm

During a preimplementation review of a newly installed network-based application, I assessed whether the password file was adequately secure. Initially, I requested that the system security administrator create a test audit user ID for me. I entered a password containing a variety of characters, including two ones. Next I found that I was able to view the password file by using a common utility program. Upon initial viewing, the user IDs were readable, but the passwords appeared scrambled in that they looked like a sequence of miscellaneous typographic symbols.

However, with the password I chose for my test audit user ID, I noted that the encrypted password had two "%" symbols in the same positions as the two ones in my password. I deduced that the password encryption algorithm was predictable. I then recorded the characters from the rest of my password with the associated encrypted characters. Next I changed my password, using other characters, and recorded the corresponding encrypted characters. Using this procedure, I was able to break the rudimentary encryption algorithm used by the application. If I had wanted to, I could have decoded the password of the system security administrator and taken over the system.

The issue was noted in the audit report; however, no recommendation to require a more secure algorithm was submitted since the application was considered to have a relatively low risk. However, it was recommended that the security weakness be communicated to the vendor so a more secure password encryption algorithm for issuance in future versions of the application could be developed.

This example demonstrates how we should not assume that encryption algorithms deployed in modern applications are even moderately secure or sophisticated. Information systems auditors should ask vendors and programmers what types of encryption are used by the application. Auditors should also attempt to crack encrypted password files and design other tests to assess the effectiveness of the cryptographic controls. (Note: These tests should be performed with the advance knowledge of the auditee management.) They also should ask whether the application has been classified according to the Common Criteria (CC) or an equivalent standard. If a CC classification has been assigned, the level of classification should be assessed for adequacy. See Appendix B for more details about the Common Criteria.

CASE STUDY 11.2

Fedwire Encryption Controls

This case study provides information about some of the encryption controls deployed by the United States Federal Reserve Bank (FRB) with its national wire transfer system, Fedwire. It is based on my experience at financial institutions that use the Fedline II microcomputer-based application to interface with Fedwire for the purpose of sending and receiving wire transfers and automated clearing house (ACH) transactions and performing other electronic communications with the FRB such as ordering cash.

Prior to interfacing with Fedwire, each microcomputer on which Fedline II has been installed must be outfitted with an encryption board supplied by the FRB. The encryption boards contain the DES encryption algorithm. The boards are manufactured with lithium batteries, which have a shelf life of 5 to 10 years. As the speed of computers continually increases, new boards must be provided periodically to financial institutions to ensure their efficient operation. In older versions of the encryption boards, the batteries could be replaced without affecting their functionality. However, to help reduce the risk of tampering and cracking of the encryption process, newer boards are designed with nonreplaceable batteries. If one attempts to replace a battery, data necessary to perform the encryption is erased from the firmware and cannot be re-created, thus rendering the encryption board useless. The type of encryption board can be determined by reading the serial number on the vertical edge of the encryption board, which is viewable from the back of the microcomputer without having to disassemble it.

Simply installing the encryption board does not activate it. To activate the board, the installer must obtain and enter synchronization information from the FRB Data Security Department. This is usually performed over the telephone during installation. This procedure prevents an unauthorized party from stealing an encryption board and copy of Fedline II software, and then spoofing a financial institution.

The FRB provides a help line, which financial institutions can call regarding installation and use of Fedline II and Fedwire. However, specific details as to the inner workings of the Federal Reserve's encryption processes are obviously kept highly secret.

NOTES

1. Winn Schwartau, *Information Warfare* (New York: Thunder's Mouth Press, 1996): 683.
2. "Student Breaks Encryption Code," *KIRO Radio News Fax* (January 30, 1997): 1.
3. "Hackers Attack Department of Defense," *Internal Auditor* (October 1996): 10.
4. "Hackers Stole Gulf War Secrets," *KIRO Radio News Fax*, (March 25, 1997): front page.
5. Dr. Dorothy E. Denning, *Manager's Guide to Cyberspace Attacks and Countermeasures* (San Francisco: Computer Security Institute, 1997), 12–13.
6. Laura Myers, "Hired Hackers Breach Nation's Computer System," *Seattle Post-Intelligencer*, April 17, 1998: A3.
7. "Code That Safeguards Internet Transactions Broken," *NewsEdge Corporation Newsbyte* (August 30, 1999); Bruce Schneier, "The 1999 Crypto Year-in-Review," *Information Security* (December 1999): 23.
8. "Lengthy Keys Are Easier to Detect," *SC Magazine* (May 1999): 17.
9. Don Clark, "Group Cracks Financial-Data Encryption Code," *Wall Street Journal* (June 19, 1997): A3.
10. From RSA's website: *www.rsa.com* (July 11, 1997).
11. "RSA's Secret-Key Challenge Solved Again," *Secure Computing* (April 1998): 14.
12. Tom Trusty, "Beware the Deep Crack Threat," *Bank Fraud* (Chicago: Bank Administration Institute, September 1998): 2; Bruce Schneier, "The 1998 Crypto Year-in-Review," *Information Security* (January 1999): 21.
13. Denning, *Manager's Guide to Cyberspace Attacks and Countermeasures*, 12.
14. In fact, Ian Goldberg did it in 3.5 hours, as mentioned at the beginning of this chapter.
15. Michael R. Anderson, *Internet Security—Firewalls & Encryption, The Cyber Cop's Perspective* (1996): 2.
16. *Http://csrc.nist.gov/encryption/aes/* (October 13, 1999).
17. "Advanced Encryption Standard Announced," *Security Wire Digest* (October 5, 2000).
18. *Http://csrc.nist.gov/encryption/aes/* (July 11, 2002).
19. Bruce Schneier, "When in Rome. . . ," *Information Security* (May 1999): 22.
20. Bank for International Settlements, *Security of Electronic Money* (August 1996): 63.
21. *Id.*
22. "Cypherpunks Unveil Netscape Flaws," *Infosecurity News* (November/December 1995): 13.
23. Denning, *Manager's Guide to Cyberspace Attacks and Countermeasures*, 13.
24. Alexander Kogan, Ephraim F. Sudit, and Miklos A. Vasarhelyi, "Implications of Internet Technology: On-Line Auditing and Cryptography," *Information Systems Audit & Control Journal* (Volume III, 1996): 46.
25. "Certificate-Authority Services Emerge," *Infosecurity News* (May 1997): 14.
26. Jon C. Graff, "Session 202: Internet Encryption," Information Systems Audit & Control Association's Computer Audit, Control, and Security (CACS) Conference (May 1997).
27. "Export Granted For 56-Bit Encryption," *Infosecurity News* (May 1997): 14.
28. John Markoff, "Netscape and Microsoft Are Cleared on Exports," *New York Times* (June 25, 1997): C8.
29. "Government Loosens Controls on Export of Encryption Software," *Seattle Times Wire Services* (July 18, 2000).
30. National Security Administration website: *www.nsa.gov* (February 27, 1997).
31. Schwartau, *Information Warfare*, 9–10.

CHAPTER 12

Computer Forensics

Humanity has become dependent on computers to store and process personal, professional, and business-related information. Even criminals cannot resist the power of the computer for maintaining records of their illegal activities. Prostitution rings maintain databases of their "Johns"; drug traffickers maintain lists of their primary customers, distributors, and suppliers; and murderers, rapists, stalkers, abusers, and other violent criminals may keep detailed accounts of their obsessive behavior and other activities. Businesses may produce volumes of data in their systems that describe in detail illegal activities such as discrimination, sexual harassment, environmental pollution or damage, antitrust activities, bribery, extortion, and a host of other legal and regulatory violations. Governmental agencies and military organizations also maintain a wealth of classified and top-secret information about their own activities as well as those of other countries. I would venture to guess that there is more information stored on all the hard drives, disk packs, floppy diskettes, compact disks, and other electronic media in the world than exists on printed matter.

Most legal systems, and especially those in the United States, have come to rely on this wealth of electronically stored information to help convict or exonerate suspects and to determine the extent of damages in civil actions. But accessing this information can be difficult, sometimes almost impossible. To hide or make incriminating evidence inaccessible, criminals often attempt to delete or erase data from their electronic storage media. They may also protect their data files using passwords, encryption techniques, or file compression software. Data can also be divided into chunks and stored in various locations on various media. Desperate crooks set their computer disks and even their computers on fire, even if it means burning down their home to avoid prosecution. Others throw their computers into rivers, lakes, and oceans to damage the evidence. The most malicious and cold-blooded criminals even resort to planting explosives on their computers so that if the wrong key is touched or if the computer is not started in the proper sequence, it explodes, thereby destroying the data and the person attempting to access it.

Experts in the field of computer forensics have come to the forefront of many legal battles to assist plaintiffs, defendants, and courts in assimilating these previously hidden facts. *Computer forensics* is the science pertaining to the relationship of computer facts and evidence to legal issues. Computer forensic experts are able to obtain and access computer information and explain it in court using legally accepted methodologies and procedures. These specialists also offer training courses to law enforcement agencies on the proper legal acquisition, handling, and storage of computer evidence.

One of the most sophisticated computer forensics companies in the world is New Technologies, Inc. (NTI), which is headquartered in Gresham, Oregon. The organization was founded in 1996 by several internationally recognized technology experts, including Michael R. Anderson, an artificial intelligence and computer forensics expert who spent 25 years performing high-tech criminal investigations and training for U.S. federal law enforcement agencies. Other members of NTI include experts in the areas of forensic computer science, forensic utility and security software development, technology trends, network issues, cryptography, risk analysis, and risk assessment. The firm's services include forensic computer science training and consulting, computer security assessments, and expert testimony in computer evidence issues. Fortunately for society, NTI works on the right side of the law, aiding law enforcement while avoiding requests for assistance from drug dealers and other criminals.

What these experts have learned is that unlike the burning of paper, erasing or deleting data on electronic storage media often does not completely remove the information. In simpler cases, erasing or deleting data only removes the computer's reference to the data's storage location. The data may remain fully intact until it has been completely overwritten by later data storage activities. Often it takes several years for data to be fully overwritten, regardless of the steps data owners take to hide or remove it. For example, one of the more detailed articles on the subject of data recovery states that "When a disk is formatted, the only data on the disk that is actually deleted is the information in the boot record, the FAT (file allocation table), and directory. The user file is still there."[1] More recent operating system versions can perform unformatting commands to help recover accidentally reformatted information. Utility software programs can also be used in some data recovery efforts. Two of the better-known utility software applications are Norton Utilities™ from Symantec Corporation and PC Tools™ from Central Point Software.

In more difficult cases, only partial file information may remain. For example, data fragments or other "electronic fingerprints" may be found in temporary storage areas and other data caches in a computer. Sometimes these fragments can be quite large. For example, "deleted" or "erased" data may be located in *file slack* areas. Anderson of NTI defines file slack as "the storage space between the end of the file and the end of the last cluster assigned to a specific space." In the case of newer operating systems, memory clusters can be as large as 32 kilobytes. Thus, if the last part of a file being saved uses only 8 kilobytes of a cluster, 24 kilobytes of file slack are available in that cluster.[2] When a computer is operating, it is continuously performing dumps of data residing in random access memory into these file slack areas. Given the vast size of hard drives in today's personal computers (PCs), the potential volume of file slack containing potentially incriminating data is enormous.

Accessing this data takes more sophisticated software and techniques. A program called SafeBack™ was developed by Sydex Corporation. According to Anderson, "obscure data segments containing binary (non-readable) data can now be filtered (using SafeBack) making the contents easily printed or displayed using simple word processing software."[2] Anderson's firm also creates its own software programs that perform highly specialized data identification and analysis functions that can reveal information that other computer experts thought was long gone.

Computer forensics experts even can match an individual diskette to the PC used to save data on it. This type of information is especially useful in the case of suspects who have diskettes in their possession that can be associated with a PC located in their home or that of another suspected criminal.

Micro Law Software, Inc., of Troutdale, Oregon, has developed a unique and interesting software package to help identify stolen computers. The software package consists of a pair of programs called Micro-ID™ and Cop-Only™. After a computer owner installs Micro-ID, the software prompts the original owner to enter personal identification information, such as name, address, phone number, and date of birth. The software also records the date of Micro-ID installation and scans the peripheral devices and other components of the computer. Micro-ID creates a record of these unique identifying features and stores the information in a secret area of the computer's hard drive. Later, if the computer is confiscated by law enforcement personnel and is suspected of being stolen, the companion Cop-Only program can be used to confirm those suspicions. Micro-ID responds immediately to Cop-Only and reveals the original owner's identifying information, date of Micro-ID loading, and recorded peripheral device information. This type of software can incriminate unsuspecting computer thieves and the people who buy stolen computers.[3] The Micro-ID software is available to the public at little or no cost. The Cop-Only software is available at nominal cost to all official law enforcement agencies with the responsibility for the recovery of stolen property.

Like any other control, this product could be outwitted by a savvy criminal. Because hard drives are easy to remove, a thief could install a replacement hard drive or swap one with another machine. Although the original identifying information may still be readable on the hard drive using Cop-Only or some other forensic software, it would not pertain to the computer in which it is now installed. As a result, the accuracy of the identification information could be placed in reasonable doubt. Yet, if there are enough instances of identifiable hard drives in a computer "chop shop," a jury may find that the evidence suggests beyond a reasonable doubt that the computers were stolen. Furthermore, there is a good chance that criminals will not chop up or destroy hard drives, because the data residing on them often is more valuable than the hard drive itself. Over time, juries will have to decide on a case-by-case basis whether the Micro-ID information can be relied on. Based on the outcomes, the product could become widely installed.

Organizations can hire computer forensic specialists to perform a variety of other services in addition to accessing and deciphering data. The specialists can provide training to internal auditors and others interested in increasing the overall security of their information systems environments. They can perform security evaluations and assessments of information systems environments and provide recommendations to help ensure that data is adequately protected against electronic invasion by criminals, competitors, and even self-incrimination. They can also help organizations develop secure data warehousing and elimination procedures so that data redundancy is minimized and unnecessary data is not stored indefinitely.

All of the aforementioned forensics issues apply to the world of corporate espionage just as easily as they apply to violent criminals. By proactively implementing the recommendations of computer forensic specialists before any crimes or espionage have been committed, organizations can significantly enhance the security of their computer systems and data as well as their legal positions in many potential court battles. Now let us examine what IS auditors can do to help secure evidence for potential use in criminal investigations.

INVESTIGATIONS[4]

Suppose a system administrator (SA) was performing a routine scan of network devices and found that a user had installed an unauthorized software program that is capable of extracting user IDs and passwords from the network and of using brute force to systematically determine most of the passwords. Suppose further that the user signed on to the network using a compromised SA user ID and password and then used the special SA privileges to extract all sorts of confidential information from the organization's network. Would the SA know what to do? Every organization should have an action plan for such discoveries. The action plan should adequately address how to handle computer evidence in such a way that it does not become tainted and include specific procedures on how to create a complete and accurate chain of evidence. The rest of this chapter focuses on these questions to help organizations become better prepared to investigate e-crime scenes before they happen.

Reality Check

The just-described scenario is not fiction. A freeware program called L0PHTCRACK (with the number 0, not the letter O), which has been around for several years, can extract the file containing the user IDs and passwords of Windows NT file servers and use brute force to determine many of them, especially the weak ones. The target files on NT operating systems are known as SAM files. Two former employees were recently charged with using L0PHTCRACK to illegally copy the SAM file from Epicor Software Corporation where they were employed and subsequently copying the company's international list of customers. Both individuals later copied the SAM file of a subsequent employer, VP Projects, Inc.[5] Programs similar to L0PHTCRACK have existed for many years and use the same approach to determine the passwords within other common network operating systems such as Unix.

Some criminals have child pornography on their computers, while others use Internet chat rooms to meet children. Patrick Naughton, former executive of Seattle-based Infoseek, was arrested by the FBI on September 16, 1999, for violating a 1994 federal law in which it is illegal to travel from one state to another with the intent to have sex with a minor. In this case, Naughton, then 34, traveled from Seattle to Santa Monica with the intent to have a sexual encounter with a minor who turned out to be an undercover FBI agent.[6] Most of Naughton's e-conversations during his seven months of luring were recorded on his personal laptop computer.

Another example of a trusted employee stealing sensitive information took place in 1997 at General Motors (GM). A high-ranking officer who was negotiating an even better position with Volkswagen (VW) in Germany copied an estimated 40,000 pages of CAD (computer-assisted-design) drawings and component specifications.[7] Although GM discovered the theft shortly after the executive started with VW, and GM received an enormous settlement after successful legal action against VW, the event was widely publicized, much to the embarrassment of GM.

These and many other types of e-crimes have become all-too-frequent news headlines. The bottom line is that despite implementation of various types of logical and physical security controls, it is not a matter of if but *when* an organization will be hit with an e-crime. As with any disaster, all organizations should be prepared to initiate an investigation that will lead to a conviction or favorable settlement if the damages are significant.

Although the legal system is gradually imposing harsher penalties for e-crimes, thus far punishments have been relatively mild and are not a significant deterrent. Complicating matters further is the difficulty in securing convictions. If evidence is mishandled or tainted in even the slightest way, the risk of the defendant being found not guilty increases substantially. So what should be done after a potential e-crime has been identified? This is where computer forensics comes to the forefront.

Evidence Handling

Fortunately for those seeking legal evidence, information on computers is extremely difficult to eradicate. Joan Feldman, owner of Computer Forensics, Inc., the Seattle-based firm that helped investigate the Naughton case, uses the analogy that computers are like tape recorders that are always running.[8] David Julian, data recovery manager of Northwest Computer Support, another Seattle-based company, says that he has recovered data from computers that have been driven over with a car, thrown into a river, and shot with a gun. Even throwing a computer into the ocean would not succeed in destroying the data.[9]

Alan Brill, global practice director for computer forensic and high-technology investigation services for Kroll and Associates in New York, reveals that "where a previously used part of a hard drive (called a cluster) is assigned to a new file, whatever space in the cluster not actually used for new data retains old data. This slack space is invisible to the operating system. And there are files (including swap files, temporary files and buffer files) where information may be stored even if the user never asked the machine to store it."[10]

Before beginning the technical analysis of computer data, many steps should be taken to help ensure a successful investigation and prosecution, if needed. The primary concept to keep in mind throughout the investigation is that the chain of evidence must be preserved, otherwise the success of any prosecution will be jeopardized. Computer forensics experts from Ernst & Young, Admiral plc (UK), and Datum eBS all concur that maintaining the chain of evidence is the "golden rule" for any computer forensics investigation.[11]

Care must be taken to ensure that a standardized, well-thought-out approach is applied. Internal information technology (IT) security professionals play a critical role in identifying e-crimes and in securing the evidence. However, allowing an untrained IT security professional to perform the technical forensics analysis could taint irreplaceable evidence, which subsequently could not be introduced in court. Walt Manning, director of the Techno-Crime Institute warns, "Being computer literate is not the same as being computer-forensics-literate."[12] Even if the internal IT security professional has the skills, the fact that computer forensics analysis could take days, weeks, or even months to complete makes it impractical and unrealistic for that individual to perform the forensics analysis—unless, of course, management chooses to hire a temporary replacement.

Furthermore, the computer forensics analyst will likely be required to testify if the case goes to trial. Again, inexperience in the courtroom can prove disastrous. Then there is the independence issue. An internal investigator testifying in court on behalf of the organization will automatically be presumed to be biased in favor of the organization, thus making the evidence less credible. For these reasons, organizations should seriously consider utilizing an independent forensics expert in cases likely to go to trial.

Michael Anderson cited a case where an internal employee was suspected of committing a major embezzlement in her company. All the evidence was in her PC. The company correctly confiscated the PC and put it in the IT manager's office. Unfortunately, the IT manager decided to perform the investigation himself. He got busy and was called out of the office for two weeks. During this time, another PC in the office crashed. His assistant, who had not been informed of the investigation, moved the computer in his boss's office into production, believing it to be unused. All evidence was tainted and thus rendered unfit for the courtroom. Extreme care must be taken so that evidence is understandable to a judge and jury as well as credible and defensible.[13]

Investigation Steps Recommended by Experts

Computer forensics should not be viewed in a vacuum. It should be part of an organization's overall computer incident response program. Even "regular" hacks may require at least some computer forensics analysis to be performed after the fact. One systems manager described the mistakes he made in a recent intrusion incident in his organization. Based on his battle scars, he compiled a 10-step "recipe for successful incident handling." Although not specific to computer forensics, this recipe provides useful guidance for those developing or assessing overall computer incident response programs:

1. Write a clear, concise statement of scope, intention, and constraints.
2. Add computing and network resource descriptions.
3. Perform an impact assessment.
4. Delegate roles and responsibilities.
5. List staff and vendor contact information.
6. Spell out incident response actions, notifications, and priorities.
7. Identify essential response resources
8. Determine incident investigation and documentation requirements.
9. Define supporting data needs.
10. Continually exercise and maintain the plan.[14]

Mark Bigler, senior information systems auditor at Pacificorp in Salt Lake City, Utah, provided similar advice. His six-step list includes:

1. Develop effective information protection policies and forensics procedures.
2. Notify your organization's legal group and possibly law enforcement.
3. Maintain a chain of custody for all evidence.
4. Prepare detailed reports and workpapers.
5. Seize suspect computer.
6. Make a mirror image copy of the hard drive.[15]

Bill Betts, a private computer security consultant in Pleasanton, California, detailed 11 steps that should be performed in consecutive order when beginning a computer forensics investigation:

1. Gain appropriate authorization to evaluate computing resources.
2. Shut down the computer (best to just pull the plug)
3. Document the hardware configuration of the system (photographs/video).
4. Transport the computer to a secure location.
5. Boot the computer from a DOS boot diskette, or remove the hard drive and install it in an isolated test computer. This step is very critical and should only be performed by experts.
6. Make a bit-stream backup image of the target drive.
7. Authenticate data on all storage devices via a hash total.
8. Document the system date and time.
9. Make a list of key search words.
10. Examine free space.
11. Examine file slack space. [16]

Mark Morris, an investigator for the Computer Forensics Investigation Service at Admiral plc in the United Kingdom and former detective in the Computer

Crime Unit at New Scotland Yard, agrees that performing a bit-stream backup is important. Morris stresses that maintaining an audit trail and comprehensive notes for any and all activities are integral steps. "No action taken by the investigator should alter the original data. This is why a bit image copy must be taken of the original hard drive, he says."[17]

Putting It All Together

Consider taking the following 13 steps in the event of an e-crime.

1. Be prepared in advance of any e-crime. Appoint a base emergency response team (ERT). The ERT should be composed of designated management, IT security professionals (e.g., network system administrators), security staff (in the event of physical intervention), fraud investigation staff, internal audit staff, and human resources staff (if an employee is the perpetrator). The ERT should include senior management in all communications.

2. Identify one or two computer forensics consultants, preferably local, who are available if their highly technical (and time consuming) skills are necessary. They should prove their expertise in both technical computer forensics analysis and courtroom testimony. Research their current and previous clients. Ensure that there is at least some knowledge transfer to your internal IS security and auditing staff so they gain valuable experience during the process. Consultants charge up to $400 per hour, so get your money's worth.[18] At some point, when internal staff members have enough experience, external consultants may only be necessary in critical, time-consuming cases going to trial.

3. Protect the network. This is network administrators' first duty upon discovery of a potential e-crime. Often they must take immediate and sometimes extreme measures without the luxury of group consultation (e.g., shutting down the entire network if a malicious attack is detected in progress or immediately resetting the passwords of all users if it is discovered the network password files have been copied).

   By the same token, system administrators must be careful not to jump the gun and alert offenders, thereby providing an opportunity for them to partially or fully destroy or remove critical evidence. As one systems manager put it, "On-the-fly response can lead to careless mistakes, which could be quite painful."[19] In the end, system administrators must make judgment calls.

4. As soon as possible after initial identification (within hours), convene the ERT. The ERT should perform a risk assessment to determine the potential damage that could or did result from the crime, which systems and data storage devices may contain evidence, and the actions that need to be performed by each team member.

5. Open a case file and begin making a physical record of every step taken during the investigation, including date and time each task was performed,

any tools used, the person performing each task, the location and controls over each piece of evidence, and any other pertinent information. Each ERT member should record his or her activities, and this information should be compiled by a single, designated ERT member to ensure a consistent and complete format.

6. If an employee is suspected of the crime: The Human Resources Department should notify the employee that an investigation is commencing and should place the person on paid administrative leave until it is determined whether or not he or she appears to have committed a crime. Extreme care should be taken not to invade the employee's privacy.

7. Disconnect the suspect computer from the network as soon as possible.

8. Collect any electronic storage media in the immediate vicinity (e.g., diskettes, CD-ROMs and CD-RWs, zip-drive cartridges) as well as any potential paper evidence and take it to a designated evidence room, which is locked and accessible only by authorized individuals. Again, take extreme care not to invade the employee's privacy. Going through purses and other personal belongings could lead to a lawsuit and much larger damages than the e-crime being investigated.

9. Copy remote electronic storage media that may contain evidence (e.g., disk storage devices connected to network file servers located either on-site or in a remote data center, CD-ROMs stored in a network "jukebox" device) using a suitable forensics tool. This step is where the computer forensics expert should be consulted.

10. Using an appropriate software tool, perform a bit-stream backup of each suspect piece of electronic storage media. Again, the computer forensics consultant should be consulted and probably be the one to perform this step.

11. Evaluate the results of the investigation with the appropriate level of management. Management should decide whether to prosecute the individual. If so, legal counsel should be notified. Appropriate law enforcement officials should also be notified, especially in cases of child pornography or other potentially violent crimes.

12. Close the case file, and archive all documents and evidence for a period of time dictated by the organization's legal counsel.

13. Conduct a case postmortem to evaluate how the overall process was handled and whether any improvements need to be made.

CONCLUSION

Computer forensics tools are, by themselves, scientific. The proper use of the various computer forensics tools and analysis of the results is both an art and a science. The steps that we as laypersons can perform amount to common sense. Nonetheless, such commonsense steps can mean the difference between a successful prosecution and a perpetrator getting away with an illegal act. It is hoped that readers will use the information in this chapter as a guide to help their organizations develop procedures that will increase the likelihood of convictions of perpetrators of electronic and other crimes. Exhibit 12.1 provides a list of common computer forensics software products and services.

EXHIBIT 12.1   COMPUTER FORENSICS SOFTWARE PRODUCTS AND SERVICES

Most computer forensics tools have been developed for private use by consultants who charge hefty fees to assist attorneys, client companies, and law enforcement agencies. Only recently have such tools become commercially available. Distribution of some of these tools still is regulated by their creators to limit the number of criminals obtaining such technology. I have compiled the following list of tools from various sources. Some are not necessarily computer forensics specific and thus have been commercially available for up to 10 years. They were included because they could assist in a computer forensics investigation.

ENCASE PRO BY GUIDANCE SOFTWARE, INC., PASADENA, CA (*www.guidancesoftware.com*)

Probably the best-known computer forensics software; originally available in 1997; sells for about $1,000; works on Windows 95/98/NT and has a graphical user interface (GUI); four-day training course available for $1,500; forensics investigation services also available; EnCase features include:

- Scan a drive on the scene, then view, copy, print unerase, and export files and folders without changing any data on the target drive.
- Switch between a Windows Explorer–type view and a database view.
- View and export any part of the hard drive, including interpartition areas, unallocated disk space and file slack, and deleted recycle bin contents.
- Scan the entire disk with cluster and sector views.
- Perform keyword and wild-card search capabilities.

EnCase creates a 128-bit MD-5 hash total from the bit-copied data. This enables the user to prove whether or not the data has been altered. If the data is examined at a later time, EnCase can create a new hash. If the data is unchanged, the two hashes should agree.

FORENSIX BY DR. FRED COHEN AND ASSOCIATES (*http://all.net*)

Created by Dr. Fred Cohen, an internationally recognized expert and instructor on computer forensics since the 1970ᶜ and currently a principal member of technical staff at the U.S. Department of Energy's Sandia National Laboratories; CD-ROM version sells for $2,000; desktop version is $7,000; ForensiX images and analyzes Mac, DOS, Windows, Unix , other disks, files, and data sources; has a graphical user interface; runs on RedHat Linux or Unix operating systems; forensics training offered through the University of New Haven, CT.

EXHIBIT **12.1** *(continued)*

INVESTIGATOR BY WINWHATWHERE CORP., KENNEWICK, WA (*www.winwhatwhere.com*)

Created by Richard Eaton and originally released in 1993, Investigator monitors and reports all computer activity, including time and usage monitoring, keystroke logging, project tracking, and Internet usage. Has stealth mode so target user is unaware of the monitoring. The information is logged for later viewing by the user. Only $100.

LEGAL DISK IMAGER, GENX, GENTEXT, GENTREE, AND IMAGER BY VOGON INTERNATIONAL, UK (*www.authentec.co.uk*)

Legal Disk Imager creates an exact replica of the original media of the target, or suspect machine. The process of imaging will not alter any information on the target machine. GenX and GenText run automatically to index and extract text from all areas of the target image. Options are also available to perform a full extraction of files from the image if required. The investigation utility, GenTree, incorporates Quick View Plus to view over 200 file formats. Identified "hits" can be viewed in their original format and printed out if required, enabling rapid identification to be made of any relevant evidence. Pricing not provided on the website. Consulting services also available.

NEW TECHNOLOGIES, INC. (NTI) SUITE, GRESHAM, OR (*www.forensics-intl.com*)

NTI was acquired by Armor Holdings, Inc. in 2000 but remains a relatively autonomous subsidiary. NTI's suite of software programs are DOS based and are not integrated, making the software less user friendly. But because they are DOS based, they are highly efficient and require minimal disk space. NTI also offers a variety of training, including an intensive three-day training course that includes the software as part of the $2,295 cost ($995 for qualifying law enforcement agencies).

NORTON GHOST 2000 BY SYMANTEC CORP., CUPERTINO, CA (*www.symantec.com*)

Ghost can clone and image partial or entire hard drives to removable media or another PC via parallel ports or NetBIOS interfaces, then restore entire images or individual files and directories as needed. Built-in error checking and image-comparison capabilities provide assurance that stored images exactly duplicate the original; compatible with all Microsoft operating systems. Single-user license, $70; enterprise licenses priced on application.

SAFEBACK, VIEWDISK, ANADISK, BY SYDEX CORP., EUGENE, OR (*www.sydex.com*)

SafeBack creates mirror-image backup files of hard disks and can make a mirror-image copy of an entire hard disk or partition. Backup image files can be

(continued)

Exhibit 12.1 (*continued*)

---

written to any writeable magnetic storage device. ViewDisk finds hidden or deleted data on computer diskettes regardless of format. AnaDisk searches, analyzes, and copies almost any kind of diskette without regard to type or format, can edit diskette data sector by sector or perform a diagnostic read of specified diskette tracks, dumps data from a selected range of tracks into a DOS file so that data from non-DOS diskettes can be examined and manipulated, and creates a date-and-time-stamped audit trail of all AnaDisk operations during a session. Prices must be requested through the website as products are made available only to "legitimate" organizations. Consulting services also available.

NOTES

1. Robert G. Bromley, "Data Recovery for Small Systems," *Information Systems Audit & Control Journal* (Volume 1, 1994): 45.
2. Michael R. Anderson, "Electronic Fingerprints, Computer Evidence Comes of Age," (1996): 1.
3. "A Stolen Computer As Star Witness," *Law Enforcement Technology* (May 1996): 58–59.
4. Parts of this section adapted from Jack J. Champlain, "Computer Forensics Investigation," *The Audit Report* (Volume 9, Issue 3, 2000): 4–8.
5. Channel 4000, "Two Face Felony Charges In Software Theft," *www.channel4000.com* (February 17, 2000).
6. Greg Miller, "Impact of Internet Sex-Predator Stings Questioned," *Seattle Times* (September 26, 1999): A6.
7. Peter Ruber, "State of Seige," *IRM Magazine* (Summer/Fall 1999): 10–11.
8. Eric Lacitis, "Secrets on a Computer: Delete Key Doesn't Make Things Clear," *Seattle Times* (September 26, 1999): L1, L8.
9. *Id.*
10. Alan Brill, "Computer Forensics: Files from the Kroll Casebook," *IRM Magazine* (Summer/Fall 1999): 8–9.
11. "Computer Forensics," *SC Magazine* (April 2000): 20–24.
12. *Id.*
13. "Computer Forensics," *SC Magazine* (October 1998): 16–21.
14. Philip Jan Rothstein, "Incident Response: Now What?" *Information Security* (May 1999): 37–41.
15. Mark Bigler, "Computer Forensics," *Internal Auditor* (February 2000): 53–55.
16. Bill Betts, "Crime Seen," *Information Security* (March 2000): 33–39.
17. "Computer Forensics," *SC Magazine* (April 2000): 20–24.
18. Lacitis, "Secrets on a Computer."
19. Rothstein, "Incident Response: Now What?"

CHAPTER 13

Other Contemporary Information Systems Auditing Challenges

The body of knowledge that encompasses information systems (IS) auditing is enormous. First, IS auditors must understand how computers work, what risks they present, and how they can best be controlled. The number and types of computers, operating systems, database management systems, and applications, each with its own unique idiosyncrasies, is staggering and continually increasing. Information systems auditors must keep current on these new technologies. Also included in the IS auditing body of knowledge are laws and regulations pertaining to the countries and industries in which organizations do business. Information systems auditors must also be fluent in traditional auditing methodologies, which have evolved from the auditing branch of the accounting profession. Knowledge of accounting principles is also extremely beneficial when examining expenditures for computer equipment and services and how they are recorded on the financial statements. A detailed understanding of business operations and high-level management issues such as strategic planning and forecasting is essential for IS auditors to communicate IS control and security issues with executives and board members. Depending on each auditor's area of specialty, additional bodies of knowledge may be encompassed. Finally, auditors must be able to apply this knowledge and information by effectively communicating in written and verbal form.

Delving into great detail on the entire body of knowledge related to IS auditing is beyond the scope of this book. However, a number of IS auditing topics were not discussed in other chapters but are important enough to discuss briefly here. These topics include computer-assisted audit techniques, computer viruses, software piracy, electronic commerce, Internet security, and information privacy.

COMPUTER-ASSISTED AUDIT TECHNIQUES

Internal and external auditors of many organizations and firms have developed and implemented computer-assisted audit techniques (CAATs) that have greatly increased the efficiency and effectiveness of their audits. Through the use of

CAATs, the productivity and value of their audits and consulting services to their clients has also increased. A CAAT can be defined as any computer program or application that has been used to enhance the efficiency and effectiveness of an audit process through the automation of previously manual procedures, expansion of the scope of audit coverage, or the creation of new audit procedures. The most powerful CAATs are the ones that independently search databases for information that could indicate the existence of significant or material control weaknesses or operational inefficiencies. Examples of tools that provide the ability for auditors to perform these types of CAATs include report-writing applications that accompany many vendor information systems; off-the-shelf database, spreadsheet and data analysis applications; and data warehouses. The keys to the successful deployment of these CAATs are the integrity and reliability of the data on which the CAATs are dependent, the independence of the method in which the data was obtained, and the timeliness with which the data is available.

Report-writing applications or modules that accompany vendor information systems have the advantage of extracting the desired data directly from production databases. Production data is not subject to the risk of data loss or corruption that could occur when production data is downloaded or extracted to another computer system for subsequent querying by a third-party application. By having the ability to create reports directly from the production database, auditors do not have to rely on data owners or other areas to run download or extract jobs and are thus able to maximize their independence. Also, the production data is available for report writers immediately upon completion of spooling, and the report writer programs can be run at any time after spooling. Download and extract programs must frequently wait until all productions jobs are completed before they are processed. Vendor report-writing applications have their drawbacks, however.

For example, obtaining access to the ability to perform vendor report writers on the production database may prove to be difficult. In some systems, report writers can bog down the production system if they require heavy processing, as in the case of numerous calculations or large history searches, or if a large number of report writers are running concurrently. As a result, data owners may be reluctant to grant report-writing ability to anyone outside their areas. Also, some vendor report-writing applications may require specialized training to use them efficiently and effectively.

To use off-the-shelf database (e.g., Access), spreadsheet (e.g., Excel), or data analysis applications (e.g., ACL, IDEA, Monarch), the data must first be downloaded from the production database. This requires the data owner to authorize the development of a report writer or program to extract the desired pool of data. If the desired pool of data is relatively small, the data owner can create a report writer to extract the data. The report output can then be electronically downloaded to the auditor's workstation or network where a database, spreadsheet, or data analysis application can be used to perform multiple queries. If the desired pool of data is relatively large, it may be more efficient to work with the programming and/or systems development departments to design an extract program that generates a database on which multiple queries can be performed. Either method reduces the independence of the auditor, but data integrity can be reasonably assured through proper systems development and change control procedures. Where possible, procedures in the audit department should require that the extracted data be balanced to the production database. Otherwise, audit results may not be as complete and accurate as expected. In some cases, data analysis applications can be configured to interrogate the production database, thereby eliminating the need to balance it. However, data owner approval must be acquired, and care must be taken to ensure that queries do not impact production application performance.

Once the data has been downloaded, the extract database has been created, or production database access has been established, auditors can perform multiple queries using their own database, spreadsheet, or data analysis applications, without affecting the performance of production central processing units (CPUs). This significantly enhances the efficiency of the computer operations area and the auditors. Keep in mind that third-party database, spreadsheet, or extract applications are only practical when auditors are going to be performing multiple queries. If only one query is required one time, then it would probably be more efficient to request a single report from the data owner.

Data warehouses (e.g., Sagent) are large databases that provide users, including auditors, the ability to access information from two or more different systems. They eliminate the need to have separate report writers or extract programs for each production system and enable analysis of entire customer relationships in one location using client software that is part of the suite of data warehouse application software. Information systems auditors can develop countless ways to interrogate a data warehouse for potential internal control weaknesses.

Risks associated with data warehouses include incomplete or inaccurate data, unauthorized or excessive data access, high cost, and inability to gain authorization to include all data in the data warehouse. As with report writers and extract programs, procedures should be in place for the data warehouse owner to balance the data within the data warehouse to its source systems to ensure that all applicable production data has been completely and accurately downloaded. Data warehouse system security administrators should also restrict access to data based on management authorization. Data warehouse technology can be very expensive, so IS management should perform an extensive needs analysis prior to initiating a data warehouse project. Senior management support is crucial to ensuring that access to all necessary data is granted so that a complete data warehouse can be created.

As new technologies are created, auditors should continue to challenge themselves to develop new and innovative audit approaches and techniques that will further enhance their efficiency and effectiveness. Literally millions of CAATs are deployed in the audit workplaces of the world. Case study 13.1 describes the development of a CAAT that significantly enhanced the efficiency and effectiveness of an audit department. Case study 13.2 describes the difficulties that can be encountered using CAATs. Although specific vendor products are mentioned, these case studies are not intended to be advertisements or promotions for the products discussed.

CASE STUDY 13.1

CAAT Using Monarch®

In the Internal Audit Department of one banking organization, we were unable to successfully utilize a vendor-supplied mainframe application to download data on production reports and report writers in "comma-delimited" format. We intended to implement CAATs that performed queries on the mainframe report data using personal computer (PC)–based spreadsheet and database applications. Unfortunately, due to faulty programming by the vendor, the data would become "tarnished" because fields in some records would become concatenated (i.e., attached) to other fields, thereby resulting in an inconsistent database format. The vendor did not have a lot of clients who required this type of capability, so correcting the faulty programming was not a high priority at the time.

Alternatively, we were able to successfully download production reports and report writers in American Standard Code for Information Intercharge (ASCII) text format, which was the only other downloading format available with the mainframe application. When these text files were imported into existing versions of PC-based spreadsheet and database software applications, however, all the fields for each record would be imported into one column. In other words, for each record, all fields were consolidated into one field. Thus, we still could not perform multiple queries on the mainframe report data with spreadsheet or database software unless a programmer was hired to design and create an extract program to correct for the vendor's faulty programming.

Instead of spending thousands of dollars and having to wait for a new download application, we decided instead to test the ability of a PC-based software application called Monarch, which is marketed by Datawatch Corporation of Wilmington, Massachusetts. Monarch can perform quite an array of functions including data querying, sorting, calculating, importing, exporting, and reporting. For us, Monarch eliminated the need for an extract program so long as the production report or report writer data in the print SPOOL could be downloaded in text format. In other words, it bridged the gap between the mainframe and microcomputer workstations without the need for costly programming efforts. The cost of Monarch software was relatively cheap—about $400 per stand-alone copy. Network versions are also available.

The most immediate need was to automate a manual monitoring process in which an individual in the Internal Audit Department examined changes to the loan and deposit databases by users from throughout the organization. The monitoring report was printed daily and was usually about 300 pages long. The auditor monitored for patterns of unusual changes that could be the result of fraud, errors, and system problems. Unfortunately, it was not humanly possible for the auditor to review the entire report every day and still have time to perform other duties. As a practical matter, the auditor would judgmentally select about 10 to 20 pages (0.3 percent to 0.7 percent) of the report activity and perform detailed examination of the data changes. The auditor spent about one hour each day reviewing the report. The remainder of the report was thrown away, with over 99 percent of the activity not being monitored.

To implement Monarch, the 300-page daily report was downloaded in ASCII text format into an Audit Department workstation. We then used Monarch to create eight different "filters" that queried the entire 300 page report. Each filter queried the data for blocks of suspicious text in selected fields and incidences of numbers exceeding predetermined parameters in other fields. We initially ran these queries separately. Then, we found that it would be more efficient to consolidate them into one filter and sort it by user ID. In this way, all suspicious or erroneous activities by each individual user could be identified.

From start to finish, including printing the Monarch reports, the auditor was now able to query 100 percent of the report activity in about 15 minutes for potentially unusual activity. The auditor then spent an additional 30 to 45 minutes each day researching the identified data change activity in detail. In this particular instance, the efficiency and effectiveness of our daily data change review was increased 1,500 to 3,000 percent. An added benefit was that the need to receive paper printouts of the data change report each day was eliminated, thereby saving about one tree each week.

Within a short time, this new daily monitoring process began to bear fruit. For example, a previously unknown yet significant internal control weakness was identified that allowed tellers to post an advance of *any amount* against a loan, even if it was closed, open with a fixed term, or in the case of lines of credit, exceeded the credit limit. During follow-up testing, a hypothetical advance of *$1 billion* was requested, and it was accepted by the system. Fortunately, before being corrected, this control weakness had been exploited for a significant amount (about $4,000) only once.

The only costs beyond that of purchasing one workstation copy of the software license were for me and one software support person from our organization to attend a local two-day Monarch training course. The training was not necessary to get started using Monarch. In fact, we had already been using the product for preparing basic reports prior to the training. The training increased our proficiency with the software and also enlightened us to some of the other potential capabilities of the software.

The first experience with Monarch was so successful that we began searching for other solutions. Our next effort was to automate a portion of the quarterly consumer loan database monitoring that we performed. Prior to implementing a Monarch solution, an auditor would spend several weeks examining a random sample of about 50 files for consumer loans that were originated during the previous quarter. However, the remainder of the consumer loan database, which consisted of about 100,000 loans, was not effectively monitored for unusual activity.

There were some custom consumer loan reports that were generated from the mainframe to identify potential exceptions, but every time we wanted to change the parameters, we had to request the changes through the Data Processing (DP) Department. In addition, if we thought of other types of queries, we again had to have the DP Department design and prepare the reports. The initial parameters usually had to be adjusted, depending on the number of

(*continued*)

reportable loans that appeared on the report writers. This could sometimes create friction between the Internal Audit Department and the DP Department. Often our requests for changes and new reports were delayed until the DP Department staff were available to process our requests.

One of our goals was to reduce our dependence on the DP Department, thereby increasing our independence and our flexibility in creating new reports and adjusting existing reports. An added benefit of our increased independence was that the DP Department staff would no longer know what attributes we were examining. We also wished to reduce the number of individual consumer loan files that were examined in detail, reduce the number of attributes that were tested for the sampled loans, and examine 100 percent of the consumer loan database for various attributes, including those that were no longer to be tested on the sampled loans.

To accomplish these goals, we worked with the DP Department to design a single, large extract report that listed all desired fields for all consumer loans. Initially we had to carefully identify all the possible consumer loan fields that we currently were interested in or that we may be interested in examining in the future. To ensure that we were aware of all fields we could potentially include, the DP Department supplied us with a current list of all the fields that existed for each consumer loan record. We then worked with the DP Department to design the final report. A procedure was also set up so that we would be notified of any changes to the attributes of existing loan fields and of the addition of new fields.

Once designed, the DP Department had to run this report only once each quarter. We would then download the report from the print SPOOL into a PC workstation and utilize Monarch to perform multiple, independent queries at our leisure. The only other time we would have to rely on the DP Department would be if the attributes of any of the fields changed or if we wished to add or remove any fields. A minor drawback was that since the report had to examine daily activity for the previous three months, it required a significant amount of CPU processing resources. Furthermore, the output was so large that it had to be separated into three data files to be reasonably manageable.

However, the benefits far exceeded these operational drawbacks. Because we were able to examine about 8 to 10 high-risk attributes for 100 percent of the consumer loan database, we were able to streamline the detailed testing performed on the manually sampled loan files. In addition, the number of loan files sampled was reduced from 50 to 20, and the manual review was directed primarily at loan documentation attributes.

Examples of the attributes we tested using Monarch included loans with interest rates outside of reasonable high and low ranges, loans with invalid collateral and purpose codes, loans that should have been written off based on the number of days the loans were delinquent, loans with amortization periods that exceeded authorized maximums, loan amounts that exceeded the original loan balance, and loan amounts that exceeded authorized limits.

We also were able to test the accuracy of a specific date calculated field. To identify delinquent loans, the Collections Department received a standard report that relied on the "number of days delinquent" field in the consumer loan database. However, if someone were granting unauthorized extensions, the loans would not show as delinquent in the "number of days delinquent" field, even though a payment may not have been made for several months. Therefore, to confirm the accuracy of the "number of days delinquent" field, we designed a Monarch filter that calculated the number of days since the last loan payment and compared it to the "number of days delinquent" field. If the difference was more than a few days, it would be reported by the filter and we would investigate further. A few instances were identified in which technically unauthorized extensions were being granted, although the reasons were found to be reasonably legitimate.

As with any type of computer program, it is extremely important to maintain documentation and backup copies of the Monarch filters and descriptions of what they are supposed to be testing. Often it is difficult to discern the purpose of a filter from its name or by examining the filter formulas. Documentation helps remind auditors of the purpose and reasoning behind each filter, provides written backup in case the original code is lost, and also assists in cross-training of other auditors. Electronic backup copies of the filters ensure that if the originals are accidentally altered or lost, they can be recovered without having to retype and re-create the original code.

The Internal Audit Department was the first in our organization to utilize Monarch. We had to strongly convince the software support group to approve the purchase and installation of the first copy of the software. Not having seen any other audit organization that had utilized Monarch, we were taking a risk in the event the software did not meet our needs. As can be seen from the above efficiencies, the potential benefits far exceeded the nominal cost of the software and training.

In fact, word of our success spread quickly throughout the organization. Since then several other operational departments that perform data analysis have installed Monarch and begun performing their own queries. As the most sophisticated user, the Internal Audit Department has become the Monarch consultant to various departments wishing to closely examine and monitor their databases.

Some of the newer spreadsheet products can perform data file importing and exporting as well as some manipulation of text data files using parsing features. However, none of them currently matches the flexibility, ease, and independence with which we were able to apply Monarch to bridge the gap between our mainframe and networked internal audit workstations.

CASE STUDY 13.2

CAAT Using FOCUS

FOCUS is a fourth-generation programming language developed by Information Builders, Inc., of New York. FOCUS databases are a source of data that enables end users to obtain information relatively quickly without having to request it through a centralized data processing report request process. FO-

(*continued*)

CASE STUDY 13.2 (*continued*)

CUS databases are created through a process in which records from the production application files are extracted by a program that subsequently copies
them in a FOCUS-readable format to a designated electronic storage address.
Since the FOCUS database is not a production database, it is extremely important that a procedure exists to balance the FOCUS database totals to the
production database totals to help confirm that the extract program performed
successfully.

I once worked in a nonaudit department of a large commercial bank in
which the FOCUS language was used to prepare numerous reports on various cross-sections of the commercial loan databases. Procedures existed to
balance the FOCUS database totals to the production database. The commercial loan application was very complex, with numerous types of loans and
credit lines, each with a myriad of distinguishing features, including rates,
collateral codes, industry codes, purpose codes, city, state, zip code, country, fees, terms, and so on. Unfortunately, the commercial loan application did
not have adequate edits to prevent the entering of invalid codes and certain
other information. This incorrect data sometimes caused significant inaccuracies in the FOCUS reports we created and submitted to senior management
and the various boards of directors throughout the corporation.

It was found that FOCUS programs could be effectively utilized to identify
exceptions to the aforementioned types of data. For example, quick and easy
routines could be written to identify loans with invalid purpose codes or collateral codes or loans with interest rates outside a predetermined range. The
applicable loan centers would then be notified so they could correct the loan
information. FOCUS programs were also written to identify loans with collateral in risky areas. For example, after an earthquake, a report was created listing
all real estate–secured loans with collateral addresses in the quake zone. Although we were in a nonaudit department, we were essentially using FOCUS
to audit the integrity of the database and to identify risky loans. In an audit
department, FOCUS could have been used to monitor the commercial loan
database on an ongoing basis.

If you do not currently have the luxury of CAAT applications, and if your
organization currently creates extract databases, you may wish to consider
inquiring as to whether your department can obtain report-writing access to
the extract databases. If so, the potentially lengthy and costly process of designing and creating a separate extract database with the systems development
group can be avoided. Users who become highly proficient with CAAT programs may be tempted to become programmers within or outside the Audit
Department. However, programming is not all glamour and can be highly
stressful, as demonstrated in the remainder of this case study.

One day, we were ordered to prepare a special rush report for an executive who wanted to have the total dollars of the commercial loan portfolio
classified into his idea of industry categories. His desired industry categories
did not exist on the commercial loan database. Instead, we had to use the
available government standard industrial codes (SICs) and map them as best
we could to the executive's industry types. By the deadline date, the resulting
report showed about $500 million of loans in the "other" category. This did

not seem too bad, considering the total commercial loan portfolio amounted to over $5 billion at the time and the executive's industry classifications left us no choice but to map a large number of loans into the "other" category. However, the executive became outraged when he saw the large "other" figure. He called our division head, a senior vice president, that afternoon and demanded that the division head personally reclassify all the loans in the "other" category by 10 A.M.. I was given the unenviable task of assisting the division head.

I had to rewrite the FOCUS program from which the figures were derived to create a detailed listing of loans in amount order within each of the executive's industry types. The program took about 30 minutes to run. If there was a programming logic error, a significant amount of time could be wasted searching for the cause of the problem and then reexecuting the program. I worked on it some that afternoon, thinking that I could complete the reprogramming by the next morning. By 9 A.M., I was still having problems getting the report to run without blowing up. The division head came over to my workstation several times and literally was standing over my shoulder, asking how much longer it would take for me to complete the job. I told him I was getting close, and the program had to finish running. In reality, parts of the program were blowing up right before his eyes. Fortunately, he did not understand the responses that were appearing in red on the computer screen. By 10 A.M., I was finally able to get the program to run and was sending the output to the printer in the back room. I had planned to compare the total amounts of the loans on the new detailed listing to the original report totals to make sure they balanced—something every programmer should get in the habit of doing. But when I went back to the printer room to retrieve the report, I was aghast to see the division head already standing there waiting for the printer to finish. On completion, he took the report into his office, shut the door, and began reclassifying the detailed listing of loans before I even had a chance to balance the output to the original report totals. After he was finished with his reclassification, he returned the printout to me. I was relieved to find that the totals of the loans on the detailed listing were within about $2 million of the $5 billion portfolio (a 99.96 percent accuracy rate). This difference was insignificant since the division head only reclassified those loans over $1 million. He left numerous loans under $1 million in the "other" category. Had the report contained a significant number of large inaccuracies, I would have had to tell the division head that he would have to tell the executive that the loan totals he had just given him were incorrect. I suspect that I would have been looking for a new job that afternoon. This experience caused me to realize that I did not belong in the report programming side of a commercial bank.

I hope you will never encounter this stressful a situation running CAAT reports for an auditing department. When programming reports, be sure to clarify exactly what the user expects on the report and to budget plenty of time for preparing, testing, and balancing reports, especially when preparing them for the first time. Time must be allowed to check the programs for accuracy, especially if they are to be used by high-level decision makers. Attention to these details will eliminate many subsequent headaches associated with rewriting reports for irate senior managers.

COMPUTER VIRUSES

With the proliferation of the Internet and other public and private networking technologies, the risk of an organization's personal computers becoming infected with a virus is significant. In fact, it is not a matter of whether the computers will become infected, but when and to what degree. Every day malicious programmers are creating new viruses. Some viruses are no more than nuisances, while others have the capability of wiping out data and causing computer operating systems to fail.

The most damaging viruses and worms in terms of economic impact in recent years according to *Computer Economics* (*www.computereconomics.com*) were "Code Red" (2001), $2.62 billion; "SirCam" (2001), $1.15 billion; "Nimda" (2001), $635 million; "I Love You" (2000), $8.75 billion; "Melissa" (1999), $1.10 billion; and "Worm.Expore.Zip" (1999), $1.02 billion.[1] Other less damaging but well-known viruses and worms include "Goner" (2001), "Anna Kournikova" (2001), "Chernobyl" (1999), and "Bubbleboy" (1999).

The risks of viruses include these costs:

- Recovering lost data
- Eradicating viruses that have infected workstations, network file servers, mainframes, diskettes, CDs, and other storage media
- Purchasing, installing, and maintaining virus detection and prevention software
- Educating users on the risks of viruses, how to test for viruses, and what to do and whom to contact when a virus is detected
- Developing and maintaining policies on virus prevention
- Reduced data processing system efficiency, or complete loss of use of system
- Adverse publicity
- Incorrect operational, financial, and other reports
- Unauthorized accesses to existing as well as other systems

According to the Computer Security Institute (CSI), a virus is a computer program that has the ability to reproduce by modifying other programs to include a copy of itself. Such programs may execute immediately or wait for a preprogrammed set of circumstances.[2] The CSI goes on to define other related threats, including bacteria, logic bombs, Trojan horses, worms, password catchers, repeat dialers, trapdoors, and war dialers.

Bacteria are programs designed to reproduce exponentially until the host central processing unit (CPU) runs out of processing capacity, memory, or storage space, thereby denying service to any other users or processes. Bacteria programs do not damage other programs.

Logic bombs are programs that activate upon the occurrence of a certain event, such as the passing of a date or the failure of its creator to reset a special counter. When the event occurs, the "bomb" is triggered and the program performs some malicious commands, such as reformatting the hard drive of a server or shutting down a host computer.

Trojan horses are programs that look and perform certain functions innocently but contain malicious code such as viruses, bacteria, and logic bombs. The innocent part of the Trojan horse program may execute routinely for the user but may be performing malicious tasks concurrently or at a later time.

Worms are programs that search for and execute themselves in available host CPU processing memory and then continuously copy themselves to other computers, usually resulting in denial of service to other users. See the Internet Security section later in this chapter for a description of the first worm released on the Internet by Robert Morris.

Password catchers, repeat dialers, trapdoors, and *war dialers* are technically not viruslike programs that can infect computer systems. However, they can be used to exploit or create security weaknesses and are therefore worthy of one's awareness and further research.

Viruses operate in a variety of ways, depending on how the creator programmed them. Roxanne Mashburn, director of the Information Technologies Group for the Eccles Institute of Human Genetics at the University of Utah, provided these descriptions of the various types of viruses:

- *Memory resident.* This type of virus stays in memory after being loaded with its host program.
- *Nonmemory resident.* This type of virus is erased from memory after the host program closes.
- *Stealth.* This type of virus can hide from antivirus scanners.
- *Encrypting.* This type of virus encrypts itself to avoid detection.
- *Polymorphic.* This type of virus mutates by altering its signature. It is the most difficult type of virus to detect.
- *Triggered event.* This type of virus is triggered by a certain event, date, time, sequence of keystrokes, or other set of circumstances.[3]

Most virus-scanning software programs on the market today enable users to peruse the list of viruses in their inventories. These virus lists usually provide brief descriptions of how each virus works, history about when each was first encountered, and how each can be eradicated. Some older examples include:

- *Gulf War Virus.* This virus was imported by an officer who brought some computer games to U.S. Gulf War headquarters in Saudi Arabia. It may have wiped out as many as half of all the chemical weapons logs maintained by the U.S. military. Incidentally, physical diskettes containing another quarter of the chemical weapons logs were lost from a safe at Aberdeen Proving Ground in Maryland and during shipment to the U.S. Central Command headquarters in Florida.[4]
- *PKZIP300.ZIP.* This virus will wipe out a hard disk and disrupt modems that operate at 14.4 kilobytes per second and faster. PKZIP300.ZIP is reportedly very difficult to eradicate. The name of this virus is intentionally similar to the genuine PKZIP and PKUNZIP file compression software written by PCWare.[5]

- *Jerusalem.* This was the first memory resident virus. While loaded, it infects or deletes *.COM and *.EXE executable files, except for the COMMAND.COM file. It was first identified at Hebrew University in Jerusalem in 1987 and was to trigger on Friday, May 13, 1988, the 40th anniversary of the last day of existence of an independent Palestinian state.[6] Later strains become active primarily on Friday the 13th but can also be active on other days, slowing systems down after each infection.
- *Michelangelo.* First appearing in 1991, this virus reformats hard drives every March 6, Michelangelo's birthday.
- *Stoned.* This virus originated in early 1988 and became prolific in 1991. Early strains did nothing more than create a message on boot-up that the PC was "stoned" and to "legalize marijuana." Later strains reformatted hard drives and may have been the culprit in the Gulf War Virus previously discussed.

Case study 13.3 describes two real-world encounters with viruses. Case study 13.4 describes a virus weakness in a Macintosh environment.

CASE STUDY 13.3

Viruses, Viruses (Two Examples)

While president of the Puget Sound (Seattle) chapter of the Information Systems Audit and Control Association (ISACA), I had requested a copy of the current bylaws from the secretary, who was employed at a regional public accounting firm. She sent me a diskette with the requested file on it. My organization's network workstations were configured to automatically check for viruses on any file read from an external drive as well as any files moving to or from the file server. The virus reference file at my organization was also updated on at least a monthly basis to detect new strains of most viruses. Therefore, my workstation detected the "ANTIEXE" virus on the diskette from the secretary. This is a memory-resident virus that can overwrite the master boot sector with a copy of the virus.

I immediately eradicated the virus and promptly informed the secretary who had sent me the infected diskette. As with all "carriers," she claimed that she had run her firm's virus-checking software on the diskette before sending it to me and found nothing. However, she also admitted that the hard drive of her laptop had "crashed" (i.e., become inoperable) a few months earlier for no apparent reason and had to be reformatted. It appears that the virus was still rampant in her organization's network, or at least on her diskettes, thereby reinfecting her laptop after it was reformatted. Furthermore, her organization's virus-detection database had apparently not been updated for some time, since it still did not detect the virus.

On another occasion, our Internal Audit Department had received a diskette with a word processing document on it from another organization's Internal Audit Department. The administrative assistant to the director of Internal Audit in our organization had received the diskette and mentioned it to someone in the network support group. The network support group requested that the foreign diskette be brought in for testing before it was even checked by the workstation. The WORD.GENERIC virus was identified on the diskette. This virus can reportedly disrupt the boot sector of workstations and can migrate throughout a network. The diskette was returned to the sender with a notification that it had contained a virus. The virus was erased on detection by our network support group.

The sender claimed that he had saved another copy of the file he wished to send us onto a different diskette and checked the diskette for viruses. The sender stated that his organization's DP Department had also examined the diskette and found no virus on it. He hand-delivered the diskette to me at a seminar and asked that I test it again to see if their virus-checking software was still not current. When I went back to work, I inserted the diskette into the A drive on my workstation and ran the virus-checking software on my workstation directly against the A drive. No virus was detected. Before opening the file, however, I decided to let our network support group test the diskette again. Once again the WORD.GENERIC virus was detected. As it turned out, the network support group's virus-checking software had a more current virus inventory database than the one to which my workstation virus-checking software referred. The virus-checking software on my workstation supposedly referred to a virus inventory database that was updated on at least a monthly basis. This time, the virus was not eradicated and the infected diskette was returned to the sender with printouts of the virus-detection software so his organization's DP Department could determine why their virus-checking software did not identify it.

Two important control recommendations can be observed from these examples. First, if possible, virus-checking software on network workstations and file servers should be configured to automatically check for viruses on any external diskette or information source and to perform a complete virus scan at least once each day. Second, the virus inventory database relied on by the virus-checking software should be updated on a regular basis (e.g., weekly or more often when new viruses are discovered). Many vendors supply periodic updates to the virus database at a reasonable charge.

CASE STUDY 13.4

Macintosh Virus Exposure

During an audit of a Windows NT network environment, we included an assessment of the network virus protection controls in the scope. We found that all NT servers and workstations were adequately protected by virus protection software. Also, the organization subscribed to automatic updates to virus pattern files. We observed that the Marketing Department used about eight Macintosh computers for graphical design projects. Each of these computers

(*continued*)

CASE STUDY 13.4 (*continued*)

was connected to the NT network for purposes of receiving e-mail and accessing the Internet. The Macs were configured with external diskette drives and internal modems, thus making them susceptible to external viruses from behind the network firewall. Because they were Macs, not PCs, the Marketing workstations were configured by the Information Technology (IT) department with a different virus protection software. At the time the virus software was installed (about six months before our audit), the current pattern files were installed. A procedure was reportedly implemented where a designated marketing user was to receive virus pattern file update notices via e-mail and to execute them via the Internet. But, as it should, the network firewall did not allow the updates to be executed remotely. Unfortunately, IT did not assist the Marketing Department in an alternative update procedure, and Marketing did not demand updates. Thus, the Macs went without virus pattern file updates for six months until the time of our audit. We recommended that the IT Department work with the Marketing Department to implement a procedure whereby virus pattern file updates could be received and installed on the Mac workstations in a timely manner.

Literally dozens of virus-detection software products available in the marketplace can detect most types of viruses. Those in charge of data security in organizations will need to determine which product best fits the organization's needs and financial resources. Keep in mind that separate virus-detection packages may need to be purchased for each platform in the organization. No matter which is purchased, these steps, at a minimum, should be followed to help reduce the risk of infections:

- Always maintain current backup copies of hard drives and data files in the event a virus causes the system to crash.
- Establish a user education program to teach users the risks of viruses, how to detect viruses based on unusual system behavior, how to operate virus-detection software, and what to do and whom to contact when a virus is detected.
- Be alert to unusual or unexplained behavior on PCs and workstations (e.g., increases in file sizes, changes in the date or time of last update, sudden decreases in the amount of disk space, or unexpected or frequently occurring disk activity).[7]
- Set virus-detection software so that it automatically checks all the files on diskettes in all external drives and any other incoming files (e.g., from the Internet or other networks). The virus-detection software should also be configured to perform a complete virus scan of all memory locations in workstations and file servers on a daily basis. Furthermore, do not assume that newly purchased software is virus free. Check all diskettes.
- Viruses, worms, and other malware are primarily transmitted via e-mail but can be proliferated by diskettes and CDs, and by copying and downloading

data files from the Internet and other networks. Therefore, an organization should have policies that prohibit the import of any external data, require the imported data to be checked for viruses by an authorized data security officer, or require users to perform virus scans on all external data they bring via diskette or download from an external source.

- The virus inventory database relied on by the virus-checking software should be updated on at least a weekly basis. Many vendors provide a service to automatically update virus pattern files at a reasonable charge.
- Avoid starting a computer with an untested diskette in an external drive.

Implementation of these steps will help ensure that the impacts of viruses, worms, and other malware to an organization are not significant. Unfortunately, like the common cold or flu, computer viruses, and malware are a necessary evil that we must all live with.

SOFTWARE PIRACY

Software piracy is the act of copying a copyrighted software program for personal use or for resale to another party, thereby denying the rightful owner royalties and any other legal benefits to which they would otherwise be entitled. In its 1991 Worldwide Report, the Business Software Alliance (BSA) reported that the annual cost of software theft worldwide ranged from $10 billion to $12 billion. The Institute of Internal Auditors (IIA) reported that an independent study commissioned by BSA and the Software and Information Industry Association (SIIA) found that, in 1996, the cost of software piracy worldwide was estimated at $11.2 billion. The study also found that about half of all new software applications used in 1996 were pirated.[8]

More recently, BSA says the total dollar losses from software piracy have actually trended down from $12.2 billion in 1999, to $11.8 billion in 2000, to $11 billion in 2001. But BSA estimated that 40 percent of all new software installed in businesses in 2001 was obtained from the black market.[9] These reductions are due to increased successes in prosecutions and settlement, sting operations, changes in domestic laws such as the U.S. Digital Millennium Copyright Act (DMCA), which was signed into law on October 28, 1998, and successes in getting foreign governments to crack down on piracy.

Because of these heavy losses, software industry trade groups have been formed in numerous countries, including Australia, Argentina, Belgium, Brazil, Canada, Chile, Columbia, the Czech Republic, Denmark, Ecuador, Egypt, Finland, France, Germany, Hong Kong, Hungary, India, Indonesia, Israel, Italy, Japan, Korea, Luxembourg, Malaysia, Mexico, the Netherlands, New Zealand, Norway, the Philippines, Portugal, Peru, Puerto Rico, Saudi Arabia, Singapore, South Africa, Spain, Sweden, Switzerland, Taiwan, Thailand, Turkey, the United Arab Emirates, the United Kingdom, the United States, and Venezuela.

The trade groups in these countries are trying to control the theft of software revenues. To help mount a united international effort to protect software copyrights, the BSA was established in 1988. Headquartered in Washington, D.C., the BSA works with government officials and national industry groups to achieve its international mission, which is to advance free and open world trade for legitimate business software by advocating strong intellectual property protection for software, increasing public awareness of the legal protection of software, and acting against unauthorized software copying in all forms.

The risks to organizations that promote or tolerate software copyright infringement include financial penalties and fines, loss of reputation due to negative publicity, and other legal remedies. In addition, software companies lose much-needed revenues, governments lose tax revenues, and communities suffer from increased drug and related crime activities fueled in part by illegal software sales. Officers and directors of organizations, as well as the individuals who performed software copyright violations, can all be held criminally accountable. In the United States, individuals convicted of criminal copyright violations can be fined up to $250,000 and face up to five years in jail. Civil lawsuits can result in the payment of actual damages (including the infringer's profits) and statutory damages up to $150,000 per infringement. In addition, pirated software can expose an organization to viruses, improperly performing software, inadequate documentation, lack of technical support, and lack of software upgrades.

Recent busts have resulted in the confiscation and prosecution of perpetrators who caused millions of dollars in lost revenues. For example, $5 million worth of pirated software was confiscated in Vancouver, British Columbia, in 2002; $100 million of illegal software in Los Angeles in 2001; $60 million in illegal software in Dallas in 2001; $2.5 million was paid in restitution by 159 firms worldwide in 2001; and $56 million in counterfeit software in California in 1999. [10]

In China, where 94 percent of all software was pirated in 2000, the government has been assisting Microsoft in piracy prevention efforts. [11] In June 1997, BSA collaborated with the Filipino National Bureau of Investigation and raided three Filipino computer companies and prosecuted two people for selling pirated software. The value of the software was approximately $2 million. The Philippines are considered a "hotbed" of piracy, with only 8 percent of software legally purchased.[12]

To avoid these risks, BSA recommends that all organizations implement these recommendations for responsible software use[13]:

- Senior management should circulate to all new and current employees a notice stating that it is illegal and against company policy to make or use unauthorized software copies. Such notice should be communicated to users via a banner page that appears during sign on. Furthermore, if an organization has a new employee training program, software copyright violations should be incorporated into the curriculum. Users should be informed that the organization is allowed to make only one backup copy of software and that the number of concurrent users allowed by network versions of software is specified in the organization's software license.
- Conduct periodic audits of all PCs and file servers so that a record of software programs installed on each machine is created. Any illegal software

copies should be deleted. Information system auditors should confirm that system security administrators are performing these audits at least annually. In the United States, SIIA provides automated tools to help inventory software. Be cognizant of the fact that the automated tools may not identify all software products on a particular device. The reason is that sophisticated users may disguise executable files to make detection difficult. Performing regular audits will alert users to the fact that the company does not tolerate illegal software. As a result, these audits will act as a deterrent and reduce the incidence of illegal software.

- Maintain a current software inventory system to record the purchase of software. Access to installation diskettes should be restricted to authorized personnel. Furthermore, centralized purchase authorization and installation can control the degree of software piracy immensely.

- Make a requisition form available to all employees so that they may submit requests for new software to their managers.

Refer to case study 6.9 for a description of a situation in which unlicensed software proliferated throughout an organization due to poor software inventory controls.

Other new control technologies are being developed to help thwart some piracy of articles and pictures on the Internet. For example, *Playboy* magazine has recently adopted Digimarc™ digital watermarks to help prevent copyright infringements of photographic images located on its website. These watermarks will be randomly embedded into some copyrighted images. To locate watermarked images downloaded by unauthorized users, *Playboy* technicians use a special software application called MarcSpider, which crawls the World Wide Web, looking at hundreds of millions of objects, in search of any that have a Digimarc watermark. The Internet addresses of identified images are recorded for follow-up investigations by *Playboy* technicians.[14]

As new and better controls are developed, and as international cooperation continues to progress so that copyright violators are sternly prosecuted, the incidence and risk of copyright violations can be reduced to reasonable levels.

ELECTRONIC COMMERCE

Electronic commerce is the process whereby goods and services are purchased through some electronic medium. Electronic commerce is becoming the desired transaction method for many businesses. It is relatively inexpensive to administer as compared to cash, check, and verbal transactions because it requires very little human labor. Many people enjoy the convenience of being able to purchase goods and services via their PCs at home or work. The primary drawback to this transaction method has been the risk of consumers having their credit card numbers, checking account numbers, and other personal information stolen or intercepted during an electronic commerce transaction and used for unauthorized purchases, especially for transactions conducted through the Internet. As a result, many potential customers are uncomfortable sending their credit card numbers and other information across the Internet or any other open electronic network.

While the growth in the number and amounts of electronic commerce transactions has been rapid in our technology-hungry society, the general acceptance of this transaction method has been much slower than expected. Encryption technologies, which were discussed in Chapter 11, have significantly increased the security of electronic transactions and are a critical aspect of electronic commerce. Several electronic commerce security technologies are described next.

VISA International and MasterCard International, which jointly have nearly 1 billion credit and debit cards in circulation worldwide, have been collaborating to develop a single technical standard for safeguarding payment card purchases made over open networks since February 1, 1996. The standard is called SET (secure electronic transaction) and is an open industry standard intended to provide financial institutions, merchants, and vendors with a reasonably secure solution to enable trusted electronic commerce to flourish. Secure Electronic Transaction relies on specially designed public key crytpography and digital certificate controls, and was jointly developed in partnership with seven technology companies: GTE, IBM, Microsoft, Netscape, SAIC, Terisa Systems, and VeriSign.

On May 13, 1997, VISA and MasterCard announced that they had contracted with CertCo and SPYRUS to provide the root certificate authority (CA) system for SET. CertCo is a leader in enabling trustworthy electronic commerce while SPYRUS is a leading provider of secure hardware crytpographic solutions. The segregation of duties enabled by a joint root CA control process provides added security, flexibility, and economy. According to the CertCo chairman:

> The security of the entire SET system depends on protection of the SET root private key. To guard that key in a single site would require lavishly expensive physical controls and heavy armoring. By splitting and distributing the root's private key fragments among independent parties, the CertCo/SPYRUS system substantially increases SET security. By making the system stronger, SET security was improved, and operating costs were reduced.[15]

VISA's website also quoted the SPYRUS CEO as stating "The deployment of the SET Root CA provides a top-level point of trust for secure credit card payments and provides the missing element necessary to jump-start electronic commerce." The number three and four credit/debit card issuers in the world, American Express and JCB Company Limited of Japan, also have both endorsed the SET standard and the selection of CertCo and SPYRUS as root CA providers. Despite the progress of SET, its commercial implementation has been slow.[16] But there is still an urgent need for SET, as evidenced by the arrest of a 36-year-old hacker who stole over 100,000 credit card numbers online.[17] For more information on the history of the development of SET, visit the website of VISA International at *www.visa.com* and the website of MasterCard International at *www.mastercard.com*.

Secure sockets layer (SSL) technology is by far the most common control used to secure electronic transactions over the Internet (see the Chapter 8 section on remote access controls for a brief description of SSL). Although adequate in many cases, SSL does not afford the same strength of security as SET.

In the interim, other technologies have been developed that significantly reduce the risk of personal information being divulged while still providing consumers with the ability to conduct electronic commerce. For example, electronic wallets and purses enable consumers to securely purchase products from retailers. One such new technology is called CyberCash Wallet.[TM] In 1997 two credit unions began offering CyberCash Wallet service to their members in conjunction with the systems developer, Digital Insight of Camarillo, California.[18] Initially credit union members load their electronic "wallets" by initiating an automated clearing house (ACH) transaction, which sends funds from their financial institution to CyberCash. CyberCash holds the funds until purchases are authorized, and then CyberCash sends the funds to the merchant's bank accounts. This service limits purchases only to those merchants who accept CyberCash, but the developers hope to enlist many merchants, thereby making CyberCash a commonly accepted electronic commerce medium.

Smart cards, e-cash, and prepaid debit cards are other types of secure electronic commerce services that are emerging. Europay, VISA, MasterCard, and other major credit and debit card issuers are planning to migrate from magnetic strip–based cards to "smart cards" that have microprocessors with mini–operating systems embedded in the plastic. These microprocessors enable a much greater degree of security than is possible with magnetic strip cards. E-cash enables consumers to exchange funds with other individuals as well as retailers. This is different from the electronic wallet services, which only allow the exchange of funds between individuals and retailers. Prepaid debit cards are also limited to acceptance by retailers. These cards are issued in limited value increments and can be discarded once the issued amounts have been used.

As with any computerized process, complete electronic commerce security is impossible. There will always be a way for criminals to perform unauthorized transactions. So long as consumers are protected and electronic commerce losses can be effectively controlled, however, the economic benefits of electronic commerce to businesses and other organizations throughout the world will far outweigh the costs. Electronic commerce will continue to grow as a standard method of purchasing goods and services for a majority of people.

INTERNET SECURITY

Description of the Internet

The Internet is a global wide-area network (WAN) consisting of millions of host computers that enable millions of local- and wide-area networks, mainframes, workstations, and personal computers located within governments, businesses, research agencies, educational institutions, and individual homes to share information utilizing various Internet services. The Internet provides a wide variety of benefits to individual users as well as organizations. These benefits include the rapid sharing, dissemination, and exchange of information and news as well as high-impact, low-cost marketing of products and services.

Computers communicating on the Internet can have any type of operating system, so long as it supports the transmission control protocol/Internet protocol (TCP/IP), which enables computers with different kinds of operating systems to communicate among themselves. (TCP/IP is explained further in the History section.) Some common Internet services include:

- *Electronic mail (e-mail)* is a low-cost mode of communication that enables users to send and receive messages. Various types of data files can be attached to e-mail messages so users can access them. E-mail is perhaps the most popular Internet service. The main benefit of e-mail is that it enables people to communicate on personal as well as business issues with anyone on the Internet, anywhere in the world, at little or no cost, any time. E-mail is easier than writing a letter by hand, addressing the envelope, buying a stamp, and mailing it. Delivery of e-mail is also much faster than conventional mail. On the negative side, e-mail is less personal and, as is the case with any Internet communications, the authenticity of messages can be brought into question if not adequately secured.
- *Telnet* is an Internet service that enables one to connect to another computer on the Internet and then use it as if one was directly connected to that computer. Remote access to computers via Telnet can be restricted via system access controls, but it is still a fairly risky service to make available to most users within an organization.
- *Gopher* is a hierarchical text database developed at the University of Minnesota and named after the university's mascot. Gopher provides interconnected links between files residing on different computers on the Internet such that they appear as directories of files on the operator's computer. It is an efficient organizer of information on related topics.
- *Usenet* is an electronic bulletin board type of news service. News groups have various articles and messages posted for public reference. As a result, Usenet can be an excellent information resource.
- *File transfer protocol (FTP)* is a file manager application for the Internet that provides the ability to upload and download data files of various format (e.g., ASCII, EBCDIC, binary) to and from other computers. File transfer protocol has drag-and-drop functionality.
- *World Wide Web (WWW)* is another highly popular service that enables users to access and exchange various types of information located on computers anywhere in the world. The World Wide Web was originally created in 1989 by researchers at CERN (the European Laboratory for Particle Physics) in Geneva, Switzerland, to facilitate the exchange of information among widely dispersed sites. Today, the World Wide Web uses hypertext transfer protocol (HTTP) to enable users to access text, graphics, multimedia such as sound and video, and information databases. Within World Wide Web documents, hypertext enables instant linking to other locations within the same document and computer, and within other documents and computers

anywhere on the Internet. Hypertext markup language (HTML) is used to format documents so that they can be properly displayed through the World Wide Web. Browser software applications make it simple for users to access the wealth of information sites available on the Internet. These sites are called websites.

Each website has a unique "address" called a uniform or universal resource locator (URL). The format of a URL is typically as follows: http://www.entity-name.ext. The name of the entity is usually the name of the organization, while the letters "ext" refer to the type of organization. The World Wide Web originally had six types of extensions:

1. .com—commercial sites
2. .org—sites of nonprofit and other organizations
3. .gov—government sites
4. .edu—educational sites
5. .mil—military sites
6. .net—Internet service provider sites

In October 1998, the Internet Corporation for Assigned Names and Numbers (ICANN) was formed by a broad coalition of the Internet's business, technical, academic, and user communities. The ICANN is a technical coordination body for the Internet. It assumed official responsibility for a set of technical functions previously performed under U.S. government contract by Network Solutions, Inc., and other groups. Specifically, ICANN coordinates the assignment of three identifiers that must be globally unique for the Internet to function:

• Internet domain names
• IP address numbers
• Protocol parameter and port numbers

In addition, ICANN coordinates the stable operation of the Internet's root server system. As a nonprofit, private-sector corporation, ICANN is dedicated to preserving the operational stability of the Internet; to promoting competition; to achieving broad representation of global Internet communities; and to developing policy through private-sector, bottom-up, consensus-based means. In November 2000, ICANN approved seven new extensions:

1. .name
2. .biz
3. .info
4. .museum
5. .pro
6. .coop
7. .aero[19]

Websites can contain a wealth of information about organizations. Most organizations have created Internet websites to provide information to interested parties, to solicit information by taking advantage of the interactive nature of the Internet, and to perform a variety of transactions. Websites are also a low-cost, high-impact marketing medium through which organizations can promote their products and services as well as describe their mission, officers, locations, communication channels, and virtually any other public disclosure information, 24 hours a day, seven days a week. Websites provide a level competitive playing field for all organizations, regardless of size. Even the smallest of organizations can have very impressive websites that outshine those of large corporations.

Consumers and potential customers find it highly desirable and efficient to visit websites to perform transactions and obtain information when it is convenient for them. Previously, consumers had to telephone an organization during business hours, explain what transactions or information they wanted, and then wait for the transaction to be completed or the information to be mailed or faxed. Through websites, consumers can quickly perform transactions or obtain much of this same information. Organizations can also request information from visitors to their websites. For example, new business opportunities can be solicited and prospective employees can be recruited. Many commercial and noncommercial websites also provide articles, references, and other highly useful pieces of information.

History

In the mid-1960s, the U.S. Department of Defense Advanced Research Projects Agency (DARPA) created an experimental network that allowed remote research and development sites to exchange information without regard to the type of computer being used. The network became known as ARPANET. Reliability was the key so that the network would remain functional even if part of the network was damaged, as in the case of military strikes and various disasters. The ARPANET was also being designed to allow new computers to be added to the network and old ones to be removed without impacting the network. One of the most important developments from ARPANET research was the creation of TCP/IP, which enables different kinds of computers to communicate among themselves and is now the computer communications protocol of today's Internet. During the 1970s, the U.S. government began encouraging educational institutions and libraries to take advantage of ARPANET. In 1983, ARPANET became the backbone computer network to which all other TCP/IP computer networks were physically connected, thereby spawning the Internet. The National Science Foundation (NSF) funded and managed the Internet backbone until 1995, at which time corporations and private foundations began managing the Internet. The Internet Engineering Task Force (*www.ietf.org*), which is a group of scientists and other technical experts, provides support on technical issues related to the Internet. The Internet Society (*www.isoc.org*), a not-for-profit organization, guides the general direction of the Internet by establishing standards and allocating certain resources.

Risks

Although the Internet is a huge global WAN, many of the risks associated with it are actually not much different from those risks faced by any computer system. The Internet has spawned an enormous number of variations of traditional IS security risks due to its open nature and the number of different hosts that data may pass through before reaching its final destination. The Internet is also relatively risky since the development of controls to protect against Internet risks is belated. This is because the Internet was originally designed to encourage widespread information sharing among researchers and educators rather than to restrict information sharing. Further complicating the situation is the fact that current legal penalties for committing crimes on the Internet are relatively mild compared to other white-collar crimes. Some of the major risks associated with the Internet are discussed next.

Data Interception or Manipulation

When information is transmitted through the Internet, the data is transformed into data packets, which are sequentially organized and tagged with identifying information. Upon reaching its destination, the data packets are pieced back together in their original order. The risk during this process is that the message can be intercepted and analyzed using data packet "sniffing" devices and programs. The data can also be altered, lost, diverted, or replaced with bogus data. These techniques are used in cases of electronic espionage in which highly sensitive and confidential information is being transmitted among key executives and high-ranking officials. These risks are also contributing to the slower-than-desired growth of electronic commerce. Many organizations have internal internets known as intranets. Data interception or manipulation can be as risky while data is being transmitted within an organization via its intranet as it is while being transmitted outside an organization.

Controls to help reduce the risk of data interception or manipulation include dedicated communication channels, and secure sockets layer (SSL) technology. SSL is a protocol used in modern web browsers to establish relatively secure communications between two computers on the Internet. It encrypts all information in both the HTTP request and the HTTP response, including the URL (see Chapter 11 for more details about SSL).

Unauthorized Access, Hacking, and Graffiti

These risks pertain to the viewing, alteration, replacement, deletion, or other damage to sensitive information while it is residing on an organization's file servers and other computers. Hackers are notorious for taking over complete systems for their personal benefit. Malicious internal users and external parties, including corporate and political spies, can also use hacking techniques to gain unauthorized access to sensitive information.

Sometimes hackers limit their activities to website damage or graffiti, as was the case when the U.S. Department of Justice's web page was changed to the "Department of Injustice." In other cases, hackers can expose innocent consumers to financial risks. For example, in April 1996, more than 10,000 credit card account numbers, names, and expiration dates were somehow obtained from First Bank in Minnesota and copied to an Internet service provider file server, where they were available on the World Wide Web. The bank contended that the numbers were randomly generated. However, all of the numbers were affiliated with Northwest Airlines, which is headquartered in Minneapolis. The bank immediately canceled all the card numbers after the problem was publicized on the local news. The method in which the numbers were obtained has not been determined.[20] After these early defacements and hacks, similar breaches have become commonplace.

The primary means for reducing the risk of unauthorized access, hacking, and graffiti include the physical and logical security controls discussed in Part Two of this book as well as firewalls, which are discussed later in this section.

Overview of Hacking

Internet websites are simply programs and data files that reside on domain file servers. Internet domain file servers are file servers which communicate directly on the Internet, as opposed to private file servers, which are not able to communicate outside the organization. Every organization with a presence on the Internet either has connected one or more of its own domain servers or has paid a service organization to connect and maintain a domain server on their behalf. Each domain server on the Internet is technically identified by a sequence of four numbers, called octets, separated by periods. In general, these octets are numbered from 0 to 255 (e.g., 123.255.0.211). These Internet protocol "addresses" are issued by domain name registration services. Organizations can register multiple sites, so long as they pay the nominal annual fees. Internet protocol addresses are of interest to Internet technical support personnel as well as hackers and their gregarious associates, who may have less than noble intentions. Obtaining an Internet protocol address is usually the first step in the hacking process.

A domain server address can be obtained in a number of ways. Some organizations may willingly divulge the Internet address of their domain server, although most prefer to just give the World Wide Web alpha-numeric address (i.e., their URL). One can also sign on to the website of an Internet domain name registration service and perform an inquiry. For example, sign on to the website of any Internet registration service and perform a "who is" search on any name. The search results will list all the domain names registered to organizations with a name matching the word or words you entered. For each domain name, the search result will include the mailing or street address of the organization, the domain name (i.e., alpha-numeric website name), the administrative contact name and phone number or e-mail address, the domain server names and Internet protocol addresses, and other information. A third way to obtain the Internet protocol addresses is through the use of special programs. PING is one such program that is widely available on the Internet. If the World Wide Web address of a particular organization is known, PING can be used to retrieve the numeric Internet protocol address.

Armed with other special programs, hackers can begin to probe the Internet protocol addresses of the identified domain servers for weaknesses and vulnerabilities. Examples of free Internet and network vulnerability analysis tools include CIS (Cerberus Internet Scanner), Nessus, nmap, nmapNT, SAINT (Security Administrators' Integrated Network Tool, version 3.2.1 or earlier), Whisker, and WinfingerPrint. As with any freeware, there are risks that the software may be buggy or may not have all the reporting bells and whistles provided in other software. More sophisticated commercial vulnerability analysis tools, which can cost several thousand dollars, include CyberCop Scanner, Internet Scanner, Retina, and later versions of SAINT.

Literally hundreds of other free and costly hacking software tools are available on the Internet. Some sites categorize exploits by operating system and version and provide descriptions of what each exploit can do. Three such sites are *www.attrition.org*, *www.hackersclub.com*, and *www.insecure.org*. I recommend visiting these sites from home or from a secure lab computer that is not attached to the organization's network. Be sure to have current virus software and at least a personal firewall (e.g., BlackICE, Tiny, ZoneAlarm, etc.) to protect yourself should you receive an infected file or an unscrupulous hacker tries to attack. If you try to visit these sites from work, the organization's firewall should block you. If you get through, you put your organization's network at risk.

Once hackers gain control over an initial defense computer like a firewall, they then have a foothold or beachhead from which to launch further attacks on each subsequent set of computers networked to the compromised one. Literally every networked computer within an organization then is at risk, including mainframes and other hosts. There are no truly safe computers.

The "holy grail" of hackers is achieving system security administrator access capability. If they succeed, they can effectively take over a system by changing the password of the system security administrator user ID they signed on with and then removing all other user IDs. The only way to recover from this situation is to disconnect the telecommunications link being used, perform an initial program load (IPL), and reinstall the computer configuration parameters, which were, it is hoped, backed up the previous day or week.

Many "Big Four" public accounting firms and other companies are marketing "network penetration testing" services. Network penetration tests are exercises that are preauthorized by organization management. During the test, a "tiger team" of experts attempt to penetrate the firewall and other controls of the organization to gain as much unauthorized access as possible, thereby simulating an actual attack on an organization's computer systems. The timing and results of their exploits are carefully recorded and detailed in a report to management. Although this service can be expensive, the results may be highly valuable in identifying weaknesses before they are discovered by spies and hackers.

Most organizations do not possess the technical and tactical expertise to take on a full-scale hacker attack. If an organization encounters a situation in which highly skilled hackers are attacking, "mercenary" services can be hired to help defend, identify, and prosecute the malicious party or parties. However, even mercenary experts may not always achieve success. In some situations mercenaries have been able only to achieve a stalemate, whereby the hackers could disappear without prosecution, leaving the specter of a possible return at a later date.

Denial-of-Service Attacks

Denial-of-service attacks typically occur when a domain server or servers must respond to huge volumes of messages or data so that they cannot process any other information. Such attacks are typically initiated by outside hackers. For example, a worm is one form of denial service attack. One of the most famous worm attacks occurred on November 2, 1988. The worm, which was written by Robert T. Morris, Jr., replicated itself onto thousands of Internet computers across the country, causing them to slow to a crawl. Ironically, Robert was the son of the chief scientist at NSA's National Computer Security Center.[21] Young Morris was sentenced to three years' probation, 400 hours of community service, and a $10,000 fine. The computer emergency responses team (CERT) was formed shortly after this event.

Denial of service can also occur internally and even by accident. A friend who works in a large corporation told me of an incident where an employee of the Human Resources Department sent a routine e-mail to over 10,000 network users during peak business hours and instructed the e-mail application to notify her when the messages were viewed. The resulting e-mail traffic congestion slowed the system to a crawl for all users.

Controls to reduce the incidence of denial-of-service attacks include strict logical security controls, restrictions on the size and priority of messages that servers will respond to, and limitations on the use and availability of Internet features such as e-mail.

Web Spoofing and Other Misrepresentations

Web spoofing occurs when one website falsely appears to be that of another website. In a web spoofing attack, the web spoofer gains unauthorized access to the victim website and changes the HTML references from the proper web address (i.e., URL) to that of the spoofing server. All information exchanges between the user and the proper website then pass through the spoofing server. When properly deployed, the user will not even realize that the original site is being spoofed. The primary goal of a web spoofer is to acquire account numbers, passwords, and other sensitive information that unsuspecting users think they are entering into a secure website. The spoofers can then sell the information or use it for their own personal gain.

A 1997 article described an example of an ingenious combination of a website scam that also employed the use of a Trojan horse. Victims were lured to sites such as *www.sexygirls.com* and *www.beavisbutthead.com*. These sites instructed users to download and execute a special viewer program called david.exe.

This program disconnected the user's computer from its existing service provider, automatically dialed a service provider phone number in Moldova, and then remained connected until the computer was turned off, thereby racking up enormous phone bills for the unsuspecting user.[22]

Unfortunately, there are no truly effective ways for Internet users to prevent web spoofing. Internet users must rely on website designers and owners to implement proper security measures so that their sites cannot be altered to direct traffic to a spoofing server. However, users can observe spoofing. For example, if the URL displayed by the web browser does not match the URL of the desired website, or if the location line no longer is visible, spoofing may be taking place.

Examples of other types of user misrepresentation that may be encountered on the Internet include web stalkers and pedophiles who spoof themselves as friendly young people to try to lure their prey into face-to-face meetings and those who violate copyrights of software, articles, graphics, and other visual images.

Information Privacy

This section examines the various information privacy risks, recent privacy laws and regulations, and a case related to website privacy. Major privacy risks include cookies, web bugs, spam, commercial availability of personal information, and identity theft and fraud.

Cookies—A Violation of Privacy?

One way that personal privacy can be violated is through the use of "cookie" files, or cookies. Cookies are text files residing on the hard drive that are created by the major web browser applications, such as Netscape and Microsoft Explorer. Some websites are programmed to write information to cookie files as well as retrieve information from cookie files when users access the site. The types of information recorded in cookies are typically personal in nature.

For example, a website may request that a user enter her name, e-mail address, zip code, area code, the type of computer being used, the organization she works for, or other identifying information. Other information copied to cookie files could include the most recent websites a user has visited. This information could be loaded into a cookie file without the user being aware of it. Cookie-seeking websites could then copy the cookie file into its internal database. The site could also record the types of information the user examined during the visit. Over time, an extensive database of the user's personal website activity and tendencies could be created and used for marketing promotions and even malicious attacks.

A *Consumer Reports* article revealed that Dilbert, Sonic the Hedgehog, Doonesbury, and other popular Internet sites "shill" for DoubleClick Network, an advertising agency, which is "collecting dossiers on the millions of people who visit dozens of popular websites daily—and who may not be aware that someone's gathering private information."[23] According to the article, "DoubleClick says it uses the information to target its clients' Web ads more effectively to receptive viewers, directing ads to particular occupations or to employees in a specific company."

One way to control dissemination of personal information via cookie files is to search the hard drive for cookie files and delete them. In Netscape 3.0 or higher, users use the sequence Options–Network Preferences–Protocols–Show and Alert Before Accepting a Cookie to get an alert that a cookie is being set. Users may also be able to download and install software like Cookie Monster, PGPcookie.cutter, and Cookie Cutter to help control cookie files.[24]

Fortunately, in June 1997, Microsoft joined Netscape, Firefly Network, Inc., and Verisign, Inc., in their alliance to more tightly control the personal information that cookies provide. The new "open profiling standard" enables computer users of Netscape Navigator and Microsoft Internet Explorer to determine what information they leave behind at websites.[25]

Web Bugs

"Web bugs" are very much like cookies in that they track Internet use and are virtually undetectable. They are clear Graphics Interchange Format (.gif) images measuring only a single pixel and are not detectable by most cookie filters. Web bugs hidden in e-mail and newsgroup postings can indicate who received them, who read them, and whether or not the e-mail was forwarded. Cutting and pasting also transfers the bugs. Bugs can even talk to existing cookies on a user's computer if they and the cookies come from the same website. The best option for preventing Web bugs is to install a firewall and configure it to block malicious code from accessing an organization's computers.[26]

SPAM

Spam is unwanted or unsolicited e-mail. Spam costs millions of dollars in time, effort, disk storage space, telecommunications bandwidth usage, and user frustration. In a 1999 Gartner Group survey of 13,000 e-mail users, 90 percent received spam at least once a week and almost 50 percent got spammed at least six times a week.[27] In an extreme case in 1998, a Philadelphia spammer named Sanford Wallace sent out as many as 25 million unsolicited ads![28] In 1999, Connect Northwest, an Internet service provider in the state of Washington, sued CTX Mortgage, a subsidiary of Centex Corporation headquartered in Dallas, for $6 million for overwhelming its network by sending 5,800 unsolicited home mortgage advertisements on April 8 and 9, 1999. This violates a Washington state law that makes it illegal to send unsolicited commercial e-mail with misleading subject lines, phony return addresses, and false headers hiding the messages' origin.[29] Many states, including Washington, have antispam laws. In 1998, Washington state sued Jason Heckel and his Salem, Oregon, firm, Natural Instincts, for using a misleading subject line: "Did I get the right email address?"[30] The law was challenged, but in 2001, the Washington State Supreme Court upheld the law.[31]

Spam is best controlled by having users avoid unreputable sites and opt out of information sharing sites. Numerous antispam software applications are available, including ePrompter (*www.eprompter.com*), which is free; and Mailbox Filter (*www.mailboxfilter.com*), which is free for a 30-day trial, then $70.

Commercial Availability of Personal Information

A significant problem prior to the implementation of various privacy laws and regulations (see section below) was that commercial entities were selling, exchanging, or otherwise making personal information available to third parties without the authorization or knowledge of consumers. For example, in 2000 Amazon.com was discovered to have been selling customer information, much to the chagrin of its customers. Amazon subsequently became the target of lawsuits claiming it violated its privacy statement posted on its website. Amazon ultimately bowed to consumer and government pressure and changed its privacy statement and certain of its information privacy practices.

In another case targeted at a specific individual, a former Snohomish County, Washington, sheriff won a $2.6 million invasion of privacy lawsuit against the Washington State Pharmacy Board after he was accused of obtaining prescription drugs illegally. In addition, his wife and children were awarded $200,000 for the pain and suffering caused by the ordeal. The court found that the Pharmacy Board had used private information in its possession to invade the privacy of the sheriff.[32]

Fortunately for consumers, lawmakers in the United States and Europe have enacted strict information privacy laws and regulations. While many organizations continue to ignore them, the largest and most reputable firms have no choice but to comply or risk damaging their reputations and subsequently losing business.

Identity Theft and Fraud

Undoubtedly the most significant privacy risk is that of identity theft and fraud. It is a scourge on society that lowlife criminals prey on the identities of law-abiding citizens to facilitate trafficking and use of illicit drugs, cashing of stolen checks, use of stolen credit cards, money laundering, and other black market operations. Some of the more notable identity theft and fraud articles include:

- Experian, one of the largest credit reporting bureaus in the United States, reported that between April 2001 and February 2002, unauthorized inquiries were made into about 13,000 credit reports. With information such as Social Security numbers, addresses, account numbers, creditor names, and payment history on credit reports, the thieves have enough information to commit credit fraud. With as many as 700,000 cases annually and 86,000 complaints reported to the Federal Trade Commission in 2001, identity theft tops the list of consumer fraud concerns.[33]
- Hijacking of personal data for fraud or theft made up 42 percent of the 204,000 fraud complaints (about 86,000) filed with the Federal Trade Commission in 2001. Identity theft complaints grew immensely from 23 percent

in 2000 when it first topped the list. Scam artists crack Internet databases, intercept mail, or bluff their way past bank tellers and credit bureaus in an attempt to gather Social Security numbers, bank account numbers, and other confidential personal information.[34]

- A major crackdown on web-based fraud has broken up pyramid schemes, phone "Beanie Bay" auctions, and other Internet scams that have cheated 56,000 people out of more than $117 million. A total of 88 people were charged and 62 arrested in Operation Cyber Loss involving 61 separate federal, state, and local investigations, the FBI and Justice Department said. The federal and state charges include wire fraud, mail fraud, bank fraud, money laundering, and intellectual property rights violations.[35]

- Two Lucent Technologies, Inc., scientists and a third man were arrested and charged with stealing the "crown jewel" of the telecommunications equipment giant's systems with the intent of transferring the information to a Chinese state-owned company. Two Chinese nationals, Lin Hai and Xu Kai, and a U.S. citizen, Chang Yong-Qing, were accused of corporate espionage by conspiring to steal source code and software associated with Lucent's PathStar Access Server, which provides call-waiting, speed dialing, and other telephone-related Internet communications.[36]

- A busboy allegedly masterminded the largest theft of identity in Internet history and is suspected of stealing millions of dollars from some of the richest people in America. Abraham Abdallah, a 32-year-old high school dropout from Detroit, duped more than 200 chief executive officers listed in *Forbes* magazine by skillfully using computers in New York libraries to obtain credit records of such luminaries as Paul Allen, Steven Spielberg, Ted Turner, Michael Eisner, Oprah Winfrey, George Soros, and Warren Buffett, to name a few. Abdullah allegedly impersonated his targets in phone calls, left call-back numbers in their home cities, then retrieved the messages using a cell phone. He used stolen credit card numbers to pay for the calls and for mailboxes he rented in the victims' names.[37]

- Western Union suffered a serious compromise in September 2000 when its website was hacked and almost 16,000 credit and debit card numbers were stolen from an unprotected database while systems underwent routine maintenance. Western Union advised all affected customers to change their card numbers and asked their banks to monitor accounts for suspicious activity. The lapse was attributed to human error. Rival Wells Fargo immediately launched a marketing campaign to tout its superior security record and plant doubt in consumers' minds about less secure firms.[38]

Since the above type of stolen information could also be made readily available to vast audiences via the Internet, including unscrupulous people and organizations, the information can be used in combination with public information about consumers to literally steal their identities. When this happens, it can take violated consumers years to fully restore their identities. As with the previous types of information privacy risks discussed, stiffer laws and regulations have been enacted to help protect consumers.

Privacy Laws and Regulations

Because private industry has been somewhat ineffective in regulating themselves with regard to information privacy, numerous consumer privacy laws and regulations have been enacted in the United States and abroad. In many cases, these laws overlap previously existing laws that require confidentiality of specific types of information. But the new privacy laws are designed to provide consumers with more comprehensive information privacy protection. Some of the most notable recent privacy laws that have significant IS security and auditing ramifications are presented next. A list of selected privacy resources available on the Internet is also provided.[39]

Gramm-Leach-Bliley Financial Services Modernization Act of 1999

Perhaps the most far-reaching and significant law with regard to information privacy and protection was the Gramm-Leach-Bliley Financial Modernization Act of 1999 (GLB). Senator Phil Gramm (R-Texas) was the lead sponsor of this act, which was signed into law by President Clinton on November 12, 1999. Among other things, this act enables organizations to offer a wide variety of financial products and services to consumers, such as deposit accounts, loans, insurance, and investments. Consumer advocates became concerned that too much information about individuals could be collected by a single organization and possibly sold to others. To help prevent such information exploitation, Senator Gramm spearheaded a consumer privacy amendment, which was added prior to the act before it was signed. Under the final version of GLB, privacy requirements were effective November 13, 2000, with full compliance required on July 1, 2001. In its more notable privacy provisions, the law:

- Requires one-time disclosure of an organization's financial privacy practices to new consumers and annual disclosures of financial privacy practices to all consumers.
- Extends privacy requirements to third-party vendors with whom organizations provide information. Since most third-party arrangements are bound by existing contracts, organizations providing financial services are allowed a two-year grandfathering period for their contracts with third-party vendors to fully safeguard member information in compliance with GLB, although early adoption is highly encouraged.
- Provides consumers the right to "opt out" if certain activities would otherwise provide nonpublic personal information to third parties.
- Requires disclosure of the types of nonpublic information organizations might provide to outside third parties.
- Requires disclosure of the types of nonpublic information provided to outside organizations allowed under the Fair Credit Reporting Act of 1970 (e.g., credit bureaus can sell information to mail and telemarketers offering preapproved credit).

- Requires organizations to disclose their information privacy and protection practices.
- Provides civil and criminal penalties for pretext calls, which typically are made by collection agencies, private investigators, and even criminals who pretend to be consumers to get additional nonpublic information about the consumers.

GLB provides the Federal Trade Commission (FTC) the authority to regulate, monitor, and enforce the information privacy and protection practices of all U.S. organizations providing financial services to consumers, except those falling under the specific jurisdiction of other federal agencies, such as the Federal Reserve Board (FRB), Federal Deposit Insurance Corporation (FDIC), Office of the Comptroller of the Currency (OCC), National Credit Union Administration (NCUA), Securities and Exchange Commission (SEC), and all state insurance commissions, which separately regulate insurance activities. These other regulatory entities must still adopt the privacy and security requirements of GLB at a minimum, but may do so within the format of their existing regulatory requirements, and may add additional privacy requirements. For example, the NCUA included the GLB privacy requirements within its previously existing Rule 716, while the GLB information security requirements were added to its previously existing Rule 748, which covers many other types of credit union security practices.

Some of the GLB requirements overlap with existing laws and regulations. Obviously, persons committing fraud by using private information gathered illegally would already have been subject to existing fraud laws. With GLB, additional privacy violation charges could be applied on top of the fraud charges. In a more specific example, the Internal Revenue Code already prohibits certified public accountants (CPAs) from disclosing specific tax return information to anyone without the consumer's permission. But since CPAs have many other types of personal information about their clients, the FTC still regulates CPAs with regard to information privacy and protection practices. Similarly, a trust company chartered under the jurisdiction of the OCC is already required to have strict standards of confidentiality under fiduciary law. In this case, any gaps in information sharing would be covered by the OCC's additional regulations implemented under the GLB requirements.

Safe Harbor Act of 2000

Europe is ahead of the United States in the information privacy and protection arena. In 1998, the European Union (EU) passed the Data Protection Directive (EUDPD). The EUDPD mandates fair information protection practices for online as well as offline data transfers from the EU before data can be transferred. Although some EU members require additional protections, the DPD provides the minimum information privacy and protection requirements. To address the EUDPD requirements, the U.S. government enacted the Safe Harbor Act of 2000

(SHA), which governs data transferred to the U.S. from the EU. As with GLB, compliance was required by July 1, 2001. The more notable SHA requirements include:

- Must clearly and conspicuously notify users about the purposes for which data will be collected, the mechanisms for limiting use and disclosure, the types of third parties to which data is disclosed, and where to direct inquires and complaints.
- Must offer users the ability to opt-out of disclosures to third parties and secondary uses.
- Must offer users the ability to opt-in for sensitive information such as medical conditions, ethnicity, political views, religion, trade union membership, sexual preference, and so on.
- Must implement reasonable precautions to protect personal information from unauthorized access, disclosure, alteration, destruction, or other loss. Regarding electronic systems and databases, "reasonable precautions" implies adequate security measures such as those discussed in this book.
- Must retain information only for the period of time necessary to fulfill purposes.
- If a third party is acting as an agent, disclosure is not required as long as the third party meets the safe harbor requirements or is already subject to the EUDPD. This verbiage should be included in any contracts between the organization and third parties.

Penalties for failure to comply with the Safe Harbor Act include economic sanctions, civil damages, and other remedies. With such motivation, many large organizations doing business in Europe are beginning to meet the SHA requirements. For example, in May 2001, Microsoft announced it would sign the safe harbor agreement.

Children's Online Privacy Protection Act of 1998

The main goal of the Children's Online Privacy Protection Act of 1998 (COPPA) is to protect the privacy of children using the Internet. The act requires commercial websites to obtain verifiable parental consent before collecting, using, or disclosing personal information from children under 13. To inform parents of their information practices, these sites are required to provide notice on the site and to parents about their policies with respect to the collection, use, and disclosure of children's personal information. President Clinton signed COPPA into law on October 21, 1998. The law became effective on April 21, 2000, with full compliance required of applicable websites by October 21, 2000. According to the FTC chairman, COPPA puts parents in control over the information collected from their children online and is flexible enough to accommodate the many business practices and technological changes occurring on the Internet. The law was enacted after a three-year effort by the FTC to identify and educate industry and the public about the issues raised by the online collection of personal information from children and adult consumers. The FTC recommended that Congress enact legislation concerning children following a March 1998 survey of 212 commercial children's websites. The survey found that while 89 percent of the sites collected personal information from children, only 24 percent posted privacy policies and only 1 percent required parental consent to the collection or disclosure of children's information. COPPA has received widespread support from industry, consumer, and law enforcement groups.

Health Insurance Portability and Accountability Act of 1996

Consumer health records are routinely transmitted over insecure networks and the Internet. Often more than the necessary amount of information is transmitted, and in some cases incorrect information is transmitted. Among healthcare organizations, this is sometimes due to inconsistent data classification schemes. These practices frequently violate the medical privacy of consumers. The Health Insurance Portability and Accountability Act of 1996 (HIPAA) was enacted to help protect and restrict consumer health information. The act provides heavy penalties and potential jail time for offenders, including corporate officers.

President Clinton signed HIPAA into law in August 1996. It includes a wide variety of requirements designed to make health insurance more affordable and accessible. With support from health plans, hospitals, and other healthcare organizations, Congress included provisions in HIPAA to require the U.S. Department of Health and Human Services (DHHS) to adopt national standards for certain electronic healthcare transactions and security. By ensuring consistency throughout the industry, these national standards will make it easier for health plans, doctors, hospitals, and other healthcare providers to process claims and other transactions electronically and to better protect personal health information from inappropriate uses and disclosures. In addition, uniform national standards are projected to save healthcare organizations billions of dollars each year by lowering the costs of developing and maintaining software and reducing the time and expense needed to process health care transactions.

A three-year deadline was set by HIPAA for Congress to enact comprehensive privacy legislation to protect medical records and other personal health information. When Congress did not enact such legislation by August 1999, HIPAA required DHHS to issue health privacy regulations. At that time, DHHS issued final electronic transaction standards to streamline the processing of healthcare claims, reduce the volume of paperwork, and provide better service for providers, insurers, and patients. The new standards establish standard data content and formats for submitting electronic claims and other administrative healthcare transactions. Most covered entities must comply with these standards by October 16, 2002.

In December 2000, DHHS issued specific rules to protect the confidentiality of medical records and other personal health information. The rules limit the use and release of individually identifiable health information; give patients the right to access their medical records; restrict most disclosure of health information to the minimum needed for the intended purpose; and establish safeguards and restrictions on access to records for certain public responsibilities, such as public health, research, and law enforcement. Improper uses or disclosures under the rule are subject to criminal and civil penalties. These rules become effective April 14, 2003.

Despite these efforts, healthcare organizations have been struggling with HIPAA compliance due to lack of enough specific requirements from DHHS. The December 2000 rules specified what kinds of records need to be protected, but DHHS still has not specified how such information is to be safeguarded. All that is known is that the requirements will be comprehensive and non–technology specific. Most healthcare organizations are attempting to be proactive by implementing common general information systems controls over their consumer data, although they will not be able to fine-tune their information privacy and protection practices until the final HIPAA requirements have been established.

Some selected privacy resources available on the Internet include:

- Department of Commerce (*www.ita.doc.gov/td/ecom/menu.html*). Safe harbor provisions
- Department of Health and Human Services (*www.hhs.gov*). HIPAA
- Electronic Frontier Foundation (*www.eff.org*). Online privacy (also see Chapter 5 for information on TRUSTe certification by EFF.)
- Electronic Privacy Information Center (*www.epic.org*). Online privacy
- Federal Trade Commission (*www.ftc.gov*). GLB and COPPA
- Online Privacy Alliance (*www.privacyalliance.org*). Online privacy
- Privacy Foundation (*www.privacyfoundation.org*). Online privacy

Case Study 13.5 discusses a situation where a bank had inadequate web disclosures.

CASE STUDY 13.5

Inadequate Web Disclosures

During an audit of a bank's Internet websites, the IS auditors tested for a variety of required consumer compliance disclosures, including the bank's information privacy statement, equal housing lender logo, FDIC-insured logo, annual percentage rate (APR) for loan rates, and annual percentage yields (APY) for deposit rates. The organization had multiple websites, including a home page, an Internet banking site, a credit card information site (non-transactional), a mortgage loan application site, a mortgage loan servicing site, and an account aggregation site. The credit card, mortgage loan application, mortgage loan servicing, and account aggregation sites were all administered by different external third-party vendors under the direction of the bank's management. The auditors found that the disclosure statements at each site were incon-

(continued)

> ### CASE STUDY 13.5 (*continued*)
>
> sistent. Some were current while others were earlier versions. Some of the sites also did not have "alt-tags" on the equal housing lender logo or the FDIC-insured logo. Alt-tags are required to present a text description of the logos when a mouse pointer is moved on top of the logos and when a consumer is using a text-only browser. Other sites were inconsistent in how they disclosed required APR and APY information, because each site was managed by a different department. These departments did not have procedures to ensure that current disclosure requirements were being followed. Also, no central monitoring function periodically verified that all of the bank's sites were consistent and correct in their disclosures. To compound matters, any time there was an update by the bank's IS Department or the external vendor's IS staff, procedures did not exist to verify that all required disclosures were properly updated and others that were not updated had not been inadvertently changed. In other words, there were inadequate change management controls.
>
> The auditors recommended that change management procedures be implemented in the bank's IS Department and at the vendor IS departments to have a business unit person verify that all required disclosures are current and function properly immediately after any updates or changes. The auditors also recommended that the bank's Compliance Department independently verify that all required disclosures are current and function properly on a periodic (e.g., monthly) basis.

Monitoring of Employee Internet Activity

In an effort to combat lost employee productivity due to non–work-related use of the Internet via company-owned computers and information systems, many firms have begun to restrict and monitor the Internet activities of their employees and to implement disciplinary actions for those employees whose activities are deemed unacceptable. Applications exist that enable system security administrators to prevent users from accessing specifically named URLs. Such applications can also create logs of URLs that have been accessed. This information can then be downloaded and queried for management reporting and productivity analysis purposes. For example, the most frequently visited URLs can be identified and the percentage of time users spend accessing non–work-related URLs can be approximated.

While the intent of monitoring controls is to help ensure that employees are productive at work, failure to adequately disclose monitoring practices can result in lawsuits by employees for violation of their privacy. The Electronic Communications Privacy Act requires employers to inform employees that their use of the Internet or other electronic communications via company information systems may be monitored.

To mitigate the risk of lawsuits by employees claiming violation of privacy, organizations should have a written policy, clearly notifying users that their activities via any company information system, including desktop and laptop computers and telephone devices, may be monitored at any time and that they may be subject to disciplinary action if company information systems are used for purposes other than those necessary to perform their work-related duties. Having users sign an acknowledgment that they have read and understand the policy helps protect the organization. The legal position of an organization can be further strengthened by programming the text of the policy into a banner page that must be read and acknowledged by users each time they sign on to company information systems.

Upon proper disclosure to employees, monitoring controls can be deployed to help reduce the incidence of lost productivity due to non–work-related activities by employees on the Internet. For example, software such as Cyber Patrol, WebSENSE, or Net Nanny can block access to pornographic and other non–business-related Internet sites.[40] Organizations can also deploy proxy file servers and specialized software to record the URLs being accessed by employees, the dates and times of access, and the user IDs of the employees accessing them. This URL traffic information can be stored for periodic examination by information security personnel. Analysis of URL traffic can reveal the percentage of work-related and non–work-related sites employees are visiting. Based on the times and dates the sites were visited, estimates of the cost of lost employee productivity could be determined and reported to management.

Case Study 13.6 discusses a situation where an employee was found to be excessively using the Internet for personal activities.

CASE STUDY 13.6

Excessive Internet Use

During a network audit, employee use of the Internet was examined. Since employees were encouraged to use the Internet for work-related tasks, senior management purposely did not want employee Internet use to be excessively restricted. However, sites classified in the software's database as sex sites and other offensive types of sites were blocked from access. A monitoring application was used to generate weekly reports of employee Internet use. The report classified total active Internet hours and total number of page hits into approximately 10 general categories (e.g., online merchant, government, entertainment, etc.). A relatively new IT nontechnical staff person was responsible for reviewing the report and notifying the vice president of IT regarding any employees who appeared to be abusing their Internet privileges. The vice president of IT was to notify the vice president above the employee in question for appropriate management action.

During the audit, we examined a report that was several weeks old. To our surprise, one employee stood head and shoulders above all others in terms of time spent on the Internet and in page hits. During the one-week period we examined, the employee logged 43 active hours on the Internet with over 16,000 page hits. Most of her hours and page hits fell into the online merchant category, yet she was also the activity champion in almost all other catego-

(continued)

> **CASE STUDY 13.6 (*continued*)**
>
> ries. Detailed investigation revealed that she was spending substantial work hours on eBay and similar non–work-related merchant sites. Examination of subsequent reports revealed similar activity, yet the IT staff person responsible for reviewing the report had not notified the vice president of IT or anyone else.
>
> We recommended that the manager over the Internet abuser be notified immediately so the abuser could receive appropriate management counseling. It was not clear how the abuser's supervisor could not have known about her excessive Internet use; surely there had been a noticeable decline in or absence of work production. The supervisor also received counseling from the manager. We also recommended that IT management review procedures with the new IT staff person in charge of reviewing.

Other Internet Risks

The number and types of risks that are possible are limited only by the imaginations of Internet users with malicious intentions.

General controls to help prevent Internet risks include environmental controls (e.g., policies, standards, user education), physical security (e.g., securing computer hardware), and logical security controls (e.g., user IDs, passwords, access controls). Each of these general types of controls were discussed in Part Two of this book. Cryptography-based controls, such as the SET and SSL cryptographic protocols, are critical if electronic commerce is to flourish. Cryptography was discussed in Chapter 11. In the aftermath of the Internet revolution, perhaps the most important type of hardware/software control that has been developed to help combat the risks of the Internet is the firewall.

Firewalls

Firewalls can be one of the most effective controls against Internet attacks. They are essential to any organization that is connected to the Internet. A *firewall* is a specialized information system designed to examine incoming and outgoing electronic transmission packets. Based on a set of rules that have been preprogrammed into the firewall configuration by the system security administrator, the firewall determines which electronic transmission packets are allowed to travel through the firewall and under what restrictions.

Although unique in their purpose, firewalls can be viewed as just another type of information system. As with any information system, a risk assessment should be performed and design requirements specified such that the business objectives of the organization can be achieved through the Internet while still enabling the IS security policies and standards of the organization to be deployed upon implementation of the firewall. As a general rule of thumb, firewalls should be designed to reject all incoming messages, unless specifically allowed. The extent to which outgoing messages are allowed is a function of organization culture and desired level of security.

Low-risk firewalls may consist of software only (e.g., ZoneAlarm®, BlackICE®, Norton®, Tiny®) or a single electronic network traffic router, which screens electronic transmission packets as they pass from the Internet directly to the destination server. More complex firewalls consisting of additional hardware components and security applications are necessary for higher-risk systems. For example, a proxy server is a separate CPU that resides between the Internet and the destination server. Using a network address translation (NAT) function, the proxy server can be configured to mask the true address of the destination server so that it appears to be that of the proxy server. In addition to protecting the destination server from outside probing, proxy servers can enable more sophisticated screening, monitoring, and logging of incoming packet traffic before it reaches the destination server. Some products provide system security administrators with warnings (e.g., via reports, e-mail messages) or alarms (e.g., via pagers) as well as encryption of outgoing messages. Since proxy servers are application specific, multiple proxy servers may need to be deployed in a firewall configuration to achieve the desired level of security for each of the Internet applications (e.g., World Wide Web, Telnet, Gopher, Usenet, File Transfer Protocol).

In simple terms, each Internet electronic transmission packet consists of a header, interface standards, and data content. The header contains characters that identify the packet as an Internet packet (i.e., "tcp"), the packet number, and the total number of packets. Packet numbering enables the message to be reassembled in its original order. Therefore, a packet with a header of "tcp;38;75;" means that the packet is an Internet packet and that it is the 38th out of a total of 75 in the transmission. The interface standards contain the Internet source address (e.g., "123.241.1.9"), the destination address (e.g., "91.239.88.7), the source port (e.g., "1776"), and the destination port (e.g., "80"). Thus, the above packet header followed by the interface standards "123.241.1.9;91.1.239.88.7;1776;80" identifies where the message came from (unless, of course, the sender is spoofing), where the message is destined, the port number used by the sender, and the source port to which the sender wishes to send the message. The data content is the message or information being transmitted. It can appear in plain or encrypted format, depending on the security applied to the message. Each network service is mapped to any one of thousands of different port numbers. There are 65,536 (i.e., 2^{16}) total ports numbered 0 to 65,535. Ports 0 to 1,023 are the well-known ports managed by the Internet Assigned Numbers Authority (IANA). Ports 1,024 to 49,151 are classified as registered, while ports 49,152 to 65,535 are classified as dynamic and/or private. Standard port numbers for a variety of selected internet services are listed next as example references:

- Ports 20,21—FTP (file transfer protocol)
- Port 23—TELNET (remote sign on)
- Port 25—SMTP (e-mail)
- Port 33—DSP (display support protocol)
- Port 43—WHOIS

- Port 69—TFTP (trivial file transfer protocol—has no security)
- Port 70—GOPHER
- Port 79—FINGER
- Port 80—HTTP (hypertext transfer, World Wide Web)
- Port 119—NNTP (network news/bulletin boards)
- Port 137—Netbios (name service)
- Port 443—SSL (secure sockets layer commonly used for e-commerce)
- Port 512—EXEC (remote process execution)
- Port 513—LOGIN (remote login)
- Port 515—PRINTER (spooler)
- Port 540—UUCP (Unix to Unix communication protocol)
- Port 2049—NFS (network file system)

By using a variety of port scanning and network administration tools, hackers will attempt to identify which Internet applications an organization is using. Port numbers can be mapped (i.e., rerouted) to other unused port numbers to make it more difficult for hackers to determine an organization's Internet applications.

Although firewalls are an absolutely necessary component of any organization's Internet and intranet security environment, firewalls can be easily circumvented by someone within the organization. For example, a network workstation or laptop computer may be outfitted with an analog modem. The user could plug the modem into an analog phone jack in the office, connect to an outside Internet service provider, and begin performing activities normally prohibited by the company's firewall. Worse yet, the user could unknowingly download a virus file and infect the entire company network. Furthermore, the workstation or laptop could be hacked and used as a launching pad for additional hacking attempts against the network.

Exhibit 13.1 provides a sample diagram of one way to configure a firewall. It is not the best way to configure a firewall by any means. Rather, it is intended to provide a general idea of how a basic firewall may be designed. There is no single best firewall configuration. The actual configuration depends on the risk of the system being protected, available financial and human resources, the types of hardware (servers, routers, etc.), operating systems, and software used, available technology, time to implement and maintain the firewall, and other constraints.

This discussion of firewalls has provided an overview. Managing and securing firewalls while still enabling an organization to do business via the Internet is very complex and has become an art as well as a science. It is no coincidence that many books have been written on the subject. To effectively audit a firewall requires a combination of experience, technical knowledge, and research into the types of hardware and software used in the configuration of the firewall being audited.

EXHIBIT 13.1 **SAMPLE SCHEMATIC DIAGRAM OF A FIREWALL FOR A CREDIT CARD PAYMENT VIA INTERNET HOME BANKING SOFTWARE**

Packet filtering router

Internet home banking client workstation

Internet

Bank's external firewall server

Internet banking application server

Bank's internal firewall server

Mainframe Databases (checking accounts debited for payment amounts, credit card accounts credited)

Internal router

Mainframe Server

NOTES

1. "2002 CSI/FBI Computer Crime and Security Survey," *Computer Security Institute* (Spring 2002): 16.

2. John O'Leary, *Manager's Guide to Computer Viruses* (San Francisco: Computer Security Institute, 1993): 2.

3. Carri Kishimoto, "Computer Viruses–Awareness Presentation," *Control Point*, Newsletter of the Utah Chapter of the Information Systems Audit and Control Association (January 1997): 8.

4. "Gulf War Chemical Logs Missing," KIRO Radio News Fax (February 28, 1997): Front Page.

5. "Warning: A New Trojan House," *Armed Forces Insurance Newsletter* (Fall 1996): 5.

6. O'Leary, *Manager's Guide to Computer Viruses*, p. 7.

7. Id., pp. 8–9.

8. "Piracy Losses Total $11.2 Billion," *IIA Today* (July/August 1997): 4.

9. "Software Piracy Increases," *Seattle News Fax* (June 11, 2002): 5; "Piracy Still Ripping Off Software Makers," *Institute of Management & Administration's Report on Preventing Business Fraud* (August 2001): 4.

10. "Alleged Software Ring Busted," *Seattle News Fax* (March 15, 2002): 3; "Northwest Business Briefs," *Seattle News Fax* (November 19, 2001): 6; "3 Sentenced for Software Piracy," *Seattle News Fax* (October 5, 2001): 6; "159 Firms Settle Piracy Charges," *Seattle News Fax* (May 22, 2001): 5; Dennis Blank, "Whatcha Gonna Do When the Bad Boy Is You?" *Information Security* (November 2000): 16; "$56M Counterfeit Court Case," SC Magazine (August 1999): 17.

11. "Microsoft Wins Anti-Piracy Pledge From China," *Seattle News Fax* (December 7, 2001): 5; Business Briefs, *Seattle News Fax* (November 12, 2001): 5.

12. "BSA Ramps Up Piracy Raids in Manila," *Secure Computing* (August 1997): 12.

13. BSA Worldwide Report, 1990–1991.

14. "Playboy Adopts Digital Watermark Technology," *Secure Computing* (August 1997): 15.

15. From Visa International's website: *www.visa.com* (July 29, 1997).

16. "Visa Finland Pilots SET Transactions," *Secure Computing* (July 1997): 16.

17. "Hacker Arrest Imparts Need for New SET Protocol," *Secure Computing* (July 1997): 11.

18. Eileen Courter, "Two CUs Introduce Electronic Cash 'Wallets' for Member Convenience," *Credit Union Times* (July 16, 1997): 31–32.

19. "Tired of .Com? Internet Names Will Be Changing," *Seattle News Fax* (May 31, 2001): 9.

20. "10,000 Credit Card Numbers Appear on the Internet," *Secure Computing* (August 1997): 20.

21. Cliff Stoll, *The Cuckoo's Egg* (New York: Simon & Schuster, Inc., 1990): 334–348.

22. "Sites Reroute Modems to Long-Distance ISP," *Infosecurity News* (May 1997): 11.

23. "Is Your Computer Spying on You?" *Consumer Reports* (May 1997): 6.

24. Peter T. Davis, "C Is for Cookie," *Secure Computing* (July 1997): 62.

25. "Microsoft Joins Netscape Plan to Protect Privacy," KIRO Radio News FAX (June 12, 1997): Business Northwest Page.

26. Cory Hamilton, "Safe Passages on the Web," *BECU Magazine* (Summer 2002): 14–15.

27. "Internet Users Bemoan Spam," *KIRO Radio News Fax* (June 14, 1999): 1.

28. "Self-Proclaimed 'Spam King' Apologizes to Victims," KIRO Radio News Fax (April 16, 1998): 5.
29. "Major Mortgage Company Sued for Sending Spam," KIRO Radio News Fax (May 21, 1999): 3
30. "Gregoire Sues Businessman Under Anti-Spam Law," KIRO Radio News Fax (October 23, 1998): 3.
31. "Northwest Business Briefs," *Seattle News Fax* (June 8, 2001): 6.
32. "Furthermore," *Seattle News Fax* (May 3, 2001): 3.
33. Myriam Bourjolly, "Consumers Put On Alert After 13,000 Credit Reports Stolen," *Credit Union Times* (May 29, 2002): 8.
34. "ID Theft Tops Consumer Fraud," *Seattle News Fax* (January 24, 2002): 1.
35. "Police Crack Internet Scams," *Seattle News Fax* (May 24, 2001): 2.
36. "3 Men Accused of Stealing Lucent Crown Jewel," *Seattle News Fax* (May 4, 2001): 5.
37. "Busboy Allegedly Stole Millions from Millionaires," *Seattle News Fax* (March 21, 2001): 2.
38. "Crackers Compromise Western Union," *Security Wire Digest* (September 14, 2000); M. E. Kabay and Lawrence M. Walsh, "The Year in Computer Crime," *Information Security* (December 2000): 30.
39. Parts of this section were derived from Jack J. Champlain, *Practical IT Auditing, 2001 Update* (New York: Warren, Gorham, & Lamont/RIA Group): Chapter B4.03.
40. Rich Andrews and Mark Bigler, "Employee Internet Use—Part II," *Control Point*, Newsletter of the Utah Chapter of the Information Systems Audit and Control Association (April 1997): 9.

CHAPTER 14

Humanistic Aspects of Information Systems Auditing

An effective internal audit function serves multiple roles within an organization. The primary function of internal audit is to assist management of an organization in achieving strategic business objectives within a framework of sound internal control practices. All internal auditors, including information systems (IS) auditors, play key roles in this ongoing process. Depending on the process or system being evaluated, internal auditors must be able to perform the role of a consultant, mediator, negotiator, investigator, facilitator, and educator. The ability of internal auditors to effectively fill these roles benefits management and therefore provides a valuable resource to many organizations. On an individual basis, auditors who are flexible enough to effectively perform multiple roles should be highly valued by their companies.

In many professions there are specialists. For example, there are a myriad of doctors in the world. Doctors can be grouped into general categories such as family doctors, surgeons, dentists, and psychiatrists. These doctors can be further divided into areas of specialty, each concentrating on perfecting their skills on a few specific parts of the human anatomy. Similarly, the legal profession is composed of many thousands of attorneys, each of whom specializes in one or a few aspects of the law. The number of doctors, attorneys, and other professionals choosing to specialize in particular fields is largely driven by the demand for skills in those areas. So it is with the auditing profession.

Auditing originated as one of the fields within the accounting profession. The accounting profession can be divided into two general categories: public accounting and private accounting. Public accountants perform a variety of services for their clients, including financial statement audits, income tax planning and preparation, financial planning, and consulting in a variety of areas, including IS controls. Private accounting encompasses accountants who work for commercial, government, not-for-profit, and other types of entities. Many of the activities of private accountants essentially mirror those of public accountants, but these activities are performed on behalf of private organizations.

As the activities in which businesses, governments, and other entities engage have become more complex, auditors have had to evolve beyond only evaluating controls directly pertaining to financial statements. Because organizations are involved in so many different types of businesses and related activities, unique sets of internal controls had to be developed within these activities. Auditors had to become highly knowledgeable about specific types of internal controls, which, if not properly deployed, could eventually impact the financial condition of an organization in a material way. As a result, auditing specialists began to appear. Examples of areas in which auditors specialized include trust, financial services, and internal and external fraud prevention. With the advent of computers, a new breed of control specialist was born—the electronic data processing (EDP) auditor.

Electronic data processing auditing was once viewed as a separate profession from other auditing in general. In fact, many EDP auditors came from technical backgrounds rooted in computer science. However, as technology continues to evolve and expand into the end-user environment, the barrier that once existed between traditional auditing and EDP auditing has shrunk enormously. In fact, traditional auditors have had to become computer literate or risk losing their livelihood.

The American Institute of Certified Public Accountants (AICPA) recognized the enormous degree to which public accountants have come to rely upon electronic evidence by issuing Statement on Auditing Standards (SAS) 80, Amendment to SAS 31, Evidential Matter, effective January 1, 1997. SAS 80 amends SAS 31 to help external auditors focus more on electronic evidence. The most significant change from SAS 31 is how risk is handled in an electronic environment. SAS 80 states that in entities in which a significant amount of information is transmitted, processed, maintained, or accessed electronically, it may be impractical or impossible to reduce detection risk to an acceptable level by performing only substantive procedures. In such circumstances, tests of controls normally would be performed to obtain evidence that would enable the auditor to achieve an assessed level of control risk sufficiently below the maximum.[1]

Traditional auditors, both internal and external, have had to reach outside their typical auditing paradigms and increase their understanding of and proficiency with computers. Conversely, EDP auditors have had to enhance their business skills to better communicate risks associated with computing systems to a more knowledgeable and computer-savvy management group. What we are witnessing is the evolution of a new breed of auditor: the IS auditor.

There will always be the need for IS auditors who are highly skilled specialists in one type of operating system, for example, IBM's OS/390 operating system. These "niche auditors" are excellent resources when a high degree of detailed expertise must be administered in an audit under severe time constraints. However, a majority of IS auditors must be able to ascertain the adequacy of controls and security in multiple IS environments because most organizations do not have the resources to employ IS auditing specialists for each computing platform they utilize. Such flexibility and diversity is what makes IS auditors so valuable to their organizations.

Heading into the first decade of the new millennium, IS auditors will be relied on to maintain a high degree of technical understanding regarding the operation and control of multiple types of computing systems. However, the required knowledge base of an effective IS auditor does not end with technical skill. The IS auditor must also possess the aforementioned skills of consultant, mediator, negotiator, investigator, facilitator, and educator. Unfortunately, many IS auditors (and non-IS auditors for that matter) experience frustration, lack of success, and even failure because of their inability to effectively communicate internal control issues with management.

The next logical question is: Where do IS auditors obtain the skills necessary to effectively audit information systems and successfully motivate management to implement internal control enhancements? The answer is through a significant investment in ongoing technical training; active participation in audit- and security-related professional associations; diligent efforts to establish and maintain networks with peers and scholars in fields pertaining to IS audit and related technologies; facing the challenge of obtaining and maintaining professional certifications related to IS audit, control, and security; a commitment to reading of books, trade journals, Internet sites, and other publications pertaining to IS audit, controls, and security; and through practical experience performing IS audits. Each of these sources of skills is discussed in the following sections. Subsequently, humanistic skills for successful auditing, as well as motivation of auditors, are discussed briefly. The chapter concludes with some interesting case studies that demonstrate various types of humanistic issues.

TRAINING

Training related to IS audit, controls, and security of new and existing technologies can be obtained from a variety of sources. For example, professional associations such as the Information Systems Audit and Control Association (ISACA), Institute of Internal Auditors (IIA), and AICPA sponsor one or more technology-related conferences and seminars each year. A host of other organizations sponsor conferences covering a wide variety of audit, control, and security-related subjects. Conferences and seminars offer several benefits. First, they provide high- to midlevel training sessions on a variety of technical subjects. These training sessions are typically grouped into several categories, or "tracks." The length of the sessions usually ranges from two to eight hours. The overall length of conferences usually ranges from three to five days, while seminars are typically one to three days.

Second, conferences and seminars offer the ability to network with peers, scholars, and experts in the field of IS controls and security. The larger conferences often attract 500 to 1,500 attendees, including speakers, some of whom travel from around the globe. The experience level of attendees ranges from the beginning IS auditor to "gurus." Some attendees may be "reformed" hackers turned consultant or even consultants who wish they could be hackers. Other attendees include managers, executives, audit committee members, vendors who sell audit-related products and services, and public accounting firms that market auditing, computer assurance, and other consulting services. As a result, conferences are one of the most effective means through which to meet numerous IS experts from a variety of industries and countries. Conference sessions with such large and diverse groups of IS auditors frequently generate enthusiasm among attendees to apply audit techniques to the applicable technologies in organizations. Conferences and seminars are also an excellent forum for sharing experiences so that each may benefit from the other's collective knowledge. Many of the information sources utilized in the writing of this book originated from grassroots networking at various conferences and seminars.

A third benefit of conferences and seminars is that they are a source of continuing professional education (CPE) credits for attendees who possess one or more certifications that require them to earn a minimum number of CPE credits annually.

Most professional associations provide the added benefit of offering brief training sessions during monthly or quarterly meetings and technical sessions sponsored by the local chapters of the associations. For example, the Puget Sound (Seattle), Washington, chapters of the ISACA and IIA sponsor monthly meetings that feature experts in auditing controls and security related to new and existing technologies. Both organizations also provide half-day and full-day technical sessions on audit-related topics. Occasionally the chapters even sponsor regional conferences or seminars featuring local and national speakers.

Independent training organizations such as the MIS Training Institute also offer highly detailed courses lasting one week or more that discuss the operations and controls pertaining to specific computing system platforms. Because these courses are relatively small by design, they provide the opportunity for hands-on exercises and direct interfacing with the instructors and other students.

Facilitation skills were traditionally not a part of the IS auditors portfolio. However, with the advent of control self-assessment (CSA), facilitation skills are becoming a must. (Control self-assessment was discussed in detail in Chapter 10.) Many training organizations and consultants offer effective facilitator courses. The people attending these courses are traditionally teachers, trainers, and educators. However, IS and other auditors should attend these courses to hone their facilitation skills in preparation for conducting CSA workshops, internal control training courses, and presentations to management and peers.

One common audit management flaw in some organizations is that audit staff are provided with training yet never assigned duties that enable them to apply the skills they have learned. For example, in one organization a number of years ago, everyone on the audit staff was provided with formalized training on how to operate new software that the organization was implementing company-wide. On completion of the training program, all auditors were considered "trained." However, they were never provided the time or opportunity to apply this new technology. Even if they used their spare time to broaden their experience, there was very little to which their creativity could be applied. For many of the "trained" auditors, the skills they had learned faded rapidly. For this reason, audit managers should develop projects prior to investing in staff members' training. In this way, they will be much more likely to recoup their investment.

Another audit management flaw in some organizations is their reluctance to budget sufficiently for training auditors. Expense control is understandable, but some organizations allow very little for any outside training, instead opting to rely on on-the-job training. In one organization, the auditors were lucky to receive mileage for driving to an off-site audit location, let alone be allowed to attend a conference or seminar or have the organization pay for membership in a professional association and the costs to attend association functions. This sort of audit management is highly unfortunate, because the auditors become "inbred." They tend to assess situations almost exclusively from the perspective of their organization. They are much less likely to directly exchange ideas and benchmark with auditors and other professionals in other organizations within and outside their industry. As a result, their creativity and enthusiasm can be stifled. A small but continuously and highly trained IS audit staff will significantly outperform a large but restricted staff. The small and highly trained staff would prove to be much more effective and valuable to their organizations than a large number of IS auditors with little or no ongoing training.

ACTIVE PARTICIPATION IN PROFESSIONAL ASSOCIATIONS

Becoming actively involved with local chapters of professional auditing associations can be one of the most important career-enhancing activities an auditor can undertake. Besides providing a forum for learning about technical subjects, active participation can contribute greatly to professional growth by allowing one to network with local auditing peers. Holding leadership positions can also provide a high profile for an organization's audit group and the organization in general. Furthermore, holding officer positions can provide valuable leadership and teamwork skills in a democratic, not-for-profit environment.

For example, I was elected to the seven-member national board of directors of the Association of Credit Union Internal Auditors (ACUIA) for the 2000–2002 term. The ACUIA is a not-for-profit volunteer-led organization primarily serving the needs of credit union internal auditors throughout the United States. Additional interested parties include members of supervisory committees (the credit union version of audit committees) and external auditors and vendors serving credit union internal auditors. As of mid-2002, the ACUIA had about 600 members.

As a volunteer board member, I have gained valuable leadership experience that I might not otherwise have been able to obtain directly in my position as an IS audit manager. My responsibilities included contributing to the long-term strategic planning of the organization, helping to formulate the annual operating budget, and providing high-level direction on designated tactical projects to assigned committees and the management firm. The ACUIA contracts with an independent management firm to perform many of the day-to-day administrative and operational functions under the direction of the board. These functions include preparation of the quarterly magazine, organization of conferences and regional meetings, administration of the website and reference library, all accounting functions, and direct management of various operational projects supported by member volunteers.

For 2002, I was elected treasurer by the other six board members. The treasurer is part of the executive committee, which also includes the chair, vice chair, and secretary. The executive committee is voted on by the board-elect each fall after board elections at the annual meeting. The treasurer is responsible for the timely and accurate preparation of the financial statements and for helping to ensure that adequate capital exists to achieve strategic objectives and to carry out ongoing association activities. The treasurer also acts as board liaison to the volunteer Audit Committee.

Directing a volunteer-run organization such as ACUIA is a very challenging task, given that the board members hold down full-time audit director or manager positions at their respective credit unions and given that the board, volunteer members, and management firm are geographically disbursed about the United States. The most important requirement to the board's success is the support provided by the chief executive officers of each of the board member's credit unions. Without their encouragement and support, we would not have the time and financial resources to perform our duties. Timely communications among the board members, volunteers, and administrative office are also essential. The board meets via conference call on a monthly basis and in-person twice each year; e-mail and telephone communications occur almost daily. Patience is a requirement since urgent matters at our primary jobs often limit the amount of time that can be devoted to our volunteer activities.

The most important board accomplishment during my tenure has been our ability to focus most of our efforts on strategic initiatives. To implement this approach, we first had to solve some key problems. Since it was founded in 1989, the ACUIA board often had to focus on daily operations, initially because it was small and was just getting started, but later because previous management firms were not performing their duties adequately. As a result, the board had to perform many day-to-day operational functions as well as correct problems caused by the management firms. The board has recently hired a promising new management firm that has been performing admirably. Other key problems that were solved included simplifying the dues structure and implementing a more effective accounting process with the management firm. We also reduced the number of committees, since many members volunteered but only a few actually produced results. Instead of requesting volunteers to serve on perpetual committees and then assigning multiple projects to the committees we now request volunteers for specific projects with specific completion dates. This change has encouraged more participation since members can volunteer for specific duties on specific projects without fear of being asked to perform multiple duties on multiple projects.

Looking further back, I served as president of the Puget Sound (Seattle) Chapter of ISACA from 1995 to 1997. During my presidency, I had the pleasure of working with IS auditors from a variety of organizations in several different industries. It was a joy and sometimes a challenge to coordinate the efforts of everyone to ensure that speakers were located for the monthly meetings, seminars, conferences, and other chapter events; the meeting facilities and equipment were properly planned for; the newsletter and other announcements were distributed in a timely manner; the mailing list was updated in a timely manner to reflect membership changes; the chapter website was updated on a regular basis; chapter finances were diligently managed; and new board members were adequately groomed to succeed outgoing board members. I can reflect back on numerous challenges and accomplishments that would not have been possible without the combined efforts of the other chapter officers and directors, as well as the support of our respective employers. I was especially proud of three successes in particular.

The most significant achievement of our chapter and board during my tenure was the successful organization, administration, and deployment of the 1997 Northwest ISACA Conference held in Seattle, Washington. Two primary goals of the conference were to provide quality education at a reasonable cost and to provide the chapter operating fund with a much-needed shot in the arm.

The conference was held during a three-day period and featured over 30 speakers on topics such as Internet security; COBIT development and implementation; controls and security of operating systems such as IBM MVS, Novell Netware 4.x, and Microsoft NT 4.0; physical security; cryptography and data security; telecommunications fraud; Internet audit resources; firewall construction; UNIX audit and control; disaster recovery; electronic commerce; and a number of sessions on industry-specific technologies. Especially interesting was a panel of chief information officers (CIOs) from six local organizations, who discussed their approaches to solving the Year 2000 problem. We were also treated to a unique guest speaker, Kirk Bailey, who founded The Agora, an association of electronic technology professionals, organizations, and others who wish to share information regarding the information security field. The Agora is based in Seattle and supports a regional membership that includes participants from the private sector, public agencies, government, and law enforcement.

The conference provided the opportunity for many talented local speakers as well as a selected group of out-of-town guest speakers to share their knowledge and skills with their peers. All of the speakers volunteered their time and resources for the benefit of the chapter and the local auditing community. Support from the organizations in which the speakers were employed was tremendous, and one corporation even donated the use of its auditorium and training facilities. Based on the survey results, attendees were very pleased with the overall quality of the presentations and the organization of the conference.

The conference was also a major financial success for the chapter. The added financial boost enabled the chapter to provide benefits to members for many years to come. For example, the chapter now has the flexibility and ability, if desired, to subsidize part or all of the cost of securing high-quality speakers from out of the area to provide half- or full-day seminars. Previously the chapter might not have been able to offer such activities without substantial cost to the members.

The second success of our chapter and board was a 13.9 percent increase in chapter membership, from 72 to 82, during the 12 months ending in April 1997. The increase was primarily attributable to membership discounts offered for conference registration and for registration in the chapter's annual Certified Information Systems Auditor (CISA) examination review course. The combined discounts were more than enough to pay for the annual membership fee in ISACA. The increase followed several years during which the number of chapter members remained stable. I am happy to report that as of mid-2002, chapter membership has grown to over 160.

The third success of which I am particularly pleased relates to one of the earliest challenges we faced—updating the chapter bylaws. The primary reason for the update was to reflect ISACA's name change from the EDP Auditors Association. Since the chapter bylaws had not been updated for several years, we took the opportunity to include a number of clarifications and corrections. This seemingly simple task turned out to be a year long ordeal. Updating the bylaws required us as a board to meet several times to prepare a draft. The draft had to be submitted to the international ISACA office for review. Next we had to prepare a final draft incorporating recommended changes from the international office. The final draft then had to be mailed to the local chapter members for ratification, and the votes tallied. As of mid-2002, the bylaws have not had to be revised again.

These professional association activities, while not directly related to our jobs as IS auditors, served the indirect purpose of contributing to the knowledge, training, and development of IS auditors and non-IS auditors in the region; providing a forum through which IS audit, control, and security experts could showcase their talents; and enabling local members and nonmembers to meet and exchange information. Without these types of activities being offered on an ongoing basis, the auditing community would suffer from a lack of quality training and interaction. As a result, the quality of auditing tools and techniques would begin to deteriorate as the rapid pace of technological changes reduces the effectiveness of previous approaches. Organizations would then begin to suffer in terms of increased exposure to risks that highly trained IS auditors might otherwise identify and resolve.

In addition to my two years as ISACA chapter president, I have also held the positions of vice president, CISA coordinator, academic relations chair, and programs director. I have also volunteered my time by assisting the local Institute of Internal Auditors chapter in locating and securing qualified speakers for its 1997 Western Regional Conference, which was held in Seattle in August, as well as performing as its academic relations chair. Other types of local and national volunteering activities in which I have participated include presentations on the subjects of wire transfer and ACH security, Year 2000, control self-assessment, and introduction to IS auditing at various conferences, chapter meetings of auditing and fraud examiners associations, graduate and undergraduate university classes, and management groups of my employer.

More recently, as the Academic Relations Committee chair of the Puget Sound chapters of both the ISACA and IIA since 2000, I am particularly proud of our recent accomplishments. Prior to 2000, the ISACA chapter had not performed any academic relations activities for at least 10 years. The IIA had only offered some small scholarships but did not see any return on their investment and was lacking in volunteer participation.

In 2000, we began sponsoring annual "Student Information Events" to promote the auditing profession as well as the ISACA and IIA organizations. The first year, we held the event in the evening at Seattle University with the help of one of its professors who was an IIA member. We promoted the event to several other large schools, including the University of Washington (UW). Deloitte and Touche sponsored the refreshments, and we had about 25 professionals on hand to share their experiences, including five who sat on a panel discussion. Unfortunately, only nine students attended, seven of whom were in a class of the hosting professor. The other two students were from the UW.

In 2001, we decided to hold the event in a lower-key venue that was convenient for students and to focus on a single campus. Since faculty sponsorship is a very important key to success, we again held our event at Seattle University. But this time we held the event during a regularly scheduled Beta Alpha Psi lunch meeting. We only scheduled three professionals to attend but were able to send our message to 17 students, an 89 percent increase over 2000.

In 2002, we again held the event at a Seattle University Beta Alpha Psi meeting, this time with 30 students in attendance to listen to six professionals. In addition, through another faculty contact, we sent three professionals to an auditing class at Seattle Pacific University and networked with seven more students. Thus we reached a total of 37 students in 2002 (a 118 percent increase over 2001).

For 2003, we plan to offer the same information at Seattle University and Seattle Pacific University. We have also secured a faculty contact at the University of Washington who is interested in having us address accounting and auditing students. We could potentially double the number of students we are reaching yet again.

All auditors should develop their technical and presentation skills and then challenge themselves by sharing their knowledge with local and national groups in the arena of IS audit, controls, and security. They should also support and become active in the professional associations of their choice. The professional associations that are best suited for an individual will depend on his or her needs for training, the financial resources available, the amount of time and resources available to volunteer for these associations and to regularly attend their activities, and the commitment of the organization to support the auditor's involvement.

Appendix A provides a detailed list of professional auditing associations and other organizations related to IS auditing and computer security. The appendix includes the address, phone number, website address, and mission statements of the listed organizations. Some related associations might have been inadvertently omitted. The list is not intended to be all encompassing but should prove to be a valuable reference tool.

NETWORKING

Networking at conferences and at professional association leadership functions was discussed in the previous section. However, networking can also be accomplished at the local level as well. Through an effective local network, one can develop contacts in a variety of different industries. These individuals can be valuable resources when one is searching for information on different auditing techniques, technical information on new and existing technologies, or simply to exchange ideas. Contacts from organizations within the same industry can provide benchmarking standards for an organization. Also, contacts from different industries can add diversity to one's perspective. The nice part about personal "local area networks" is that one can physically meet these people for lunch or at some other informal venue to discuss topics of interest.

Networking opportunities of a different nature occur when one is an active chapter board member. For example, the ISACA International office helps facilitate the development of chapter leaders throughout the world by hosting annual leadership conferences. ISACA's North American Leadership Conference is usually held during the weekend prior to the annual Computer, Audit, Control, and Security (CACS) Conference. Chapter delegates usually include the president, vice president, and selected other board members. The conferences enable leaders of chapters of all sizes to network and exchange ideas on all aspects of chapter operations, as well as international operations. The willingness of chapters with healthy finances to provide financial assistance to small chapters in need was especially impressive. I also appreciated the fact that we all spoke candidly about our opinions and experiences. Since we only had a relatively short time to discuss matters, we held very open, honest, and respectful discussions on all issues.

To provide an additional opportunity for leadership development, the chapters from the West Coast of the United States organized their own regional leadership conferences. These conferences were usually held about halfway in between the North American Leadership Conferences to ensure that significant issues affecting chapter operations could be discussed semiannually instead of just annually. I found these regional leadership conferences to be highly productive and to provide an opportunity to really get to know the other chapter leaders within the same geographic region upon whom we often relied for the exchange of vital information.

A perfect example of how our chapter benefited from such networking pertained to the 1997 Northwest ISACA Conference. Our chapter wanted to mail conference brochures to as many potential attendees on the West Coast as possible. We were able to coordinate with each West Coast chapter to mail brochures to everyone on their respective mailing lists, which encompassed thousands of individuals. At the preceding regional leadership conference, I was able to coordinate in advance what steps I would need to perform in order to send a conference brochure to everyone on the mailing lists of all chapters on the West Coast. As previously mentioned, the conference was a great success.

Both the international and regional leadership conferences generate teamwork, camaraderie, and fun among the attendees through group social functions and outings. I have made many contacts at these functions, many of whom have also become good friends.

PROFESSIONAL CERTIFICATIONS RELATED TO INFORMATION SYSTEMS AUDIT, CONTROL, AND SECURITY

Professional certifications related to the field of IS audit, control, and security attest to the holder's knowledge and experience. In general, these professional designations are designed to achieve these objectives:

- To evaluate individual competence in the field
- To provide a mechanism for maintaining such competence
- To provide management objective criteria for personnel selection and promotion

Earning and maintaining professional designations provide many benefits to the certificate holders. These benefits include:

- Demonstrate expertise and competence in the field
- Attain career recognition
- Enhance career through promotions
- Establish professional credibility and qualification across industry lines
- Encourage professional growth

To earn a professional certification, candidates are typically required to pass an examination, or series of examinations, which tests their mastery over a particular body of knowledge. By passing the examination, candidates attest that they have attained the required knowledge level. Although professional certifications are not a substitute for practical experience, most audit-related certifications require candidates to provide proof of at least a few years of practical auditing experience. By requiring proof of a few years of practical auditing experience, the overall competence of the certificate holder is supplemented.

After earning a professional designation, certificate holders are expected to maintain a current proficiency by earning a certain number of continuing professional educational (CPE) credits each year. A CPE credit is typically equivalent to 50 minutes of contact time. Continuing professional educational credits can be earned by attending seminars, conferences, college courses, and some correspondence courses and tests; meetings of audit-related professional associations; writing books, articles, and research papers; performing oral presentations; and participating as an officer or committee member in an audit-related professional association. The number of CPE credits allowed for these types of activities varies among each certification sponsor.

In some cases, the certificate renewal period may be two or even three years, with a minimum number of CPEs required to be earned in each year. In addition, most professional certifications stipulate that the holder must adhere to a specific ethical code of conduct. Although codes of conduct are reliant upon the honesty and integrity of the certificate holders, I believe that the existence of the codes of conduct help certificate holders question or refrain from activities that they might otherwise have participated in. The risk of being stripped of one's certifications, and thus of one's livelihood, is an additional consideration that certificate holders must consider before engaging in questionable activities. Some certificate-sponsoring organizations also promulgate professional auditing standards to which certificate holders are expected to adhere.

Numerous certifications can be earned in the field of IS audit, control, and security, and auditing in general. The extent of technical knowledge and experience in IS audit, control, and security varies widely among the certifications. Nevertheless, the importance of IS controls is apparent in the bodies of knowledge required to obtain these certifications. Following are brief descriptions of a few of the most prominent certifications. Not every professional designation that relates to the IS audit, control, and security field is included. This is not intended to be a comprehensive list. Rather, it is to provide information on some of the better-known, non–industry-specific professional certifications. Please refer to Appendix A for more details on auditing, control, and security-related organizations.

Certified Information Systems Auditor

The CISA designation is sponsored by ISACA. There are currently over 26,000 ISACA members in over 100 countries. The CISA designation was first established by ISACA in 1978. There are currently more than 14,000 CISAs worldwide.

To earn the CISA designation requires candidates to pass a four-hour-long examination consisting of 200 multiple-choice questions covering seven areas:

Process-based Area

1.   The IS Audit Process

Content Area

2.   Management, Planning and Organization of IS
3.   Technical Infrastructure and Operational Practices
4.   Protection of Information Assets
5.   Disaster Redcovery and Business Continuity
6.   Business Application System Development, Acquisition, Implementation, and Maintenance
7.   Business Process Evaluation and Risk Management

In addition to passing the examination, candidates must submit proof of five years of IS audit, control, or security experience. One year of the experience requirement may be waived if the candidate has an associate degree, and two years of the experience requirement may be waived for a bachelor's degree. One year of the experience requirement may be substituted for one year of general audit or IS experience. In essence, a seasoned auditor with a bachelor's degree must possess two years of IS audit, control, or security experience to earn certification. To provide educators with certification opportunities, one year of the experience requirement may be substituted for each two years as a full-time university instructor in a related field.

To maintain the CISA designation, certificate holders must earn a minimum of 120 CPE credits over a fixed three-year period, with a minimum of 20 CPE credits earned each year. Certificate holders must adhere to a code of professional ethics.

Certified Internal Auditor

The Certified Internal Auditor (CIA) designation is sponsored by the Institute of Internal Auditors (IIA). There are currently over 75,000 IIA members in over 120 countries. The CIA designation was first established by the IIA in 1974. There are currently over 35,000 CIAs worldwide.

Earning the CIA designation requires candidates to pass a four-part examination administered over a two-day period. Each part is 210 minutes long, for a total examination length of 14 hours. Each part consists of 80 multiple choice questions, broken down into four parts:

- Part 1—Internal Audit Process
    Subjects: Auditing, Professionalism, Fraud

- Part 2—Internal Audit Skills
    Subjects: Problem Solving and Evaluating Audit Evidence, Data Gathering, Documentation, and Reporting Sampling and Mathematics

- Part 3—Management Control and Information Technology
    Subjects: Management Control, Operations Management, Information Technology

- Part 4—Audit Environment
    Subjects: Financial Accounting, Finance, Managerial Accounting, Regulatory Environment

In addition to passing the examination, candidates must hold a bachelor's degree or equivalent from an accredited college-level institution. In some cases, other professional designations may be accepted as equivalent to a bachelor's degree. A character reference must also be submitted from a responsible person, such as a supervisor, manager, educator, or CIA. Finally, candidates must possess two years of internal audit or equivalent experience. A master's degree can be substituted for one year's work experience.

To maintain the CIA designation, certificate holders must earn a minimum of 80 CPE credits over a fixed two-year period. Certificate holders must adhere to a code of professional ethics.

Certified Public Accountant

The Certified Public Accountant (CPA) designation is sponsored by AICPA, which has over 330,000 members across the United States. The Uniform CPA Examination was first administered in 1917. There are currently over 400,000 CPAs in the United States. Although membership in most sponsoring organizations is not mandatory to maintain certification, it is interesting that the number of CPAs far exceeds the number of AICPA members. This is due to the fact that a CPA license is mandatory for those practicing public accounting. To earn a CPA designation requires candidates to pass a four-part examination administered over a two-day period. Each part is from 180 to 270 minutes long, for a total examination length of 15.5 hours. Each part consists of multiple choice and/or essay questions, broken into four parts:

- Part 1—Business Law & Professional Responsibilities; Information Technology (70–80 percent multiple choice/objective, 20–30 percent essay)
- Part 2—Auditing (70–80 percent multiple choice/objective, 20–30 percent essay)
- Part 3—Accounting & Reporting—Taxation, Managerial, Governmental and Not-for-Profit Organizations (100 percent multiple choice/objective)
- Part 4—Financial Accounting & Reporting (70–80 percent multiple choice/ objective, 20–30 percent essay)

After passing the examination, candidates must also pass an ethics examination. In addition, candidates must hold a bachelor's degree or equivalent from an accredited college-level institution and have completed a minimum number of specific accounting courses.

In the United States, most state boards of accountancy have adopted a requirement that raises the minimum number of educational credits required for certification from 120 hours to 150 hours. This requirement essentially requires candidates to attend college for an additional year. However, the curriculum during the additional year of education does not need to be in the area of accounting or auditing. The effective date of this requirement varies by state. In the State of Washington, the 150-hour requirement went into effect on July 1, 2000.

The number and types of CPE credits required to maintain the CPA designation varies slightly by state, but not significantly. In the State of Washington, CPAs must earn a minimum of 120 CPE credits over a fixed three-year period, with a minimum of 20 CPE credits earned each year. Of the 120 CPE credits, 4 must be in ethics and 116 in technical or non-technical areas. However, no more than 24 CPE may be in non-technical areas. Certificate holders must adhere to a code of professional ethics.

Certified Information Systems Security Professional

The Certified Information Systems Security Professional (CISSP) designation is sponsored by the International Information Systems Security Certification Consortium, Inc. (ISC^2). The CISSP designation was first established by the ISC^2 in 1992. There are currently about 8,500 CISSPs worldwide.

To earn the CISSP designation requires candidates to pass a six-hour-long examination, consisting of 250 multiple-choice questions covering 10 domains:

1. Security Management Practices
2. Security Architecture and Models
3. Access Control Systems and Methodology
4. Application Development Security
5. Operations Security
6. Physical Security
7. Cryptography
8. Telecommunications, Network, and Internet Security
9. Business Continuity Planning
10. Law, Investigations, and Ethics

In addition to passing the examination, candidates must attain at least three years of IS security-related experience as a practitioner, auditor, consultant, vendor, investigator, or instructor who requires IS security knowledge and involves the direct application of that knowledge. Effective January 1, 2003, candidates must possess four years of experience, or three years with a college degree or equivalent life experience.

To maintain the CISSP designation, certificate holders must earn a minimum of 120 CPE credits over a fixed three-year period. Certificate holders must adhere to a code of professional ethics.

Certifications in Canada, United Kingdom, and Australia

The Canadian Institute of Chartered Accountants (CICA) and the Institute of Chartered Accountants in England and Wales (ICAEW) both sponsor a designation known as the *Chartered Accountant* (CA). Each is independently administered and subject to unique and independent certification requirements. There are over 76,000 members of the CICA and 120,000 members of the ICAEW.

In Australia, there are two somewhat competing professional accounting bodies: the Institute of Chartered Accountants in Australia (ICAA) and the Certified Practising Accountants of Australia (CPAA), formerly known as the Australian Society of Certified Practising Accountants (ASCPA). The ICAA has over

37,000 members, while the CPAA has over 105,000 members. Each is an independent association that sponsors separate professional certifications: Chartered Accountant (CA) and Certified Practising Accountant (CPA), respectively. For purposes of establishing standards and guidelines, the two organizations have created the Australian Accounting Research Foundation (AARF), with representatives from each organization comprising the Joint Standing Committee, which oversees the foundation's board of management. The National Institute of Accountants (NIA) is yet a third organization with over 14,000 members. The NIA does not sponsor a separate ertification but offers several levels of memberhisp based on experience and education.

Other Certifications

A list of other audit, control, and security-related professional designations follows. The eligibility and maintenance requirements of each of these certifications is similar to the aforementioned professional designations.

- *Certificate in Data Processing (CDP)*, sponsored by the Association of Information Technology Professionals (AITP). Prior to 1996, the AITP was known as the Data Processing Management Association (DPMA).
- *Certified Management Accountant (CMA)*, sponsored by the Institute of Management Accountants (IMA).
- *Certified Fraud Examiner (CFE)*, sponsored by the Association of Certified Fraud Examiners (ACFE).
- *Certified Financial Services Auditor (CFSA)*, sponsored by the National Association of Financial Services Auditors (NAFSA). In mid-2002, NAFSA merged with the Institute of Internal Auditors (IIA). The CFSA certification will continue to be offered through the IIA.
- *Certified Government Auditing Professional (CGAP)*, sponsored by the Institute of Internal Auditors (IIA).
- *Certification in Control Self Assessment (CCSA)*, sponsored by the Institute of Internal Auditors (IIA).
- *Global Information Assurance Certification (GIAC)*, sponsored by the SANS Institute. GIAC is a program where candidates can earn up to 10 different GIAC certifications in differing areas of specialization.
- *Systems Security Certified Practitioner (SSCP)*, sponsored by the International Information Systems Security Certification Consortium (ISC²).
- *Certified Protection Professional (CPP)*, sponsored by the American Society for Industrial Security (ASIS).

A Few Thoughts about Professional Certifications

Professional designations are an important and valuable credential in any auditor's portfolio of skills. They provide a wide array of opportunities to enhance one's career, whether it is through promotions, outside job opportunities, or more creative opportunities, such as consulting and writing. Although professional certifications are not a guarantee of the holder's ability to perform, they definitely provide a solid foundation from which holders can be evaluated and from which they can catapult their careers.

Organizations that hire IS auditors with professional designations and encourage and support their uncertified IS auditors to attain these designations are helping to ensure that their internal control environments are being adequately evaluated by qualified individuals. With the rapid advances in information technology come opportunities for new types of internal control weaknesses and operational inefficiencies to slow the progress of organizations. As we head further into the new millennium, auditors with professional certifications will play an important role in helping their organizations achieve their strategic objectives.

There are already many audit-related certifications available. One concern is that the number of independent auditing associations and certifications is continuously expanding. Each association has its stated purpose and objectives, and each association typically wishes to become nationally or internationally recognized. Unfortunately, one of the methods through which they choose to attain such recognition is through the creation of new certification programs. As more and more audit-related associations and certifications are established, there will become an increasingly overlapping body of knowledge. As a result, the certification tests will inevitably be repetitive to those who take them. To maintain the appearance of credibility in an industry-specific auditing association, an otherwise completely qualified holder of one or more different certifications will be indirectly forced to earn additional professional designations to the point where they become an administrative nightmare. In addition, the cost of maintaining them will become prohibitive, especially to those whose employers do not supplement their certificate holders. Typically, each sponsoring professional association requires certificate holders to pay an annual certificate maintenance fee. In addition, if the certificate holder wishes to be a member, he or she must pay additional annual membership dues. Multiple certificate holders are forced to select only one or a few certifications and memberships, when they may otherwise be highly qualified and proficient in other audit-related areas. In some cases, this could place them at a competitive disadvantage when seeking job opportunities and promotions, even though they may in fact be more highly qualified than their competition.

It is hoped that each new audit-related professional association chooses to earn its recognition through other means. Proficiency of members in these associations can be established through existing certifications. Granted, there are specific technical areas in which there is a need for auditors to gain specialized knowledge, but there is a limit as to how much granularity of specialization is needed in the auditing field. Therefore, recognition of new professional auditing associations can be better achieved through active research, publications, and other activities that will expand and promote the specific technical knowledge they wish to be added to the field of auditing. Instead of creating more and more certifications with overlapping bodies of knowledge, new associations can take at least two strategic approaches. One would be to lobby the existing certification sponsors to incorporate critical areas of knowledge into their existing bodies of knowledge. Another alternative would be to establish a more specific and inexpensive credential that tests only a highly focused and specific body of knowledge, without overlapping into more general bodies of knowledge that are already tested and evaluated by the existing audit, control, and security-related professional certifications.

As mentioned earlier, Appendix A provides a detailed list of professional auditing associations and other organizations related to IS audit, control, and security.

READING

Because of the rapidity with which information technology changes, one must budget as much time as reasonably possible to read various publications pertaining to IS audit, control, and security, as well as new technologies. The reading regimen should be something done on a daily basis. Often, new control weaknesses may be identified about information systems currently being used in an organization or that one is preparing to examine. Since new technologies are constantly being implemented within organizations, one of the most timely and effective means for one to stay current is through reading. Among the types of publications that provide current information about new technologies and IS audit, control, and security techniques are books, trade journals, magazines, national and local newspapers, various business news services, newsletters from professional auditing associations and their local chapters, and industry-specific bulletins, newsletters, flyers, and regulatory updates. Many of these publications are available on the Internet. In fact, some publications are available only on the Internet. One thing to keep in mind is to not overwhelm yourself by thinking you have to read every word of every technology-related publication. There are more publications than you can reasonably read and still be able to perform your job. The key is to be selective in what you read. Choose a few publications to read on a regular basis, including some that are pertinent to your organization's industry. Read other publications on a more piecemeal basis, being alert to key topics. As you begin to subscribe to various publications and become a member of various professional auditing and security associations, be prepared to be inundated with flyers inviting you to attend conferences, seminars, and other educational events, and to purchase all kinds of audit- and security-related products and services.

Most professional associations issue periodic newsletters. In addition, the larger associations publish magazines and trade journals as well as Internet publications. Some of the larger publications, with the name of the professional association or organization that publishes them in parentheses; include:

- *Information Security* (TruSecure Corporation)
- *Internal Auditor Journal* (Institute of Internal Auditors)
- *IS Audit and Control Journal* (Information Systems Audit & Control Association)

- *Journal of Accountancy* (American Institute of Certified Public Accountants)
- *Secure Computing* (West Coast Publishing Company-UK)

I literally have piles of these publications, but at least they are organized in chronological order. I even have labeled tabs on the notable articles within each issue. Another publication I read more infrequently due to time constraints but that contains interesting IS audit, control, and security related articles is *EDPACS* by Auerbach Publications. *2600* magazine is popular among those interested in the world of hacking.

If you are looking for opportunities to educate your peers, or to voice your opinion on IS audit–related issues, you may be able to move beyond the limitation of just reading IS audit–related trade journals and magazines and into the realm of writing articles and submitting them for publication. Most editors of such publications are constantly searching for fresh ideas and topics pertaining to IS audit, controls, and security. Many accomplished writers have had their works published, but there is always a demand for new writing talent. I challenge each of you to contribute to the literary body of knowledge in the field of IS audit, control, and security, and auditing in general.

PRACTICAL EXPERIENCE

There is no substitute for practical experience auditing information systems, new technologies, and related processes. At some point, your training, professional affiliations, networking, certifications, reading, and other education must be applied to real-world situations in order to recoup your and your organization's investments of time and financial resources. Application of these skills is where your organization will reap the benefits of a significantly more secure IS control environment. As the numerous examples within this book attest, theory alone is no substitute for the reality of practical experience. The human factor is the great unknown in the deployment and controlling of all information technologies. Humans are what create an unpredictable IS environment. Our role as auditors and IS security professionals is to continuously evaluate IS controls to minimize the risk presented by the human factor. As you gain more and more practical experience, you will become progressively more comfortable and adept at auditing the logical security, physical security, and operational aspects of a variety of applications, database management systems, operating systems, and related processes. You will also become a valuable consulting resource for your organization when IS control and security issues arise, as in the case of development and implementation of new technologies, or resolution of recently identified IS control weaknesses or operational deficiencies.

HUMANISTIC SKILLS FOR SUCCESSFUL AUDITING

One of the most often overlooked but essential skills for IS auditors and any other type of auditors to possess are those pertaining to communication and interpersonal relations. Skills such as a high-level business understanding, verbal and written communication skills, analytical skills, and negotiation skills are equally as important as the technical skills necessary to effectively evaluate IS control environments.

Historically, auditors were often perceived as technical recluses who dealt with people only after they had identified errors, irregularities, and other violations of policies, procedures, laws, or regulations. The recommendations in audit reports were often perceived as stern, robotic, and difficult to revise. Auditors needed only to be able to identify weaknesses with limited regard as to how they were presented to the auditee management. This autocratic approach to auditing was the old school of thought. Thankfully, modern auditing has progressed to more of a consultative role. Under the modern internal control frameworks (see Chapter 10), auditee management is encouraged to look to auditors for suggestions as to how to improve operations and achieve strategic objectives.

Auditors must be able to act as a liaison between management and staff and between management of different departments that rely on each other but may be experiencing common difficulties. They must be able to present findings and effectively interact with staff at all levels of the organization, from executive management down to the individual workers, and at every level in between. This interaction may be in the form of verbal conversations, written or electronic correspondence, and/or a combination of the two, as in the case of a presentation to management or the performance of a CSA workshop.

All auditors must have a high-level business understanding to assess the potential significance of operational and control issues and to communicate the effects of these issues to management. Auditors must also be likable, approachable, and able to befriend people. These skills are especially important when dealing with line workers. Line workers are frequently an excellent source of detailed information of which management may not be aware, especially when evaluating efficiency/effectiveness issues. I even recommend approaching audits as if you are forming alliances with the process owners. If successful, you will be able to go to them for information, and they will be much more likely to seek you out for information. Such an approach promotes teamwork and helps to minimize the adversarial environment that is often created when an individual or group of individuals are having their process evaluated by an outsider.

Excellent writing ability is one of the most important of all the nontechnical skills that auditors must possess. Half of my time is spent writing. Examples of written documents common to all types of auditing include memos, risk assessment descriptions, narratives describing how systems or processes work, audit programs, audit reports, and summary reports. Poor grammar and spelling can be frustrating to the reader, whether it is auditee management or even one's own supervisor. Poor writing skills inevitably lead to reduced effectiveness because the reader may not get a clear idea of what the control issue is or exactly how the auditor proposes to resolve an issue. This kind of confusion wastes time by causing documents to be revised or reworked more frequently than necessary. Poor writing also includes unnecessary verbiage and detail, which distract the reader from the point that is trying to be made.

Negotiation skills are rarely associated with an auditor's skill set. However, because of the sometimes sensitive nature of the control weaknesses encountered and the recommendations to resolve them, negotiation skills are highly desirable. Sometimes I have to play the role of a diplomat when presenting sensitive control recommendations, especially when the recommendation involves action by two or more separate operating units. However, this role can be very rewarding. At times I have been able to assist in opening the communication channels between two or more operating units that previously viewed each other as the reason that a particular control issue existed. By carefully presenting recommendations so that neither party is being identified as the cause, the odds of successfully implementing a solution are greatly enhanced.

Even in the case of sensitive recommendations submitted to management of a single operating unit, negotiation skills are frequently necessary. For example, it is often more effective to "soften" the description of a control issue to increase the likelihood of implementing the solution. Taking a hard line by harshly describing a control weakness usually results in an immediate and sometimes irreversible desire on the part of auditee management to refuse to implement a recommendation or to implement it on a limited basis. If this is allowed to happen, the organization suffers. To avoid confrontations, auditors must be able to "read" the nonverbal signals of auditee management as well as line workers. People are highly sensitive, especially in the workplace. Many auditors are technically proficient but fail miserably because they offended someone they were auditing. All it takes is one negative confrontation, and the communication channels between the auditee and the auditor can be irreparably damaged. Therefore, it is very important for auditors to act in a professional and diplomatic manner, even in the face of situations in which they would like to speak what they are truly thinking.

MOTIVATION OF AUDITORS

Motivation of auditors is as complex a subject as for any group of individuals. Everyone has different wants, needs, and desires, and is therefore motivated by different factors. To delve deeply into human psychology and management theory as to all of the possible motivating factors that exist would be far beyond the scope of this section. Instead, I focus on two factors that can be highly successful at motivating auditors if effectively implemented: creativity in one's job and goal-oriented financial incentives.

Job Creativity

Many people, including auditors, are motivated by a certain degree of creativity in their jobs and other aspects of their lives. In auditing, creativity may mean the freedom to pursue new approaches to auditing a particular process; to learn about new technologies, tools, and techniques; to earn new certifications; to create new training tools; to perform research and write about the results; and the like. In short, creativity means the ability to search outside the standard methodology that may have been previously established. Sometimes the risk of allowing this sort of creativity may not result in the most efficient deployment of audit resources. However, if granted within reasonable constraints, the ability to practice creativity can often produce significant rewards to the organization through creative solutions as well as the auditors' satisfaction in terms of job fulfillment.

Therefore, successful audit managers should not try to view and deploy their auditors as robots, even in large audit departments. I recently learned of a case of robotic audit management at one large multistate banking organization. This organization had directed that standard audit programs be utilized for audits of the same processes in each subsidiary, even if they are in different states or countries. While this approach might seem to make sense on the surface as far as efficiency is concerned, it does not allow for adjustments in scope and approach due to local and regional IS environments, corporate and social cultures, and other intangibles, including auditor motivation. This sort of tunnel-vision approach to managing inevitably stifles the creativity of any IS or non-IS auditor. Successful audit management should be encouraging risk analyses to be performed during audit planning so that local and regional differences can be evaluated and necessary adjustments can be incorporated into the audit approach.

As we move further into the new millennium, the results arising from a narrow-minded, autocratic, Theory X approach to audit management will be inherently less effective than a flexible approach that allows the audit process to quickly adapt to a dynamically changing environment. It is extremely difficult to function effectively in an autocratic type of environment. It is hoped that most audit managers will encourage, or even require, at least a certain degree of creativity in the jobs of every auditor.

Financial Incentives for Auditors

Financial incentives can be a two-edged sword in terms of motivation. While working in a non–audit department several years ago, I participated in an incentive plan that was totally discretionary. There was no written description as to how the plan was to be administered or how rewards were to be earned. Each year people went about their normal business, but they were always concerned about doing something that might negatively influence their incentive. The incentives were issued in secret, and one either received an envelope or did not. Nothing was said if one did not. I found that even after receiving an incentive during the first year, the positive effect of the reward wore off after about one week. I was then faced with the thought of toiling in the unknown for another year, wondering if I would be lucky enough to receive another one. There were no specific goals or objectives on which to set my sights. I would classify this type of incentive plan as highly demotivating.

However, I have participated in a financial incentive plan while employed as an auditor that I found to be an excellent motivational tool. The plan was developed jointly by a project team of members throughout the organization, but under the direction of a professional consultant who had helped develop and implement numerous incentive plans. The incentive plan participants included supervisors, managers, directors, and nonmanagement professionals such as auditors. Final approval of the plan design was granted by senior management. Briefly, the plan based the participants' annual financial incentive on three criteria.

One criteria, which accounted for 25 percent of the total incentive award, was based on individual performance as specified in the individual's written annual performance appraisal. The direct manager was responsible for performing this evaluation. As far as motivation is concerned, this facet of the plan was equally as effective as a typical annual performance assessment.

The second criteria, which also accounted for 25 percent of the total incentive award, was based on two to three company goals that were established by senior management at the beginning of each year. This goal was awarded to all plan participants equally, regardless of what department they worked in and regardless of what effect they might have on the award. For example, one year the organization established one company goal designed to encourage safety and soundness and another to encourage expense control. The safety and soundness goal was measured by the ratio of total average reserves to total average assets. The expense control goal was measured by the ratio of total expenses to total average assets. For each ratio, minimum, target, and maximum performance levels were established by senior management. If the organization was below the minimum performance level for a particular ratio, no incentive was awarded for that goal. If the ratio was at or above the maximum performance level, then the highest incentive was awarded for that particular goal. Incentives were awarded on a prorated basis if the ratios were somewhere between the minimum and maximum performance levels.

From the motivational viewpoint of an auditor, I did not think about the company goals on a regular basis. They encouraged us to develop recommendations that I would consider typical objectives of auditing; namely, to control expenses and to operate in a fiscally conservative manner. But this part of the incentive package provided the psychological benefit that all participants are part of a large team, all striving to achieve the same goal, with the same reward for everyone. I found this aspect of the incentive plan to be refreshing, and it helped motivate me to work together with my peers.

The third criteria is where auditor motivation can be maximized. It is also under this criteria that the organization can benefit the most. This criteria consisted of three to four departmental goals, which accounted for 50 percent of the total incentive award. These goals were originally developed by participants in their respective departments at the beginning of each year and then approved by senior management. Qualifying goals were required to support one or more of the objectives of the organization's annual operating plan or long-term operating plan. Exhibits 14.1–14.6 discuss examples of goals that have been found to be highly motivating and beneficial to organizations.

Exhibit 14.1   Efficiency/Effectiveness Recommendations

Since one of the goals of the COSO (Committee of Sponsoring Organizations of the Treadway Commission) control framework was to help enhance the operational efficiency and effectiveness of the organization, a goal was developed to increase the percentage of efficiency and effectiveness recommendations submitted to management. Recommendations were examined from the previous two years. It was found that about 11 percent of the recommendations pertained to operational efficiency and effectiveness. A minimum performance level for the year was established at 15 percent and a maximum performance level at 20 percent. At first I was apprehensive about whether we could even achieve the minimum performance level for this goal. By the end of the year, however, 34 percent of all the recommendations we submitted to management pertained to enhancing the efficiency and effectiveness of operations. The interesting part about the results is that weak or insignificant recommendations were not included in the measurement. Only those recommendations included in the audit reports were counted. I am not sure whether the department could maintain a 34 percent efficiency/effectiveness recommendation ratio on an ongoing basis. If that was our goal, I am sure that we could easily sustain a level far above the 11 percent average of the previous two years.

   Audit department goals related to efficiency and effectiveness of operations enhance the consultative role of internal auditing. The old school of auditing, in which internal auditors act like police, still exists in some organizations. However, these auditors are not providing value-added ideas to their organizations. Internal auditors are in an ideal position to identify and communicate new ideas to management and effect positive change within their organizations. They are independent of the politics within and across departments that may be hampering progress. They are able to assess operations from a big-picture perspective, avoiding the common "We've always done it that way" roadblock. They can provide ideas and examples of how other companies are performing similar operations. As can be seen, an audit department incentive to encourage ideas that improve business operations can significantly benefit an organization.

Exhibit 14.2   Development of CSA Program

When CSA was an emerging audit approach, we wanted to be on the leading edge. Therefore, our goal one year was to establish a CSA program. (See Chapter 10 for a detailed analysis of CSA.) We had seen and read a lot of literature on the subject but were struggling with taking the plunge and

EXHIBIT 14.2 (*continued*)

committing the resources necessary to develop the program. By adopting the CSA program as a departmental goal, we were much more highly motivated and committed to accomplishing the goal. Minimum, target, and maximum performance levels were established, based on when development of the CSA program was completed and how many CSA workshops had been conducted.

Although we did not achieve the maximum performance level by the end of the year, we succeeded in developing an internal control training course as well as a formal CSA workshop methodology. In addition, we conducted two CSA workshops as part of regularly scheduled audits, and the audit staff received a significant degree of training in CSA theory and facilitation techniques.

EXHIBIT 14.3   RISK EXPOSURE REDUCTION AND PRODUCTIVITY INCREASES

An audit department goal was established to achieve a certain dollar level of risk exposure reduction and productivity increases. This goal was measured by totaling the annual dollar amounts in four categories.

1. Exposure reductions from audit recommendations that resolved or eliminated significant internal control weaknesses or compliance violations
2. Significant errors that were identified and corrected as a result of audits
3. Revenue increases resulting from implementation of audit recommendations
4. Expense reductions and cost savings resulting from implementation of audit recommendations

This goal rewarded the Audit Department for identifying financially significant issues. It helped auditors avoid the temptation of latching on to issues of principle that may be insignificant or immaterial to the organization as a whole. The difficulty of this goal was what dollar amounts to set. Lofty dollar goals were set for minimum, target, and maximum performance levels. As it tuned out, early in the year a control weakness in the wire transfer system security parameters was identified that exposed the entire amount of all wire transfer transactions to potential losses reaching into the billions. Thus, by submitting a recommendation to resolve this one weakness, the maximum dollar goal for the entire year was exceeded.

Exhibit 14.4 Reduce the Incidence of Exceeding Budgeted Audit Hours

One of the common struggles of audit management is accurately estimating how long it will take to perform an effective audit. Often, to complete an audit in the allotted time, certain steps are omitted, the scope of testing is reduced, or creative investigation into unusual or puzzling activity that could identify potentially significant control weaknesses is forgone. It can be especially difficult to determine an adequate budget for first-time audits of new processes. Often the complexity of the system or process is not fully known until after the auditors have completed a narrative description and flow chart of the process.

Proper planning for audits and limiting the scope to high-risk areas can help reduce the degree to which budgets may be exceeded, but sometimes unforeseen events occur that can extend the length of an audit beyond what is planned. For example, if a significant control weakness is identified, additional testing may be required to determine the full extent of the exposure. Unplanned vacations or family emergencies by auditee staff or management can also delay completion of an audit. Another common reason for exceeding budgeted hours is when emergency projects or special investigations arise that take priority over the audit. An auditor may be temporarily reassigned to the unplanned project for a few days or weeks. When he or she returns to complete the audit, communications with auditee management and staff must be reestablished and the testing worked into the auditee's schedule. As a result the efficiency of the audit is reduced, and budgeted hours can be exceeded. For these reasons, I have never been a fan of strict audit budgets. However budgeting audit hours is necessary for management planning purposes. Estimated budgets are essential for developing the annual audit plan and, to a certain extent, for monitoring auditor performance.

Therefore, we developed a goal to balance the management need to adhere to budgeted audit hours and the challenge faced by auditors in performing effective audits within budgeted hours. The percentage with which actual audit hours had exceeded budgeted hours during the previous two years was estimated first. A vast majority of the audits were completed over budget. The degree to which audit budgets were exceeded varied widely by auditor and type of audit. Some were exceeded by an embarrassingly high percentage. Therefore, the minimum performance level of this goal was for the total number of actual hours spent on audits to exceed the budgeted hours by no more than 20 percent. The target performance level was for the total number of hours spent on audits to match the number of budgeted hours. To earn the maximum performance level, the total number of hours spent on audits would have to be 10 percent less than the total number of budgeted hours. By the end of the year, Audit Department performance was only slightly above the minimum, but the desired effect was achieved. A significantly greater number of audits were completed within or close to the number of budgeted hours as compared to the previous two years.

EXHIBIT 14.4   *(continued)*

During the development of this goal, an interesting budget planning methodology was developed that resulted in a more effective and accurate method of estimating hours. Because of the uncertainly in estimating the number of hours necessary to perform first-time audits of new processes, it was agreed that, for purposes of calculating goal performance, the number of budgeted hours would be reassessed after completion of the risk assessment and system or process narrative description. At this point, the scope could be determined with much greater precision, and the resulting budget could be much more accurate.

The Audit Department of one company prepared an annual audit plan that only forecast six months into the future. This concept is useful because it provides flexibility to audit resources. As unforeseen projects, investigations, rescheduling, and other events occur, previously scheduled audits can be extended into the third or fourth quarter. Thus, the overall impact on the audit plan would be minimal. If for some unusual reason the six-month plan is completed as scheduled, an additional six-month plan can be formulated at midyear. Some audit managers may wish to consider employing this audit-planning approach.

EXHIBIT 14.5   ORGANIZATION-WIDE SYSTEM IMPLEMENTATION GOAL

An all-new deposit and loan transaction system was being developed to replace a 15-year-old legacy system. After a one-year preliminary phase to analyze alternatives and to identify vendors who could fulfill the design requirements, implementation was scheduled for October of the current year. The new system actually consisted of four separate applications from four separate vendors. Each application used one of three different database management systems and one of two different operating systems. All business units had to reengineer their processes to fit the models of the new applications, with the customer contact areas being the most affected. Communications had to be prepared and delivered to account holders at the appropriate times. Literally every department in the institution was impacted by the project. Some were involved directly with the project. Others were impacted indirectly due to reduced availability of staff dedicated to the new system project or reduced financial resource availability for other projects.

To motivate everyone in the organization to contribute to the success of the project, the CEO required every department, including Internal Audit, to formulate at least one annual goal related to the project. The Internal Audit Department goal was to help ensure that all significant risks associated with

(continued)

EXHIBIT 14.5 (*continued*)

---

project management and with the new deposit and loan processes were adequately mitigated. The auditors identified numerous risks and associated controls and then performed monitoring tests throughout the project to help ensure that the controls were functioning adequately.

EXHIBIT 14.6 INTERNAL CUSTOMER SURVEY GOAL

To attempt to measure the effectiveness of audits, a goal was established whereby internal customer surveys were developed and sent to auditee management immediately after each audit. Among other areas, the survey questions focused on whether the audit was completed in a timely manner, the audit objectives were clearly communicated, the auditor understood the business, the audit recommendations were useful, and the audit report was clearly written. The surveys were returned to the director of Internal Audit, not the audit managers. Survey responses of "agree" and "strongly agree" were desired and were rewarded in the goal, while responses of "disagree" and "strongly disagree" were undesirable. At the end of the year, the combined average survey responses were calculated and compared to the goal percentages.

The goals described in exhibits 14.1–14.6 are just a few of the ones that could be developed to help motivate auditors and to invoke desired results for audit management in terms of the overall effectiveness of the audit process. Overall, the aforementioned incentive plan was highly motivational and effective. It was easily measurable, clear, concise, and promoted teamwork within the department as well as among peers throughout the organization. As consultants to management, auditors should be included in some form of management financial incentive program, but the program must be designed so that goal performance, while difficult, should be reasonably achievable. Most important, the incentive program must be designed to motivate all participants to work together as a team toward the common good of the organization.

In summary, this chapter has discussed a variety of topics that pertain to the humanistic side of IS auditing and auditing in general. These topics include training; active participation in professional associations; networking; professional certifications related to IS audit, control, and security; reading; practical experience; humanistic skills for successful auditing; and motivation of auditors. Each of these topics plays an important role in the overall audit process and the development of auditors. To increase their individual value and their value to their employers, auditors must be well rounded and versatile. After all, auditors are human beings too. The chapter concludes with three case studies of interesting situations that demonstrate some of the humanistic issues likely to be encountered in the IS auditing arena and how they can be addressed.

CASE STUDY 14.1

Negotiation of Audit Recommendations

An external IS audit manager for an organization in which I was employed as an internal IS auditor supported implementation of a number of IS security standards, which we in the internal IS audit function had identified as lacking in the organization. For example, there were no standards requiring a minimum password length, password expiration, or suspension of a user ID after a predetermined number of unsuccessful sign-on attempts. These and other IS security controls were deployed haphazardly throughout the organization. We strongly recommended immediate development and implementation of a comprehensive set of standards to apply to all existing and planned information systems. In addition, other less important IS security enhancements were proposed. However, IS management was reluctant to implement all of the audit recommendations at one time, not so much because of the difficulty of implementing them but more because of a desire to resist change.

Since the external auditor firm concurred with the need for the IS security enhancements, we collaborated with it to attempt to convince IS management of the need to adopt these changes. During a planning session I attended with the external audit manager, he outlined a strategy that, in retrospect, was very profound. As part of their annual audit, the external audit firm would prepare a letter to the organization that supported implementation of most of the control improvement recommendations the internal IS audit group had identified. The external IS audit manager was fully aware that the likelihood of IS management implementing all of them was slim. However, he believed that IS management could be expected to implement half or more of the recommendations, especially the most important ones. If so, we would have accomplished our goal for the year.

When I stepped back and analyzed this approach, I could see the psychological wisdom within it. In the view of IS management, they would not feel as if they had conceded to all of the audit recommendations. By implementing the primary internal control enhancements, however, the strength of the organization's overall control environment would be significantly increased. As a result, a win-win situation was created in the first year. The following year, the same approach could be used to recommend that the next tier of internal control improvements be implemented. Using this strategy over time, an organization could make significant progress toward enhancing its IS control environment. In fact, that is exactly what transpired at this organization.

The lesson I learned from this experience is that, although fully implementing all audit recommendations is preferred and optimal, demanding or insisting that they all be implemented immediately often promotes conflict. By taking a long-term approach to enhancing the control environment, an open and respectful team approach between the IS function and the internal and external IS auditors can be preserved and nurtured. As a result, IS management will be much more likely to implement recommendations submitted by the internal and external IS auditors. This type of working relationship obviously provides significantly greater benefits to the organization as compared to the "traditional" adversarial approach.

CASE STUDY14.2

What to Do When Testing Requirements Are Met with Resistance

During an audit of a microcomputer-based voice response banking application, we had planned to inspect the hard drives of each of the three microcomputers that housed the application to test for unauthorized software and/or data files. On our request to schedule a time to investigate the hard drives, we were initially denied access to perform our tests by the manager of the department responsible for the voice response application. One of the reasons given was that it would disrupt the availability of the service to customers since each microcomputer serviced multiple concurrent calls. We acknowledged this issue and offered to perform the tests during a weekend or evening and to examine only one machine at a time to minimize such disruption. The manager of the voice response system still did not grant permission.

I then escalated the issue to the Internal Audit Department manager, who also attempted to obtain authorization from the IS director to whom the manager of the voice response application reported. Again we were denied access for the same reasons. After some heated exchanges, the IS director eventually gave us permission to examine one of the three microcomputers, but she was to specify which one we could examine. She stated that since each of the central processing units (CPUs) were configured in exactly the same way, we did not need to look at all three. Obviously, allowing the IS director to dictate our testing parameters would result in a severe lack of independence. Therefore, we did not accept this offer and escalated the problem to the Internal Audit director.

As a matter of note, this was not the first time that the IS director had put up strong resistance to IS audit procedures. In her defense, much of her resistance was a manifestation of the brute-force approach used by a previous IS auditor. He had succeeded in almost completely "burning the bridge" between the Internal Audit Department and the IS group. That is why he was no longer with the organization.

The Internal Audit director jokingly grumbled about having to deal with this situation on a Friday afternoon. Begrudgingly, he closed the door to his office and called the IS director. After about five minutes, the Internal Audit director emerged and notified us that we could call the manager of the voice response application and schedule a time to examine all three microcomputers. We were astounded at how rapidly he had succeeded in securing permission to view all three CPUs.

He stated that he had discussed the issue with the IS director and told her that he was tired of bickering about the scope of every IS audit. He further stated that if she did not want us to look at them, then we would accept that position. However, he stated that we would specify the limitation in scope in the audit report and let senior management, including the president and the Audit Committee of the board of directors, assess the ramifications of such limitations. The IS director obviously did not want to commit political suicide, so she relented in her attempt to limit the scope of the audit.

We did not identify any significant issues during our examination of the hard drives of the three microcomputers used for the voice response application. However, we knew that PCs can be like people in that no two (or three) PCs are exactly alike. Despite identical hard drive sizes and hardware configurations, we found that the amount of available disk space was slightly different for each of the three PCs we examined. In fact, we identified a few minor exceptions. For example, using a utility software program, we identified public domain file compression software and several other miscellaneous files that were not authorized on each of the three PCs. The unauthorized software and files were subsequently deleted as a result of our audit.

The lesson in this scenario is that when encountering difficulties with management of any area that is being audited, it is fruitless to butt heads and argue over scope limitations. Instead, the professional approach is to attempt to accommodate the concerns of management over the area being audited. If this is unsuccessful, then escalate the issue to the appropriate levels of management. If resistance is still encountered, invoke the leverage of issuing a qualified opinion due to scope limitation. I have yet to see anyone in management willing to report to a curious Audit Committee and president as to why he or she limited the reasonable scope of an audit.

This situation also clearly demonstrates the need for the internal audit function to be functionally independent of all other areas in the organization. Independence is achieved by an organization structure in which the internal audit function reports directly to the president. With this type of reporting structure, the directors of the areas being audited cannot exert undue influence over the activities of the internal audit function. Some purists argue that the internal audit function should report directly to the Audit Committee of the board of directors so that even the president cannot exert undue influence over the internal audit function. However, from an administrative viewpoint, having the internal audit function report directly to the president is much more practical. The president is much more familiar with the day-to-day activities of the organization and is therefore in a much better position to supervise the activities of the Internal Audit director. Audit Committee members are not employees of the organization and typically convene on a monthly basis to review the status of the annual audit plan and the results of audit activities. The role of Audit Committee members is more typically that of making decisions on higher-level issues, although they should have some input as to the performance of the Internal Audit director. There are debates going on as to which is the preferred reporting structure.

CASE STUDY 14.3

To Whistle-blow or Not to Whistle-blow

Several years ago during an audit of an internally developed credit card processing application, I identified a flaw in the module that calculated the annual percentage rate (APR) that was disclosed to credit card holders on their

(continued)

CASE STUDY 14.3 (*continued*)

monthly statements. The flaw resulted in the understatement of APRs on statements in which the card holder had performed a cash advance transaction during the period covered by the statement. At the time, the financial institution assessed a fee for each cash advance transaction. A U.S. government banking regulation (Regulation Z: Truth-in-Lending) required that such fees be treated as finance charges, along with interest, for the purpose of calculating APR. The weakness pertained to the fact that when a cash advance fee was assessed to a card holder, the resulting APR calculation on the card holder's statement was often understated by more than the one-eighth of 1 percent tolerance allowed by the regulation. Although the actual amount of interest and cash advance transaction fees assessed were correct, the regulation is very specific in its disclosure requirements. The penalties for violating the regulation included a maximum fine of $500,000 in the event of a class-action lawsuit, associated attorneys' costs, the costs of notifying each potentially affected card holder, and the repayment of "overcharged" finance charges for every month that disclosed APRs were understated. The overcharged finance charges were the amounts that would need to be repaid to each affected card holder to render each of the incorrectly disclosed APRs accurate. Determining these amounts would involve recalculating tens of thousands of APRs and finance charge amounts, at a significant cost to the financial institution. In addition, a potentially more costly penalty would be the loss of public confidence in the accuracy of the other services offered by the financial institution.

When I initially identified the calculation flaw, I had only judgmentally sampled a few statements, finding one that appeared to be understated. Because of the potential significance of the problem, I was granted additional time to perform a detailed analysis of the extent of the problem. From a computer-generated random sample of 59 card holder accounts that had one or more statements with a cash advance transaction during the previous four months, I found that 27, or 45.8 percent, had been sent one or more statements with an understated APR. The total number of accounts with one or more cash advance transactions during the same period was nearly 50,000. Thus, well over 20,000 accounts were likely to have been impacted.

The above-sampled accounts were discussed at great length and tested in great detail in conjunction with the senior managers of the credit card operation. Yes, the top credit card management performed recalculations of our recalculations and performed some of their own independent recalculations. We all reached a consensus as to the existence of the flaw. Senior management of the credit card operation authorized the Application Programming Department to develop a correction to the APR calculation module, which amounted to a very simple change to one line of code. The revised code was successfully tested and was simply awaiting a final authorization from the general counsel of the financial institution. The general counsel was ultimately responsible for responding to all regulatory compliance violations.

Only at this point did the general counsel decide to perform his own tests. I learned that his testing consisted of a 15-minute phone call to a "friend" at the Federal Reserve Bank. During that call, the general counsel determined that the APR calculation flaw was actually correct, despite what I considered irrefutable evidence from the testing performed that I and the senior managers of the credit card operation I had performed. The general counsel responded in writing that the audit finding was flawed and even provided his own example. The Internal Audit director asked me to read the general counsel's response and draft a written "rebuttal" response. I found that the general counsel's response used the same logic as the flawed APR calculation module in the credit card application. I stated in my written rebuttal that the general counsel's example was flawed and submitted my response to the Internal Audit director. That was the last official contact I had regarding the issue. Normally, the Internal Audit director would obtain a final written response from the general counsel, but each time I inquired about it, I was told that one was pending. A written response was never submitted. I do not believe that my rebuttal response was ever submitted to the general counsel for consideration.

I do know that the issue was examined by the external auditors during their quarterly review of internal audit reports and that they briefly discussed the issue with the Audit Committee. Nothing further ever came of it, though, and the credit card application continued to create thousands of statements with what I considered to be flawed APR disclosures.

In discussions with my peers and senior managers of the credit card operation, we all believed that the issue was swept under the carpet by the general counsel and the Internal Audit director. The head of the credit card operation, who had been with the organization for many years, confided that I had done my job and that there was nothing further that could be done. At the time, I was relatively inexperienced and was mentally unprepared to deal with a situation that I felt very strongly about. These types of situations are not addressed in the curriculum of auditing classes. I had even considered communicating the issue outside of the organization, at the risk of my own job. Thankfully, I did not.

As it turned out, the issue dissolved over time. First of all, after about two years, a new credit card application was developed to replace the previous one. This replacement application was later eliminated after the organization was acquired in a merger and the credit card accounts were consolidated into the acquiring financial institution's credit card system. I was glad that I did not succumb to my young and eager intentions by taking the issue outside the chain of command.

In retrospect, this situation demonstrates a valuable lesson. The head of the credit card operation was correct that I had done my job. One of the responsibilities of internal auditors is to identify significant issues and submit them to senior management. It is the responsibility of senior management, the Audit Committee, and the board of directors to make decisions as to how to resolve the issues. If they choose to ignore significant issues, they do so at the risk of their jobs and professional reputations. Furthermore, they can be held legally liable for the ramifications of their actions or lack thereof. I suppose if the issue were related to matters of life and death of human beings, I would have to consider the moral and ethical aspects of the issue and whether I could

(continued)

CASE STUDY 14.3 (*continued*)

live with myself for not doing anything. I would have to consider the potential ramifications of whistle-blowing on my career, my family and friends, and my conscience. Many people who were aware of sensitive issues in the U.S. government have made the decision to contact news services to have the issues publicized. Early whistle-blowers were rewarded by being blacklisted and unable to secure employment. Although there are now laws protecting whistle-blowers to a certain extent, it is still a difficult proposition to do so.

As IS auditors, there is only a remote possibility that we may be faced with such a dilemma. However, it would behoove all of us to contemplate what we would do in such a situation before it happens. Although your final actions will depend on the actual situation, you will at least have developed a thought process and methodology for guiding your actions. It is to be hoped that you will make a decision that you can live with.

NOTE

1. *Journal of Accountancy* (January 1997): 14–15.

CHAPTER 15

Information Systems Project Management Audits[1]

New electronic products and services are being introduced into the marketplace at an increasing pace. Computers have evolved to the point where new applications can be created and implemented quickly, often before they have been thoroughly evaluated for control weaknesses. Because of the sheer number of new products and services companies are deploying, and because of limitations on the size of many auditing staffs, it is becoming increasingly difficult to find enough time and resources to perform effective audits of new systems and processes using traditional auditing methodologies. To adapt to this changing systems development environment, information systems (IS) auditors must adjust their approach.

As with any audit, a risk assessment should be one of the first steps to be completed when examining a new process. The risk assessment will help determine whether the process warrants expending a significant amount of audit resources on the project. The scope of the audit depends on the risk. But even for high-risk systems, the scope should be limited to testing the critical internal controls upon which the security of the process depends.

Throughout the development of any new process, IS auditors can provide expertise not only on internal control issues, but also on issues that ensure that systems and related policies and procedures can be performed efficiently and effectively and conform to applicable laws, regulations, and other standards to which management wishes to adhere. Depending on the scope of the audit, auditors can also confirm that the development, implementation, and hardware costs of the new process are properly recorded and reported in the financial statements. Auditors should also assess the adequacy of the overall project management. Project management oversight can stymie a project just as quickly as an internal control weakness or operational difficulty.

Many information systems development project management (ISPM) controls were formally developed during the early days of computers and are still applicable in today's IS environments. However, the number of cases in which these controls need to be applied has literally exploded, especially over the last 10 years. Virtually all organizations have become highly dependent on computer information systems to achieve their strategic business objectives. To maintain and enhance their competitive positions, these organizations must continue to maintain and upgrade their existing computer systems. They must also continue to develop and implement new systems. Over the last five years, many organizations have deployed new e-commerce products and services to remain competitive, often at significant costs. The Gartner Group predicts that global information technology (IT) spending will reach $3.3 trillion in 2002.[2] Furthermore, the total dollar amounts and transaction volumes processed by these systems are increasing at an exponential rate.

All large projects are faced with a myriad of potential risks. The project management body of knowledge is vast, and volumes have been written about project management. It is no wonder that project management is considered a separate profession.

Information systems project risks affect all areas of an organization, either directly or indirectly, and thus pertain to all components and objectives of the COSO (Committee of Sponsoring Organizations of the Treadway Commission) internal control model. Entire books have been written just on the subject of ISPM. Therefore, this chapter focuses on the major risks of IS development projects and briefly discusses important ISPM controls that auditors should be able to identify within their organizations. While this chapter is targeted more specifically at IS projects, the concepts presented can be applied to virtually any type of project within almost any organization.

PRIMARY INFORMATION SYSTEMS PROJECT RISKS

The chapter discusses these specific ISPM risks:

- IS project failure (complete or partial)
- Vendor goes out of business
- Poorly worded contracts or agreements
- External contractor risks
- Financial statement risks

Each of these risks is discussed in a separate section, with an emphasis on the IS project failure risk. Within each section, internal controls designed to mitigate the risks are presented.

PROJECT FAILURE

The primary risk of any IS development project is that of project failure. Failure can be total or, more commonly, partial. Partial failure includes completing the project late, over budget, with fewer features, or some combination of these.

In a 2000 survey of 1,375 North American IT professionals, the Gartner Group found that about 40 percent of IT projects do not produce their intended results. The study found that a canceled IT project lasted only 14 of the 27 weeks for which it was scheduled, caused organizations to spend an average of $1 million annually for unsatisfactory results, and caused IT professionals to spend 10 percent of their time on tasks that produced no business benefit. Project staff could predict project cancellation by six weeks, with team members knowing their efforts would be ultimately fruitless.[3]

Similarly, the Standish Group, an IT market research firm, found that only 16.2 percent of all computer software projects are completed on time and within budget; 52.7 percent are finished late, over budget, and with fewer features than promised; and 31.1 percent are canceled.[4] Here are some real-world examples of total and partial project failures:

- In 1993, after investing $49 million, the California Department of Motor Vehicles canceled an upgrade to its licensing systems after it learned that the project would actually cost $175 million.[5]
- In 1997, the Washington State Department of Licensing canceled a car and boat licensing system after spending $40 million.[6]
- In 1991, a consortium made up of Hilton Hotels, Marriott, Budget Rent-A-Car, and American Airlines canceled a joint reservation computer system after investing $165 million.[7]
- In 2000, the Executive of King County, Washington, requested $7 million to shut down a combined finance and payroll computer system project that had already cost the county $38 million. Completing the original project would have cost an additional $30 million. Only a partially operational payroll system was deployed.[8]
- A City of Seattle utilities billing computer system project began in June 1998. In January 1999, the estimated completion cost was $18 to $20 million and implementation was scheduled for February 2000. By September 1999, the estimated cost to complete the project was $26 million and project implementation was rescheduled for May 2000. By February 2001, the final cost estimate was $40.2 million. The system was finally implemented in April 2001.[9]

Numerous controls exist that can be implemented to help prevent these types of IS project failures. Some of the most important controls are listed below. Each is examined in detail since they are the focus of the chapter.

- Deployment of a standardized ISPM methodology
- Project oversight groups
- Training of project team members
- Change controls
- Early trademark searches
- A method of classifying organizational projects versus low-risk projects

Standardized Information Systems Project Management Methodology

Every organization should develop and implement a standardized ISPM methodology. An ISPM methodology is a major control that helps ensure that IS development projects are completed in a consistent, timely, efficient, and effective manner. It also helps prevent scope creep, or the tendency to keep adding additional features to a system during the design phase beyond that which was originally planned. Without a standard approach, IS projects are left under the direction of individual project managers. This may be acceptable and successful if the same person manages all IS projects and is sufficiently skilled in ISPM. However, in most organizations, ISPM duties are performed by a number of different people, each with a different background, philosophy, and ISPM style. If a standardized ISPM methodology is lacking, the risk of IS project failure, or at least inconsistent results, is significantly increased.

Many variations of ISPM models exist. Tukwila, Washington, based Boeing Employees' Credit Union (BECU) uses a classical ISPM model consisting of seven phases (see Exhibit 15.1). Each phase consists of several high-level tasks. Each task essentially can be viewed as a separate internal control. Some of the tasks seem obvious, but inadequate attention to the tasks can be disastrous to a project. Many organizations use standardized ISPM models similar to BECU's. But what varies extensively among organizations, and even among projects within organizations, is the implementation of the ISPM methodology. Regardless of the ISPM methodology used, poor project management implementation can doom a project within a very short time. Two of the more notable tasks of the ISPM model are choosing appropriate team members and performing quality reviews.

Selection of the appropriate team members is a critical control to help ensure that the project fulfills its intended purposes, on time, and within budget. Each

---

EXHIBIT 15.1 BECU IS PROJECT MANAGEMENT METHODOLOGY

I. Initiation
  A. Identify project sponsor
  B. Identify project manager
  C. Identify stakeholders
  D. Form project team
  E. Form project structure
  F. Develop scope
  G. Develop customer and business requirements
  H. Conduct initiation quality review

II. Analysis
  A. Research existing processes and tools
  B. Identify alternatives
  C. Evaluate alternatives

Exhibit 15.1 (*continued*)

       D. Recommend solution
       E. Update scope document
       F. Update requirements document
       G. Conduct analysis quality review
       H. Select vendor(s)

  III. Design
       A. Develop product design
       B. Develop integration plan
       C. Develop product communication plan
       D. Develop data conversion plan
       E. Complete project schedule
       F. Develop project budget
       G. Conduct design quality review
       H. Confirm go-ahead with project sponsor

  IV. Development
       A. Build products
       B. Acquire products
       C. Set up products
       D. Finalize process changes
       E. Develop product communication materials
       F. Conduct development quality review

  V. Test
       A. Develop test plans
       B. Obtain test resources
       C. Conduct testing
       D. Document test results
       E. Conduct testing quality review
       F. Confirm go-live date

  VI. Implementation
       A. Develop implementation plans
       B. Conduct user training
       C. Deliver product communication
       D. Convert data
       E. Conduct go-live setup
       F. Conduct acceptance testing
       G. Conduct readiness review
       H. Go live

  VII. Postimplementation Support
       A. Monitor processes and systems
       B. Resolve remaining issues
       C. Validate customer and business value driver achievement
       D. Evaluate project
       E. Turn over to sustaining operations

team member, including the IS project manager, should have the proper skill set and level of training to successfully perform his or her duties. In many cases, it may be necessary to hire external contractors or consultants to supplement the internal team roster.

The project should contain a quality review process to help ensure that each project phase is properly completed and documented. The quality review may be informal but should require some sort of management approval or acceptance. At BECU this step is conducted by a separate IS Quality Assurance Department.

While ISPM models provide a conceptual framework from which to conduct IS development projects, the steps within each phase do not occur in exact chronological order. Often, steps occur out of order due to delays and other events. Auditors must be aware of major delays and problems that may cause the project to be delayed by a significant amount of time or to be significantly over budget. When identified by an auditor, major delays and problems should already be addressed by the project manager if internal controls are functioning properly. If not, the auditor should bring the problems to the attention of the project manager immediately in writing.

Project Oversight Groups

Project oversight groups such as steering committees and applicable project subcommittees are often overlooked. The 2000 Gartner Group survey found that 61 percent of projects lacked a supervisor charged with ongoing evaluation of a project's viability and, where appropriate, the timely termination and reassignment of staff to other activities.[10] Project oversight groups perform valuable monitoring functions to help determine when projects are falling behind or are going over budget. They are responsible for implementing measures to rectify project problems in a timely manner. Such measures include retention and replacement of key project personnel. In the King County, Washington, example cited earlier, project failure was attributed to turnover in several key positions and poor planning and controls.[11]

Training of Project Team Members

The 2000 Gartner Group survey stated that 60 percent of organizations did not offer project management training.[12] Without adequate project management training, internal team members will not be as productive as desired and can actually be a detriment to their projects. One potential source of project management training is the Project Management Institute (PMI), an international organization devoted exclusively to the field of project management. The PMI provides training, education, networking, and other resources related to the project management field, and sponsors two related professional certifications (see Exhibit 15.2 for more details). The IS project budget should also provide adequate funding for technical training, especially for technical staff who may be implementing a new oper-

---

EXHIBIT 15.2   PROJECT MANAGEMENT INSTITUTE

Many professional associations can provide project management information. However, the Project Management Institute (PMI) is the only one devoted exclusively to the field of project management. The PMI, which is headquartered near Philadelphia, was founded in 1969 and has grown to over 86,000 members in 45 countries worldwide. It has over 170 professional chapters and nine student chapters. The PMI provides training, education, networking, and other activities related to the project management field. It also sponsors the Project Management Professional (PMP) designation. The PMP requirements include experience, education, following a code of ethics, and passing a 200-question test covering five areas of knowledge: initiating processes, planning processes, executing processes, controlling processes, and closing processes. In 2002, the PMI began offering a Certified Associate in Project Management (CAPM) designation. Practitioners who have demonstrated fundamental project management knowledge and experience by supporting projects using project management tools, techniques, and methodologies are eligible for this designation. See *www.pmi.org* for additional information.

---

ating system or database management system or updated versions of existing systems.

Since there is no guarantee that external contractors, consultants, and vendor representatives are adequately trained, project managers should request that external personnel provide evidence of their qualifications prior to engaging them. Such qualifications should include adequate work experience, education, and applicable certifications.

Change Controls

Upon completion of testing, system access controls should exist to ensure that the transfer of approved software programs into the production environment is performed by an area independent of the software development group. This segregation of duties helps ensure that programmers do not introduce unauthorized programs and changes into the production environment. Change controls are not unique to new IS development projects. In fact, routine procedures should already exist to ensure that all new and updated software programs are subjected to quality reviews and that programmers do not move new and updated programs into the production environment.

Early Trademark Searches

Project managers should ensure that any necessary trademark searches and applications are performed early in a project. Failure to secure a trademark could cause project delays and force marketing areas to spend excessive funds to re-create advertisements and other promotional materials. Case study 15.1 describes just such a problem.

CASE STUDY 15.1

Trademark Snafu

A financial institution was eagerly anticipating the rollout of a new automated service to its customers. The project team had seemingly completed all necessary steps. The information systems had been programmed and tested, operational procedures were developed, a name had been selected for the process, marketing and promotional literature had been designed, the vendor contract had been executed, and vendor processes and procedures had been tested. All that was left was to schedule the printing of promotional and advertising literature. Near the end of the project, the Marketing Department decided to perform a trademark search on the selected name, although no competitors were known to use the same name.

Trademark searches in the United States are simply a matter of searching the database of names maintained by the Patent and Trademark Office (PTO) of the U.S. Department of Commerce. But before a trademark can be officially registered, a trademark application must be completed and submitted to the PTO. If the application meets the minimum requirements, a filing date and serial number are assigned. About four months after filing, an examining attorney at the PTO reviews the application to determine whether the trademark is already registered under another owner. If the examining attorney believes that the trademark is already registered or that there could be confusion between the applicant's trademark and a registered trademark, the application is suspended and a notification is sent to the applicant. The applicant can either apply for a different trademark or submit a letter describing how the trademark is different from the one already registered. A second review is performed, and the examining attorney may accept the application or deny it again.

Upon acceptance, the trademark on the application is published in the *Official Gazette*, a weekly PTO publication. Any party who believes that the new trademark may damage or infringe on their position has 30 days to file an opposition to the registration. Any opposition is heard before the Trademark Trial and Appeal Board. If no opposition is encountered, and the applicant has already been using the trademark in commerce, the PTO issues a trademark registration certificate. If the applicant has not yet used the trademark in commerce but has a bona fide intention to use it, the PTO issues a Notice of Allowance. The applicant has six months from the date the Notice of Allowance was issued to submit a Statement of Use, which declares that the applicant has used the trademark in commerce, or to request a six-month Extension of Time to File a Statement of Use. Upon approval of the Statement of Use, a registration certificate is issued.

Clearly the trademarking process is quite lengthy. Therefore, it should begin early in the development of any new product or service. Unfortunately for the financial institution in this example, the trademark application process revealed that the trademark name applied for was already registered to another financial institution. As a result, another name had to be selected and a new trademark application had to be submitted. Because the original trademark application was submitted late in the project and was rejected, rollout of the new service was delayed by several months while a new name was selected and the examining attorney at the PTO made an initial determination of the trademanrk's viability.

As part of our testing of the development of any new product or service, ensure that the organization has submitted a trademark application very early in the project to allow time to react in the event the original name has been used. The organization may even choose to apply for one or two alternate names in case the first one is denied.

The following additional controls and project milestones should be examined, where applicable, during reviews of the development and implementation of new products and services to help prevent oversights. The order in which the steps occur can be changed to suit individual project variations. For each step of the project, management approval and authorization should be documented before proceeding further. In addition, throughout the project, appropriate levels of management and staff should be kept informed of the progress of the project and the potential impact to their respective areas.

- Management should formulate the objectives of the new product or service. Then a preliminary market analysis should be performed to determine possible product acceptance. A detailed assessment of the possible risks and returns should also be prepared.
- The financial and operational feasibility of the proposed product or service should be researched, including financial resources necessary to develop and implement the product or service, staffing requirements, technical requirements, time-to-market estimates, and equipment requirements. Based on the outcome of the research, necessary adjustments to the product or service should be made, or the project should be killed.
- A detailed market analysis of customer wants and needs for the product or service should be prepared. An analysis of competing products and services should also be performed. All areas of the organization should be consulted to secure their early acceptance of the development of the product or service. The financial and operational feasibility should be revised based on current information.
- A project leader should be assigned, and a project team of qualified staff from all significantly impacted areas of the organization should be selected. The responsibilities of the project team should be defined. Project timelines and milestones should be prepared.
- Any legal and regulatory issues should be researched and resolved, and applications for any patents and trademarks should be submitted. Contracts with vendors should be drafted, reviewed by legal counsel, and executed by the appropriate level of management. If management has decided to purchase the services of an outside vendor or service organization, com-

(continued)

petitive bids should be solicited. Each bid should be carefully reviewed and documented. Audited financial statements and service auditor reports (if applicable) for each vendor and service organization should be reviewed.

- The information systems supporting the product or service should be designed. Design should allow for future expansion. Other standard information systems design controls should be incorporated, including system edits to help reduce data input errors, segregation of duties, audit trails, logical security controls to prevent and detect unauthorized access to systems or compromise of information (e.g., encryption controls, password length, password expiration, access restrictions, logging and review of unusual activity), physical security to protect hardware and data, and disaster recovery plans and testing. Programming should commence based on the approved designs.

- Upon completion of programming, testing procedures should be performed to ensure that all operational, financial, and control processes are functioning properly.

- Training programs should be designed so that all impacted staff members are adequately trained prior to system implementation.

- End users and other staff impacted by the project should be surveyed shortly after implementation to determine whether any significant operational or control issues materialized during or after implementation. If so, steps should be taken to resolve the issues and to help ensure that they are avoided in future projects. Another post-implementation review should be performed about three to six months after the initial postimplementation review.

In addition to these steps, the traditional controls critical in the mainframe environment should continue to be assessed, where applicable. Programs must be adequately tested and documented. For programs developed in-house, access control software must restrict transfer of programs from the development and testing environment to the production environment so that the changes can be performed only by change control personnel. Computer operations personnel should not have access to production programs. Access to computer hardware, output files, and printouts should be adequately restricted to prevent tampering and unauthorized access to restricted information. Information systems auditors involved in systems development projects should be aware of these basic segregation-of-duties controls.

Management of all organizations should proactively include IS auditors on their project teams. The auditors should function primarily as observers, advisors, facilitators, and consultants on the design of internal controls. In this role, IS auditors can help ensure that the project team is aware of all major risks, that the risks are being adequately addressed through the design of automated controls and manual control procedures, and that any significant internal control issues are communicated in a constructive manner to the project team and appropriate levels of management. The final design and implementation of the new process or system should remain the responsibility of the project team and management of the organization. Case study 15.2 describes a major project where management included an IS auditor on the team.

CASE STUDY 15.2

A Well-Managed Project

A project team was assembled at a large bank with the responsibility of consolidating operations at data processing centers in three states into one large regional data processing center. The highly experienced project manager requested that a member of the IS audit staff be included on the project team. Thus I was added to the team, which consisted of over 40 managers and directors from all three states. My role was to monitor the progress of the project by attending all meetings and reviewing all correspondence. I provided internal audit management with weekly progress reports and a description of any potentially significant issues. Although no significant control issues materialized during the 12-month project, the project team was concerned about whether an additional large check-processing machine compatible with existing systems could be secured by the time the data center consolidation was completed. At the time, the manufacturer was designing a new model, so no new machines were being manufactured. As a result, demand for any used or even leased machines was high, making their availability very scarce. In the end, the necessary machine was secured so that operations were not impacted at the time of conversion. Overall, due to the experience and expertise of the project team and the project leader, the project was completed successfully.

Organizational Projects versus Low-Risk Projects

Some projects may be too low risk to be recognized as organizational projects and to warrant applying a formal ISPM methodology to them. Organizations should develop criteria to help define when a new project should be officially recognized as an organizational project. The estimated project budget is the most common criteria. The dollar amount will vary depending on the size of the organization. Smaller organizations may recognize new projects with estimated budgets of $50,000 while large organizations may require a budget of $1 million or more. But even in large organizations, a process should exist to divide and further subdivide the overall project budget among the applicable subsidiaries and operating units so that proper accountability is maintained.

Project duration is another potential project classification criteria. Projects that must be completed within two months may not have the luxury of formally applying the standardized ISPM methodology, even if they have large budgets. These types of projects may not technically be "organizational," but they can still be high risk. For these types of projects, the project manager can still apply many of the ISPM steps, while documenting only the most critical ones (e.g., management approval of large expenditures, and management acceptance of final testing results).

Exhibit 15.3 provides information about rapid project implementation techniques developed by Murrell G. Shields.[13]

EXHIBIT 15.3   RAPID PROJECT IMPLEMENTATION TECHNIQUES

In his book *E-Business and ERP: Rapid Implementation and Project Planning*, Murrell G. Shields, describes several rapid project implementation techniques which he applies to e-business and enterprise resource planning (ERP) development projects.[14] He contends that it is possible to implement ERP products in a third or less of the time than it has taken in the past, yet in a way that better manages the risks associated with these products. The author presents the following key success factors for rapid implementations:

   a. Make quick decisions.
   b. Make technology infrastructure available in day 1.
   c. Have small, cross-functional project teams.
   d. Do not start the clock until the team is ready.
   e. Use *time boxing* and scope management.
   f. Start with preconfigured versions of the software.
   g. Select the right package.
   h. Pick the right consultants.
   i. Take a process-driven approach.
   j. Conduct concurrent/parallel activities.
   k. Manage for speed.

Shields defines *time boxing* as deciding, up front, how long the project will be allowed to take and managing the scope of the project to get it done in that time frame. He compares time boxing to Pareto's 80/20 rule. In this case, implementing the most useful 20 percent of a package's functions can contribute toward rapid implementation, with the remaining functions being implemented at a later time. Shields provides additional ideas that contribute to rapid project implementation, including:

- To reap major benefits requires changes in people, processes, and technology.
- Top management must be fully supportive.
- Capture and communicate lessons learned from the project.
- Evaluate the financial stability of the vendor.
- Select a vendor with good support, system documentation, and data conversion tools.
- Perform reference checks as part of due diligence and risk management.
- There is a project trade-off among time, resources, and scope.
- An experienced project manager is a key for successful rapid implementation.
- Projects usually fail because of people problems, so select a team of the right people from applicable cross-functional areas, not just IT, then manage the soft issues.
- A 1998 Deloitte & Touche survey cited the top four barriers to project success: resistance to change, inadequate sponsorship, unrealistic expectations, and poor project management.

EXHIBIT 15.3 (*continued*)

- Use consultants from vendor and external organizations where necessary to supplement the project team.
- Change management levers consist of communication, involvement, training, and job design.
- Make implementations business driven and process driven
- Eliminate non-value-added steps, design for flexibility, and leverage the capabilities of the package.
- Having adequate bandwidth after system implementation is a common oversight.
- Ten project accelerators are: rapid methodology, process models, preconfigured software, just-in-time core team training, hosted applications, user procedures, online support, end user training, configuration support, and automated interfaces.

Unfortunately, Shields does not provide many ideas for the inclusion of logical security controls in a rapid project implementation, does not go into much detail regarding project risk management, and does not emphasize contracts and how a poorly written contract will impede and potentially stop the progress of a project, or that contracts should not be signed until all essential design requirements have been clearly documented and accepted by the vendor. (See Part III and Chapter 6 for more information about vendor contracts). There is obviously a tradeoff between project implementation speed and the inclusion of adequate security controls and proper contract management. The project team must assess the risks of not including certain logical security controls and of accepting a less than optimal contract.

VENDOR GOES OUT OF BUSINESS

As evidenced by the recent dot-com bust, there are no guarantees that prospective vendors will remain in business. If a vendor goes out of business or significantly reduces staff, the success of any IS development project will be in jeopardy. Therefore, due diligence is an important control that organization management should perform prior to expending significant IS resources and prior to signing any contracts or agreements. After obtaining competitive bids, due diligence efforts should include:

- Reviewing audited financial statements of vendors for the last two or more years (see Chapter 6 for more details).
- Contacting current and former clients to assess customer satisfaction.
- Reviewing vendor privacy policies displayed on their websites.
- For organizations which are external service providers or IS security vendors, reviewing the last two or more SAS 70s or other applicable IS secu-

rity certification results (e.g., TruSecure, CPA SysTrust, CPA WebTrust, BBBOnline, TRUSTe). See Chapter 5 for more details on each of these types of audits and certifications.

Outsourced technology services create significant enough risks to financial institutions that the Federal Financial Institutions Examination Council (FFIEC) issued a guidance letter to members, including banks, thrifts, and credit unions, on November 28, 2000. The letter, entitled "Risk Management of Outsourced Technology Services," provides a general overview of risk management controls. It also includes a seven-page appendix identifying specific controls and procedures that financial institutions should consider. Organizations in other industries can easily apply these controls. Auditors should review this letter and confirm that applicable internal controls are being applied within their organization. The letter can be obtained at the FFIEC website (*www.ffiec.gov*).

POORLY WORDED CONTRACTS OR AGREEMENTS

Contracts and agreements play a critical role in the development and ongoing success of information systems. Optimally, contracts and agreements should be finalized before significant IS project resources have been expended. A formal contract management process within the organization will help ensure that standard provisions are included in all IS contracts and that they have been reviewed by legal counsel. Like project management, contract management is actually a separate field with its own vast body of knowledge, as evidenced by the many attorneys who specialize in the field. However, it is important to highlight a few critical provisions which should be contained within all software license, maintenance, and support agreements. They include:

- The exact amounts of software license, maintenance, and support fees and payment terms.
- Service levels to be provided by the vendor (e.g., 24/7 availability for critical problems; 10/5 for noncritical ones). These provisions are often referred to as service-level agreements. They may be a separate agreement or contained within the maintenance and support agreement.
- Confidentiality/nondisclosure statement providing recourse against the vendor company in the event of theft or divulging of proprietary information or other information privacy breaches. This statement is usually included within the master agreement or contract.
- A section requiring the current version of the application source code to be held in escrow at an independent third party. This section should specify the conditions under which the source code will be released to the client (e.g., vendor ceases operations, vendor breaches contract).

Chapter 6 contains additional details regarding vendor contracts.

EXTERNAL CONTRACTOR RISKS

External consultants, contractors, and vendor representatives working on-site expose organizations to increased risks of unauthorized system access, unauthorized expense payments, theft of intellectual property, and information privacy violations. These contractors are often placed in high-profile ISPM positions and other positions of high trust. Some staff-level employees may perceive them as having management authority and may unwittingly perform duties that are not authorized by organization management. They also often have physical access to sensitive areas of the contracting organization.

In larger organizations, the problem is magnified. Typically a large number of IS projects are in process at any time. Often a steady stream of external consultants, contractors, and vendors revolves through the IS department, performing various IS project duties. In this type of environment, strangers are often taken for granted as just another external contractor. Five controls can help mitigate external contractor risks:

1. Expenditures should follow the contracting organization's standard accounts payable process, which includes requiring signed authorization by organization management for expenses and researching vendors for legitimacy and potential conflicts of interest. Since contractors are not employees, they should not be allowed to act as agents of the organization or otherwise contractually obligate the organization.
2. The contractor's direct report should provide a current list of individual contractors who are deployed at organization locations to the Human Resources Department. The list should include for each person: full name; name of their direct report within the organization; contact information (phone number, e-mail address); the project or projects being worked on; and the start and end dates at each organization location. This list should be made available to all staff via e-mail and/or intranet in the event a particular contractor's presence or purpose is questioned.
3. Each individual contractor, consultant, or vendor representative who is deployed at any of the contracting organization's locations should sign a confidentiality/nondisclosure agreement, even if the vendor company has already signed one. The reason is that on-site personnel may come into contact with private information unrelated to the project. Thus, they must be held individually accountable for their actions. This agreement should state, among many potential legal limitations, that during the course of their contractual duties they will not divulge any information they develop, observe, or otherwise become aware of to any outside parties without written permission from the contracting organization's management. The agreements should be included as part of the project documentation or maintained within the Human Resources Department.
4. Every outside person who is going to be on-site for an extended period of time (e.g., more than one week) should be provided a one- to two-hour

training session on evacuation routes and procedures during fires and disasters, location of first aid and other safety equipment, and whom to contact in the event unauthorized activities by the client organization's employees or other contractors are observed. Such training serves to help protect the safety of contractor personnel.

5. As always, the Human Resources Department should be aware of the types of activities and durations of stays of external personnel to reduce the risk of them claiming they are actually acting as employees of the organization.

FINANCIAL STATEMENT RISKS

Information systems projects present several financial statement risks due to the relatively large dollar budgets associated with them. Obviously, project cost overruns rank at the top of the list. Two additional risks warrant discussion.

The risk of unauthorized expenses from external contractors has been mentioned. The same risk exists for internal IS employees. For example, a former Starbuck's IS employee was charged with embezzling $3.7 million by forging her supervisor's signature on a fictitious consulting services agreement. This enabled her to begin drawing funds to pay over 100 invoices she created in the name of the fictitious business for services that were never rendered.[15]

A lesser-known generally accepted accounting principle is AICPA Statement of Position (SOP) 98-1 entitled "Accounting for Costs of Computer Software Developed or Obtained for Internal Use." SOP 98-1, which was issued on March 4, 1998, specifies various costs that should be capitalized and amortized over the estimated useful life of an internal-use system. Typically, the most difficult of these costs to measure is the hours spent by internal staff on software development. The reasons are that many developers abhor keeping track of the hours they spend on projects, and the system used to track the hours is inadequate.

These controls can help mitigate the aforementioned financial statement risks:

- General ledger entries for IS project expenses should be recorded with enough detail so that reports comparing all applicable IS project expenses to all budgeted expenses can be prepared in a timely and accurate manner for review by the IS steering committee and other project oversight groups. Project expenses should include payments to IS project vendors for items such as contractor hours for labor and internal staff training, software license fees, software maintenance and support fees, and on-site contractor travel costs (airfare, hotel, meals, rental cars, taxi, "other"). This type of monitoring activity should occur on a monthly or more frequent basis.
- Expenditures should follow the contracting organization's standard accounts payable process, which includes requiring signed authorization by organization management for expenses and researching vendors for legitimacy and potential conflicts of interest.

- An accurate process should exist for recording all hours spent by internal staff on software development as well as recording all other software development costs.[16] Optimally an automated time-keeping application should exist, and developers should be required to enter the applicable hours they spend on various software development projects on a regular basis. The Accounting Department should have procedures to properly classify these and other IS project expenses on the financial statements.

Chapter 6 contains additional information regarding the accounting treatment of computer hardware and software.

CONCLUSION

The body of knowledge pertaining to IS project management is so vast that this chapter can only provide a primer on the subject. My goal was to provide information to enable auditors to identify control weaknesses that could lead to significant failures in IS development projects. Such failures weaken an organization's ability to achieve its strategic business objectives and can eventually lead to its total demise. Auditors are responsible for reporting significant weaknesses to applicable organization management and recommending solutions. Because IS project management is both an art and a science, it will always be a challenge to maintain adequate controls over major IS projects. Just a few poor IS project management decisions can negate even the best-intentioned internal controls. Ultimately, it is the organization's senior management who is responsible for ensuring that major IS projects are being completed on time and within budget on a consistent basis.

This chapter concludes with two case studies. In case study 15.3, a project audit uncovered a significant security weakness. In case study 15.4, an audit identified significant project management deficiencies.

CASE STUDY 15.3

Project Audit Identifies Security Weaknesses

During a consulting audit of a PeopleSoft financial accounting and accounts payable project implementation, my objective was to assess the adequacy of the logical security controls over the entire system, including the PeopleSoft application, Oracle database management system (DBMS), and the Unix operating system. Each was administered by different individuals. I requested a meeting with the project team and each of the three system administrators near the end of the testing phase of the project so that any logical security deficien-

(continued)

CASE STUDY 15.3 (*continued*)

cies identified could be resolved prior to implementation. The meeting room was to be equipped with a workstation that could access the development server for testing purposes.

At the start of the meeting, I had the PeopleSoft system administrator log-on and began questioning her about general logical security controls. It quickly became evident she was very inexperienced with the application's logical security controls. The database administrator (DBA) took over and was able to demonstrate the existence of various logical security controls, most of which were actually controlled by the DBMS. For example, he was able to demonstrate that the file containing the encrypted passwords of the application users was located within the DBMS. We did this by having him create a test user ID and password. Upon viewing the contents of the file containing the passwords, we were able to view the test user ID but the password appeared only as a fixed-length hash and did not appear to be easily discernible.

Interestingly, the Unix security administrator was observing the DBA and interjecting how various Unix production job scripts needed to include the DBMS superuser password in order to access confidential areas. The DBA concurred and stated that the Unix security administrator technically had more power than the DBA since he could view Unix production job scripts and determine the DBMS superuser password, then access the DBMS. Furthermore, because these job scripts contained hard-coded DBMS passwords, a password expiration control could not be implemented for the DBMS superuser ID. Doing so would cause production jobs to terminate without completing processing.

I recommended that a variable field reference be inserted in each production job script containing a hard-coded password. In this way, the password could be changed in one location without having to locate the password in multiple production job scripts. The Unix security administrator also needed to create a tickler to remind him to change the password in the variable reference field every 60 days, since the DBMS did not have an automatic password expiration feature.

This case demonstrates how an effective audit test can be performed in a very short meeting so long as key people are present.

CASE STUDY 15.4

Poorly Managed Applications Development Department

During a consulting audit of a department that included about eight applications developers and eight database administrators, I began by requesting from the management team a variety of documents that would be considered management tools. These included a department charter or mission statement, a summary or list of significant accomplishments during the last six to 12 months, an internal procedures manual, written standards for application programming code and database-stored procedures, an inventory list of all applications that contained custom programming code and databases that contained custom-stored procedures, log of hours spent by developers and DBAs on various projects, job descriptions, and individual and department goals required to receive annual incentive bonuses.

I found that there was no mission statement for the applications developers and only a partially completed mission for the DBAs; there was no list of accomplishments (existing application fixes, new applications developed, database stored procedures completed, new departmental efficiencies, etc.); no internal procedures manual; unwritten standards for programs and stored procedures; no inventory lists of applications with custom code or databases with custom-stored procedures; and no log of hours spent by staff on various projects. Furthermore, the incentive goals were an atrocity. Some were so poorly worded that all the person had to do was attend a training conference to attain the maximum bonus. Others were not approved by senior management as required, while some were not approved until November (they should have been approved by March). Nearly all employees in the department had to achieve only one goal, although the incentive bonus plan specified three to five goals are required. One manager put it succinctly; "I know we are extremely busy all the time, but we just can't prove it."

Obviously, I recommended the implementation of all the controls mentioned above so that management could be able to monitor staff productivity. Since management controls were so significantly lacking, the need to perform detailed testing of programming code and database stored procedures was considerably reduced; there were no written standards to audit against. The few programs and stored procedures sampled were found to be reasonably documented and tested. Once the basic management controls have been implemented, more extensive testing of programs and stored procedures will be conducted.

NOTES

1. Parts of this chapter have been adapted from Jack Champlain, "IT Project Management Risks and Controls," *The Audit Report* (Volume 11, Issue 1, 2002): 14–18.
2. "Research Shows High Failure Rate on IT Projects," *Journal of Accountancy* (February 2001): 24.
3. Roberto Sanchez, "Software Projects Often Don't Compute," *Seattle Times* (June 12, 2000): B1, B4.
4. Ibid.
5. Ibid.
6. Ibid.
7. Ibid.
8. Roberto Sanchez, "Sims: $7 Million to Pull Plug," *Seattle Times* (June 23, 2000): B1,B4.
9. *www.cityofseattle.net/audit/00-CCSS_Security.pdf.*
10. "Research Shows."
11. Sanchez, "Sims."

12. "Research Shows."
13. Murrell G. Shields, *E-Business and ERP, Rapid Implementation and Project Planning* (New York: John Wiley & Sons, 2001).
14. Shields, *E-Business and ERP*.
15. Joshua Robin, "Is Packed House Evidence of Illness or Crime?" *Seattle Times* (October 3, 2000): A1, A14.

CHAPTER 16

Conclusion

This book has attempted to view information systems (IS) auditing from a practical viewpoint, applying many existing concepts to a variety of real-world situations, thereby providing readers with useful examples of what they might expect to encounter in audits that they perform or oversee. There have been many excellent books written on the subject of IS auditing that cover the concepts in this book plus many others in much greater detail. This book is designed to provide readers with information, suggestions, and examples of real-world IS issues that I have encountered in the business world and to identify issues that are pertinent within the IS auditing field.

The previous chapters have discussed many important IS auditing concepts that are critical to performing effective audits as we move further into the new millennium. These include the basics of computing systems; identification and creation of computing systems inventories; a generic IS audit program; IS policies, standards, and guidelines; auditing of service organizations, including their financial stability and contracts; accounting treatment of computer equipment and hardware; physical and logical security controls; IS operations; control self-assessment (CSA); encryption and cryptographic controls; computer-assisted audit techniques; computer viruses; software piracy; computer forensics; electronic commerce; auditing system development projects; Internet security; and the humanistic aspects of contemporary IS auditing.

The IS auditing theories, checklists, case studies, exhibits, references, and other information discussed in this book by no means encompass the entire body of knowledge surrounding the field of IS auditing, nor are they meant to be presented in scientific detail. They represent a microcosm of the IS auditing universe and are intended to be a primer on the realities of IS auditing. They are general by design and are intended to stimulate readers' curiosity as to whether all significant IS-related internal control issues have been addressed by their organizations. The concepts are also intended to help readers think about creative approaches to addressing new and traditional risks that their organizations are facing as the technology age rolls on. It is hoped that readers will share their newfound knowledge, thereby helping to advance the body of knowledge encompassed by IS auditing. One final intention is that readers will realize that auditing is a profession that has a wealth of highly skilled and knowledgeable individuals and resources available for the taking. All one has to do is take the initiative and begin the fascinating and rewarding journey through the profession of helping organizations control the risks posed by the never-ending supply of new IS technologies being introduced in the marketplace. In fact, one of the biggest challenges IS auditors face is keeping knowledge current with rapidly changing technology while still monitoring the controls and security over existing technologies.

NEW TECHNOLOGIES

In 1998, when the first edition of this book was published, the broadband Internet-in-the-Sky network of over 840 satellites envisioned by the Teledesic LLC of Bellevue, Washington, seemed a certainty. But by mid-2002, according to their website (*www.teledesic.com*), the concept called for a total of only 30 satellites, with an initial launch of 12. Service is slated to begin in 2005. The reduced number of satellites is undoubtedly due in part to the economic downturn, the dot-com bust, and subsequent lack of additional venture capital. It remains to be seen whether primary investors such as Bill Gates, Craig McCaw, and the Boeing Corporation will be successful with their $9 billion–plus investment and whether it will ever reach its originally planned constellation of interlinked medium-Earth orbit, low-cost satellites that can provide true global access to a broad range of telecommunications services such as computer networking, broadband Internet access, interactive multimedia and high-quality voice. If successful, this technology will present some interesting risks, including eavesdropping or intentional disruption of the data transmitted throughout the network. It also seems possible that hackers could wrest control of the satellites and alter or terminate their orbits.

A simpler technology holds more immediate promise. Microsoft is researching password technology whereby users click on a number of points within a screen of images. The points correspond to pixels, which are then converted into a random number that is stored in the computer. Users only have to remember where on the images they clicked and in what sequence. They will essentially be creating a 20- or more character password without having to remember it. This technology sounds promising, but auditors must be alert to obvious potential risks, such as whether or not the file containing the 20-character passwords is encrypted and whether the passwords are encrypted while in transit across networks or the Internet.[1]

Biometric technologies are gaining in reliability and costs have come down. Therefore, applications of biometric technologies to access controls that help prevent fraud and help ensure security are becoming more commonplace. One credit union is using hand-image verification in conjunction with a personal identification number to provide unescorted access to safe deposit boxes. Similar technologies are becoming available for automatic teller machines, airport security devices, driver's licenses, and state-issued identification cards.[2] The National

Aeronautics and Space Administration has been using an Internet outsourcing service from eTrue, Inc., which authenticates users for both Web and local network log-on through multiple biometrics, such as face and fingerprint verification.[3] Iris recognition systems such as those developed by Iridian Technologies (*www.iridiantech.com*) have been used in prisons and airports. Facial recognition is also becoming a reality now that the public is more open to deploying such technology for passive surveillance and possibly a national identification card system.[4] The International Biometric Group, a biometric consulting group, estimates that sales will grow from $58 million in 1999 to $594 million in 2003, with 65 percent of the market being in the United States.[5] Since this prediction was written prior to the events of September 11, 2001, I suspect that demand for biometric security devices will increase even more rapidly.

While biometric controls will likely replace or at least supplement passwords and additional controls, they, too, can be circumvented. A Japanese researcher recently found that he could create fake fingers from gelatin and fool fingerprint readers an average of 80 percent of the time.[6] Perhaps a more critical concern would be theft of the electronic "prints" of innocent people and subsequent usage of the information to steal identities. Therefore, IS auditors will need to be alert to the limitations of the biometrics that they encounter in their organizations.

Nanoscience, which is the study of materials smaller than 100 nanometers (1/10th the width of a human hair), has come to the forefront of technology circles within the last year. One application of the technology is to create computer circuits based on single molecules. In August 2001, IBM reported that its researchers had built a logic circuit that can perform processing functions using tiny cylindrical structures, called carbon nanotubes, as semiconductors. The nanotubes are about 100,000 times thinner than a human hair, about 10 atoms across, and about 500 times narrower than current silicon processors. This nanotechnology could render the existing silicon-based semiconductors obsolete. At the current rate of progress, silicon-based chips are projected to have a 10- to 15-year life cycle because it will no longer be possible to make them smaller, thereby limiting improvements in chip size and speed.[7]

In fact, nanotechnology has such great potential, it could rival and eventually exceed the human brain in processing and learning power. Nanoscience could also lead to other unexpected properties, such as lightweight breathable fabrics that stop bullets.[8] Even more mind-boggling, in September 2001 physicists in Denmark made two samples of trillions of atoms that interact at a distance. This breakthrough could lead to real-life quantum communications systems and computers, even teleportation.[9]

But nanotechnology is not without its risks. Stephen Hawking, the world-renowned physicist, projects that computers could develop intelligence and potentially take over the world, given enough time. This is because, in contrast to our own intellects, computer performance has been doubling every 18 months. Hawking suggests that one solution to combat this threat would be to use genetic engineering to increase the complexity of human DNA and improve human beings.[10] With regard to IS auditing, the general risks and controls will be the same so long as nano-based computers function on the binary system. However, the almost incomprehensible speed and beyond-microscopic size of the individual processors will undoubtedly present risks that we can not even imagine. It will be up to future IS auditors to help create controls that can help mitigate these new risks.

CONSTANT RISKS

As I mentioned in the introduction, terrorism has redefined the way most of us view risk. We must never forget what happened on September 11, 2001, and we must implement controls to help our organizations and our government prevent such atrocities from ever happening again.

But we must not forget about the traditional weaknesses and challenges that we face on a daily basis. In its popularly quoted but nonscientific 2002 Computer Crime and Security Survey of practitioners in a variety of U.S. corporations, government agencies, financial institutions, and universities, the Computer Security Institute (CSI) found that 223 of the 503 respondents were willing and able to quantify their computer crime losses at $456 million. The actual loss figure within the United States is most certainly many orders of magnitude larger since many organizations are reluctant to share loss information. The most common loss categories cited by CSI were theft of proprietary information ($171 million), financial fraud ($116 million), insider abuse of Internet access ($50 million), and viruses ($50 million).

While the CSI survey references insider abuse of Internet access, insider abuse is a farther-reaching problem. There have been many incidents of insiders causing astronomical harm, some even jeopardizing the security of the United States. The following cases are just a sampling of many cases of insider abuse.

- Robert Hanssen, a FBI agent with high security clearance, was one of the most damaging spies in U.S. history. Hanssen was convicted of espionage by spying for Russia for 22 years. Hanssen said that security was so lax at FBI headquarters that he never worried about being searched. He combed the FBI's computer system to obtain and disseminate over 6,000 classified documents and even to check whether he was under suspicion. He was quoted as saying "Any clerk in the bureau could come up with stuff on that system. It was pathetic." The FBI reportedly canceled a classified computer system fearing Hanssen, a skilled computer programmer, might have planted malicious code or a back door into the system.[11]
- John Rusnak, a once-promising currency trader for the U.S. branch of Allied Irish Banks, tried to conceal an estimated $691 million in trading losses in 2001 while simultaneously receiving bonuses of $100,000 to $200,000 on top of his $85,000 salary. This case closely mirrors that of Nick Leason, who lost over $1.4 billion and caused the collapse of England's Barings Bank in 1995.[12]

- Frank Gruttadauria, a former Lehman Brothers Holdings, Inc., stockbroker manager, admitted in 2002 to bilking investors out of $277 million over the past 15 years. He simply shifted money from one account to another, systematically looting each one.[13]
- Timothy Lloyd, a former New Jersey computer programmer for Omega Engineering Corporation, was convicted in May 2000 of causing about $12 million in damages. Prior to being fired in 1996, Lloyd planted a logic bomb that erased all Omega's contracts and the proprietary software used by the company's manufacturing tools. One Omega manager said that it would "never recover." Lloyd's actions also caused the layoff of 80 employees.[14]
- Bill Conley, former president of U.S. Computer Corporation of Redmond, Washington, pled guilty to federal wire-fraud charges and agreed to pay Hewlett-Packard (HP) $1.5 million after admitting he had paid an HP employee to reveal competitors' bids on used computer servers, thereby enabling him to buy the equipment by submitting slightly higher bids.[15]
- Five former security employees for Nordstrom were charged with stealing $140,000 by falsifying receipts and returns for cash at out-of-state stores.[16]
- Two former Lucent Technologies scientists, Hai Lin and Kai Xu, and an accomplice, Yong-Qing Cheng, were charged with stealing trade secrets from Lucent and selling them for $1.2 million to a Chinese company. The three formed a joint venture with a Chinese government-owned company called Datang Telecom Technology Co., Ltd., of Bejing.[17]
- Aaron Blosser, an obsessed contract computer consultant for Qwest, was charged in 1998 with hacking into the U.S. West (now Qwest) computer system and diverting 10.63 years of processing power from 2,585 computers toward his effort to solve a 350-year-old math problem of finding a new prime number.[18]
- Martin Frankel bilked insurance companies in five states out of over $200 million. He pled guilty to 20 counts of wire fraud and various other crimes under the Racketeering Influenced Corrupt Organizations (RICO) Act.[19]

These cases are only those that involved insiders. Even more common are cases of fraud and identity theft by criminals external to organizations. To help combat the threats of terrorism, insider abuse, external fraud, identity theft, and other major risks, all organizations must be more diligent about implementing internal controls, including computer security and physical security, operational and accounting controls, and employee and consultant background checks. Organizations must also work in harmony with applicable governmental agencies so that offenders can be charged and any necessary changes can be made to applicable laws and regulations. In extreme cases, such cooperation could even help military leaders determine where to deploy support.

Another constant hurdle is that internal and external IS developers continue to program applications with weak security. There will continue to be new systems that allow minimum password lengths to be under eight characters, that fail to have password expiration, that do not have logging capabilities, that do not provide sufficient encryption of passwords and other critical information, that allow concurrent sign-on by nonsystem administrators, and that do not provide automatic session time-outs. Security continues to be an afterthought for these developers. We as IS control and security professionals must be constantly on the lookout for these types of systems. Too often, management in information systems and end-user areas falsely presume that the developers always design adequate IS security features into their applications.

Since the culture and operational practices of each organization and within each country are different, it is up to the internal and external auditors of all organizations to ensure that management is aware of the IS risks mentioned in this book, any risks that are unique to their organizations and countries, and the new risks posed by emerging technologies and terrorism. Once risks are identified, internal controls can be tailored to mitigate them and to result in healthy and thriving IS environments within their organizations, as well as a safer world for all of us.

NOTES

1. "Microsoft Password Research Looks to Images," *Seattle News Fax* (March 25, 2002): 6.
2. "Texas CUs Install Latest Biometrics Safe Deposit Technology," *Credit Union Times* (May 15, 2002): 25.
3. "NASA Logs on to Biometric Service," *www.ecomworld.com* (January 2, 2001).
4. Simon L. Garfinkel, "Biometrics: The Face of Post-Sept. 11 Security," *Information Security* (November 2001): 62–63.
5. "Real-time Kiosks, SAFLINK Bring Biometrics to Credit Unions," *Credit Union Times* (March 7, 2001): 14.
6. "Biometrics Fail Sticky Test," *Security Wire Digest* (May 19, 2002).
7. "IBM Molecular Circuit May Mean Tiny Chips," *Seattle News Fax* (August 27, 2001): 5.
7. Matthew Fordahl, "Atom-Sized Circuitry the Next Step," *Maui News* (September 10, 2001): B7.
9. "Teleporting Closer to Reality," *Seattle News Fax* (September 28, 2001): 9.
10. Associated Press, "Hawking: Smart Computers Pose a Challenge to Humans," *Seattle Times* (September 2, 2001): A9.
11. "Hanssen Report Raps Lax FBI," *Seattle News Fax* (April 5, 2002): 2; "Feds Try to Estimate Computer Damage Caused by Accused Spy," *Security Wire Digest* (March 8, 2001).
12. "Business Briefs," *Seattle News Fax* (March 11, 2002): 5; "Business Briefs," *Seattle News Fax* (February 21, 2002): 5; "Business Briefs," *Seattle News Fax* (February 12, 2002): 5; "Irish Bank Calls in FBI Over Suspected Fraud," *Seattle News Fax* (February 7, 2002): 5; "Top Irish Bank Accuses Its U.S. Trader of Fraud," *Seattle Times* (February 7, 2002): A6.
13. "Stockbroker Charged with Fraud," *Seattle News Fax* (February 12, 2002): 2; "Fugitive Stockbroker Gives Up," *Seattle News Fax* (February 11, 2002): 2.
14. "Business Briefs," *Seattle News Fax* (February 27, 2002): 5; "Security Breaches,"

Information Security (September 2000): 48; MacDonnell Ulsch, "Lloyd's Lesson," *Information Security* (July 2000): 30; "By the Numbers," *Information Security* (June 2000): 16.

15. Luke Timmerman, "Redmond Businessman Admits Fraud in HP Case," *Seattle Times* (October 31, 2000): D4.

16. "Furthermore. . . ," *Seattle News Fax* (January 3, 2001): 3.

17. Andrew Backover, "Feds: Trio Stole Lucent's Trade Secrets," *USA Today* (May 4, 2001): 1B.

18. "US West Hacker Hunts for New Prime Number," *Seattle News Fax* (September 16, 1998): 5.

19. "Financier Frankel Pleads Guilty," *Seattle News Fax* (May 16, 2002): 5.

APPENDIX A

Professional Auditing Associations and Other Organizations Related to Information Systems Auditing and Computer Security

American Institute of Certified Public Accountants (AICPA)
1211 Avenue of the Americas
New York, NY 10036-8775, U.S.A.
www.aicpa.org
Phone: (212) 596-6200
Mission: To provide members with the resources, information, and leadership that enable them to provide valuable services in the highest professional manner to benefit the public as well as employers and clients.

American National Standards Institute (ANSI)
1819 L Street NW, Suite 600
Washington, DC 20036, U.S.A.
Phone: (212) 642-4900
www.ansi.org
Mission: To enhance both the global competitiveness of U.S. business and the U.S. quality of life by promoting and facilitating voluntary consensus standards and conformity assessment systems, and safeguarding their integrity.

American Society of Industrial Security (ASIS)
1625 Prince Street
Alexandria, VA 22314-2828, U.S.A.
Phone: (703) 519-6200
www.asisonline.org
Mission: To establish, develop, and promote excellence in the security profession by assuring high-quality education programs, responsiveness to members' needs, standards for professional and ethical conduct, a forum for debate and exchange of ideas, promotion of the organization and profession, and strategic alliances with related organizations.

Association of Credit Union Internal Auditors (ACUIA)
PO Box 1926
Columbus, OH 43216-1926, U.S.A.
Phone: (614) 221-9702, 1-866-254-8128
www.acuia.org
Mission: To unify and encourage cooperative relationships among credit union internal auditors to facilitate the exchange of information and ideas; to promote and maintain high professional standards for internal auditors in credit unions; to provide educational opportunities for developing audit and leadership skills; to provide guidelines for auditing

credit unions; to aid in the development of internal audit functions at credit unions; and to communicate professional opportunities for internal auditors within the credit union industry.

Association of Certified Fraud Examiners (ACFE)
The Gregor Building
716 West Avenue
Austin, TX 78701 U.S.A.
Phone: (800) 245-3321 (USA & Canada only); (512) 478-9070
www.cfenet.com
Mission: To reduce the incidence of fraud and white-collar crime and to assist the membership in its detection and deterrence.

Association of Information Technology Professionals (AITP)
(formerly the Data Processing Management Association [DPMA])
315 South Northwest Highway, Suite 200
Park Ridge, IL 60068-4278, U.S.A.
Phone: (800) 224-9371, (847) 825-8124
www.aitp.org
Mission: AITP offers opportunities for Information Technology (IT) leadership and education through partnerships with industry, government and academia. AITP provides quality IT-related education, information on relevant IT issues, and forums for networking with experienced peers and other IT professionals.

Australian Accounting Research Foundation (AARF)
Jointly established by the Institute of Chartered Accountants in Australia (ICAA) and CPA Australia (CPAA)
Level 10/600 Bourke Street
Melbourne, Victoria 3000, Australia
AARF Phone: (61) (3) 9641-7433
www.aarf.asn.au
Mission: To improve the quality of auditing and assurance services in Australia through the development of auditing and assurance standards and guidance; to contribute to the development of international auditing and assurance standards and guidance; to contribute to the development of legislation and regulation in Australia in respect of commercial law, including corporate governance, financial reporting, and auditing matters.

BBBOnLine, Inc.
4200 Wilson Boulevard, 8th floor
Arlington, VA 22203, U.S.A.
Phone: (703) 247-9370 or 9336
www.bbbonline.com
Mission: To promote trust and confidence on the Internet through the BBB*OnLine* Reliability and Privacy Seal Programs.

Business Software Alliance (BSA)
1150 18th Street Northwest, Suite 700
Washington, DC 20036, U.S.A.
Phone: (202) 872-5500
Anti-Piracy Hotline: 1-888-NO-PIRACY
www.bsa.org

Mission: The Business Software Alliance (BSA) is the foremost organization dedicated to promoting a safe and legal online world. We are the voice of the world's software, hardware, and Internet sectors before governments and with consumers in the international marketplace. BSA members represent the fastest-growing industries in the world. BSA educates computer users on software copyrights and cybersecurity; advocates public policy that fosters innovation and expands trade opportunities; and fights software piracy.

Canadian Institute of Chartered Accountants (CICA)
277 Wellington Street West
Toronto, Ontario M5V-3H2, Canada
Phone: (416) 977-3222
www.cica.ca
Mission: To enhance decision making and improve organizational performance through financial management, assurance, and other specialized expertise. We act with integrity, objectivity, and a commitment to excellence and the public interest.

Certified Practising Accountants of Australia (CPAA)
(formerly the Australian Society of Certified Practising Accountants [ASCPA])
Level 28, Bourke Street
Melbourne, VIC 3000, Australia
Phone: (61) (3) 9606 9700
www.cpaonline.com.au
Mission: For CPAs to be leaders in finance, accounting, and business advice.

Computer Crime & Intellectual Property Section (CCIPS)
U.S. Department of Justice, Criminal Division
John C. Keeney Building, Suite 600
10th & Constitution Avenue Northwest
Washington, DC 20530
Main (202) 514-1026
www.cybercrime.gov
Mission: The Computer Crime and Intellectual Property Section (CCIPS) attorney staff consists of about 24 lawyers who focus exclusively on the issues raised by computer and intellectual property crime. Section attorneys advise federal prosecutors and law enforcement agents; comment on and propose legislation; coordinate international efforts to combat computer crime; litigate cases; and train all law enforcement groups. Other areas of expertise possessed by CCIPS attorneys include encryption, electronic privacy laws, search and seizure of computers, e-commerce, hacker investigations, and intellectual property crimes.

Computer Emergency Response Team (CERT) Coordination Center
Software Engineering Institute
Carnegie Mellon University
Pittsburgh, PA 15213-3890, U.S.A.
Phone: (412) 268-4793
www.cert.org
Mission: To provide a reliable, trusted, 24-hour, single point of contact for emergencies; to facilitate communication among experts working to solve security problems; to serve as a central point for identifying and correcting vulnerabilities in computer systems; to maintain close ties with research activities and conduct research to improve the security of existing systems; and to initiate proactive measures to increase awareness and under-

standing of information security and computer security issues throughout the community of network users and service providers.

Computer Incident Advisory Capability (CIAC)
7000 East Avenue, L-303
Livermore, CA 94550, U.S.A.
Phone: (925) 422-8193
www.ciac.org/ciac/
Mission: To apply cybersecurity expertise to prevent, detect, react to, and recover from cyberincidents for the Department of Energy, National Security Agency, and other national stakeholders. We value teamwork, integrity, competence, communication, responsibility, and reliability.

Computer Security Institute (CSI)
600 Harrison Street
San Francisco, CA 94107, U.S.A.
Phone: (415) 947-6320
www.gocsi.com
Mission: To serve and train the information, computer, and network security professional; and to aggressively advocate the critical importance of protecting information assets.

Credit Union Internal Auditors Association (CUIAA)
No specific street address or phone - see website for board contacts
www.cuiaa.org
Mission: To support and enhance the professional development of credit union internal auditors and the internal audit function as it continues to develop in credit unions.

Critical Infrastructure Assurance Office (CIAO)
1401 Constitution Avenue Northwest, Room 6095
Washington, DC 20230, U.S.A.
Phone: (202) 482-7473
www.ciao.gov
Mission: CIAO's major initiatives are to coordinate and implement the national strategy; to assess the U.S. government's own risk exposure and dependencies on critical infrastructure; to raise awareness and educate public understanding and participation in critical infrastructure protection efforts; and to coordinate legislative and public affairs to integrate infrastructure assurance objectives into the public and private sectors.

Defense Information Systems Agency (DISA)
Falls Church, VA 22041, U.S.A.
Phone: (703) 681-2234
www.disa.mil
Mission: To be the preeminent provider of information systems support to our warfighters and others as required by the Department of Defense, under all conditions of peace and war.

Disaster Recovery Institute International (DRII)
111 Park Place
Falls Church, VA 22046-4513, U.S.A.
Phone: (703) 538-1792
www.drii.org

Mission: To serve the educational, certification, promotional, and standards needs of the institute's Certified Business Continuity Professionals.

Electronic Frontier Foundation
454 Shotwell Street
San Francisco, CA 94110, U.S.A.
Phone: (415) 436-9333
www.eff.org
Mission: To help civilize the electronic frontier; to make it truly useful and beneficial, not just to a technical elite but to everyone; and to do this in a way that is in keeping with society's highest traditions of the free and open flow of information and communication.

Federal Computer Incident Response Center (FedCIRC)
7th & D Streets SW, Room 5060
Washington, DC 20407, U.S.A.
Phone: (202) 708-5060
www.fedcirc.gov
Mission: To provide civil agencies with technical information, tools, methods, assistance, and guidance; to be proactive and provide liaison activities and analytical support; to encourage the development of quality products and services through collaborative relationships with federal civil agencies, Department of Defense, academia, and private industry; to promote the highest security profile for government information technology resources; and to promote incident response and handling procedural awareness within the federal government.

Federal Financial Institutions Examination Council (FFIEC)
2000 K Street NW, Suite 310
Washington, DC 20006, U.S.A.
Phone: (703) 516-5588
www.ffiec.gov
Mission: To prescribe uniform principles, standards, and report forms for the federal examination of financial institutions by the board of governors of the Federal Reserve System (FRB), the Federal Deposit Insurance Corporation (FDIC), the National Credit Union Administration (NCUA), the Office of the Comptroller of the Currency (OCC), and the Office of Thrift Supervision (OTS); and to make recommendations to promote uniformity in the supervision of financial institutions.

Foundstone, Inc.
27201 Puerta Real, #400
Mission Viejo, CA 92691, U.S.A.
(877) 91-FOUND
(949) 297-5600
www.foundstone.com
Mission: To provide continuous security intelligence through each stage of the security life cycle to help clients prevent, respond to, and resolve enterprise security issues.

High Tech Crime Investigators Association (HTCIA)
1474 Freeman Drive
Amissville, VA 20106, U.S.A.
(540) 937-5019
www.htcia.org

Mission: To encourage, promote, aid, and effect the voluntary interchange of data, information, experience, and knowledge about methods and processes among the membership of HTCIA; to establish, encourage, and enforce observation of a code of ethics and standards of professional conduct; to publish and distribute books, pamphlets, periodicals, papers, and articles supportive of activities and purposes of HTCIA; to conduct surveys and studies and hold conferences, symposiums, seminars, and forums; to arrange for the presentation of lectures and papers on matters and problems of interest; to foster, promote, encourage, study, research, facilitate discussion, collect, and disseminate information of service or interest to the members of HTCIA or the public at large.

Information Systems Audit and Control Association (ISACA)
(formerly the Electronic Data Processing Auditors Association [EDPAA])
3701 Algonquin Road, Suite 1010
Rolling Meadows, IL 60008, U.S.A.
Phone: (847) 253-1545
www.isaca.org
Mission: To support enterprise objectives through the development, provision, and promotion of research, standards, competencies, and practices for the effective governance, control, and assurance of information systems and technology.

Information Systems Security Association (ISSA)
7044 South 13th Street
Oak Creek, WI 53154, U.S.A.
Phone: (414) 768-8000, (800) 370-ISSA
www.issa-intl.org
Mission: To provide education forums, publications, and peer interaction opportunities that enhance the knowledge, skill, and professional growth of its members.

Information Technology Association of America (ITAA)
1401 Wilson Boulevard, Suite 1100
Arlington, VA 22209, U.S.A.
Phone: (703) 522-5055
www.itaa.org
Mission: The ITAA is the leading trade association of this nation's information technology industry. Its over 500 direct member companies create and market products and information services associated with computers, communications, and data. ITAA sponsors a wide range of services, meetings, and activities that enhance an information technology firm's ability to remain competitive in the marketplace. Through its advocacy efforts, ITAA helps to foster an environment conducive to the health, prosperity, and competitive nature of the IT industry and to help its members succeed in delivering the benefits of IT to their customers. With the aid of its four divisions, the association represents the IT industry's interests in issues such as intellectual property protection, government procurement, telecommunications policy, taxation, and privacy.

Institute of Chartered Accountants in Australia (ICAA)
37 York Street
Sydney, NSW, 2000, Australia
Phone: (61) (2) 9290 1344
www.icaa.org.au
Mission: To be the organization of first choice for leading business, finance, and knowledge management professionals.

Institute of Chartered Accountants in England & Wales (ICAEW)
Chartered Accountant's Hall
PO Box 433 Moorgate Place
London EC2P 2BJ, England
Phone: (44) (020) 7920-8100
www.icaew.co.uk
Mission: To advance the theory and practice of accountancy in all its aspects, including in particular auditing, financial management, and taxation; to recruit, educate, and train a body of members skilled in these arts; to preserve at all times the professional independence of accountants in whatever capacities they may be serving; to maintain high standards of practice and professional conduct by all its members; and to do all such things as may advance the profession of accountancy in relation to public practice, industry, commerce, and the public service.

Institute of Electrical and Electronics Engineers (IEEE)
3 Park Avenue, 17th Floor
New York, NY, 10016-5997, U.S.A.
Phone: (212) 419-7900
www.ieee.org
Mission: To promote the engineering process of creating, developing, integrating, sharing, and applying knowledge about electro- and information technologies and sciences for the benefit of humanity and the profession.

Institute of Internal Auditors (IIA)
247 Maitland Avenue
Altamonte Springs, FL 32701-4201, U.S.A.
Phone: (407) 830-7600
www.theiia.org
Mission: To be the primary international professional association, organized on a worldwide basis, dedicated to the promotion and development of the practice of internal auditing.

Interagency Operations Security (OPSEC) Support (IOSS)
6411 Ivy Lane
Greenbelt, MD 20770, U.S.A.
Phone: (301) 982-0323
www.ioss.gov
Mission: To promote and maintain OPSEC principles worldwide by assisting customers in establishing OPSEC programs, providing OPSEC training, and conducting OPSEC surveys.

International Criminal Police Organization (Interpol)
General Secretariat
200, quai Charles de Gaulle
69006 Lyon, France
Fax: (33) 4 72 44 71 63
www.interpol.int
Mission: To be the world's pre-eminent police organization in support of all organizations, authorities, and services whose mission is preventing, detecting, and suppressing crime.

International Federation of Accountants (IFAC)
535 Fifth Avenue, 26th floor
New York, NY 10017, U.S.A.
Phone: (212) 286-9344
www.ifac.org
Mission: To develop the profession and harmonize its standards worldwide to enable accountants to provide services of consistently high quality in the public interest.

International Information Systems Security Certification Consortium, Inc. (ISC²)
860 Worcester Road, Suite 101
Framingham, MA 01702, U.S.A.
Phone: (508) 875-8400
www.isc2.org
Mission: A not-for-profit consortium dedicated to training and certifying information security professionals worldwide.

International Organization for Standardization (ISO)
1, rue de Varembé, Case postale 56
CH-1211 Geneva 20, Switzerland
Phone: (41) 22 749 01 11
www.iso.org
Mission: To promote the development of standardization and related activities in the world with a view to facilitating the international exchange of goods and services and to developing cooperation in the spheres of intellectual, scientific, technological, and economic activity.

Internet Corporation for Assigned Names and Numbers (ICANN)
4676 Admiralty Way, Suite 330
Marina del Rey, CA 90292-6601, U.S.A.
Phone: (310) 823-9358
www.icann.org
Mission: To coordinate the stable operation of the Internet's unique identifier systems. In particular, ICANN coordinates the allocation and assignment of three sets of unique identifiers for the Internet: domain names (forming a system referred to as DNS); Internet protocol (IP) addresses and autonomous system (AS) numbers; and protocol port and parameter numbers. ICANN also coordinates the operation and evolution of the DNS's root name server system.

Internet Engineering Task Force (IETF)
1895 Preson White Drive, Suite 100
Reston, VA 22091, U.S.A.
Phone: (703) 620-8990
www.ietf.org
Mission: To identify and propose solutions to pressing operational and technical problems in the Internet; to specify the development or usage of protocols and the near-term architecture to solve such technical problems for the Internet; to make recommendations to the Internet Engineering Steering Group (IESG) regarding the standardization of protocols and protocol usage in the Internet; to facilitate technology transfer from the Internet Research Task Force (IRTF) to the wider Internet community; and to provide a forum for the exchange of information within the Internet community among vendors, users, researchers, agency contractors, and network managers.

Internet Society (ISOC)
1775 Wiehle Avenue, Suite 102
Reston, VA 20190-5108, U.S.A.
Phone: (703) 326-9880
www.isoc.org
Mission: To assure the open development, evolution, and use of the Internet for the benefit of all people throughout the world.

MIS Training Institute
498 Concord Street
Framingham, MA 01702-2357, U.S.A.
Phone: (508) 879-7999
www.misti.com
Mission: The international leader in audit and information security training, with offices in the United States, the United Kingdom, and Asia. MIS's expertise draws on experience gained in training more than 100,000 delegates across five continents. MIS presents seminars and conferences in the areas of internal and information technology audit, information security, networks, e-commerce applications, operating platforms, and enterprise applications.

National Infrastructure Protection Center (NIPC)
J. Edgar Hoover Building
935 Pennsylvania Avenue NW
Washington, DC 20535-0001, U.S.A.
Phone: (202) 323-3205; 1-888-585-9078
www.nipc.gov
Mission: To serve as the U.S. government's focal point for threat assessment, warning, investigation, and response for threats or attacks against our critical infrastructures, which include telecommunications, energy, banking and finance, water systems, government operations, and emergency services.

National Institute of Accountants
Head Office
Level 8, 12-20 Flinders Lane
Melbourne, Victoria 3000, Australia
www.nia.org.au
Mission: To provide members and the business community with quality resources and support required for success, through professional recognition, education and professional development, business and technical advice, alliances with business service providers, and advocacy to government and agencies.

National Institute of Standards and Technology (NIST)
100 Bureau Drive, Stop 3460
Gaithersburg, MD, 20899-3460, U.S.A.
Phone: (301) 975-6478
www.nist.gov
Mission: To develop and promote measurements, standards, and technology to enhance productivity, facilitate trade, and improve the quality of life.

National Security Agency/Central Security Service (NSA/CSS)
9800 Savage Road
Fort George G. Meade, MD 20755-6000, U.S.A.
Phone: (301) 688-6524
www.nsa.gov

Mission: To design cipher systems that will protect the integrity of U.S. information systems and to search for weaknesses in adversaries' codes.

National Security Institute (NSI)
57 East Main Street, Suite 217
Westborough, MA 01581, U.S.A.
Phone: (508) 366-5800
www.nsi.org
Mission: To provide a variety of professional information and security awareness services to defense contractor, government, and industrial security executives throughout the United States. NSI's central business is helping clients interpret and implement government security directives and establish sound security strategies that effectively safeguard classified and proprietary information through the publication of newsletters, special reports, seminars, and electronically via the World Wide Web and online security awareness programs.

New Technologies, Inc. (NTI)
2075 Northeast Division Street
Gresham, OR 97030, U.S.A.
Phone: (503) 661-6912
www.forensics-intl.com
Mission: To develop state-of-the-art computer forensics and risk assessment tools and provide computer forensics training and computer evidence consulting. NTI provides consulting services to some of the largest law firms and corporations in the world concerning e-commerce evidence and general computer evidence issues. NTI also provides software tools and advisory services to military and intelligence agencies in computer security risk identification and the elimination of such risks.

Office of Foreign Assets Control (OFAC)
U.S. Department of the Treasury
Treasury Annex
1500 Pennsylvania Avenue NW
Washington, DC 20220
Phone: (202) 622-2490
www.treas.gov/ofac
Mission: Administers and enforces economic and trade sanctions against targeted foreign countries, terrorism-sponsoring organizations, and international narcotics traffickers based on U.S. foreign policy and national security goals. OFAC acts under presidential wartime and national emergency powers, as well as authority granted by specific legislation, to impose controls on transactions and freeze foreign assets under U.S. jurisdiction.

Project Management Institute (PMI)
Four Campus Boulevard
Newtown Square, PA 19073-3299, U.S.A.
Phone: (610) 356-4600
www.pmi.org
Mission: To establish project management standards and provide seminars, educational programs, and professional certification that more and more organizations desire for their project leaders.

RSA Data Security, Inc.
174 Middlesex Turnpike
Bedford, MA 01730, U.S.A.
Phone: (781) 515-5000, 1-877-RSA-4900
www.rsasecurity.com
Mission: As the inventor of leading security technologies, RSA Security is focused on four core disciplines of e-security: authentication, web access management, encryption, and digital signatures.

SANS (System Administration, Networking and Security) Institute
5401 Westbard Avenue
Bethesda, MD 20816
Phone: (540) 372-7066, 1.866.570.9927 (U.S. & Canada)
www.sans.org
Mission: To support various programs and products, including SANS computer and information security training; the Global Incident Analysis Center (GIAC) certification program; SANS resources; incidents at the Internet Storm Center; Center for Internet Security, and SCORE; and the SANS/FBI top-20 list.

Software & Information Industry Association (SIIA)
(formerly the Software Publishers Association [SPA])
1090 Vermont Avenue NW, 6th floor
Washington, DC 20005
Phone: (202) 289-7442
Software Piracy Hotline: 1-800-388-7478
www.spa.org
Mission: The SIIA is the principal trade association for the software and digital content industry. SIIA provides global services in government relations, business development, corporate education, and intellectual property protection to the leading companies that are setting the pace for the digital age. Its principal mission is to promote the common interests of the software and digital content industry as a whole, as well as its component parts; to protect the intellectual property of industry members and advocate a legal and regulatory environment that benefits the industry; and to serve as a resource to member companies on a wide range of topics.

TruSecure Corporation
(formerly the International Computer Security Association [ICSA])
13650 Dulles Technology Drive, Suite 500
Herndon, VA 20171
Phone: (703) 480-8200, (888) 627-2281
www.trusecure.com
Mission: TruSecure® Corporation is a worldwide leader in security assurance solutions for Internet-connected organizations. Hundreds of leading companies rely on TruSecure to help them identify, correct, and continuously mitigate risks to mission-critical systems and information. TruSecure's cost-effective programs generate improved returns on security investments and provide the assurance that organizations can confidently and safely pursue their Internet-based initiatives.

TRUSTe
1180 Coleman Avenue, Suite 202
San Jose, CA 95110, U.S.A.

Phone: (408) 494-4950
www.truste.org
Mission: To build users' trust and confidence on the Internet and, in doing so, accelerate growth of the Internet industry.

USENIX (Advanced Computing Systems Association)
2560 Ninth Street, Suite 215
Berkeley, CA 94710, U.S.A.
Phone: (510) 528-8649
www.usenix.org
Mission: The USENIX Association and its members are dedicated to problem-solving with a practical bias; to fostering innovation and research that works; to communicating rapidly the results of both research and innovation; and to providing a neutral forum for the exercise of critical thought and the airing of technical issues.

VeriSign, Inc.
487 East Middlefield Road
Mountain View, CA 94043, U.S.A.
Phone: (650) 961-7500
www.verisign.com
Mission: To be the leading provider of digital trust services that enable everyone, everywhere to engage in commerce and communications with confidence.

World Information Technology and Services Alliance (WITSA)
1401 Wilson Boulevard, Suite 1100
Arlington, VA 22209, U.S.A.
Phone: (703) 284-5333
www.witsa.org
Mission: WITSA is a consortium of 46 information technology (IT) industry associations (including ITAA) from economies around the world. WITSA members represent over 90 percent of the world's IT market. As the global voice of the IT industry, WITSA is dedicated to advocating policies that advance the industry's growth and development; to facilitating international trade and investment in IT products and services; to strengthening WITSA's national industry associations through the sharing of knowledge, experience, and critical information; to providing members with a vast network of contacts in nearly every geographic region of the world; to hosting the World Congress on IT, the only industry-sponsored global IT event; and to hosting the Global Public Policy Conference; and the Global Information Security Summit.

World Wide Web Consortium (W3C)
Massachusetts Institute of Technology
Laboratory for Computer Science
200 Technology Square
Cambridge, MA 02139, U.S.A.
Phone: 1 (617) 253-2613
www.w3c.org
Mission: To make the web accessible to all by promoting technologies that take into account the vast differences in culture, languages, education, ability, material resources, and physical limitations of users on all continents; to develop a software environment that permits each user to make the best use of the resources available on the web; and to guide the web's development with careful consideration for the novel legal, commercial, and social issues raised by this technology.

APPENDIX B

Common Criteria for Information Technology Security Evaluation

Note: The following reference information was obtained from the official Common Criteria website (*www.commoncriteria.org*). Please refer to the site for complete details. Detailed documents are available for download in portable document format (PDF). Some can be quite large. I examined one that was 368 pages and over 1 megabyte in size.

BACKGROUND

The Common Criteria (CC) was created to harmonize various information technology (IT) security evaluation standards in the United States, Europe, and Canada. The Common Criteria includes concepts of the U.S. Trusted Computer System Evaluation Criteria (TCSEC, 1985, also known as The Orange Book); the European Information Technology Security Evaluation Criteria (ITSEC, 1991), and the Canadian Trusted Computer Product Evaluation Criteria (CTCPEC, 1993). Version 1.0 of the CC was published for comment in January 1996. Version 2.0 was published in May 1998. The International Organization for Standardization (ISO) reviewed version 2.0 and adopted a revised version 2.1 of the CC as an international standard (#15408) in June 1999.

SPONSORING ORGANIZATIONS

The seven organizations sponsoring development of the CC are:

- Communications Security Establishment (Canada)
- Service Central de la Securite des Systemes (France)
- Bundesamt fur Sicherheit in der Informationstechnik (Germany)
- Netherlands National Communications Security Agency (Netherlands)
- Communications-Electronics Security Group (United Kingdom)
- National Institute of Standards and Technology (USA)
- National Security Agency (USA)

OVERVIEW

The Common Criteria (CC) is presented as a set of distinct but related parts. **Part 1, Introduction and General Model**, is the introduction to the CC. It defines general concepts and principles of IT security evaluation and presents a general model of evaluation. Part 1 also presents constructs for expressing IT security objectives, for selecting and defining IT security requirements, and for writing high-level specifications for products and systems. In addition, the usefulness of each part of the CC is described in terms of each of the target audiences.

Part 2, Security Functional Requirements, establishes a set of security functional components as a standard way of expressing the security functional requirements for Targets of Evaluation (TOEs). Part 2 catalogs the set of functional components, families, and classes. The eleven functionality classes are:

- Audit
- Cryptographic Support
- Communications
- User Data Protection
- Identification and Authentication
- Security Management
- Privacy
- Protection of the Target of Evaluation Functions
- Resource Utilization
- Target of Evaluation Access
- Trusted Path/Channels

Part 3, Security Assurance Requirements, establishes a set of assurance components as a standard way of expressing the assurance requirements for TOEs. Part 3 catalogs the set of assurance components, families, and classes. It also defines evaluation criteria for Protection Profiles (PPs) and Security Targets (STs) and presents evaluation assurance levels that define the predefined CC scale for rating assurance for TOEs, which is called the Evaluation Assurance Levels (EALs).

MORE ON CC PART 3, SECURITY ASSURANCE REQUIREMENTS

Security assurance requirements are grouped into classes. Classes are the most general grouping of security requirements, and all members of a class share a common focus. Eight assurance classes are contained within Part 3 of the CC:

- Configuration Management
- Delivery and Operation
- Development
- Guidance Documents
- Life Cycle Support
- Tests
- Vulnerability Assessment
- Assurance Maintenance

Two additional classes contain the assurance for Protection Profiles (PPs) and Security Targets (STs). Each of these classes contains a number of families. The requirements within each family share security objectives but differ in emphasis or rigor. For example, the Development class contains seven families dealing with various aspects of design documentation (e.g., functional specification, high-level design, and representation correspondence). Each family contains one or more components, and these components are in a strict hierarchy. For example, the Functional Specification family contains four hierarchical components, dealing with increasing completeness and formality in the presentation of the functional specification. The CC has provided seven predefined assurance packages, on a rising scale of assurance, known as Evaluation Assurance Levels (EALs). These provide balanced groupings of assurance components that are intended to be generally applicable. There are seven EALs.

EAL1—Functionally Tested

EAL1 is applicable where some confidence in correct operation is required, but the threats to security are not viewed as serious. It will be of value where independent assurance is required to support the contention that due care has been exercised with respect to the protection of personal or similar information. This level provides an evaluation of the Target of Evaluation (TOE) as made available to the consumer, including independent testing against a specification, and an examination of the guidance documentation provided.

EAL2—Structurally Tested

EAL2 requires the cooperation of the developer in terms of the delivery of design information and test results, but should not demand more effort on the part of the developer than is consistent with good commercial practice. As such it should not require a substantially increased investment of cost or time.

EAL2 is applicable in those circumstances where developers or users require a low to moderate level of independently assured security in the absence of ready availability of the complete development record. Such a situation may arise when securing legacy systems or where access to the developer may be limited.

EAL3—Methodically Tested and Checked

EAL3 permits a conscientious developer to gain maximum assurance from positive security engineering at the design stage without substantial alteration of existing sound development practices. It is applicable in those circumstances where developers or users require a moderate level of independently assured security and require a thorough investigation of the TOE and its development without incurring substantial reengineering costs.

An EAL3 evaluation provides an analysis supported by "gray box" testing, selective confirmation of the developer test results, and evidence of a developer search for obvious vulnerabilities. Development environmental controls and TOE configuration management are also required.

EAL4—Methodically Designed, Tested and Reviewed

EAL4 permits a developer to maximize assurance gained from positive security engineering based on good commercial development practices. Although rigorous, these practices do not require substantial specialist knowledge, skills, and other resources. EAL4 is the highest level at which it is likely to be economically feasible to retrofit to an existing product line. It is applicable in those circumstances where developers or users require a moderate to high level of independently assured security in conventional commodity TOEs and are prepared to incur additional security-specific engineering costs.

An EAL4 evaluation provides an analysis supported by the low-level design of the modules of the TOE and a subset of the implementation. Testing is supported by an independent search for vulnerabilities. Development controls are supported by a life-cycle model, identification of tools, and automated configuration management.

EAL5—Semi-Formally Designed and Tested

EAL5 permits a developer to gain maximum assurance from security engineering, based upon rigorous commercial development practices, supported by moderate application of specialist security engineering techniques. Such a TOE will probably be designed and developed with the intent of achieving EAL5 assurance. It is likely that the additional costs attributable to the EAL5 requirements, relative to rigorous development without the application of specialized techniques, will not be large. EAL5 is therefore applicable in those circumstances where developers or users require a high level of independently assured security in a planned development and require rigorous development approach without incurring unreasonable costs attributable to specialist security techniques.

An EAL5 evaluation provides an analysis that includes all of the implementation. Assurance is supplemented by a formal model, a semiformal presentation of the functional specification and high-level design, and a semiformal demonstration of correspondence. The search for vulnerabilities must ensure resistance to attackers with a moderate attach potential. Covert channel analysis and design are also required.

EAL6—Semi-Formally Verified Design and Tested

EAL6 permits developers to gain high assurance from the application of security engineering techniques to a rigorous development environment in order to produce a premium TOE for protecting high-value assets against significant risks.

EAL6 is therefore applicable to the development of security TOEs for application in high-risk situations where the value of the protected assets justifies the additional cost.

An EAL6 evaluation provides an analysis that is supported by a modular and layered approach to design and a structured presentation of the implementation. The independent search for vulnerabilities must ensure resistance to attackers with a high attack potential. The search for covert channels must be systematic. Development environment and configuration management controls are further strengthened.

EAL7—Formally Verified Design and Tested

EAL7 is applicable to the development of security TOEs for application in extremely high risk situations and/or where the high value of the assets justifies the higher costs. Practical application of EAL7 is currently limited to TOEs with tightly focused security functionality that is amenable to extensive formal analysis.

For an EAL7 evaluation, the formal model is supplemented by a formal presentation of the functional specification and high-level design, showing correspondence. Evidence of developer "white-box" testing and complete independent confirmation of developer test results are required. Complexity of the design must be minimized.

APPENDIX C

The International Organization for Standardization: Seven-Layer Open Systems Interconnection (OSI) Reference Model

7 Application Layer   User-level and application-specific services and procedures: distributed application support, e-mail, access security checking, information validation. Application dialog.

6 Presentation Layer   Representation of information: formats, codes; transformation, encryption. Modification for syntactic compatibility.

5 Session Layer Session management: "conversation" initiation, initial screening, access security checking; sychronization, abnormal recovery. Dialog between workstations (processes, users, etc.).

4 Transport Layer   Sending messages. End-to-end control across networks: session and network selection, virtual circuit management, flow control; message error checking, packet assembly/disassembly (PAD); enterprise-wide addressing; user-O/S interface. Creating a robust path.

3 Network Layer   Sending packets or streams (of data). Network management: routing, switching, traffic monitoring, and congestion control; initiating an end-to-end pathway. Control of network logical topology.

2 Data Link Layer   Sending blocks/frames (of bits). Link management: framing into transmission blocks; synchronization, bit error detection/ correction. Control of a single point-to-point, error-free, sequential channel.

1 Physical Layer   Sending bits. Functional and procedural interface to the medium: activate, maintain, deactivate the physical connection; modem control; signal multiplexing. Signaling topology, that is, signaling energy connectivity. Test equipment. Transmits bits over channel.

0 Physical Medium   The medium that carries the energy that carries the information. Physical topology (connectivity) as indicated in appropriate diagrams and drawings. Electrical/optical/ mechanical specifications are considered part of the medium.

Source: Copyright 1999 Holocon, Inc.

The ISO-OSI model was created in 1983 to be a universal reference model that could be applied to any computing environment to conceptually describe how two computer processors transmit data between each other. Since it is a conceptual model and not one applied to a specific physical processing environment, it can still be applied to all of today's computer processing environments and any foreseeable ones. In fact, it is included within the common bodies of knowledge for both the CISA and CISSP certifications.

ISO-OSI MODEL REFERENCES

1. Many classes and seminars apply the OSI model to data processing environments. One of the OSI developers, Stuart Holoman, presents several intermediate and advanced IS auditing classes through the MIS Training Institute; the classes teach IS auditors how to understand and apply the model to IS audits.
2. Peter T. Davis, "C/S Auditing, One Bite at a Time," *Information Security*, (June 1999): 50–55.
3. Trivia: You may be wondering why the International Organization for Standardization is called ISO, not IOS. The reason is that there are members of ISO from many different countries. Since the name does not always translate into the same acronym in different languages, the name ISO was chosen. ISO was derived from the Greek word *isos,* which means "equal" and is consistent with the ISO mission of developing standards. Thus, ISO adopted its name so that it could be consistently used in all languages and that it would not be an acronym.

Selected References

Bruce Schneier, *Applied Cryptography*, 2nd ed., (New York: John Wiley & Sons, Inc., 1996).

Bruce Schneier, *Secrets & Lies, Digital Security in a Networked World* (New York: John Wiley & Sons, Inc., 2000).

Cliff Stoll, *The Cuckoo's Egg* (New York: Simon & Schuster, Inc., 1990).

Computer Security Alert, published monthly by the Information Systems Security Association, Glenview, IL.

Control Objectives for Information and Related Technology (COBIT), Copyright © 1996, 1998, and 2000 by the Information Systems Audit & Control Association, Rolling Meadows, IL.

CSI/FBI Computer Crime and Security Survey, published annually by Computer Security Institute, San Francisco, CA.

Current Issues in Bank Auditing, published monthly by Bank Research Associates, Boise, ID.

EDPACS, The EDP Audit, Control, and Security Newsletter, published monthly by Auerbach Publications, New York, NY.

Federal Financial Institutions Examination Council (FFIEC) Information Systems Examination Handbook, 1996 edition. Available from the Office of the Comptroller of the Currency, PO Box 70004, Chicago, IL 60673–0004.

Information Security, published monthly by TruSecure Corporation, Norwood, MA.

ISACA Journal, published bimonthly by the Information Systems Audit & Control Association, Rolling Meadows, IL.

Joel Scambray, et. al., *Hacking Exposed, Network Security Secrets & Solutions,* 2nd Ed., (Berkeley: Osborne/McGraw-Hill, 2001).

Manager's Guides (to various technologies, series of seven pamphlets), published and issued free of charge by Computer Security Institute, San Francisco, CA.

Murrell G. Shields, *E-Business ERP: Rapid Implementation and Project Planning* (New York: John Wiley & Sons, 2001).

Secure Computing, published monthly in the United States by West Coast Publishing Company of the United Kingdom. *Infosecurity News* was published bimonthly by MIS Training Institute, Framingham, MA, until June 1997, when it formed an alliance with Secure Computing.

Systems Auditability and Control (SAC), Copyright © 1977, 1991, 1994, by the Institute of Internal Auditors, Altamonte Springs, FL.

Unix: Its Use, Control, and Audit, Copyright © 1995 by the Information Systems Audit and Control Foundation, Rolling Meadows, IL, and the Institute of Internal Auditors Research Foundation, Altamonte Springs, FL.

Glossary

AARF   Australian Accounting Research Foundation.

ACFE   Association of Certified Fraud Examiners.

ACH (automated clearing house)   A process whereby debit and credit transactions initiated by various vendors (e.g., utilities, businesses) and government agencies (e.g., the Social Security Administration) are electronically transmitted by originating financial institutions to accounts at other financial institutions.

ACUIA   Association of Credit Union Internal Auditors.

adverse opinion   An independent auditor's opinion that financial statements do not present fairly the financial position, results of operations, or cash flows of an entity in conformity with generally accepted accounting principles.

AES (advanced encryption standard)   A replacement of the DES algorithm that has variable block and key lengths of 128, 192, or 256 bits. The Rijandel algorithm won an international competition and in December 2001 was announced by NIST as Federal Information Processing Standard (FIPS) 197. It became effective on May 26, 2002.

AGS 1026 (Auditing Guidance Statement #1026)   An auditing guidance statement issued by the AARF that provides guidance to external auditors on the preparation of reports on the internal controls of superannuation (pension) funds.

AICPA   American Institute of Certified Public Accountants.

AITP   Association of Information Technology Professionals.

algorithm   A step-by-step procedure for solving a problem in a finite number of steps. As applied to encryption, an algorithm is a secret formula used to encrypt and decrypt messages.

ANSI   American National Standards Institute.

applets   Small packets of computer program code that can be summoned when needed through the World Wide Web.

application   A program that enables a computer to perform general business functions such as word processing, spreadsheets, and data analysis, as well as specific functions in virtually all industries.

ASCII (American Standard Code for Information Interchange)   An ANSI standard for representing English characters as numbers, with each letter assigned a number from 0 to 127. In the standard ASCII character set, each character uses 7 bits.

ASIS   American Society of Industrial Security.

asymmetric algorithm   An algorithm that uses different but mathematically related keys for encrypting and decrypting messages.

audit program   A checklist of the various tests that auditors must perform to determine whether key controls intended to mitigate significant risks associated with a system or process are functioning as designed.

audit trail   A method by which each person involved in a process is accountable for the task or tasks they performed. In computer systems, secure user IDs are the most common form of audit trail.

audited financial statements   Financial statements upon which an independent auditor expresses a written opinion as to whether they accurately represent the financial condition of the organization, in all material respects, in conformity with generally accepted accounting principles.

authenticity   A condition whereby a message recipient can be reasonably sure that it was originated by the entity that appears to have originated it.

automated job scheduling software   A program or set of programs that can significantly enhance the operational efficiency of computer operations by automatically initiating the next scheduled production program immediately upon completion of the previous program.

bacteria   A program designed to reproduce exponentially until the host central processing unit (CPU) runs out of processing capacity, memory, or storage space, thereby denying service to any other users or processes. Bacteria programs do not damage other programs.

batch program   A program that is submitted by the user and executed by the system when data processing resources are available. Submitting jobs in batch frees the user ID to perform other interactive functions without having to wait for the job to complete.

BBBOnline   A division of the Better Business Bureau that offers two website certifications, one for business reliability and one for information privacy.

biometric lock   A lock that is activated when an authorized person is authenticated by recognizing one or more unique physical features of the accessing individual, such as fingerprints, palm prints, retinal images, or voice recognition.

brute-force attack   A technique whereby all possible keys to an algorithm are systematically tested until the correct one is identified.

BSA   Business Software Alliance.

business resumption program (BRP)   A documented set of key procedures and processes necessary to ensure that critical functions of an organization are restored to minimum operating levels after the occurrence of a disaster or other significant business interruption.

CA (chartered accountant)   A professional designation sponsored in Canada by the Canadian Institute of Chartered Accountants, in the United Kingdom by the Institute of Chartered Accountants in England and Wales, and in Australia by the Institute of Chartered Accountants in Australia.

CAAT   *See* computer assisted audit techniques.

Cadbury Committee   The Committee of the Financial Aspects of Corporate Governance of the Institute of Chartered Accountants in England and Wales. Cadbury published *Internal Control and Financial Reporting* in 1994 to build on the internal control concepts developed by the Committee of Sponsoring Organizations of the Treadway Commission (COSO).

carbon nanotubes   Computer semiconductors that are about 100,000 times thinner than a human hair, about 10 atoms across, and about 500 times narrower than current silicon processors. IBM is a leading pioneer in the technology, which could render current silicon-based semiconductors obsolete.

CCSA (Certification in Control Self Assessment)   A professional designation sponsored by the Institute of Internal Auditors.

CDP (certificate in data processing)   A professional designation sponsored by the Association of Information Technology Professionals.

central processing unit (CPU)   A box of interconnected electronic circuits that form the heart of a computer.

centralized CSA   A variation of control self-assessment (CSA) whereby an internal audit department or other designated department within an organization performs CSA workshops.

CERN   The European Laboratory for Particle Physics in Geneva, Switzerland. The World Wide Web was created there in 1989.

CERT   Computer Emergency Response Team.

certificate authority   An organization that certifies the authenticity of public keys, identifies public/private key creators, and distributes public keys via digital certificates.

CFE (certified fraud examiner)   A professional designation sponsored by the Association of Certified Fraud Examiners.

CFSA (certified financial service auditor)   A professional designation sponsored by the Institute of Internal Auditors.

CGAP (Certified Government Auditing Professional)   A professional designation sponsored by the Institute of Internal Auditors.

Childen's Online Privacy Protection Act (COPPA) of 1998   A U.S. law enacted to protect the privacy of children using the Internet. The law became effective on April 21, 2000, with full compliance required of applicable websites by October 21, 2000.

CIA (certified internal auditor)   A professional designation sponsored by the Institute of Internal Auditors.

CIAC   Computer Incident Advisory Capability.

CIAO   Critical Infrastructure Assurance Office.

CICA   Canadian Institute of Chartered Accountants.

cipher lock   A lock that is activated by entering a secret set of numbers and/or characters on a keypad next to the door.

CISA (certified information systems auditor)   A professional designation sponsored by the Information Systems Audit and Control Association.

CISSP (certified information systems security professional)   A professional designation sponsored by the International Information Systems Security Certification Consortium, Inc. (ISC²).

CMA (certified management accountant)   A professional designation sponsored by the Institute of Management Accountants.

COBIT (control objectives for information and related technology)   An internationally developed, comprehensive information technology evaluation tool published in 1995 by the Information Systems Audit and Control Foundation.

CoCo   Criteria of Control Board of the Canadian Institute of Chartered Accountants. CoCo published *Guidance on Control* in 1995 to build on the internal control concepts developed by Cadbury and COSO (the Committee of Sponsoring Organizations of the Treadway Committee).

cold site A facility that is equipped only with the basic infrastructure necessary to operate a primary information processing system. The basic infrastructure includes lights, electrical wiring, air conditioning, and related supplies, but does not include computer equipment.

Common Criteria (CC) A set of common information technology (IT) security best practices developed by seven European and North American countries to harmonize various IT security evaluation standards in the United States, Europe, and Canada. ISO (the International Organization for Standardization) adopted version 2.1 of the CC as an international standard (#15408) in June 1999.

compiled financial statements Financial statements about which an independent auditor states that the information contained in them are the representation of management and that the auditor does not provide any form of assurance over them.

Computer-assisted audit techniques (CAAT) A computer program or application that has been used to enhance the efficiency and effectiveness of an audit process through the automation of previously manual procedures, expansion of the scope of audit coverage, or the creation of new audit procedures.

computer forensics The science pertaining to the relationship of computer facts and evidence to legal issues.

computer maintenance A set of procedures designed to protect computer hardware against failure over the expected useful life of the equipment. The procedures are usually specified in the contract with the hardware vendor and must be performed in order for the manufacturers' warranties on the equipment performance to remain in effect.

computer operations A set of automated and manual processes that help ensure that input data is processed in an efficient and effective manner to support the strategic objectives and business operations of an organization.

computing system Any computer software application that performs a business function, the hardware on which it resides and which provides access to the application, and the operating system that controls the hardware.

concurrent sign-on A feature of many computer systems that allows users to be signed on from two or more workstations at the same time.

confidentiality A condition in which only intended recipients of transmitted information can read it.

control total A common form of integrity/completeness check whereby the sender provides the recipient with a mathematical total that the recipient can confirm by recalculating the total from the data actually received.

cookie A text file residing on a user's hard drive that contains personal information which may be retrieved by some websites.

COSO Committee of Sponsoring Organizations of the Treadway Commission, which was officially called the National Commission on Fraudulent Financial Reporting. The commission was originally established in 1985 to identify the primary causes of fraudulent financial reporting in the United States. COSO published *Internal Control—Integrated Framework* in 1992 to provide a model definition and framework of internal control.

CPA (certified practising acountant)   A professional designation sponsored by the Australian Society of Certified Practising Accountants.

CPA (certified public accountant)   A professional designation sponsored by the American Institute of Certified Public Accountants.

CPAA   Certified Practising Accountants of Australia.

CPP (Certified Protection Professional)   A professional designation sponsored by the American Society for Industrial Security.

CRSA (control and risk self-assessment)   Essentially synonymous with control self-assessment (CSA), with slightly more emphasis on risk assessment.

cryptography   The art or science of encrypting and decrypting messages using secret keys or codes.

CSA (control self-assessment)   A leading edge process in which *auditors* facilitate a group of *staff members* who have expertise in a specific process, with the objective of identifying opportunities for internal control enhancement pertaining to critical operating areas designated by *management.*

CSI   Computer Security Institute.

CUIAA   Credit Union Internal Auditors Association.

data warehouse   A large database that provides users the ability to access information from two or more different systems, thereby eliminating the need to have separate report writers or extract programs for each production system and enabling analysis of entire customer relationships in one location using client software.

database administrator (DBA)   One who is responsible for maintaining, securing, and generally managing a database management system.

database management system (DBMS)   A suite of programs used to define, query, secure, and generally manage large volumes of data. Benefits include the flexibility to change applications without affecting the data, the ability to eliminate data redundancy formerly required by nonopen applications, and the ability to better secure and monitor the data.

decryption   The act or process of translating a hidden message into its original, readable form. Decrypt is synonymous with the term *decipher.*

Deep Crack   A single computer developed by the Electronic Frontier Foundation (EFF) in July 1998 that used brute force to break a 56-bit DES encrypted message in 56 hours after testing about 18 quadrillion out of a possible of 72 quadrillion keys. Deep Crack had a total of 36,864 microprocessors, each of which could test 2.5 million possible keys per second.

DES (data encryption standard)   Based on the data encryption algorithm, DES was adopted as a federal information processing standard for sensitive but unclassified information by the U.S. government in 1977.

detective control   A control that helps identify the occurrence of a risk. A detective control is less desirable than a preventive control.

digital certificate   An electronic block of data received from a trusted certificate authority that certifies the authenticity of the sender's public key, identifies the creator of the sender's public/private key, and contains the sender's public key

Digital Millennium Copyright Act (DMCA)   A U.S. law enacted to help protect owners of digital information such as computer programs, digital images, and sounds from piracy and other unauthorized usage and sales. The law became effective on October 28, 1998.

digital signature   The block of data resulting when a message digest is encrypted using the sender's private key.

DISA   Defense Information Systems Agency.

DRII   Disaster Recovery Institute International.

EBCDIC (Extended Binary Coded Decimal Interchange Code)   An IBM standard for representing English characters as numbers, with each letter assigned a number from 0 to 255 and with each character using 8 bits. EBCDIC is used mainly on larger IBM computers.

edit checks   Automated controls programmed into an application to help prevent invalid or unreasonable data from being entered.

EFF   Electronic Frontier Foundation.

electronic access badge lock   A lock that is activated when the holder of an authorized magnetically encoded badge places it on a badge reader plate.

electronic commerce   The process whereby goods and services are purchased through some electronic medium.

e-mail   An Internet service that enables users to send and receive electronic messages.

emergency power system   A system consisting of a generator and the necessary hardware to automatically provide limited electrical power to critical operational areas within a facility in the event of a power loss.

encryption   The act or process of translating a message into hidden form using a secret formula, or algorithm, with the goal of ensuring message confidentiality. Encrypt is synonymous with the term *encipher.*

ENIAC (Electronic Numerical Integrator and Computer)   The first digital computer, which was developed by the U.S. Army in 1945 and publicly revealed in 1946.

environmental controls   General controls surrounding an information system including information systems security policies, standards, and guidelines; the reporting structure within the information systems processing environment (including computer operations and programming); procedures to assess the financial condition of service organizations and vendors; vendor maintenance contracts and warranties; and procedures to assess the status of computing system policies and procedures placed in operation at service organizations, if applicable.

eSAC (Electronic Systems Assurance and Control)   A contemporary information systems control model published in 2001 by the IIA Research Foundation. It modernizes its predecessor model called SAC.

European Union Data Protection Directive (EUDPD) of 1998   A European Union directive that mandates fair information protection practices for online as well as offline data transfers from the EU before data can be transferred. Although some EU members require additional protections, the DPD provides the minimum information privacy and protection requirements.

extract program   A program that copies selected data from a production database to another database to enable subsequent data analysis, reporting, and/or processing.

FedCIRC   Federal Computer Incident Response Center.

FFIEC   Federal Financial Institutions Examination Council.

file transfer protocol (FTP)   A file management application for the Internet.

FIPS (Federal Information Processing Standard)   A series of standards established by the U.S. government for processing electronic information.

firewall   A specialized information system designed to examine incoming and outgoing electronic transmission packets.

firmware   Computer memory chips that contain frequently used operating programs and data so they can be processed more rapidly than if the programs and data had to be loaded and executed in random access memory (RAM). Unlike RAM, the programs and data in firmware are not erased when the power is turned off.

FIT 1/94   A technical release issued by the Faculty of Information Technology of the Institute of Chartered Accountants in England and Wales (ICAEW), which provides guidance to external auditors in the United Kingdom on the preparation of reports on the processing of transactions by service organizations.

FRAG 21/94   A guidance document issued by the Financial Reporting and Auditing Group of the Institute of Chartered Accountants in England and Wales (ICAEW), which provides guidance to external auditors on the preparation of reports on the internal controls of investment businesses.

GIAC (Global Information Assurance Certification)   A professional designation sponsored by the SANS Institute.

gigabyte (GB)   One gigabyte is equivalent to 1 billion bytes of electronic data.

gopher   An Internet service that provides interconnected links between files residing on different computers on the Internet such that they appear as directories of files on the operator's computer.

Gramm-Leach-Bliley (GLB) Financial Services Modernization Act of 1999   A U.S. law enacted to require, among other things, that financial institutions fully disclose their practices regarding the distribution of personal financial information of their customers, distribute such customer information only if customers give them permission, and implement adequate security practices to protect personal customer information. Full compliance with GLB information privacy and protection requirements was required by July 1, 2001.

granularity   The degree of specificity with which system access control parameters can be controlled.

halon   A gas that rapidly removes oxygen from the air and is thus used in fire suppression systems. Halon dissipates quickly, leaves no residue, is nontoxic, and, because of its inert properties, does not damage equipment. Negative side effects include damage to the earth's ozone layer of the atmosphere and harm to humans when exposed for prolonged periods. For these reasons, halon gas is heavily taxed in some cities and jurisdictions.

hard drive   The physical device within computers that contains storage memory. The term *hard drive* is synonymous with *hard disk, fixed disk*, and *fixed drive*.

hash total   A common form of integrity/completeness check whereby the sender of data provides the recipient with a mathematical total, based on a key nonnumeric field, which the recipient can confirm by recalculating the total based on data actually received.

hashing   The process of calculating a control total based on nonnumeric data with the goal of ensuring message integrity.

Health Insurance Portability and Accountability Act (HIPAA) of 1996   A U.S. law enacted to help protect and restrict consumer health information. The act provides heavy penalties and potential jail time for offenders, including corporate officers. The HIPAA was signed into law by President Clinton in August 1996. After extensive delays and difficulties in establishing standards for data content and formats for submitting electronic claims and other administrative healthcare transactions, most covered entities had to comply with these standards by October 16, 2002.

hot site   An information processing facility that is fully equipped and configured with lights, electricity, air-conditioning equipment, computer equipment, and supplies such that it can be fully operational in less than 24 hours.

HTCIA   High Tech Crime Investigators Association.

HTML (hypertext markup language)   A language used to format documents so that they can be properly displayed through the World Wide Web.

http (hyper text transfer protocol)   A protocol that enables World Wide Web users to access text, graphics, multimedia such as sound and video, and information databases.

HVAC (heating, ventilation, and cooling) systems   Systems that provide warmth, air circulation, dust reduction, and cooling to computer users and computer equipment.

hybrid CSA   Application of centralized control self-assessment (CSA) in some areas and pure CSA in others.

IANA   Internet Assigned Numbers Authority.

ICAA   Institute of Chartered Accountants in Australia.

ICAEW   Institute of Chartered Accountants in England and Wales.

ICANN   Internet Corporation for Assigned Names and Numbers.

IDEA   International Data Encryption Algorithm.

IEEE   Institute of Electrical and Electronics Engineers.

IETF   Internet Engineering Task Force.

IETF (Internet Engineering Task Force)   A group of scientists and technical experts who provide support on Internet-related technical issues and who help develop Internet standards.

IFAC   International Federation of Accountants.

IIA   Institute of Internal Auditors.

information systems auditor   A specialized auditor who is skilled in assessing the adequacy of environmental, physical, and logical security controls over information systems.

information systems security guidelines   Minimum criteria, rules, and procedures established by senior management that may or may not need to be implemented to help ensure the achievement of the information systems security policy. In some firms, management may direct staff to implement only those guidelines which they judge to be pertinent or useful. In other firms, guidelines may be treated as the equivalent of standards.

information systems security policy   A high-level overall statement describing the general goal of an organization with regard to the control and security over its information systems. Policies are usually established by management and approved by the board of directors.

information systems security standards   Minimum criteria, rules, and procedures established by senior management that are required to be implemented to help ensure the achievement of the information systems security policy. Staff (e.g., system security administrators and users) implement IS security standards under the direction of management.

initial program load (IPL)   The process of installing an operating system or application program for the first time or reinstalling the operating system and/or application software due to computer hardware failure, virus, malicious attack, or other event.

integrity/completeness check   A control that helps provide reasonable assurance that the data recipient or user has received all the data intact, without any alterations or missing information. Control totals and hash totals are common examples.

internal control   A process, effected by an entity's board of directors, management, and other personnel, designed to provide reasonable assurance regarding the achievement of objectives in three categories: effectiveness and efficiency of operations; reliability of financial reporting; and compliance with applicable laws and regulations.

International Organization for Standardization (ISO)   An international organization that develops international standards for a wide variety of products and services, including computing systems. ISO adopted its name from the Greek word *isos,* which means "equal" so that it could be consistently used in all languages and that it would not be an acronym.

Internet   A global wide-area-network consisting of millions of host computers that enable millions of local- and wide-area networks, mainframes, workstations, and personal computers located within governments, businesses, research agencies, educational institutions, and individual homes to share information utilizing various Internet services.

Interpol   International Criminal Police Organization.

IPL   *See* initial program load.

IPSec (Internet Protocol Security)   A dominant virtual private network (VPN) protocol standard developed by the Internet Engineering Task Force.

ISACA   Information Systems Audit and Control Association.

ISC^2 International Information Systems Security Certification Consortium, Inc.

ISO   International Organization for Standardization.

ISOC   Internet Society.

ISPM   Information Systems Project Management.

ISSA   Information Systems Security Association.

ITAA   Information Technology Association of America.

jukebox   A device that stores and retrieves arrays of CD-ROMs to enable users to access a wide range of information stored on the CDs.

Kerberos   An authentication system first developed at the Massachusetts Institute of Technology in the 1970s. Kerberos helps enable network users to exchange private information across an otherwise open network. The kerberos server assigns a unique key to each authenticated user and embeds it in messages to identify the sender of the message.

kernel   The central module of an operating system which loads first and remains in random access memory (RAM). It manages memory utilization and other critical computer processes.

L0PHTCRACK   A freeware program that can extract the file containing the user IDs and passwords of Windows NT file servers and use brute force to determine many of them.

logic bombs   Programs that activate upon the occurrence of a certain event, such as the passing of a date or the failure of its creator to reset a special counter. When the event occurs, the "bomb" is triggered and the program performs some malicious commands, such as reformatting the hard drive of a server or shutting down a host computer.

logical security controls   Controls that restrict the electronic access capabilities of users of a system and prevent unauthorized users from electronically accessing a system. Logical security controls may exist within an operating system, application program, or both.

maiden password   A password that authenticates the system user ID when a computer system is activated or initialized for the first time.

malware   software designed to perform a malicious function.

megabyte (MB)   One megabyte is equivalent to 1 million bytes of electronic data.

megahertz (MHz)   One megahertz is equivalent to 1 million operations per second. Computers operating speed is usually measured in terms of MHz.

message authentication code (MAC)   The block of data resulting when an electronic message and a cryptographic key are processed through a one-way hash function.

message digest   The block of data resulting when an electronic message is processed through a one-way hash function.

MIPS   Machine instructions per second.

Moore's Law   A reference to Intel cofounder Gordon Moore, who prophetically predicted in 1965 that each new memory chip could perform about twice as many processes as its predecessor, and each new chip would be released within 18 to 24 months of the previous chip.

NACHA (National Automated Clearing House Association)   An association that establishes operating rules, regulations, and standards for the efficient, effective, and consistent processing of electronic transactions.

nanoscience   The study of materials smaller than 100 nanometers (one-billionth of a meter).

NIA   National Institute of Accountants.

NIPC   National Infrastructure Protection Center.

NIST   National Institute of Standards and Technology.

nonrepudiation   A condition whereby senders of a message cannot refute the fact they sent it.

NSA   National Security Agency.

NSI   National Security Institute.

ODBC (Open Database Connectivity)   A database programming interface protocol developed by Microsoft that provides a common language for most applications to access data in most database management systems.

OFAC   Office of Foreign Assets Control.

one-way hash function   A mathematical formula that uses an electronic message as its input to create a block of data from which the original message cannot be determined.

Open Systems Interconnection (OSI) Reference Model   The seven-layer ISO-OSI model was created in 1983 to be a universal reference model that could be applied to any computing environment to conceptually describe how two computer processors transmit data between themselves. The seven layers, from the top down, are: application, presentation, session, transport, network, data link, physical.

operating system   A set of programs that are required in order to make computer hardware devices function. Operating systems typically include an assortment of utility programs that assist in the functioning, maintenance, and security of the various hardware devices.

output media   Physical items or devices on which electronic output are stored. Examples include paper printouts, microfiche, microfilm, magnetic tapes, diskettes, and disk storage devices.

password expiration   A control in a computer system whereby a user is automatically required to enter a new password after a predetermined time period.

password masking   A control that prevents password characters from appearing on the video terminal screen as they are entered by the user.

peripheral devices   Computer hardware that assists in storing, accessing, and transmitting data and also in the production of information output.

physical security controls   Controls that protect computer hardware (central processing units and peripheral devices) against physical damage.

piggybacking   When an authorized person unlocks a door and then allows another person to follow them through it without using a personal access method.

platform   The type of computer hardware and operating system upon which one or more application programs reside.

PMI   Project Management Institute.

preventive control   A control that helps prevent the occurrence of a risk. A preventive control is more desirable than a detective control.

problem management   The process of resolving and monitoring system problems to help ensure that their impact on the operations of an organization are minimized.

pure CSA   A variation of control self-assessment whereby operating units within an organization are responsible for conducting their own CSA workshops on an ongoing basis.

qualified opinion   An independent auditor's opinion that, except for the effects of matters to which the qualification relates, financial statements present fairly, in all material respects, the financial position, results of operations, and cash flows of an entity in conformity with generally accepted accounting principles.

random access memory (RAM)   Memory space that is utilized by a computer during processing but that is erased after turning the computer off. RAM is also referred to as processing memory, or temporary memory. The amount of RAM available in computers is commonly stated in terms of megabytes (MB).

reciprocal site   An information processing facility located within another organization.

Two organizations make an agreement in which each agrees to allow the other to utilize its information systems resources in the event that one or the other experiences a business interruption.

repeat dialer   A device that repeatedly dials the same number to prevent others from making a connection thereby causing denial of service.

reviewed financial statements   Financial statements for which an independent auditor provides only limited assurance that they are free of material misstatement because the scope of the tests performed was significantly less than would be performed during an audit.

S/MIME (Secure Multi-purpose Internet Mail Extension)   An e-mail specification for formatting non-ASCII messages (graphics, audio, video) so that they can be sent securely over the Internet. It utilizes public key encryption technology from RSA Security Corporation.

SAC (systems auditability and control)   A comprehensive tool that provides guidance on internal control and audit of information systems. It was the first internal control framework to focus primarily on information technology. SAC was originally published by the Institute of Internal Auditors in 1977, with a significant update in 1991 and a further revision in 1994.

Safe Harbor Act (SHA) of 2000   A U.S. law enacted to conform to the European Union Data Protection Directive (EUDPD) of 1998. SHA governs data transferred to the United States from the European Union. As with the Gramm-Leach-Bliley (GLB) Financial Services Modernization Act, compliance was required by July 1, 2001.

SANS   System Administration, Networking and Security Institute.

SAS 70 (Statement on Auditing Standards #70)   An auditing standard issued by the American Institute of Certified Public Accountants that provides guidance to external auditors in the United States on the preparation of reports on the processing of transactions by service organizations. SAS 70 was effective for service auditors' reports dated after March 31, 1993.

SAS 78 (Statement on Auditing Standards #78)   An auditing standard issued by the American Institute of Certified Public Accountants that amends SAS # 55 by providing guidance to external auditors in the United States regarding the impact of internal controls on financial statement audits. SAS 78 was effective for audits of financial statements for periods beginning on or after January 1, 1997.

SAS 80 (Statement on Auditing Standards #80)   An auditing standard issued by the American Institute of Certified Public Accountants that amends SAS # 31 by helping external auditors in the United States focus more on electronic evidence. SAS 80 was effective for audits of financial statements for periods beginning on or after January 1, 1997.

SAS 94 (Statement on Auditing Standards #94)   An auditing standard issued by the American Institute of Certified Public Accountants, that amends SAS 55 and SAS 78 to add significant new sections regarding the effect of information technology on internal control. SAS 94 was effective for audits of financial statements for periods beginning on or after June 1, 2001.

Section 5900   A section of the Canadian Institute of Chartered Accountants *Handbook of Auditing* that provides guidance to external auditors in Canada on the preparation of reports on the processing of transactions by service organizations.

secure sockets layers (SSL)   A protocol used in web browsers to establish relatively secure communications between two computers on the Internet.

segregation of duties   Separation of tasks in a process to reduce the risk that one person can perform an action that may expose an organization to significant risks.

service bureau   *See* service organization.

service organization   An external company that provides business applications and/or data processing resources that would otherwise be too expensive or time consuming to develop and maintain internally. The term *service organization* is synonymous with service bureau and third-party processor.

SIIA   Software & Information Industry Association.

software piracy   The act of copying a copyrighted software program for personal use or for resale to another party, thereby denying rightful owners royalties and any other legal benefits to which they would otherwise be entitled.

SPAM   Unwanted or unsolicited e-mail that costs millions of dollars in time, effort, disk storage space, telecommunications bandwidth usage, and user frustration.

spoofing   A situation whereby one entity misrepresents itself as a different entity.

SPOOL (simultaneous peripheral operation online)   A temporary queue consisting of electronic output files awaiting printing, downloading, or other action specified by the data owners.

SQL (Structured Query Language)   A standard language used to request and process data in a database.

SSCP (systems security certified practitioner)   A professional designation sponsored by the International Information Systems Security Certification Consortium, Inc.

SSL   *See* secure sockets layer.

Statement of Position (SOP) 98-1   A statement by the American Institute of Certified Public Accountants entitled "Accounting for Costs of Computer Software Developed or Obtained for Internal Use." SOP 98-1 specifies various costs that should be capitalized and amortized over the estimated useful life of an internal-use system. It was issued on March 4, 1998.

storage memory   Memory space in which electronic data can be stored on the hard drive of a computer. In most computers storage memory is usually measured in gigabytes.

symmetric algorithm   An algorithm that uses the same key to encrypt and decrypt a message.

system console   A special terminal connected to a central processing unit (CPU) that enables the operator to execute various operating system commands that control the CPU (e.g., to run production jobs, copy and print output, perform backup procedures, etc.).

system security administration   The process through which an information system is protected against unauthorized access and accidental or intentional destruction or alteration.

system software   A collection of computer programs including the operating system and associated utility programs.

system user ID   A user ID with system administration capabilities that a computer system recognizes when it is activated or initialized for the first time.

SysTrust   A service jointly developed by the American Institute of Certified Public Accountants and the Canadian Institute of Chartered Accountants that enables qualified public accountants with the necessary information systems skills to provide assurance that a client's system is in fact reliable.

targeted CSA   A variation of control self-assessment (CSA) whereby an internal audit department performs CSA workshops on a limited basis.

TCP/IP (transmission control protocol/Internet protocol)   A protocol that enables computers with different kinds of operating systems to communicate among themselves. It is the standard protocol for the Internet.

Teledesic   A corporation whose primary investors are Bill Gates, Craig McCaw, and the Boeing Corporation. It plans to mobilize a constellation of about 30 interlinked low–Earth orbit, low-cost satellites to provide global access to a broad range of voice, data, and video communications capabilities.

telnet   An Internet service that enables a user to connect to another computer on the Internet and then use it as if he or she were directly connected to that computer.

teraflop   One teraflop is equivalent to 1 trillion operations per second. Currently, only a few supercomputers are capable of operating at these speeds.

Third-party processor   *See* service organization.

Trojan horse   A program that looks and performs certain functions innocently but contains malicious code such as viruses, bacteria, and logic bombs.

TruSecure® Corporation   A company that helps Internet-connected organizations identify, correct, and continuously mitigate risks to mission-critical systems and information. TruSecure was one of the first organizations to offer a website certification service.

TRUSTe   An independent, nonprofit privacy organizations whose mission is to build users' trust and confidence in the Internet. TRUSTe issues two different "trustmarks," standard privacy and children's privacy.

uninterruptible power supply (UPS) system   An arrangement of batteries and supporting hardware components that are configured to provide smooth, continuous power to computer equipment. The UPS system acts as a buffer between the outside power source, so that power surges and spikes are minimized. Also, in the event of primary power loss, a UPS system continues to supply electricity to the computer equipment until the emergency power system can fully activate.

unqualified opinion   An independent auditor's opinion that financial statements that have been audited present fairly, in all material respects, the financial position, results of operations, and cash flows of an entity in conformity with generally accepted accounting principles.

URL (uniform or universal resource locator)   An alpha-numeric description of the location of an item on the Internet. It contains the host name, directory path, and file name.

usenet   An Internet electronic bulletin board service that facilitates public exchange of data and conversations.

USENIX   Advanced Computing Systems Association.

virus   A computer program that has the ability to reproduce by modifying other programs to include a copy of itself.

VPN (virtual private network)   A network that enables secure Internet sessions between remote computers and the network server. A VPN gateway server commonly protects the network server; the remote computer must have the corresponding VPN client application in order to establish a secure channel (sometimes referred to as a "tunnel") for the purpose of electronic data interchange or exchange.

W3C   World Wide Web Consortium.

war dialer   a device that rapidly dials phone numbers in sequential order to identify those which could be potential hacking targets.

web bugs   Graphics Interchange Format (.gif) images measuring only a single pixel that are similar to cookies in that they track Internet use and are virtually undetectable by most cookie filters.

WebTrust   A family of services jointly developed by the American Institute of Certified Public Accountants and the Canadian Institute of Chartered Accountants that enables qualified public accountants with the necessary information systems skills to provide assurance that client websites that conduct business-to-consumer and business-to-business electronic commerce transactions meet standards for one or more of various principles. A client must earn an unqualified opinion letter before it can display the WebTrust seal on its website.

WITSA   World Information Technology and Services Alliance.

World Wide Web (WWW)   An Internet service that enables users to access and exchange various types of information.

worm   A program that searches for and executes itself in available host central processing unit (CPU) processing memory and then continuously copies itself to other computers, usually resulting in denial of service to other users.

WORM (write-once-read-many) drive   A storage device that permanently saves onto compact disks or other permanent storage media.

Year 2000 problem   A problem in which a computer program incorrectly performs mathematical and data calculations or sorts data based only on the last two digits of the year.

Index